Dear Delia

2nd Lt. Henry Falls Young, Seventh Wisconsin Infantry (Wisconsin Veterans Museum, Image ID 0052.1006)

Dear Delia

THE CIVIL WAR LETTERS OF

Captain Henry F. Young,

SEVENTH WISCONSIN INFANTRY,

1861–1864

Edited by

Micheal J. Larson and John David Smith

THE UNIVERSITY OF WISCONSIN PRESS

Publication of this book has been made possible, in part, through support from the Anonymous Fund of the College of Letters and Science at the University of Wisconsin–Madison.

The University of Wisconsin Press
1930 Monroe Street, 3rd Floor
Madison, Wisconsin 53711-2059
uwpress.wisc.edu

Gray's Inn House, 127 Clerkenwell Road
London ECIR 5DB, United Kingdom
eurospanbookstore.com

Printed in the United States of America

This book may be available in a digital edition.

Library of Congress Cataloging-in-Publication Data

Names: Young, Henry Falls, 1824–1902, author. | Larson, Micheal J., editor. | Smith, John David, 1949–, editor.
Title: Dear Delia: the Civil War letters of Captain Henry F. Young, Seventh Wisconsin Infantry / edited by Micheal J. Larson and John David Smith.
Description: Madison, Wisconsin: The University of Wisconsin Press, [2019] | Includes bibliographical references and index.
Identifiers: LCCN 2018045752 | ISBN 9780299323608 (cloth: alk. paper)
Subjects: LCSH: Young, Henry Falls, 1824–1902—Correspondence. | United States. Army. Wisconsin Infantry Regiment, 7th (1861–1865) | Soldiers—Wisconsin—Correspondence. | United States—History—Civil War, 1861–1865—Personal narratives.
Classification: LCC E537.5 7th .Y68 2019 | DDC 973.7/8092 [B]—dc23
LC record available at https://lccn.loc.gov/2018045752

For Carl N. Larson, my dear friend Chad Brownell, and the men and women of our Armed Forces who selflessly defend our nation each and every day.

—M. J. L.

For Dr. Hans-Jürgen Brandt and Petra Brandt—with affection.

—J. D. S.

Contents

Illustrations

Editorial Statement

The editors transcribed all of Captain Young's letters, and they appear in this edition in their entirety. While Young certainly was literate and wrote clearly and precisely, he generally followed the literary conventions of his day and provided little in the way of modern punctuation. For example, Young frequently concluded his sentences with commas or semicolons but often failed to employ periods or question marks. To clarify Young's intentions, the editors have modernized the text, silently capitalizing the start of each sentence, inserting a period or question mark at the end of sentences where they deemed such punctuation to be appropriate, and indenting paragraphs. The editors have retained Young's original spelling and capitalization and have refrained from inserting the intrusive [*sic*] to identify his misspellings. In rare instances they have inserted square brackets to indicate missing pages, to note where his words were illegible, or to render words intelligible to a modern reader. Young's letter to his wife of November 21, 1861, was incomplete; the editors have identified the start and end of the missing material with ellipsis points. To retain the flavor and integrity of Young's prose, the editors have retained his abbreviations (such as Capt for Captain) and his cross-outs of words or phrases.

The editors have made every effort to identify or describe in annotations all persons, places, and events Young mentioned in his letters. However, they have resisted annotating uniformly well-known persons, places, or events (such as the Battle of Gettysburg) that, in their opinion, require no further explanation. In instances where the editors could obtain no credible evidence to assist in verifying individuals, locations, or events, they noted such in an annotation. In the notes the editors also have identified as many persons as possible whom Henry Young mentioned in passing in his letters home.

The editors thank the Wisconsin Historical Society for granting access to the Papers of Henry Falls Young, 1861–1902, that serve as the basis of *Dear Delia*.

Micheal Larson acknowledges the support of Dr. Gwen Walker, University of Wisconsin Press, and Professor John David Smith, University of North Carolina at Charlotte, for their expertise and encouragement throughout the process. Mike also wishes to thank his parents, Jim and Donna Larson, for their immeasurable support and assistance. He also thanks the staff of the Southwest Wisconsin Room, Karrmann Library, University of Wisconsin–Platteville, for their generous assistance. He offers a special thank you to James Hibbard, archivist at the University of Wisconsin–Platteville, for their conversations on Captain Young early in the editorial process.

John David Smith thanks Dr. Gwen Walker, University of Wisconsin Press, for inviting him to join Mike Larson as coeditor of Young's letters; to Amanda Binder, librarian at the University of North Carolina at Charlotte, for her research assistance; to Professor Randall M. Miller, St. Joseph's University, for his always sage advice; and to those who help keep the fires burning on the Charlotte home front—Sylvia A. Smith and Max—for their unceasing encouragement, love, and support.

The editors also wish to thank copyeditor Jeri Famighetti and managing editor Adam Mehring for their valuable assistance in publishing their book.

Introduction

In November 1861, 2nd Lt. Henry F. Young of the Seventh Wisconsin Volunteer Infantry wrote, "I would rather spend the last drop of blood I have and let my wife and children have the free government of the united states to live in than to have our government broken up." In letters to his wife, Delia, and to his father-in-law, Jared Warner, in Wisconsin, Young often mentioned duty, family, and patriotism. These were among his core values. He was more than willing to sacrifice his life if necessary to suppress the Confederate rebellion nine hundred miles away.[1]

Dear Delia: The Civil War Letters of Captain Henry F. Young, Seventh Wisconsin Infantry chronicles the story of this thirty-seven-year-old soldier as told through his 155 letters home. Young's correspondence from the Virginia front relates and reveals the beliefs, observations, and opinions of a junior officer from the Midwest who fought in one of the Civil War's most battle-tested units. Over time, the Seventh Wisconsin became one of the most highly decorated regiments of the war, accumulating the third highest number of total losses (281 killed in action and died of wounds) among Northern regiments.[2]

Henry Young's letters make clear why and how he fought to keep the Union intact. They emphasize his emerging sense of community pride, duty, loyalty, nationalism, and intense patriotism. Serving in the military also signified a citizen's right and a citizen's responsibility. Beyond these qualities, the correspondence documents the volunteer soldier's life, his connections with home and comrades, the meanings of courage, and the brutal realities of war—what Walt Whitman termed "the black infernal background of countless minor scenes . . . of the Secession war." These, he noted, constituted "the real war," and he predicted that they "will never get in the books."[3]

Young's insights, often poignant and powerful, enable readers to witness the Civil War as he did. Few topics avoided Young's careful eye. Bluntly honest about his emotions and opinions, he left little doubt as to where he stood on the questions of the day. His correspondence—candid, contemplative, thorough, and occasionally humorous—provides a clear window into everyday events, as well as into war, society, and politics. Young's letters reveal the perspective of an officer from America's western heartland. The ideas and thoughts of midwesterners—also then known as westerners—provide a regional perspective underrepresented in Civil War–era documentary editing projects and collections that focus on the Northern states. Also, Young, unlike many soldiers, shared with his wife at least some of the horrors of war.

No doubt midwestern recruits shared many characteristics with soldiers who came from the northeastern and border states. Their regiments, and even more so the companies in which they served, were what the historian Randall M. Miller has termed "extensions of the community" that had sent them to war. As such they were "closely watched and worried over." Soldiers like Young believed that they "represented" their communities' interests and values—always conscious of their connections and obligations to home, especially in their moral conduct and physical courage. To a certain degree, then, the Civil War soldier was away from home without being truly away.[4]

Westerners tended to come from local communities "comprised [of] a mixed population of northerners and southerners in a way that people from the states of the northeast and south could not claim." For them the Civil War and their military service in suppressing the slaveholders' rebellion took on a special meaning, becoming, according to the historians Ginette Aley and J. L. Anderson, "the central event of Midwestern history" but also a nationalizing experience as they became part of the nation in action and came to know men from other regions and backgrounds. Recent scholarship suggests that Iowans, for example, subscribed to a "cult of unionism" that "approached something of a religious obsession in their newly adopted state." They feared that the South's secession, and possible future secessions by rebels in other regions, would lead to mass government dysfunction, thereby threatening individual liberty and signaling "a failure of the

American experiment with democracy." Iowans and other midwesterners considered the Union to be sacred. For them it signified "the only successful democracy in a world plagued by tyranny." Its destruction would usher in economic and political chaos, American stagnation, and retrogression. Above all, westerners prided themselves on their loyalty to and identification with the Union.[5]

Young's correspondence covers many topics during the first three years of the Civil War, including innumerable details of military service—the brutality of internecine "hard war"; camp life; camaraderie, pettiness, and thievery among the troops; equipage; and food shortages. Young also addressed military leadership, maneuvers and tactics, rumored troop movements, and what he considered the strengths and weaknesses of African American soldiers. The letters provide invaluable glimpses into the texture of everyday military life: building earthworks, ducking incoming artillery barrages, maintaining camp sanitation, and obtaining medical care. Young's correspondence additionally documents his business affairs on the home front and wartime inflation. From newspapers he retained a firm grasp of Wisconsin and national politics. In his letters he often remarked on reports of graft and corruption and offered pointed opinions regarding the controversial 1864 presidential election between President Abraham Lincoln and the Democratic candidate, George B. McClellan. Young agreed with Lincoln that in this contest it was "not best to swap horses while crossing the river."[6] *Dear Delia* further contains gossip and information about other enlistees from Young's rural Wisconsin community who served in his unit, Company F. Above all, Young's communications highlight his unflagging patriotism—his fierce determination to preserve the Union no matter the cost.

Significantly, Young's letters also illumine how the men in Company F retained their community ties. In his opinion their conduct in the field reflected community values back home. In his correspondence Young described how his compatriots trusted one another on the basis of longstanding shared ideals and experiences, especially pertaining to such mid-nineteenth century values as bravery, courage, personal and family honor, idealism, manliness, and pride. Like many of his time and place, he sought to be a stalwart man. Young often expressed his antipathy toward men he judged to be dishonorable and unmanly—cowards, war profiteers, slackers, and traitors. He frequently aimed barbs at Northern newspaper editors whom he judged had criticized unfairly, at a safe distance from the conflagration of war, both the army's leadership and its rank and file.

Young's devotion to family and place—his wife, Delia, and his young children and home—runs through his letters home, capturing the heartfelt concerns of a young husband and father separated from his loved ones by the war. Repeatedly Young expressed his loneliness and his desire to return home and offered advice to his wife on raising their children. Having done so, he nonetheless repeatedly underscored his commitment to his role as an officer and his determination to stay the course until the Union Army proved victorious in restoring the nation. Far away from home, he frequently complained about the dearth of letters from his wife and how much he longed for Delia and their children. Correspondence from the home front boosted his morale. In his letters Young also frequently addressed his concern for providing for his family and honoring his financial obligations to Jared and other business associates back home. Readers will find Young as conscientious in meeting his familial and financial obligations as he was in serving the Union Army—even after experiencing three years of war weariness and personal sacrifice. And in all, Young showed that wartime service made him, like many soldiers, more aware of the obligation to be a man—steady, strong, principled, and caring. Having to explain the war to his "dear Delia" and others, as well as to himself, also forced Young to ponder his place in a world bigger than the one he had left in Wisconsin.

As a company commander, Young was responsible for conveying orders to his men, keeping them in line, and moving them forward in battles and skirmishes. His correspondence also suggests the degree to which he cared deeply for his soldiers, many of whom came from his community and had been neighbors before the war. After his first brush with combat, in August 1862, Young emphasized the pathos of war. Attending to the dead and wounded following the Battle of Cedar Mountain, Virginia, he explained, constituted "one of the most horrible jobs i ever was in. Oh it is awful to look on and assist those wounded soldiers . . . shot and mangled in every conseiveable manner." Young admitted that "the battle field has its allurements and excitement but not so after it is over." Several days later he informed Delia that "from the papers you can never know the horrours of the battle field. The excitement of battle wears of after it is over and when it comes to going out and burying the dead by hundreds after they have lain in the sun for three or four days."[7]

Young devoted himself fully to the Union cause, its army, and its famed Iron Brigade, in which he served. At one point Young declared, "our army is composed of the best stuf in the world." On another instance he praised the men of Company F "as good and brave a set of boys as ever shouldered a gun." That said, Young nonetheless often criticized the Union war effort and those who orchestrated it, charging officials in Washington with mismanaging the army, playing favorites in assigning commands, politicizing the process of recommending men for promotion in Madison, and colluding with war contractors who reaped immense profits from supplying the troops. Early in 1863 he summed up the problem: "The whole thing is one infernal scramble for promotion political power, and money." In Young's opinion, "Those three things will ruin us yet, at least i fear so."[8]

He found most outrageous the petty jealousies between high-ranking general officers—Young dubbed them "infernal *Jealous curses*"—that made them unwilling to work together and thus diminished the Union's war effort. In mid-1862, for example, Young summarized what he considered the "bitter feeling" in the ranks against Union major general Irvin McDowell. In his opinion the men judged McDowell "a perfect curse to the army and every officer under him would leave his Divission if he could." Following the Union defeat at Second Bull Run in late August 1862, Young informed his father-in-law, Jared Warner, that "There is no use in disguising the truth. We were completely out Generald at every turn and Gen [John] Pope & McDowell, are completely played out." In contrast, Young praised the legendary Confederate major general Thomas J. "Stonewall" Jackson and his men, who, in his opinion, "fight like Devils. I have seen them charge right up the cannons mouth when they were being killed by scores. They think Jackson can do any thing he undertakes."[9]

Following Lincoln's removal of McClellan, then a major general in command of the Army of the Potomac, on November 10, 1862, Young informed Jared that he and his men would support "the old flag and will suppoart the [Lincoln] Administration" regardless of who commanded them. Although clearly sympathetic toward retaining McClellan, whom he praised highly for drilling, organizing, and instilling discipline in his command, as head of the Army of the Potomac, Young insisted "that the American Soldier is true to his country, true [to] his oath, and resolved to fight the rebellion to the bitter end no difference who commands." Determined to explain his support of McClellan to his father-in-law, Young declared, "I am not A McClellan man, A Burnside man, A [Joseph] Hooker man. I am for the man that leads us to fight the Rebs on any terms he can get." Young also criticized Northern newspaper editors who, from a safe distance and while totally unfamiliar with the changing fortunes and challenges of combat, faulted Union troops for failing to defeat the Rebels. In March 1863 he informed Delia, "I wish that every northern editor had to march just one day in mud with a knapsack on his back with gun and sixty rounds cartridges, just what our men have to carry. You would never hear them advocating a move in the mud again."[10]

Like soldiers in other wars across time and space, Young held thoughts of home, family, and friends most dear. In his letters to his wife he addressed the most minute details of life, instructing Delia on which crops to plant, how to manage their finances in his absence, how to raise their children, and how she could claim his back pay and pension should he die in combat.[11] And, typical of war letters, Young's complained about the paucity of details about life back home, about his rations (he yearned for Wisconsin vegetables), about the infrequent visits from the regimental paymaster, about his family's finances and property, and, predictably, about the weather—especially the Virginia mud and damp ground, which worsened his chronic rheumatism. Ever mindful of his financial obligations, Young fretted constantly and obsessively over the sawmill he operated with his father-in-law, over honoring the debts he owed to merchants in Grant County, Wisconsin, and over conducting business and the vagaries of sending money home on a regular basis.

He also possessed a dry-as-dust sense of humor and was unafraid of poking fun of himself or reprimanding others, including his father-in-law, if the situation warranted it. In mid-1864, for example, Young wrote to Jared about having not changed his clothes, including his undergarments, for thirty-five days. "Talk about being lousy & dirty, *Oh ye Gods*," he quipped. Later that month, writing from the Petersburg, Virginia, trenches, Young informed his father-in-law that "I feel fine this morning for be it known that I got a clean shirt and drawers on yesterday the 2d change I have had since the 3d of May. And I not only shed my duty clothing but i sent off a good crop of lice with them." He predicted, however, that by the following day "I will have [a] new and more hungry set for the whol country is covered with them." Upon learning that Delia had enjoyed a pleasant Fourth of July in Wisconsin, Young joked that for him and his men in the trenches the holiday was anything but festive; rather, it "was dull as a Quaker meeting." Writing to Delia during an unusually cold October in Virginia, he complained that he had to share his "scant bedding" with his "bedfellow" Capt. George S. Hoyt of Company K. It was so chilly, he explained, "that I Devilish near froze last night. And every time I waked up cold my mind would wander off to Wisconsin to where I had a good bed and a bedfellow that dont go on picet."[12]

More frequently, Young addressed more serious matters in his letters to Delia and Jared, including the contemplation of his own mortality. In April 1864, anticipating a "terriffic conflict," a major offensive against the Confederate stronghold of Richmond, Virginia, Young wrote his wife "that the position of the true soldier and patriot is to look the danger in the face and nerve himself to meet it. Yes meet it with the cool determination to conquer or die. This is no fancy picture." Soon after he informed her that should he fall during the coming struggle, "it will be in the line of my duty as becoms a true soldier, And I will have the proud satisfaction that I have been true to my wife and family as well as to my country." Should he die in the war, Young continued, Delia must provide their children "a good substantial education & teach them to be true Patriots." Several months later, following the Union disaster at the Battle of the Crater, in Petersburg's outer defenses, he admitted to his father-in-law that he was weary of the war. "I am heartily tired & sick of the service," he admitted, but added, "this is no time to whine or back down I see and hear to much of that and I almost get the blues sometimes and yet I know that the true soldier should never get downhearted." Much earlier in the war, Young explained in a letter to friends, "I am going to see this war through if I come out not worth the first damed red cent."[13]

Henry Falls Young was born on September 23, 1824, in the western Pennsylvania town of New Castle. Unfortunately he left a sparse record of the years before 1850, when he relocated to Wisconsin. Young's parents, William and Rachel Falls Young, died when he was eight years old, leaving many unanswered questions about Henry's early life. An aunt, the sister of either William or Rachel, raised Henry until he reached adulthood. As a young man he clerked for a few years in one of the stores in New Castle, and sometime in 1850 he made the move west, making his first stops along the Mississippi River at Rock Island and Moline, Illinois. Piloting a river raft for lumber companies on the Kickapoo River, Henry rode as far south as St. Louis. The outbreak of the Mexican-American War in 1846 led Young to enlist in the army, but the war ended and his volunteer unit disbanded before he saw combat.[14]

Young's employment on the Mississippi River undoubtedly put him into contact with Jared Warner, his future father-in-law. Warner was born in Canfield, Ohio, on December 6, 1811. He relocated to Millville, Grant County, Wisconsin, in 1838, with his young family and that of his father, Ehilu. The Warners were among the first settlers to inhabit Millville. There in 1840 father and son built the first sawmill in Grant County. Another mill, built in 1844, proved successful enough to turn out between two thousand and three thousand board feet of lumber daily. Jared Warner operated this mill until he moved to a farm, just north of Patch Grove, Wisconsin, in the late 1850s. Jared was very active in politics in Grant County and Wisconsin generally; in 1860 constituents elected him representative to the Wisconsin State Assembly. He also held a wide number of county and town positions, including supervisor, assessor, treasurer, constable, and county commissioner. Jared dedicated himself to serving his community and state until near the end of his life. He died in 1880.[15]

Henry Young, then twenty-eight-years old, first went to work for Jared Warner in November 1852, laboring at his mill for a salary of "13 pr month." Soon after, Henry and his brother, William E. Young, purchased a tract of land for $2,000 in Patch Grove Township, in northern Grant County, located in Wisconsin's southwestern corner. A quit claim deed for $1,000 filed on December 31, 1852, made Henry the sole proprietor of the property. Shortly thereafter, he purchased "3 yds shirting & linen" and "800 ft fensing," a move signaling the appearance of someone new in his life—Jared Warner's eldest daughter—Miss Delia Warner. It is impossible to say exactly when Henry and Delia met, but most certainly they came to know each other thanks to Young's employment with and his proximity to the Warner household.[16]

Delia Warner, born in Canfield, Ohio, on May 13, 1836, moved to Wisconsin with her family in 1838. Five years later her mother died, and for a time Delia lived with an aunt, Jared's sister Rebecca Mills. Rebecca was the second of Warner's sisters to marry the prosperous Lancaster lawyer, Joseph Trotter (J. T.) Mills. The 1850 census listed Delia among the residents of the Millses' household, exposing her to a highly refined and learned atmosphere and leading her to seek an education beyond the Millses' home. As a young woman, she received an uncommonly first-class education for her day. Delia attended the Platteville Academy and the seminary for girls in Galesburg, Illinois, the institution that later became Knox College. At the seminary she studied mathematics and science, courses unlike those taken by her male counterparts, whose course of study at Knox focused on the classics. Delia's extraordinary educational experiences, unusual for even most elite women of her time, no doubt contributed to her ability to communicate so clearly and directly with Henry in her letters to him. Close reading of Henry's responses reveals his many references to Delia's interest in the popular magazines and newspapers of their day. He also promised to bring books home to his children when he returned on furlough.[17]

Delia and Henry married on March 1, 1853, in Patch Grove, and the couple first settled in that township. Their marriage, lasting nearly forty-nine years, was, from all appearances, a happy one, demonstrated by their correspondence during the war. Following the Battle of Antietam, for example, Henry admonished Delia not to "fret yourself to death" over his safety because "it will do no good, for we are all creatures of circumstance over which we have no control, and your fretting about my getting killed, wont help the matter." Henry sustained only minor wounds during his three years of military service. In his letters to Delia, Young reminisced about their warm Sundays together picking early spring flowers in the Wisconsin countryside. Their first two children, Jared and Laura, were born while the couple lived in Patch Grove. A third child, May, arrived on December 11, 1860. Outside the home, Young participated actively in local affairs and served as Patch Grove township supervisor and, in 1861, as superintendent of schools for Cassville Township.[18]

In 1858 an opportunity arose that offered the Youngs a chance to move up the economic ladder. On September 3, Henry and Delia sold their tract of land in Patch Grove to Nathaniel Austin for $6,000. With some of the proceeds, they purchased one-half ownership of a flour mill in Cassville Township from Oliver P. Wetmore. The mill had been a joint operation between Wetmore and Jared Warner until Wetmore became ready to part with his share in the unfinished project. A memorandum in Warner's ledger for December 25, 1858, recorded that "Henry F. Young did on the 15th day of Sept. 1858 purchase all the right title and interest of O. P. Wetmore in a flour mill in the town of Cassville Grant Co. Wis. then being built by J. Warner and O. P. Wetmore." He went on to note that in constructing the mill, Warner expended $7,416.10 to Young's $3,749.69. Young agreed to make up the amount he owed Warner by paying Wetmore $2,000 for the land in Cassville Township and transferring four notes to Warner for a total of $1,925. The mill, at least initially, proved profitable. The 1860 Census recorded that it produced 2,400 barrels of flour at a value of $12,000. During the war, Young's neighbor Cornelius Furman rented one-half of the mill, a business arrangement that became the focus of many of Young's letters home to Jared and Delia.[19]

Young's domestic tranquility changed dramatically when Confederates attacked Fort Sumter, a federal military installation in Charleston Harbor, in the early hours of April 12, 1861. Even before this attack, in early 1861, Wisconsin had authorized $100,000 to raise state troops in case war came. Badgers rushed to volunteer. In one Wisconsin town 111 of the 250 men who were registered to vote enlisted. The five states carved out of the Old Northwest Territory—Michigan, Wisconsin, Illinois, Indiana, and Ohio—contributed one million men, or 14 percent of their total 1860 population. This number constituted 21 percent of the total number of men who wore the Union blue.[20]

Soon after the Rebel attack on Fort Sumter, Young commenced training several of his neighbors and, later, a small squad in nearby Cassville. As summer approached, some of the men Young trained went to nearby Prairie du Chien to join the newly formed Sixth Wisconsin Volunteer Infantry. On June 29 Young presided over and served as marshal at a patriotic pole and flag-raising ceremony before a large audience at Cassville school, an event that featured the Beetown Home Guards "in uniform, armed with rifles and fowling guns." Young was trout fishing in Millville when news arrived of the Confederate victory at the July 21, 1861, Battle of Bull Run. This Union defeat inspired him to take formal steps to enlist in the federal forces. Soon after, he and his squad, along with other enlistees, formed the Lancaster Union Guards. That unit came under the command of Capt. John B. Callis, a native of Lancaster, Wisconsin. In August the men of the Lancaster Union Guards elected Young second lieutenant.[21]

Upon assembling in Lancaster, the company drilled for an hour and then reportedly "marched to the several hotels about town" where the citizens of Lancaster served the recruits dinner. Following their meal, J. W. Blanding, Esq., administered the company members their oath of service. Young, commissioned a second lieutenant on August 30, 1861, departed for Madison, where state authorities mustered Company F, composed of men from Grant County, into the Seventh Wisconsin Volunteer Infantry. The regiment, originally composed of 1,022 officers and men, organized in ten companies and drilled at the state's training site, Camp Randall, from late August 1861 until the third week of September. Other regiments dubbed the Seventh Wisconsin "the Huckleberries" because, according to one veteran, the men "liked to talk about pies and things to eat." It was destined to become a highly honored unit, fighting in at least twelve major engagements, from the Second Battle of Bull Run to the Battle of Five Forks. According to one authority, the Seventh Wisconsin's service, although often ignored by Civil War scholars, "may be the most exceptional of the five Iron Brigade regiments."[22]

On September 21, 1861, nearly one thousand men of the Seventh Wisconsin regiment stood in attention near the gate at Madison's Camp Randall, which became a major recruitment center for the Badger State. The men, hailing from all parts of Wisconsin but especially from its southern and central parts, had begun trickling into the training camp after mid-August to commence their transition from civilian to military life. Three of the companies—the Lancaster Union Guards, Platteville Guards, and Grant County Badger State Guards—came from Grant County. Seven other companies—the Lodi Guards, Marquette Sharpshooters, Badger State Guards, Columbia County Cadets, Grand Rapids Union Guards, Waushara North-Western Tigers, and Beloit Badger Rifles—completed the regiment. By all appearances the men of the Seventh Wisconsin looked fit and ready for what awaited them in their new militia gray uniforms—uniforms manufactured in their home state. As the war progressed, the Wisconsin units substituted standard Union blue uniforms for the gray ones to avoid being confused with Rebel troops. The men from Grant County, with their previous training, had a leg up on others in the regiment, many of whom were drilling for the first time. As for drilling, one of Young's men remarked, "We have the best officers of any Co in the Regt for understanding drill. Our second Lieutenant [Young] is the best drill master in the Regt. . . . Some of the boys didnt like him at first because he was so strict but as they have more experience in what must be done, they like him verry well now and I like him better all the time." Observing the regiment's training, a Madison resident described the unit as "a remarkably intelligent and determined looking set of men." They awaited orders that would take them to battles half a country away to the battlefields of Virginia in a war many men worried might be over before they even left home.[23]

The first commander of the regiment, Col. Joseph Vandor (alternatively spelled Van Dor), was a native of Hungary and an aristocrat. A graduate of the Hungarian Military Academy in Vienna, Austria, he fought in the

Hungarian Revolution of 1848 and, upon emigrating to the United States, served as a professor at Captain Partridge's Military School in Brandywine Springs, Delaware. In 1856 Vandor moved to Milwaukee, where he practiced law. Thanks to recommendations from the mayor of Milwaukee and other prominent citizens, on June 24, 1861, Gov. Alexander W. Randall commissioned Vandor as commander of the Seventh Wisconsin. Vandor set out to make an immediate mark on the regiment.[24]

In an unusual move Colonel Vandor took a public oath of temperance and applied his personal pledge to the entire Seventh Wisconsin. Assessing the impact of forbidding alcoholic beverages in camp, a local newspaper reported that the regiment's commander "has entirely prohibited their sale on the camp ground, either to soldiers or visitors, and declines presents of intoxicating drinks, under all circumstances." No doubt adding insult to injury for many of the Wisconsin volunteers, Vandor turned down a keg of beer offered as a present to the regiment. However unpopular his prohibition of alcohol proved to be, Vandor nonetheless justified his abstinence policy on the grounds that a soldier had recently died in an accidental shooting in another regiment, the Fourth Wisconsin. The court-martial investigating the death determined that "Liquor was at the bottom of the difficulty." While it was not uncommon early in the war for recruits to take a vow of abstinence, officers nonetheless could purchase whiskey from the regimental commissary without permission. As Young reported in his letters home, he did not rigidly follow the lead of his commanding officer, at least in terms of alcohol. In October 1864 he confessed jokingly that he considered "the great equalizer in the army is forty rod Lightning comesary Whiskey." He added: "I have seen it bring Genls down as low and flat as Privates could *get*, and I have seen it elevate the lowest till they felt as big as the President." Vandor, whose limited English and autocratic ways irritated Young and others of his command, ultimately had little impact on the Seventh Wisconsin. Because of his stubbornness and problems resulting from his limited English proficiency, Vandor became a tragicomical figure. After leading the regiment to the Washington, DC, area, he resigned on January 30, 1862, to accept the post of US consul to the Tahitian Islands.[25]

Lt. Col. William W. Robinson, a resident of Sparta, Wisconsin, served as the Seventh Wisconsin's executive officer and assumed command of the regiment following Vandor's resignation. Robinson was a likable, efficient, and able officer, one who Young considered far superior to his erratic and eccentric predecessor. An experienced soldier, Robinson had served in the

Mexican-American War under Maj. Gen. Zachary Taylor, commanding Ohio volunteers. Maj. Charles A. Hamilton was third in line in command of the Seventh Wisconsin as the regiment embarked for Washington. The grandson of Alexander Hamilton, Charles Hamilton practiced law in Milwaukee before the war and was severely wounded at the Battle of Gainesville (or Brawner's Farm), Virginia, on August 28, 1862, wounds that led to his resignation on March 3, 1863.[26]

Company F, as it formed on the Camp Randall parade grounds, listened for instructions from its first commander, Captain Callis, who led the company for its first fifteen months in service. He gained promotion to major of the Seventh Wisconsin on January 5, 1863. Six months later Callis suffered a severe wound at Gettysburg, taking a bullet in his lung. Callis made an improbable recovery and returned to the regiment in February 1865, during the waning moments of the war, as a lieutenant colonel of the Veterans Reserve Corps. Callis's promotion led to Young's appointment as captain of Company F on January 5, 1863. He commanded the company until his resignation on December 3, 1864. Writing to Delia about his promotion, Young remarked proudly, "I have been commisseoned and assumed the title of Capt. Young. . . . Wont you congratulate me? The col said it was well earned and truly deserved which makes it in my case better still."[27]

The waning days of August 1861 finally brought the Seventh Wisconsin to full strength, with all companies in camp and ready to complete their training. In fact, Grant County sent more men than the regiment could accept, forcing some men to return home. By early September the regiment, according to an observer, was "becoming quite proficient in drill. The men are making good use of their time, and the officers are devoting themselves with much energy and efficiency to the fitting of the men for service."[28]

As elsewhere across the northern and western states, women supported their troops. In Madison they baked pies and cakes and served the regiment these treats with supper as the date of their departure from Camp Randall neared. Miss Hannah Ewbank of Marquette, Wisconsin, a vivandiere, joined the regiment to support the men as they readied to go off to war in Virginia. She even participated in a dress parade with the troops. "Her uniform is very neat, and . . . consists of a Zouave jacket, of blue merino, trimmed with military buttons and gold lace," a correspondent reported. According to the *Janesville Daily Gazette*, she made the journey with the regiment at least as far as Chicago.[29]

On September 20, 1861, the men of the Seventh Wisconsin received orders to "strike tents at 5 o'clock tomorrow morning, and be ready to take the cars at nine." In a steady rain, the men spent their last full day at Camp Randall parading unarmed. "Each man has been supplied with ten rounds of ball cartridges and instructed to use them against secessionists only," explained one report. After the troops had packed their equipage and eaten breakfast, Louis P. Harvey, secretary of state and future governor of Wisconsin, addressed the men, giving them a spirited patriotic address. Around 10 a.m. the regiment boarded first-class train cars amid the cheers and the roar of a cannon salute. Clattering out of the depot, the train passed through Stoughton and Edgerton, reaching Janesville after one o'clock on September 21. Residents of that city, many of whom had waited for two hours merely to catch a glimpse of the volunteer troops, were not disappointed when the regiment arrived. Commanding two full trains, the men of the Seventh Wisconsin came to a brief halt in Janesville. There welcoming residents treated them to refreshments.[30]

The regiment arrived in Chicago at eight o'clock that evening. The men detrained, formed ranks, and marched through the city to a rousing cheer. Forming with the men were police officers, a Light Guard Band, and "the Ellsworth Zouaves with dashing costume," until, finally, the regiment arrived at the Fort Wayne Railroad Depot. Boarding a train of the Chicago, Fort Wayne, and Pittsburgh Railroad, the Seventh Wisconsin regiment continued its travel east, reaching Fort Wayne, Indiana, at nine o'clock the next morning. A company of thirteen women greeted the regiment's train at Pittsburgh early on September 23, ladling hot coffee for the soldiers into canteens for the men to drink. Physicians and other citizens alike offered their services to the men before they departed again at 11 a.m., reaching Harrisburg, Pennsylvania, at 7 p.m. on September 24.[31]

There Pennsylvania governor Andrew Curtin reviewed the regiment and complimented their soldierly bearing. As the regiment's next train approached Maryland, the men observed armed guards lining the railroad tracks—their first visible signs of war. The unit next entered Baltimore, a city deeply divided between those loyal to the Union and those sympathetic to the Confederacy. It was the final stop of the regiment before the men of the Seventh Wisconsin reached the nation's capital, where loyal citizens provided them with coffee and rations. After five days on the rails, the regiment finally reached Washington, DC, at 1 p.m. on September 26. Forged into a unit in under one month of drilling, the Badgers nevertheless were confident that they were prepared for the vicissitudes of war—challenges that would test every man in the momentous years to come.[32]

Upon their arrival in the nation's capital, Young and his men joined the Army of the Potomac and initially manned Washington's defenses. Their first brigade commander was a Milwaukeean, Brig. Gen. Rufus King, followed in May 1862 by Brig. Gen. John Gibbon, a West Point graduate and regular army artillery officer who worked relentlessly to improve the unit's discipline and training. One historian has described Gibbon as "blunt, calm, fair, and ambitious who found no glory in war." A contemporary considered him akin "to cold steel for his wintry manner and the strict discipline he maintained among his men." According to another scholar, "Western troops were reported to be undisciplined, but Gibbon had the right touch and the men were apt pupils." His soldiers "were westerners in an eastern army and felt they had something to prove about the soldierly virtues of people in their part of the country." Beyond this, the men who came to constitute the hardscrabble Iron Brigade defined themselves as possessing more grit, more determination than their foes. Over time they believed in their "invincibility"—that they "were able to storm objectives or hold positions against fire and in the face of losses that would have broken most regiments."[33]

When, in March 1862, McClellan established the French corps military unit, composed of two or more divisions, the Seventh Wisconsin and its sister regiments joined McDowell's First Corps, Army of the Potomac. The Seventh Wisconsin, brigaded since October 1, 1861, with the Second and Sixth Wisconsin and the Nineteenth Indiana, spent much of the first year's duty (from October 1861 to August 1862) in camp, parading and training, not fighting, as part of Washington's defensive perimeter and later (during McClellan's Peninsula Campaign) in reserve at Fredericksburg, Virginia. Upon observing the Seventh Wisconsin in October 1861, an officer in a rival Wisconsin unit judged it "the finest body of soldiers yet sent from our State. . . . The men are not only of good size and hardy looking, but they have an intelligence and smart look, which is assurance that they bring brain as well as muscle to the work." In July 1862 another observer, an enlisted man from the Second Wisconsin, informed Madison's *Wisconsin*

Daily Patriot that the Seventh regiment "puts on the least style of" any of the regiments "and crow[s] the least. It is now the largest regiment in the brigade and well drilled."[34]

Soon after arriving in the Washington area, Young commented on his surroundings. Encamped at Washington by the famous Chain Bridge, he explained: "I had not time to look round Washington, (but give me the west) in preference to any place i have seen yet for I consider this a cussed poor country nigers and all. Every thing is verry high priced particularly provisions." Two months later, tired of camp life, Young had a chance to familiarize himself with Washington. Writing to his family, he explained that he used a twenty-four-hour pass to "take a turn through the Capital and Grounds . . . run round the White House; take a look at the green house, with its Oriental Plants, Flours, & Shrubbery, Fruits & c. Then go to Willards or the National, take a grand dinner; listen to the members of Congress and other big bugs that live on the Public Crib; talk poletics speculate about the war & after supper go to the Theatre if there is any thing worth going to see."[35]

In May 1862, following months of drilling during the winter of 1861–62 at Fort Tillinghast, near Arlington, the army assigned Young (in April 1862 he was promoted to the rank of first lieutenant), along with a few other men from Company F, to detached service with McDowell's bridge-building Construction Corps in Fredericksburg. Their job was to assist in building railroad bridges. He remained with the engineers throughout the summer of 1862, witnessing his first battlefield casualties after the Confederate victory at the Battle of Cedar Mountain on August 9. While building bridges, the engineers found themselves in the thick of the action of another hard-fought Confederate victory during the Northern Virginia Campaign at the Second Battle of Manassas or Bull Run (August 28–30, 1862) where, at Groveton, Virginia, Young received his real baptism into combat. There the Seventh Wisconsin bore part of the brunt of the Confederate attack and experienced stand-up fighting for two hours at a distance of one hundred yards. Both sides suffered overwhelming causalities. The Union troops lost about one-third of their operatives.

Young had strong opinions about how the Union commanders, especially Maj. Gen. John Pope, had mismanaged that campaign. "After Pope made the fatal mistake of letting Jackson turn his right flank and get in his rear, he and McDowell acted like men that were perfectly bewildered and went it blind. And yet they knew Jackson was turning our flank. Every officer in the army knew it, but we supposed that Pope was letting Jackson turn our flank for the purpose for getting him in a trap. But when Mannasses was captured with all our supplies and ammunition for the use of the army then these Generals appeared to wake up, for they run us to the right then to the left, marching day and night till they had their army scattered from hell to breakfast." Writing about the August 28, 1862, engagement at Brawner's Farm, near Gainesville, Rufus R. Dawes, lieutenant colonel of the Sixth Wisconsin, explained: "in the history of war, it is doubtful whether there was ever more stubborn courage than was displayed by the second and seventh Wisconsin and nineteenth Indiana regiments on this field of battle." At Brawner's Farm, the Iron Brigade's first real action, the Seventh Wisconsin and its sister regiments clashed with Stonewall Jackson's Rebels. Within a three-week span Young's brigade participated in five battles, including Second Bull Run, and lost 58 percent of its original manpower.[36]

Young rejoined Company F to participate in the Maryland Campaign on September 16, two days after the Union victory at the Battle of South Mountain, the fight that showcased the army's only all-western infantry brigade, composed of the Nineteenth Indiana, the Second, Sixth, and Seventh Wisconsin and, later, following the Battle of Antietam, the Twenty-fourth Michigan regiments. The latter unit provided the brigade with much-needed reinforcements while retaining its all-western esprit de corps. According to the historian Alan T. Nolan, the Iron Brigade's "regional identity played a large part in sustaining the morale of the men."[37]

After South Mountain and Antietam, on September 17, near Sharpsburg, Maryland, McClellan gave the combined units their sobriquet the "Iron Brigade of the West." This unit became known as one of the most famous and tenacious fighting brigades in the war. Because of its distinctive, high-crowned, black felt Model 1858 headgear of the US Army Regulars, with one brim pinned up and sporting a black cockade, contemporaries dubbed the brigade the Black Hat Brigade. It also had the unfortunate distinction of leading all federal brigades in its percentage of battle deaths. According to the historian Jeffry D. Wert, over a span of almost eleven months, from mid-August 1862 to July 1863, the Iron Brigade constituted "the best combat unit in the Army of the Potomac. . . . Numbers testify to its unmatched stature. Nearly 1,750 brigade members lost their lives to disease or in combat. Of that figure, 1,150 were either killed or mortally wounded." Young's regiment, the Seventh Wisconsin, had 281 of its men killed or mortally wounded.[38]

The Iron Brigade enhanced its reputation as one of the hardest fighting units in the Army of the Potomac at Antietam. This constituted the bloodiest one-day battle in the Civil War. At Antietam Creek, Young and the men of the Seventh Wisconsin were at the center of the action fighting against the Confederacy's Texas Brigade, led by Brig. Gen. John Bell Hood, west of farmer David Miller's cornfield. In Young's opinion, Antietam "was the most terrible fight that ever was fought on this continent and our Brigade was in the thickest of it. I went into the fight with only 14 men and lost 6 of them. 2 were killed, and 4 wounded and missing." It signified "the great fight of the Rebellion."[39]

The Iron Brigade's next major campaign was manning the extreme left flank of the federal line at the Union defeat at Fredericksburg, Virginia, December 11–15, 1862. Young described his troops' advance on the town as a complete disaster. Refusing to mince words, on December 17, 1862, he complained to his father-in-law, "I wont try to describe to you the perfect contempt i feel for the man or men that run us into such a place as we have just got out of. Got out did I say? Yes, but there is thousands of brave fellows that did not get out, that were sacrificed and butchered." Explaining the debacle to Delia, Henry portrayed the Fredericksburg assault as "the damedest blunder i ever heard of a General making. To think of crossing here and storming those fortified heights, when they could have been easily flanked by the right or left." Following the Battle of Fredericksburg and Maj. Gen. Ambrose Burnside's disastrous and demoralizing January 20–23, 1863, "Mud March," the brigade spent winter quarters at Belle Plains, Virginia, on the bank of the Potomac River, until the start of the spring 1863 campaigns.[40]

For Young (promoted to captain of Company F in January 1863) and the rest of the Iron Brigade, the 1863 spring campaigns began in earnest in late April at the Battle of Chancellorsville, Virginia (April 30–May 6, 1863). The brigade crossed the Rappahannock River at Fitzhugh's Crossing in the early morning hours of April 29 and endured most of its casualties for the campaign in its successful taking of the opposite bank. Many in the regiment, including Young, could not believe that they were defeated in the battle. Writing to Jared, he explained, "We had a terrible fight up there [at Chancellorsville]. The Rebs were hurled back at every charge. They did not charge our Brigade, but I seen them charge on our left with five lines of battle three times in all of which they were repulsed with terrible loss." Among the losses Young recounted was the killing of Confederate general

Stonewall Jackson. According to Young, "The famous Reb Jackson is dead. So much for the fight of Chancellorsville. He was worth twenty thousand men to the Rebs in a fight." Weary from battle and yearning to visit family and friends, in May 1863 Young received a fifteen-day leave of absence. He caught up with the regiment in early June as it made its way to Gettysburg, Pennsylvania, where it fought in the bloody three-day battle (July 1–3, 1863) that historians consider the "high-water mark" of the war. According to the historian Lance J. Herdegen, at Gettysburg the five regiments of the Iron Brigade "earned a distinguished place in American military history."[41]

The brigade, then designated as the First Brigade, First Division, First Corps, and commanded by Brig. Gen. Solomon Meredith, was one of the first Union units to take the field at Gettysburg. In doing so, it impeded the Confederate advance until more regiments from the Army of the Potomac arrived, despite experiencing catastrophic and devastating losses, especially on the battle's first day, when the brigade was almost decimated. For its part the Seventh Wisconsin exhibited its fighting spirit, battling furiously against a Confederate force, first along McPherson's Ridge prior to moving to Seminary Ridge, west and northwest of the town of Gettysburg. The regiment lost one-half of its operatives in the intense fight while the brigade lost two-thirds of its 1,800 effectives. Three days later, Jerome A. Watrous, a member of the Sixth Wisconsin, recalled, "Nearly every survivor had lost from one to a dozen of his company comrades. It [July 4, 1863] was a day like a funeral, a quiet day, save the labor called for in burying the dead and caring for the wounded." Forced backward through Gettysburg, the brigade eventually dug in south of town, near Culp's Hill, for the last two days of the battle.[42]

Writing to Delia, Young summarized succinctly his opinion of the fighting at Gettysburg. "We have had three days terrible fighting. Our victory is complete. Our Brigade suffered terribly. . . . Our men fought splendid. We are all in good spirits but—tired and hungry." For all its heavy fighting, the Iron Brigade sustained the highest proportion of casualties among Union troops at Gettysburg. One of every two men in the Seventh Wisconsin was killed, wounded, or missing. "Against 28 percent overall Union casualties," at Gettysburg "the Iron Brigade suffered 61 percent casualties." While the Iron Brigade continued to function as a unit following Gettysburg, "it never recovered its former punch," a point Young recorded in his correspondence home.[43]

A week later Young assessed his company's losses at Gettysburg, informing Jared that "In fact it was impossible for several days to tell who was killed and who was taken prisnors in falling back the last time, for men were falling thick and fast around us and there was no time to pick them up or look to see who they were." As the smoke of the three-day battle at Gettysburg cleared, Young reported how the regiments had withstood staggering casualties; only twenty men remained in his company—although he wrote proudly that they were "All tough and hearty." The battle fatally weakened the First Corps, Army of the Potomac. As for himself, Young wrote, "I got off with a mear scratch on the sole of my right foot, but there was one shell came so close to me that it tooke the heads of the two men in front of me scattering their brains all over my chlothes." That said, several months following Gettysburg one of Young's men, Pvt. William R. Ray, a blacksmith from Grant County prior to volunteering, remarked that his company commander was "rather unwell and looks bad as he has for a number of weeks."[44]

For the remainder of 1863, the Iron Brigade engaged in the Bristoe and Mine Run campaigns (October 9–December 2, 1863). In early 1864 Young received another furlough and returned to Wisconsin until February 1864. While home, he recruited volunteers for the Seventh Wisconsin, hopeful of supplanting the serious losses sustained by his regiment in battle the previous year. By July 1864, eastern troops, including draftees and substitutes, joined the Iron Brigade as veterans left the service as their enlistments expired. The raw nonwestern enlistees strengthened the unit's numbers but changed the brigade's unique regional identity.[45]

For Young and others of his regiment, the 1864 Overland Campaign tested their endurance beyond all previous challenges. From early May through the middle of June, the Iron Brigade was in almost constant combat, including at the battles of the Wilderness (May 5–7, 1864), where Young suffered minor wounds; Laurel Hill (May 8, 1864); Spotsylvania Court House (May 7–19, 1864); North Anna River (May 23–26, 1864); and Cold Harbor (May 31–June 12, 1864); they also participated in the assault and siege of Petersburg and the Petersburg mine explosion (June 15–July 30, 1864). During the Battle of the Wilderness alone Young's unit sustained astounding losses, including 217 men killed, wounded, or missing. This total exceeded those of any other regiment or battalion in his brigade. Even though Young's initial enlistment terminated in the summer of 1864, probably because of unit pride and loyalty he elected to see the fight through to the end, joining 210 of his comrades in "veteranizing"—enlisting in what became the Seventh Wisconsin Veteran Volunteers. Following the battle at Spotsylvania, the Rev. Samuel Eaton, chaplain of the Seventh Wisconsin, noted that officers like Young, who heretofore appeared youthful and in good health, seemed "older by years than before the campaign." Young's letters underscore the degree to which the exhaustion of the army, from the almost constant combat from the Wilderness to Cold Harbor, rendered the battles more confused and longer than they otherwise might have been.[46]

While exhausted from the constant strain of his service and suffering from rheumatism, Young nonetheless felt a higher calling and was determined to see the Southerners' rebellion to its end. The August 1864 Battle of Weldon Railroad proved to be Young's final engagement. A month later he wrote to Jared, explaining his determination to stay in the army. "I dont feel like leaving the service now," he explained. "Some how my hope is large, and I still hope to see the Rebellion crushed before winter. The draft and Recruits will fill up the army by Nov, then I look for the Election of Lincoln which in its self will be a crushing blow at the Rebellion. Let him be elected and at the same time let Grant, Sherman, & Sherridan be heavily reinforced and ready to strike the decisive blow and down will the Rebellion. At all events this is not the time to falter while the Govt is calling for men. Is not the time for me to leave the service. Although i am free to confess i am tired of it and some times verry home sick." Young's faith in Lincoln and his determination to suppress the rebellion by force proved to be well served. Following the November 1864 presidential election, he wrote to Delia: "The Election is over. Our Brigade cast 1291 votes of which Lincoln received 946 & Mc 345 giving Lincoln 645 majority. The rest of the army voted about the same. Tomorrow we will begin to get the news of how the states went. I am looking for Lincoln to have a larger majority than at his 1st Election."[47]

Events at home, however, quickly captured Young's attention and convinced him to conclude his service. In early November he received devastating letters from both Delia and Jared, informing him that Laura, his middle child, had died. Despondent over the sad news, Young wrote to Jared and explained that he would settle his official business and muster out as soon as possible. "I think I will go out of the service next month. I owe it to my family and I will go. I have faithfully served my [country for] over three years and my wife has nobly performed her part, but now she says come home and a man must not neglect his family." Homesick and heartbroken, Young applied for and received his military discharge on December 3, 1864, near Petersburg. He then began the long trek homeward to Cassville, Wisconsin. Unlike his comrades from the Seventh Wisconsin, Young thus failed to witness the surrender of Confederate general Robert E. Lee at Appomattox Court House on April 9, 1865.[48]

Young's letters to Delia and her father reveal a man unafraid of sharing his innermost thoughts, often sharply and directly, on the men and measures of the day, including insightful and often harsh assessments of famous Union and Confederate leaders. Not surprisingly, Young slowly changed his opinions as his wartime service progressed. Like men in all wars, Young matured, gaining perspective and context, especially after "seeing the elephant"—experiencing combat. While his physical stamina and zeal for combat waned over time, not so his commitment to the Union.[49]

On several occasions, however, Young expressed a disdain for the politics and political infighting that lay behind the Union war effort and that raged among the generals who commanded President Lincoln's army. Early in 1862, for example, he wrote to Jared from Camp Arlington, Virginia: "i have been perfectly satisfied that if it was not for the money that is made by many, and the intrigueing for Military and political power by others this war would be terminated in six weeks. You may think I am gassing but I know it is truth I write. Every person about washington in any kind of business is getting rich."[50]

Also Young, like many of his peers throughout the North, stated clearly that they were fighting to suppress the Southern rebellion and to keep the Union intact—not to free the South's four million slaves. On December 23, 1861, for instance, he explained to Jared adamantly that "We are fighting for to crush out rebellion, not for the abolition of slavery." He added: "And every man of comon sence knows that as the army advance, the slaves of every Rebble will be set free, and what is the use of their forever harping on the question in Congress. It does us more harm than fifty thousand men in the Rebble army could possibly do. The fact is i wish those agitators of slavery were placed in the ranks to fight. I think that would cure their radical ideas." A fellow soldier in the Seventh Wisconsin shared Young's opinion of Lincoln's emerging emancipation project. "Ask almost any solider," he wrote to the *Wisconsin Daily Patriot*, "what he thinks of the war; he will answer, 'I don't like to fight for the damned nigger. It's nothing but an abolition war, and I wish I was out of it.' You can hear it everywhere, let those deny it who may. It is the truth, and why hide the truth. That is the sentiment go where you will."[51]

Young, like many Yankee volunteers, thus was slow to consider the Rebels' rebellion as a war of black liberation. In early November 1862, weeks after Lincoln issued his preliminary Emancipation Proclamation, Young informed Delia that he had no intention of commanding black troops because he considered them "the infernalist set of cowards in the world. We cant trust them as Ambulance drivers, or Amunition drivers, or in fact any where that there is danger, and i would not fight with them for the same reason. It is not on account of their coulour, but on account of their cowardice. There are exceptions but they are rare. The great majority of them would prefer to be slaves rather than fight for their liberty."[52]

Significantly, Lincoln's preliminary edict made no mention of arming black troops. Rather, it proclaimed that if the Confederates failed to cease their insurrection effective January 1, 1863, slaves held in states or parts of states then in rebellion against the United States would be freed.[53] According to the historian Harry S. Stout, "For Lincoln, emancipation and union were not contradictory goals. They were the same goal." While African American slaves initiated the emancipation process, fleeing their masters the moment that federal troops penetrated the Confederacy, the president's proclamation was absolutely necessary—"and he knew it. He realized the enormity of what he was doing. He caught the thunderbolt."[54]

Young was slow to do so, however. In November 1862, he explained to his wife that he remained convinced that African Americans would provide little help in defeating the Rebels. In his opinion they lacked "ambition enough about them to fight for their own rights." He nonetheless hoped—but was far from convinced—that Lincoln's proclamation might force the Confederates to stop fighting "to save their negroes." As January 1 approached, Young remained skeptical that southern blacks possessed "any ambition to help them selves." He regretted this because, as he explained to Delia, "if they would raise a little disturbance in the cotton states it would soon disperse Lees Army from Fredricksberg." Well into 1863 Young seemed determined to suppress the Rebels without a firm commitment to emancipation—to "whip them back into the union with or without negroes just as we please."[55]

That said, at times Young seemed to favor emancipation. On September 26, 1862, four days after Lincoln issued his preliminary emancipation edict, Young, then stationed near Sharpsburg, Maryland, asked Jared: "What do you think of Old Abes procklamation? It takes well with the Army here. Now the Rebs, will have to die dog or eat the hatchett." While Young remained uncertain how Confederates would respond to Lincoln's emancipation decree, he considered "it . . . just what was wanted." Young insisted that if the Rebels "dont lay down their arms we will have to annihilate them, niggers cotton and all." Cognizant that emancipation would lead temporarily to "hard times" for white Southerners, he informed Delia that Lincoln's proclamation nevertheless was a positive step, one that would "forever settle the everlasting slavery question."[56]

Similar to many western-state volunteer soldiers, late in the war Young gradually came to interpret emancipation more as a means to an end than an end unto itself. He reasoned that freeing and utilizing black persons for the federal army would disrupt the Confederacy's ability to wage war effectively and interrupt the South's agriculture. Like Young, these western-state volunteers believed that, should the Rebels continue their insurrection without slave labor, the Confederate revolt would become untenable. To be sure, only a minority of northern white persons considered themselves abolitionists, but, as the Civil War dragged on, a majority came to see the value of freeing and arming the South's slaves as a necessary war measure. Beyond that, as Private Ray recorded on January 1, 1863, the day Lincoln's final Emancipation Proclamation took effect, "the Blight of Slavery" rendered poor white Southerners ignorant, "worse than any Negro that had been in the North 6 months." He also endorsed Lincoln's edict.[57]

For his part, Young's letters late in the war suggest a slight change of heart, especially a certain amount of respect for the fighting ability of African American soldiers and the larger cause—freedom and true equality for all Americans—for which the approximately two hundred thousand African American soldiers and sailors who served in the Union Army and Navy fought. In early March 1863, Young asked Delia a rhetorical question and then answered it. "What do I think of the nagur? Now, I say arm and equip them giving them the same pay and all the rights and privileges of white soldiers with the same rewards fo merit, and if there is any fight in them let us have the benefit of it." He added: "Let the loyal people of every section, of every coulour, of every polittical party raise in their might, burry their party strife, and come to the suppoart of the administration and we will end this monstrous Rebellion the coming summer." Over time, then, Young thus came to accept black persons, at least as soldiers, if not as equals. Ultimately, he came to consider them necessary in suppressing the Confederate insurrection.[58]

That said, Young exhibited a common racial bias of his day against African Americans, criticizing candidly what he judged to be the poor performance of black troops at the July 30, 1864, Battle of the Crater. There Pennsylvania coal miners burrowed surreptitiously more than five hundred feet under Elliott's Salient, a Confederate fort in the outer defenses of Petersburg, Virginia, and packed four tons of black powder in the tunnel's lateral galleries. The subsequent explosion, Young reported to Delia, "was the thrilling sight perhaps ever witnessed," burying hundreds of Rebel soldiers in the wreckage. Although nine regiments of U.S. Colored Troops had trained in special maneuvers necessary to charge the breach created by the explosion, federal commanders, fearful of the political implications of black troops being massacred, ordered white troops under Brig. Gen. James H. Ledlie into the huge sheer-sided crater 130 feet long, 60 or 70 feet wide, and 25 to 30 feet deep in the Confederate lines. Brig. Gen. Edward Ferrero's division of U.S. Colored Troops constituted the next wave to enter the pit, hopeful of driving the stunned Rebels back to Petersburg.[59]

In a letter to Delia, Young reported that the black troops "went forward in good order till they came to the first breast work when they met a stuberon resistance. Instead of overcomeing . . . they broke and fled like a flock of sheep or huddled together behind the enemy's breast works to be cut to pieces by the enemys grape & canister. The enemy seeing their demorralized condition charged them in front and . . . succeeded in scaring a way the coloured Divison." Ultimately the white troops, lacking support, withdrew and "Thus was lost the fruits of near a months labour" in the federal army's drive to capture Petersburg.[60]

Young blamed the black troops, whom he considered unable to think and act without the direction of white officers, at least in part for the debacle at The Crater. Their white leaders also shouldered responsibility for the humiliating Union defeat, he said. In his opinion, had General Burnside "kept his negroes away we would have carried Petersberg." He reasoned that once the black troops and their white officers entered close quarters with the enemy, the Confederates purposely shot their leaders, "knowing that the negroes would be worth nothing without their officers." In the end, however, Young sympathized with the African American troops. He explained to Delia that "We cant blame the negroes for they will go whereever their officers lead them, but an officer of a couloured Regt is a conspicuous mark to what the same officer would be in a white Regt. And the Rebs have learned that all is necessary to defeat the couloured troops is to shoot down their officers and they will act upon it."[61]

Two days later Young wrote to Jared, explaining that he had viewed the fiasco at The Crater first hand. "Had there been no couloured troops in the assault I am confident we would have carried the entire line on the left, fortifications, and Petersberg, into the bargain," he remarked. Having said this, Young nonetheless again defended the black troops. "I have nothing to say against the courage of the negro Division. But in such a place as that where everything depends on quick manouvres no troops should be pushed forward as storming party without thoroughly understanding what is expected of them. And then they should be troops that can be handled and ma[n]ourved on the run." He credited Ferrero's men with carrying the first line of Confederate troops "in good style." But once the Rebels shot virtually all of their white officers, Young explained, "The negroes . . . huddled together like a lot of sheep and instead of charging over and carrying the next line became perfectly demorralized and run back right in the way of the suppoarting column." Young believed "That had they had sense enough to lay down behind the works five minutes would have saved them and the works too. But in their hasty retreat they forced back the suppoarting column which was compelled to break to let the couloured Division through."[62]

Although Young proved ambivalent about the employment of black troops in the Union Army, as the war dragged on he grasped the central place of slavery and, implicitly, of race in the white Southerners' rebellion. Significantly, he based his views not on ideology per se but rather on his direct experiences, observations, and self-interest. For example, writing to Jared from south of Petersburg in early November 1864, he commented on the hotly contested debates within the Confederate government over its arming of the slaves and its implication for Southern nationhood. "I see from a Richmond paper that there is likely to be a regular split amongst the Rebs about the arming of the negroes," Young noted. Confederate president "[Jefferson] Davis and his gang have grown Desperate for anything and now go in for freeing and arming two hundred & fifty thousand negroes. The Planters & Slave owners cant see it as they contend that it will ruin the institution of slavery forever. The other side contend that in case of the reelection of Lincoln they will have neither Confederacy Slaves or anything else soon if they dont do it." Northern voters overwhelmingly reelected Lincoln—whose candidacy Young supported enthusiastically—in November 1864. Both the infant Southern republic and its "peculiar institution" fell soon thereafter.[63]

What led Young to endure the hardships of war—what he termed "the contagion" of war weariness? To be sure, his devotion and loyalty to his comrades and to the Union remained firm throughout his three years service despite the immense bloodletting he witnessed. But foremost was his ideological and patriotic commitment to ensuring that the republic would survive the rebellion so that Delia and his children would enjoy the fruits of American democracy. Writing to his wife in late January 1863, he explained: "tis the thought of dear loved home that keeps me up. Was it not for the loved ones there and the pictures of them that i continually build in my immagination little would i care what became of me." These thoughts, Young insisted, kept his "honour unsullied." He admitted that "It nerves my heart to perform my duties," but "It makes me just and honourable with those that are under my command, for never will wife or child of mine have cause to be other than proud of the husband or Father while an officer in the Federal Government." Like other Civil War soldiers, then, Young fought for "country, duty, honor, and the right."[64]

Young's wartime experiences also altered him. He and his brothers in arms found a home away from home in the Seventh Wisconsin and in the Iron Brigade. Despite the severe challenges posed by combat and military life, "they did not waver in their allegiance to the restoration of the Union. They saw beyond themselves to the greater good, and accepted the sacrifices."[65]

In October 1864 Young informed Delia that he felt "verry lonesome" because one of the brigade's sister regiments, the Nineteenth Indiana, was being consolidated with another unit and leaving what he termed "the famous Old Iron Brigade." Commenting on the bonds forged in military service, Young wrote: "The friendships that are formed in camp and on the field of danger are stronger than they are in civil life. I seen officers and men of the gallant Old 19th shed tears this morning in parting with us, and I have seen those same men stand firm and swing their hats and cheer when charging on the enemy amidst a perfect storm of bullets." As the historian Lorien Foote has explained, "The struggle to save the Union forged intense bonds between men with very different ideals of manhood. A common ideology about what the Union stood for and why it must be saved brought men together in moments that counted. Shared hardships created comrades who truly loved one another." In the war's aftermath, Young stayed in touch with his men.[66]

He believed that for all its brutal horrors and destruction, the war nonetheless accomplished an essential purpose—saving the nation and establishing degrees of understanding and resolution between Northerners and Southerners. Ultimately the crucible of a brothers' war altered all participants, transforming the meaning of "the Union" from an assemblage of plural states into "the nation," a unitary whole, one certainly not without racial and sectional prejudices but one finally liberated from the manacles of chattel slavery. As the *Washington Post* editorialized in 1887, "The surrender of Mr. Davis and Gen. Lee meant a transition from the plural to the singular."[67] Following his service at Gettysburg, while on picket duty on the south side of Virginia's Rappahannock River, Young reflected on conversations he heard between Yankee and Rebel pickets separated by only about two hundred yards. He concluded that "The stories that the north and the south could not live peaceably is all noncence. The war has changed the oppinons of the mases of the South. They knew nothing of the character of the people of the north. They were led to beleive the people of the north were every thing that was low cowardly and mean but the war has taught them better. Their leaders will never fool them again."[68] Not only did the internecine conflict serve to redefine sectional boundaries and identities; it also "widened the war's purpose from the restoration of the Union to proclaim emancipation, enlist black men as soldiers, embrace black people as citizens, and reconstitute the government itself on a more democratic basis."[69]

In December 1864 Henry Young thus looked forward to returning to Wisconsin. He eagerly sought to reunite with his grieving family, to celebrate what he assumed would be a long overdue Union victory, and to find his way in the reunited union—a new nation, quite literally, the United States of America.

NOTES

1. Henry F. Young to Friends, November 15, 1861, Papers of Henry Falls Young, 1861–1902, Wisconsin Historical Society, Madison. Young addressed Warner as

"Father" in his letters. All letters from Henry cited in this introduction derive from this collection and appear in this book. Readers should consult the Editorial Statement in this book for the editors' policies concerning capitalization, punctuation, and spelling.

2. William F. Fox, *Regimental Losses in the American Civil War, 1861–1865* (Albany: Albany Publishing Company, 1889), 3; Alan T. Nolan, *The Iron Brigade: A Military History* (New York: Macmillan, 1961), 381n66.

3. Walt Whitman, *Specimen Days & Collect* (1883; reprint, New York: Dover, 1995), 80.

4. Randall M. Miller, "Introduction," in *Union Soldiers and the Northern Home Front: Wartime Experiences, Postwar Adjustments*, ed. Paul A. Cimbala and Randall M. Miller (New York: Fordham University Press, 2002), xii.

5. Ginette Aley and J. L. Anderson, "The Great National Struggle in the Heart of the Union: An Introduction," in *Union Heartland: The Midwestern Home Front during the Civil War*, ed. Ginette Aley and J. L. Anderson (Carbondale: Southern Illinois University Press, 2013), 3, 11; Thomas R. Baker, *The Sacred Cause of Union: Iowa in the Civil War* (Iowa City: University of Iowa Press, 2016), 59, 50, 37, 8–9; Matthew E. Stanley, *The Loyal West: Civil War & Reunion in Middle America* (Urbana: University of Illinois Press, 2017), 82, 91.

6. Lincoln quoted in *Washington Evening Star*, June 9, 1864.

7. Young to Delia, August 10, 15, 1862.

8. Young to Delia, April 23, 1862; Young to Father & Friends, September 26, 1862; Young to Delia, December 31, 1862; Young to Father, January 9, 1863.

9. Young to Father, July 5, 1862; Young to Delia, June 18, 1862; Young to Father, September 9, 1862.

10. Young to Father, December 1, 1862; Young to Delia, March 1, 1863.

11. On the disadvantages Wisconsin women on the home front experienced, see Ginette Aley, "Inescapable Realities: Rural Midwestern Women and Families during the Civil War," in Aley and Anderson, *Union Heartland: The Midwestern Home Front during the Civil War*, 129, and J. L. Anderson, "The Vacant Chair on the Farm: Soldier Husbands, Farm Wives, and the Iowa Home Front, 1861–65," in Aley and Anderson, *Union Heartland*, 163.

12. Young to Father, June 8, 27, 1864; Young to Delia, July 15, October 22, 1864. Here Young referred to performing picket duty.

13. Young to Delia, April 17, May 1, 1864; Young to Father, August 6, 1864; Young to Friends, November 15, 1861.

14. "Henry Falls Young," *The Weekly Teller* (Lancaster, WI), February 20, 1902.

15. Consul Willshire Butterfield, *History of Grant County Wisconsin, Containing an Account . . . of the United States* (Chicago: Western Historical Company, 1881), 868–69, 880–81; Castello N. Holford, *History of Grant County Wisconsin . . . and a History of the Several Towns* (Lancaster, WI: The Teller Print, 1900), 120–21, 144–48, 163, 617–20, 651–53.

16. Day Book, 1849–1854, vol. 2, 430, 442, Jared Warner Papers, 1836–1880, Wisconsin Historical Society (hereafter cited as Warner Papers); Grant County Register

of Deeds, *Grantor/Grantee Indexes, 1837–1901*, vol. S, 547, vol. U, 356–57; James Hibbard, "Introduction," email attachment to Micheal J. Larson, June 4, 2009.

17. "Mrs. Delia Young," *Bloomington Record* (Bloomington, WI), March 5, 1924; Grant Forsberg, "Women's Education at Knox," accessed September 23, 2017, https://www.knox.edu/about-knox/our-history/perspectives-on-knox-history/womens-education; 1850 United States Census, District 24, Grant County, Wisconsin, digital image s.v. "Delia Warner," Ancestry.com.

18. Holford, *History of Grant County*, 603, 618; Butterfield, *History of Grant County*, 858; Grant County Genealogical Society, *Marriages for Grant County*, comp. by the Grant County Genealogical Society, vol. 2, 1987; Young to Delia, October 4, 1862.

19. Grant County Register of Deeds, *Grantor/Grantee Indexes, 1837–1901*, vol. G.2, 584; Day Book, 1854–1880, vol. 3, 87, Warner Papers; 1860 United States Census, Schedule 5, Products of Industry Census, Town of Cassville, Grant County, 2; Hibbard, "Introduction," June 4, 2009. It is not known whether the $2,000 paid by Young to Wetmore constituted part of the $3,749.69, but Warner, in lieu of these arrangements, made Young an equal partner in the mill on Christmas Day 1858.

20. Phillip Shaw Paludan, *"A People's Contest": The Union and Civil War, 1861–1865* (New York: Harper & Row, 1988), 15, 157; Paul W. Gates, *Agriculture and the Civil War* (New York: Knopf, 1965), 229.

21. *The Weekly Teller*, February 20, 1902; Edwin Bentley Quiner, *Quiner Scrapbooks: Correspondence of the Wisconsin Volunteers, 1861–1865*, 10 vols., electronic reproduction (Madison: Wisconsin Historical Society, 2010), vol. 1, 270 (hereafter cited as *Quiner Scrapbooks*); "Lancaster Union Guards—Positive Service," *Grant County Herald*, June 27, 1861; "Pole and Flag Raising at McCartney's-Cassville-Beetown," *Grant County Herald*, July 3, 1861; "New Companies," *Grant County Herald*, August 14, 1861. On Young's election by his peers, see "Capt. Callis' Company," *Grant County Herald*, August 21, 1861. Sources disagree on when Young enlisted in the state forces. Wisconsin, Adjutant General's Office, *Roster of the Wisconsin Volunteers, War of the Rebellion, 1861–1865*, Blue Books, 2 vols. (Madison: Democrat Printing Press, 1886), 1:558, reports that he enlisted on June 27, 1861 (hereafter cited as *Roster*).

22. *Quiner Scrapbooks*, vol. 1, 270; Lance J. Herdegen, "Introduction: William R. Ray, the Seventh Wisconsin, and the Iron Brigade," in *Four Years with the Iron Brigade: The Civil War Journals of William R. Ray, Co. F., Seventh Wisconsin Infantry*, ed. Lance Herdegen and Sherry Murphy (Cambridge, MA: Da Capo Press, 2002), xvi. Over the course of the war more than seventy thousand troops trained at Camp Randall. On the "Huckleberry" nickname, see Lance J. Herdegen and William J. K. Beaudot, *In the Bloody Railroad Cut at Gettysburg: The 6th Wisconsin of the Iron Brigade and Its Famous Charge* (El Dorado Hills, CA: Savas Beatie, 2015), 102. The Seventh Wisconsin also had another nickname: "the bully seaventh." See Ray journal entry, October 31, 1861, in Herdegen and Murphy, eds., *Four Years with the Iron Brigade*, 16. In 1861–62 Wisconsin sent eleven infantry regiments to the federal armies.

23. "Troops at Camp Randall," *Wisconsin State Journal* (Madison, WI), August 15, 1861 (hereafter cited as *WSJ*); "Matters at Camp Randall," *WSJ*, August 16, 1861;

"Matters at Camp Randall," *WSJ*, September 5, 1861; "The Seventh and Eighth Regiment," *WSJ*, September 12, 1861; "At the Camp," *WSJ*, September 20, 1861; Ray journal entry, December 23, 1861, in Herdegen and Murphy, eds., *Four Years with the Iron Brigade*, 37; *Quiner Scrapbooks*, vol. 1, 274.

24. "Colonel of the 7th Regiment," *WSJ*, June 25, 1861; "A Hungarian Colonel in Wisconsin," *Wilmington Clinton Republican* (Wilmington, OH), July 5, 1861; *Roster*, 1:538.

25. "Matters at Camp Randall," *WSJ*, August 16, 1861; "The War and Temperance," *Manitowoc Daily Tribune* (Manitowoc, WI), August 28, 1861; "Acquitted," *Daily Milwaukee Press and News*, September 11, 1861; Gerald F. Linderman, *Embattled Courage: The Experience of Combat in the American Civil War* (New York: Free Press, 1987), 120; Young to Father, October 21, 1864; Herdegen and Beaudot, *In the Bloody Railroad Cut at Gettysburg*, 107. In his journals William R. Ray of Company F, a temperance man, recorded several instances of Young drinking alcohol excessively. See entries of January 28, April 19, 1862, and July 4, 1864, in Herdegen and Murphy, eds., *Four Years with the Iron Brigade*, 45–46, 80, 287.

26. "Regimental Appointments," *WSJ*, August 15, 1861; "Matters at Camp Randall," *WSJ*, September 5, 1861; *Quiner Scrapbooks*, vol. 1, 269; *Roster*, 1:538.

27. *Roster*, 1:538, 558; Young to Delia, March 10, 1863.

28. "Notes from Camp Randall," *WSJ*, September 13, 1861.

29. Ethel Alice Hurn, *Wisconsin Women in the War between the States* (Madison: Wisconsin History Commission, 1911), 100–102, electronic reproduction, Wisconsin Historical Society, 2005; "The Vivandiere of the Seventh Regiment," *WSJ*, September 19, 1861; "The Seventh Regiment in Chicago," *Janesville Daily Gazette* (Janesville, WI), September 25, 1861; Lance J. Herdegen, *The Men Stood Like Iron: How the Iron Brigade Won Its Name* (Bloomington: Indiana University Press, 1997), 28. A vivandiere performed all manner of duties, including washing, cleaning, and nursing sick or injured soldiers. Another noted vivandiere, Miss Eliza Wilson, of Dunn County, accompanied the Fifth Wisconsin Regiment, composed of men from Menomonie and nearby counties.

30. *Quiner Scrapbooks*, vol. 1, 274; "At the Camp," *WSJ*, September 20, 1861; "The Seventh Regiment," *Janesville Daily Gazette*, September 21, 1861.

31. *Quiner Scrapbooks*, vol. 1, 272–75.

32. *Quiner Scrapbooks*, vol. 1, 272–75.

33. Stephen R. Taaffe, *Commanding the Army of the Potomac* (Lawrence: University Press of Kansas, 2006), 198; Richard Slotkin, *The Long Road to Antietam: How the Civil War Became a Revolution* (New York: Liveright, 2012), 205; Richard Slotkin, *No Quarter: The Battle of the Crater, 1864* (New York: Random House, 2009), 101. Following Gibbon's promotion to division command in November 1862, Brig. Gen. Solomon Meredith commanded the Iron Brigade.

34. Lance J. Herdegen, *The Iron Brigade in Civil War and Memory: The Black Hats from Bull Run to Appomattox and Thereafter* (El Dorado Hills, CA: Savas Beatie, 2012), 70–71; Robert K. Beecham in *Wisconsin State Patriot*, July 9, 1862, p. 1, quoted in Alan D. Gaff, *On Many a Bloody Field: Four Years in the Iron Brigade* (Bloomington: Indiana University Press, 1996), 141.

35. Young to Delia, October 2, 1861; Young to Delia and Eva, December 1, 1861.

36. Young to Father, September 9, 1862; Herdegen, *The Men Stood Like Iron*, 103; Gaff, *On Many a Bloody Field*, 156; Mark M. Boatner III, *The Civil War Dictionary*, rev. ed. (New York: Vintage Books, 1991), 427.

37. Wisconsin, Adjutant General's Office, *Regimental Muster and Descriptive Rolls, 1861–1866*, Red Books (Madison: State Militia, Adjutant General's Office, 1865), reel 3, 7th Infantry; Allan [*sic*] T. Nolan, "Iron Brigade," in *Encyclopedia of the American Civil War: A Political, Social, and Military History*, ed. David S. Heidler and Jeanne T. Heidler (New York: Norton, 2000), 1040.

38. Herdegen, *The Men Stood Like Iron*, 146; Herdegen and Beaudot, *In the Bloody Railroad Cut at Gettysburg*, 131; Jeffry D. Wert, *A Brotherhood of Valor: The Common Soldiers of the Stonewall Brigade, C.S.A., and the Iron Brigade, U.S.A.* (New York: Simon & Schuster, 1999), 316, 317; Herdegen, "Introduction: William R. Ray, the Seventh Wisconsin, and the Iron Brigade," xv.

39. Young to Delia, September 18, 1862; Young to Father, September 20, 1862.

40. Young to Father, December 17, 1862; Young to Delia, December 17, 1862.

41. Nolan, *The Iron Brigade*, 210–11; Young to Father, May 13, 1863; Herdegen, "Introduction: William R. Ray, the Seventh Wisconsin, and the Iron Brigade," xiv.

42. Herdegen, *The Men Stood Like Iron*, 4; Jerome A. Watrous quoted in Herdegen, *The Men Stood Like Iron*, 9.

43. Young to Delia, July 4, 1863; Lance J. Herdegen, "John F. Reynolds and the Iron Brigade," in *Giants in Their Tall Black Hats: Essays on the Iron Brigade*, ed. Alan T. Nolan and Sharon Eggleston Vipond (Bloomington: Indiana University Press, 1998), 112; Jean Huets, "The Iron Brigade," *New York Times*, July 23, 2013; Boatner, *The Civil War Dictionary*, 428.

44. Young to Father, July 11, 27, 1863; William R. Ray journal entry, September 25, 1863, in Herdegen and Murphy, eds., *Four Years with the Iron Brigade*, 220.

45. On March 24, 1864, the army discontinued the First Corps, Army of the Potomac, reassigning it to the Second and Fourth divisions, Fifth Army Corps. According to the historian Richard J. Sommers, "Devastating in attack, unshakable in defense, well led, the I Corps was destroyed by its own achievements." See RJS [Richard J. Sommers], "Union Corps," in *Historical Times Illustrated Encyclopedia of the Civil War*, ed. Patricia L. Faust (New York: Harper & Row, 1986), 172.

46. Table 4, Return of Casualties for First Brigade, May 5–7, 1864, in Nolan and Vipond, eds., *Giants in Their Tall Black Hats*, 205n151, 270; Herdegen, *The Iron Brigade in Civil War and Memory*, 451; Nolan, *The Iron Brigade*, 270; James M. McPherson, *For Cause & Comrades: Why Men Fought in the Civil War* (New York: Oxford University Press, 1997), 84; Chaplain Samuel Eaton quoted in Gaff, *On Many a Bloody Field*, 352; Mark Grimsley, *And Keep Moving On: The Virginia Campaign, May–June, 1864* (Lincoln: University of Nebraska Press, 2002).

47. Young to Father, September 19, 1864; Young to Delia, November 10, 1864.

48. Young to Father, November 20, 1864.

49. Young to Father, January 11, 1862, December 23, 1861.

50. Young to Father, January 11, 1862.

51. Young to Father, December 23, 1861; *Wisconsin State Patriot*, February 4, 1863, p. 2, quoted in Gaff, *On Many a Bloody Field*, 215–16. Despite this soldier's remark, the historian Chandra Manning uncovered a case in November 1861 where a member of Young's regiment, then stationed at Arlington Heights, Virginia, declared that "every private in the ranks" condemned slavery—"that system which tramples on the honor of man, and makes merchandise of the virtue of women." Chandra Manning, *What This Cruel War Was Over: Soldiers, Slavery, and the Civil War* (New York: Knopf, 2007), 49.

52. Young to Delia, November 2, 1862. On the ambivalence of the men of the Iron Brigade toward the Emancipation Proclamation, see Herdegen, *The Iron Brigade in Civil War and Memory*, 290–91.

53. Fearful of alienating border-state Unionists, especially white Kentuckians, Lincoln chose not to unveil his plan to recruit African Americans for armed military service until he issued the final Emancipation Proclamation on January 1, 1863. See John David Smith, *Lincoln and the U.S. Colored Troops* (Carbondale: Southern Illinois University Press, 2013), 23–24.

54. Harry S. Stout, *American Aristocrats: A Family, a Fortune, and the Making of American Capitalism* (New York: Basic Books, 2017), 276.

55. Young to Delia, November 15, December 31, 1862, February 14, 1863.

56. Young to Father & Friends, September 26, 1862; Young to Delia, October 4, 1862.

57. Ray journal entry, January 1, 26, 1863, in Herdegen and Murphy, eds., *Four Years with the Iron Brigade*, 167, 165. On this metamorphosis on the part of Union troops, see Chandra Manning, "Wartime Nationalism and Race: Comparing the Visions of Confederate, Black Union, and White Union Soldiers," in *In the Cause of Liberty: How the Civil War Redefined American Ideals*, ed. William J. Cooper Jr. and John M. McCardell Jr. (Baton Rouge: Louisiana State University Press, 2009), 87–104.

58. Young to Delia, March 10, 1863.

59. Young to Delia, August 4, 1864.

60. Young to Delia, August 4, 1864.

61. Young to Delia, August 4, 1864.

62. Young to Father, August 6, 1864.

63. Young to Father, November 7, 1864. On Confederate emancipation, see Robert F. Durden, *The Gray and the Black: The Confederate Debate on Emancipation* (Baton Rouge: Louisiana State University Press, 1972); Bruce Levine, *Confederate Emancipation: Southern Plans to Free and Arm Slaves during the Civil War* (New York: Oxford University Press, 2006); and Philip D. Dillard, *Jefferson Davis's Final Campaign: Confederate Nationalism and the Fight to Arm Slaves* (Macon, GA: Mercer University Press, 2017).

64. Young to Delia, February 14, January 25, 1863; McPherson, *For Cause & Comrades*, 92, 6.

65. Wert, *A Brotherhood of Valor*, 317–18; Gaff, *On Many a Bloody Field*, 364.

66. Young to Delia, October 13, 1864; Lorien Foote, *The Gentlemen and the Roughs: Violence, Honor, and Manhood in the Union Army* (New York: New York

University Press, 2010), 179; Herdegen and Beaudot, *In the Bloody Railroad Cut at Gettysburg*, 251.

67. J. M. McK., "'The United States Has' and 'Remarks,'" *Washington Post*, April 24, 1887.

68. Young to Father, August 23, 1863.

69. Edward L. Ayers, *The Thin Light of Freedom: The Civil War and Emancipation in the Heart of America* (New York: Norton, 2017), 20.

Dear Delia

CHAPTER ONE

"Old Abe looks first rate, and is not a homely man by any means"

August 31 to December 27, 1861

Camp Randall Aug 31 1861

Dear Delia

I have been from home A whole week, and have not time to write but a few lines at that. We arrived here on Thursday afternoon. The men had to be mustered into the service of Unkle Sam and get into their uniform and arms so that we have been verry busy. I was up in the town yesterday to get mesured for my uniform is the only time I have been out of camp.[1]

I have to pay for all my chlothes. So do all commissioned officers. The captain & S Woodhouse went with me. We left the men in camp to change their chlothes, and when we came back we hardley knew our own men. They had all got on their uniforms and are the finest looking company in camp.[2]

We are all well and enjoy ourselves verry much. We are well fed have plenty to eat. The drum is beating for officer drill, and i must close in order to send this to day. Kiss the babies for me and except all the love for your self that can be sent in a letter.

yours affectionately

H F Young

I will write you full account of all we have and do soon.

NOTES

1. Many Wisconsin regiments trained during the Civil War were sent to Camp Randall. Named Camp Randall by the colonel of the Second Wisconsin, the site was

Camp Randall Aug 31 1861
Dear Delia
I have been from home
a whole week, and have not time
to write but a few lines at that
we arrived here on Thursday afternoon
the men had to be mustered into the
Service of Unkle Sam and get their
uniforms and arms so that we have
been very busy I was up in
town yesterday to get mesured for
my uniform is the only time I have
been out of Camp
I have to pay for all my clothes
so do all commissioned officers
the captain & I Woodhouse went with
me, we left the men in Camp to
change their clothes,
and when we came back we hardly
knew our own men they had all
got on their uniform and are the
finest looking company in Camp

2nd Lt. Henry Falls Young, August 31, 1861, letter to Delia (Wisconsin Historical Society, Henry Falls Young Papers, 1861–1902)

We are all well and enjoy ourselves
verry much we are well fed have
plenty to eat

The drum is beeting for officer
drill and i must close in order to
Send this to day

Kiss the babies for me
and except all the love for
your self that can be sent in
a letter

Yours affectionately

H J Young

I will write you a full account
of all we have and do soon

originally the State Agricultural Society's fairground. Other training grounds in the state were in Milwaukee (Camp Scott), Racine (Camp Utley), and Fond du Lac. Initially issued a gray uniform, many men were upset that the burden of paying for the uniforms rested on their shoulders. Richard N. Current, *The History of Wisconsin*, vol. 2, *The Civil War Era, 1848–1873* (Madison: State Historical Society of Wisconsin, 1976), 337–38.

2. Samuel Woodhouse enlisted as a first lieutenant in Company F of the Seventh Wisconsin on June 27, 1861. In the fall of 1861 Young had three children, Jared, Laura, and May. At the time of his departure from home, Young was thirty-six years old, while his wife, Delia, was twenty-five. Wisconsin, Adjutant General's Office, *Roster of the Wisconsin Volunteers, War of the Rebellion, 1861–1865*, Blue Books, 2 vols. (Madison: Democrat Printing Press, 1886), 1:558 (hereafter cited as *Roster*); 1860 United States Census, Cassville, Grant County, Wisconsin, digital image s.v. "Henry Young," Ancestry.com.

Camp Randall Sept 6 1861

Dear Delia

I have received no letter from you not yet and I want one so very much. I am well and have more work on hand than I can well attend to.

Now for my routine of duty. There is the ten Companies of the Seventh here and the Companys of the 8 wich I suppose will be full this week which will make 2000 men in the encampment. The tents of each company are set accorded to the plot I send you. Six men to each tent. the capt, 1 tent. The two Lieuts one tent between them. We are called at daylight by firing of the canon. Then roll call ½ hour to wash comb hair and c. Then drill to 7 oclock. Then breakfast. We all eat together. Each company at its own table. You would laugh to see two thousand men march intwo the cook house and all sit down to a meal at once and all talking at the same time. After breakfast we march to our tents. Dismiss at 8 oclock. We have to attend officer drill, at half past 9. We have to Drill our companys untill the drum beat for dinner. At two oclock we have to attend sword drill. At three we have to commence to drill the men. We drill to 5 oclock, then supper. After supper dress parade which is over by sunset, from that to 9 oclock we studdy military tactics.[3]

There now you have it. Tell Furman to write and write your self.[4]

Kiss the babies for me. Oh how I would like to see them and i will if I can before we leave. And now dear keep in good heart.

your affectionately

H F Young

NOTES

3. The Eighth Wisconsin training overlapped with the Seventh Wisconsin at Camp Randall. One of their recruits, "Old Abe," the war eagle of the Eighth Wisconsin, was brought to Madison by the Eau Claire Badgers (later Eagles), a company of men from west-central Wisconsin. Old Abe served with the regiment for the entire war. The men did not train for a long time before they were sent to the theater of war; training was similar in the North and South and kept the men busy each day with squad, company, and battalion drill and dress parade. "The Seventh and Eighth Regiments," *Wisconsin State Journal* (Madison, WI), September 12, 1861; Gerald F. Linderman, *Embattled Courage: The Experience of Combat in the American Civil War* (New York: Free Press, 1987), 118.

4. Cornelius Furman purchased a small tract of land next to Young's in Cassville Township, and during the war he rented half of the mill in Young's absence. His wife, Caroline, was mentioned in many of Young's letters home. His last name, Furman, was alternately spelled Firman or Farman in different census documents and on his marriage certificate; for uniformity, Furman will be used in the subsequent annotations. 1860 United States Census, Cassville, Grant County, Wisconsin, digital image s.v. "Cornelius Furman," Ancestry.com; 1870 United States Census, Wisconsin, digital image s.v. "Cornelius Firman," FamilySearch.org; Wisconsin, County Marriages, 1836–1911, digital image s.v. "Cornelius T. Furman"; Grant County Register of Deeds, *Grantor/Grantee Indexes, 1837–1901*, vol. N.2, 82, 84.

Camp Randall Sept 15 1861

Dear Wife & Babies

I would have writen this letter sooner, but i have hoped to get home, which i am afraid is no go as there is no furloughs granted for longer than forty Eight hours which would be to short for me to get home and return. We are ordered to leave for Washington next wendsday. If the order should be countermanded i will try and get home. Father has been here. He left this morning. I sent my chlothes with him. There has been quite a number of acquaintances here from Grant County. I will get my Photograph taken and send it home as soon as i get my full uniform. I have got all now but my sword & sash. I get one month extra pay which will give me all the money I want at present. I get that for helping raise the company. Woodhouse gets the same.[5]

Our boys are all well and in good spirits. Wm Ray met with an accidint. We were drilling on the double quick when one of the boys fell down, and Wm ran against his bayonett, but he is able to be about and will be all right in a few days. I have plenty of hard work to do but i get along first rate. I have not been found fault with by an officer yet which is saying a great deal, for Col Vandor is a good deciplinarian. If i could only get home and see you and the babies i would be perfectly satisfied. Through the day when i am hard at work i do not think much of home or any thing else except the drill, but i lie down on my cot at night i go to sleep thinking of the Dear old girl and the babies.[6]

And now i must scold a little for i have received but one letter in this place. It is not so bad for i hear from home every few days but i want you to write as often as twice a week after we leave here, and i will write as often as i can find time. Direct to Lieut H F Young Company F 7 Reg Wis volunteers. You can send your letters to Madison and they will follow us wherever we go until you get a letter from me. I have got two uniforms. One grey and one blue. The two cost fifty five dollars without the caps. My sword sash & belt will cost $34.50 and i have to buy a trunk and revolver and then i am thoroughly equipt. The men are furnished two suits apiece all round, but the officers have to buy theirs. If i have any money to spare after i get my outfit i will send you some. When i get east i will send you and the children some presents.[7]

Tell Furman to write to me and let me know how he gets along with the mill. If you want a girl get one and i will send you the money to pay her, and if Eva cannot stay with you i want you to get some good girl to stay with you and live at mill. I cannot bear the idea of your leaving our dear old home. Kiss the babies for me.[8]

yours in all things

H F Young

NOTES

5. Young referred to Jared Warner as Father in his letters. Warner represented Grant County in the Wisconsin State Assembly in 1861. Wisconsin, *A Manual of Customs, Precedents and Forms, . . . The Rules, The Apportionments, and Other Lists and Tables for Reference, With Indices,* comp. D. H. D. Crane (Madison: E. A. Calkins & Company, 1861), 35 (hereafter cited as *Blue Book* by year).

6. William Ray was in Company F of the Seventh Wisconsin. The wound was not serious enough to interrupt Ray's drilling, and he returned to the company soon. Col. Vandor was a strict disciplinarian, a trait that did not sit well with some of the officers in the regiment. From the moment they reached Washington, DC, he ceased to actively lead the regiment. This fractured relationship, as well as accusations of corruption, eventually led to his resignation in January 1862. "Accident at the Camp," *Wisconsin State Journal*, September 13, 1861; "Our Washington Correspondence," *Wisconsin State Journal*, November 22, 1861; "Trouble in the Regiments," *Janesville Daily Gazette* (Janesville, WI), October 31, 1861; *Roster*, 1:560; Alan T. Nolan, *The Iron Brigade: A Military History* (New York: Macmillan, 1961), 26–27.

7. The state provided gray uniforms to the first eight regiments. Issued blue uniforms once they were manufactured, the men paid for the new ones at their own expense. Current, *The Civil War Era, 1848–1873*, 2:339.

8. Joseph Trotter Mills, an early pioneer of Grant County, whose first wife was the sister of Jared Warner, Evalina. When she died, he married Warner's youngest sister, Rebecca. The 1860 Federal Census shows a daughter by the name of Evalina, Eva for short, age fourteen, who was Delia's first cousin. This was the Eva that Young referred to throughout the letters. J. T. Mills was a lawyer, judge, district attorney, and state assemblyman throughout much of his life. 1860 United States Census, Lancaster, Grant County, Wisconsin, digital image s.v. "J. T. Mills," Ancestry.com; Castello N. Holford, *History of Grant County Wisconsin . . . and a History of the Several Towns* (Lancaster, WI: The Teller Print, 1900), 113–15.

Camp Randall Sept 17 1861

Dear Delia

I have received but one letter from you yet i am well and right side up with care. I send you my Photograph and $20 and two cents for Jared & Laura. Mrs Ramsey will take them to you. Use the money. I have kept plenty to do me.[9]

We are expecting to leave here every day now.

I will write as soon as we get to Washington. Write often and keep in good spirits for i will come back some day. I have sent your father and Rebecca each a likeness just like the one i send you. Kiss the babies for me and my love to your self.[10]

Henry

NOTES

9. Jane Ramsey, Cassville Township, lived with her husband, William, a carpenter. 1860 United States Census, Cassville, Grant County, Wisconsin, digital image s.v. "Jane Ramsey," Ancestry.com.

10. According to a family tree drawn by James Hibbard, archivist in the Southwest Room at the University of Wisconsin–Platteville, Rebecca S. Warner may be Young's reference to "Susan" throughout the letters. She was the younger sister of Young's wife, Delia. James Hibbard, hand drawn family tree to Micheal J. Larson, undated; 1860 United States Census, Patch Grove, Grant County, Wisconsin, digital image s.v. "Rebecca Warner," Ancestry.com.

Washington Sept 28 1861

Dear Delia

We are encamped one mile & a half East of the capital on capital hill. We left Camp Randall 21 at 5 oclock in the morning and arrived at Washington on 27 at 3 oclock PM. All safe and sound. We had some hard time and some verry plesant on the trip. In most places we were received with great entusiasm particularly at Pittsburg and Baltimore. The citizens that are loyal turned en masa. You would have thought is the most loyal city in the union. In washington all is quiet. You hear far more news out west than we do here but you must recolect it is most of it guess work, for to fill the papers. I have not had the to look round yet.[11]

Capt McKee came to see us yesterday. His men are well. You here of no army movements here only when they have been executed. When you read in the papers about washington being in danger you must not believe it for there is no danger. Our General George McClelan would just like for the rebbles to actact washington. I received your second letter the night before we left madison and it done me more good than any thing in the world could have done except to have had a furlough.[12]

And now write often for Cornel Vandor says we now belong to the government and must attend to our duties as officers first. I like the life of the soldier first rate.

I will write some again. I am writing this on the back of a knapsack as we have not got our camp equipage yet. Kiss the babies and write. Keep in good heart and all will be well. Give my love to all but your self in particular.

Henry

NOTES

11. The Seventh Wisconsin left Camp Randall at 11 a.m. on September 21, 1861, and arrived in Washington, DC, on the afternoon of September 26. They received a

rousing welcome along the route to Washington. Treated well in Baltimore, despite its questionable loyalty to the Union, the soldiers marched through the city to affectionate cries from the citizens. "Don't you dare come back here without Jeff. Davis' head!" was heard by one soldier in the regiment. Edwin Bentley Quiner, *Quiner Scrapbooks: Correspondence of the Wisconsin Volunteers, 1861–1865*, 10 vols., electronic reproduction (Madison: Wisconsin Historical Society Digital Collections, 2010), vol. 1, 274–75.

12. Capt. David McKee, Company C of the Second Wisconsin, was promoted in March 1862 to lieutenant colonel of the Fifteenth Wisconsin. Maj. Gen. George B. McClellan assumed command of the Army of the Potomac on August 29, 1861. *Roster*, 1:363; 2:804; United States, War Records Office, *War of the Rebellion: A Compilation of the Official Records of the Union and Confederate Armies*, 128 vols. (Washington, DC: Government Printing Office, 1885–1901), ser. 1, vol. 5, 1 (hereafter cited as *OR*).

Chain Bridge Oct 2 1861

Dear Delia

We are encamped at the famous chain bridge you have heard so much about. We broke up camp yesterday and marched down to washington, and was sent out here. We are encamped with the Second and Sixth wis. We have seen all the boys from old grant. I thought some of them would have went crazy when we marched in yeterday. John Bergess L Showwalter look hearty & stout. So do all the rest of the boys. You can stand in our encampment and see the tents of twenty Regiments of men encamped. The Rebels have fallen back in their fortifications but they wont get us to follow them this time. I had not time to look round Washington, (but give me the west) in preference to any place i have seen yet for I consider this a cussed poor country nigers and all. Every thing is verry high priced particularly provisions.[13]

The land all round us belonged to Secesionists and is confiscated. We have good watter in this camp and the only sickness we have is measles which if there is enough to go round will go through the regiment. I am making poor writing this morning but if you could see me on my marrow bones beside my trunk you would not wonder at it. We have not our tent fixed up yet. I went over last night and took supper with Herman Ganter, C Okey, B Moris, J Babcock and L Parsons, & J Richards, of the Sixth and this morning George Stephenson came for me to Eat breakfast with them. I went over and found him L Shoualter, Cook, Jimmy Hughs, Stephenson fom Muscalunge George Hallowway, in one mess in the Second. They are a jolly set of fellows and enjoy them selves firstrate. I must close this quick for the drum is beating for Drill. Kiss the babies and give my love to all. I want a letter verry bad. I have received none since i left Camp Randall.[14]

yours Truly

H F Young

Direct to Washington DC

NOTES

13. Spanning the Potomac River, Chain Bridge provided the army access to the countryside from Washington, DC. 2nd Lt. Levi Showalter and John H. Burgess were both in Company C of the Second Wisconsin. Company C of Second Wisconsin counted many men from Grant County among its ranks. Another regiment, Company C of the Sixth Wisconsin, also enlisted many men from Grant County. Nolan, *The Iron Brigade*, 31; *Roster*, 1:353–54.

14. A constant throughout the war was the loss of men to sickness and disease. A February enumeration of the brigade showed 263 of 3,669 men as sick. Each man mentioned in this letter lived in Grant County and enlisted in either the Second or the Sixth Wisconsin. Showalter, Michael Cook, James Hughes, George Stephenson, and George W. Holloway were in Company C of the Second Wisconsin, while Herman Ganter, Cornelius Okey, Braeton B. Morris, Cuyler Babcock, Luke Parsons, and John Richards were in Company C, Sixth Wisconsin. Muscalunge was a small village in Beetown Township, Grant County. Nolan, *The Iron Brigade*, 35; "From the Seventh Regiment," *Janesville Daily Gazette*, February 1, 1862; *OR*, ser. 1, vol. 5, 718; *Roster*, 1:353–55, 505–7.

Arlington Heights Oct 6 1861

Dear Delia

Here we are on the famous ground you have heard so much about. But first let me tell you I rec your long letter of the fifteenth. It was a long time on the road as I got it yesterday morning but the news of how well you were getting along was almost satisfaction for having to wait so long. I had more confidence in your ability to get a long than you had and i am perfectly satisfied with the result. Tell Jared I am glad he is such a good boy and as soon as i can have a chance I will send him a popgun. Tell Laura that papa would like to rock his little girl to sleep once more verry much but be a good girl to moma and when papa comes home he will bring her something nice.

And Dear little may. You will have to kiss her for me, as I expect she would not know me if i was to go home now. O how i would like to see you all this morning, but the soldier is a Machine ~~o~~ so said Napoleon. And he toled the truth to a certain extent.[15]

We were at Chain bridge above Washington when I wrote you last. Day before yesterday just at dark we (that is to say Kings Brigade) which consists of the Wisconsin 2, 6, 7, Indiana 19 making 4 Reg, were ordered to strike tents yesterday morning at 8 oclock *am*, and march to Georgetown cross the Potomac and join Mc Dowls Division on arlington heights. And here we are where the woods are so thick you cant see out but by looking right straight up, but these woods are full of forts, and masked Bateries all ready for a fight with the Secesh as soon as they show themselves. And as I wrote you before there is no danger of Washington at present.[16]

But every thing indicates a forward movement on the enemies lines. We expect to move on in a day or two or we may receive orders to move within the next hour, as we know nothing of a movement intill we get orders to march. I must again caution you not to beleive what you see in the dalie papers for they are not allowed to publish army movement of any importance. You may form some idea of how strict the orders are when one of us officers cant get a permit to visit the city, unless it is some special duty connected with the army. All private business must be laid asside for the present, and we all feel satisfied that it is the only way to keep out the enemies from our lines. This is the hotest weather I ever experienced for the time of year. Yesterday many of the men gave out. Our Reg stood it better than the Second. We arrived here before dark but the bagage did not get along so we rolled ourselves in our blankets and went supperless to bed, and I did not hear one word of a grumbling from either men or officers. Such is the life of the soldier when on active duty. I would not live here if i had the best farm in the country. I dont like it at all. I do not like the country East half as well as the west. The fields rivers and every thing is so different from the west.

U tell Firman I have not received any letter from him yet. Tell him the rough soldier life agrees with me for I have gained seven pounds since I left the mill, and now I will tell you what we have to eat. Yesterday morning we had potatoes coffee, fat pork, and Bread. For dinner I had Bread and water that I carried in my Haversack and canteen. Last night I had no supper. This morning we had coffee fat pork and bread, and we eat it like a set of hungry bears. And we are all satisfied no one wishes to leave while he is

Brig. Gen. Rufus King (Library of Congress, Prints & Photographs Division, Civil War Photographs, LC-DIG-cwpb-6711)

well, but is is a hard place on a person that is sick to be piled away in a wagon and hauled over these rough roads. Tell him not to wait for me to write for i postively have not the time to spare.

Give my love to Caroline and all the friends. Wilcox left here yesterday. He said he would call and see you. John Bergess and all the boys of the Second are well.[17]

your with true affection

Henry

NOTES

15. John Parke Custis, the stepson of George Washington, built Arlington Heights, the home of Robert E. Lee. The Lees evacuated Arlington at the onset of

hostilities. Brig. Gen. Rufus King used the house as his headquarters when his brigade encamped nearby. Lance J. Herdegen, *The Men Stood Like Iron: How the Iron Brigade Won Its Name* (Bloomington: Indiana University Press, 1997), 31.

16. General King, originally from New York City, graduated from West Point in 1833 and moved to Wisconsin in 1845. He helped draft the Wisconsin State Constitution, was part owner and editor of the *Milwaukee Sentinel and Gazette*, and was the first commander of the brigade. Saddled with the defeat of Union forces at the First Battle of Bull Run, Maj. Gen. Irvin McDowell, in a demotion, was given command of the First Corps, which included King's Division and the Seventh Wisconsin. "Secesh" was a slang term that referred to the secessionists, the Southern states that had seceded from the Union. Nolan, *The Iron Brigade*, 24–25; Herdegen, *The Men Stood Like Iron*, 31; Lance J. Herdegen, *The Iron Brigade in Civil War and Memory: The Black Hats from Bull Run to Appomattox and Thereafter* (El Dorado Hills, CA: Savas Beatie, 2012), 44–45; *OR*, ser. 1, vol. 5, 18, 755.

17. Franklin Wilcox was in Company K of the Sixth Wisconsin. *Roster*, 1:536.

Camp Arlington Oct 20 1861

Dear Delia

Here we are yet in the same camp as when I wrote you last with good health and as the saying is all anxious to meet the Secsh.[18]

The weather is warm with no sign of frost yet, but when it rains we have an abundance of mud of the stickiest kind.

We had a grand review day before yesterday of our whole brigade, which was a verry grand affair, and we all acquitted ourselves well. Besides Gen McDowells staff King & staff. There were a number of distinguished visitors on the ground, Wm H Seward, Prince DeJoinvelle, and many others.[19]

I have not been to Washington but once since i came on this side of the river as it hard to get a pass except on important business. Captan Mckee is verry sick and is at the hospital at Georgetown. They have telegraphed to his wife to come and see him. Our company is all able to be about. We have had some severe cases of measles but they are all better. On friday evening while we were on dress parade we noticed a baloon coming in our direction. We see them frequently but this one was coming straight for us and come down about a mile from our camp. Then it was best fellow for most. We run the guards and run all the way to it, and found Lamountam with his balloon Saritoga instead of the Secesh we had hoped. And we have incidents occurring every day which keeps up the excitement.[20]

I would like to see you all this pleasant Sunday morning. Verry verry much indeed. Tell Jared and Laura that papa never sees any children but what he thinks of them. I received your letter and hope to get another soon.

yours ever

H F Young

NOTES

18. The brigade wintered at Camp Arlington, Virginia, in 1861–62. Nolan, *The Iron Brigade*, 31.

19. King's Brigade was reviewed by Secretary of State Seward; the ministers of France, England, and Spain; and Francois-Ferdinand-Philippe-Louis-Marie d'Orleans, more commonly known as Prince de Joinville. A French aristocrat who fell out of favor with Napoleon III, Joinville eventually found his way to the United States and offered his services to President Lincoln at the beginning of the war. "Distinguished Visitors," *Evening Star* (Washington, DC), October 19, 1861; *Encyclopedia Britannica On-line*, s.v. "Prince de Joinville," accessed April 6, 2016, http://www.britannica.com/biography/Francois-Ferdinand-Philippe-Louis-Marie-dOrleans-prince-de-Joinville.

20. Saratoga, an observation balloon, piloted by Professor La Mountain, made many reconnaissance missions near the nation's capital in the fall of 1861. "A Successful Balloon Ascension," *Evening Star*, October 19, 1861.

Camp Arlington Oct 26 1861

Father & Friends

We are still on the heights with rations cooked, and a standing order to be ready to march at a moments notice. If it was not for the hard work they give us by Drilling us 6 hours every day we would all get the blues. We get up at 6. Breakfast at 7. Batallion Drill comes on at 9 to 12 oclock. 2 oclock Brigade Drill in which the 4 Reg. all drill under Gen. McDowl, or Gen. King. 5 oclock Dress parade. So you see wee are kept busy.

You will have heard of the army movements and the death of Baker. It seem to be the intention of the Rebbles to kill all of our officers in all the skirmishing our men have with them. Their aim is to shoot down the officers first. You are near enough to the seat of the war, and I hope it may never get any nigher my home than it is now. If you would see the destruction of property you would feel like dying on the field of battle if you could prevent a war from coming near your home. If the Rebbles would only try to mak good their threat of attacting us we would make short work with them. It would take all the men they could raise and that doubled to do any thing with our position.[21]

We have forts commanding every bit of ground between Falls Church or munsons hill and Washington, and they are placed in such position that if a fort falls into the hands of the enemy, the inside forts in the rear of the ones taken can immediately destroy them. Many of them are mounted with 64 colunabiads. Besides this was all a heavy timbered country, and we have cut all the timber down for miles all round falling it with the tops out in all directions leaving only the roads clear which makes it impossible for an army to advance on us without first clearing the timber and brush out of the way in which they would lose thousands of men. So you may have some idea of what we have got to fight against, for the Rebbles have made their positions as strong as our own. And yet we still feel confident that we can whip them and will do it yet. But many brave fellows will have to bite the dust for our enemies besides being strongly fortified shoot well. And well they may, for they have their guns like our own ranged so that every ball from their big guns count. The trouble with our men is they are two anxious for a fight. Officers want to distinguish themselves and think to do it by running themselves and their men into unnecesary danger. That is why we lose so many in our skirmishing. They dont take half men enough. It sounds big for one of our men to whip four or five of theirs and some of the officers act on that supposition, and some times win. But when they dont; they get their command cut to peices or taken prisoners.[22]

You say you recommended Shiriff More for Lt Col of one of the Reg. I hope he is capable of filling it with honnour but I do not know him. But for Gods sake never reccommend a man for a position in the army unless he has the experience or is well calculated for the place, for no man would except a position if he knew what he has to go throug. Unless he knew himself quallified to fill it.[23]

We have trouble on our own hands. All the commissioned officers but one in the Reg. has signed a petition to Col Vandor to resign his command of the regiment. And I do not know how it will end for if he dont Resign many of the other officers will. The trouble is he cant command americans: he cant explain any thing so that we can understand it, and since we have been drilling in Hardees Tactics he is worse. He get the movements and commands mixed up so that all hell cant tell what he is driving at. Then he gets mad as thunder and raves and belows like a mad bull; and abuses all the officers for not anticipating his damned dutch command.[24]

I hope you will be returned to the Legislature this winter. Then I can give you some items of the way our great state of Wis. is spending their money. If the government ever pays back all the money that the governour is fooling away on his frends they will be a darned set of fools. The boys are all well. I see that M K Y is good for being senator.[25]

My love to all.

Write soon.

H F Young

Capt McKee is better. His wife is in Washington.

NOTES

21. The death of Col. Edward D. Baker near Leesburg, Virginia, at the Battle of Ball's Bluff on October 21, 1861, was a profound blow to the president. Baker and Lincoln enjoyed a long friendship that dated to their time in Illinois, and at the time of his death Baker was a sitting senator from Oregon. The "Lincoln's were devastated by the news and received no White House visitors the next day." In the aftermath of the disasters at Bull Run and Ball's Bluff, a Joint Committee on the Conduct of the War was formed to investigate the causes of the defeat. *OR*, ser. 1, vol. 5, 291; James M. McPherson, *Battle Cry of Freedom: The Civil War Era* (New York: Oxford University Press, 1988), 362–63; Doris Kearns Goodwin, *Team of Rivals: The Political Genius of Abraham Lincoln* (New York: Simon & Schuster, 2005), 380–81; David Herbert Donald, *Lincoln* (New York: Simon & Schuster, 1995), 319.

22. Munson's Hill, occupied by Confederate forces early in the war, was across the Potomac River from Washington, DC. A columbiad is a large-caliber, muzzle-loaded, smooth-bore cannon. Skirmishes in October occurred at Springfield Station, Virginia; Edwards Ferry, Maryland; Little River Turnpike, Virginia; Harper's Ferry, Virginia; and Occoquan, Virginia. *OR*, ser. 1, vol. 5, 2–3; Frederick H. Dyer, *A Compendium of the War of the Rebellion Compiled and Arranged from Official Records . . . and Other Reliable Documents and Sources* (Des Moines, IA: Dyer Publishing Company, 1908), 896 (hereafter cited as *Dyer's Compendium*).

23. Jonathan B. Moore was the sheriff of Grant County in 1861–62 and was later appointed colonel of the Thirty-third Wisconsin in August 1862. Holford, *History of Grant County*, 140; *Blue Book*, 1861, 58; *Roster*, 2:501.

24. Vandor's welcome with the regiment did not last long because of two primary factors. His limited English made it difficult for the men to understand his orders, and his brusqueness toward his officers did not help matters. A letter, drafted by Capt. Samuel Nasmith, signed by the officers of the regiment, requested that he resign his commission. Further complicating matters, the letter made its way around the entire brigade and division and even reached the governor. According to the *Wisconsin State Journal* on November 22, "Col. Vandor has not yet resigned, but does not pretend to command his Regiment or even visit them."

Effective control of the regiment passed to Lt. Col. William W. Robinson. *Hardee's Rifle and Light Infantry Tactics*, written by William Joseph Hardee, was used by both sides to drill soldiers during the war. Initially published in 1855, by the start of the war it was considered essential reading for military leaders. Hardee resigned from the cavalry at the beginning of the war and rose to the rank of lieutenant general in the Confederate Army. Herdegen, *The Iron Brigade*, 99–100; Nolan, *The Iron Brigade*, 26; Herdegen, *The Men Stood Like Iron*, 32; "Our Washington Correspondence," *Wisconsin State Journal*, November 22, 1861; Douglas Southall Freeman, *Lee's Lieutenants: A Study in Command*, vol. 1, *Manassas to Malvern Hill* (1942; New York: Charles Scribner's Sons, 1970), 709.

25. Elected to the State Assembly in 1860, Jared Warner served the Seventy-ninth District through 1861. His bid for a second term came up short as he lost to Samuel Newick of Beetown. It is not exactly clear what Young was referring to in the last paragraph of this letter. The problems for Gov. Alexander Randall were many in 1861. A banking crisis came to a head in 1861, which did little to help an already fragile system in Wisconsin. Wildcat banks in the state did not have the requisite funds to cover notes they had issued. By the end of 1861 Wisconsin's banks notes were valued at a mere one-third of what they had been worth on January 1 of that year. A poor bond market and the discrediting of banks notes from forty institutions made matters worse. Rules for banking operations stabilized the crisis by the end of 1861, but it took two years to recover from the crisis. Each of these problems may have contributed to the decision by Randall to forgo another run for governor in the fall of 1861. Milas K. Young served in the Wisconsin State Senate from 1862 to 1865. He was active in local politics and also served as board chairman and superintendent of schools. *Blue Book*, 1861, 10, 35, 1862, 115, 1867, 182; Frank L. Klement, *Wisconsin and the Civil War: The Home Front and the Battle Front* (Madison: State Historical Society of Wisconsin, 1997), 21; Current, *The Civil War Era, 1848–1873*, 2:296, 302, 304; Frederick Merk, *Economic History of Wisconsin during the Civil War Decade* (Madison: Wisconsin Historical Society, 1916), 187, 189, 194–95, 205; Holford, *History of Grant County*, 123; Consul Willshire Butterfield, *History of Grant County Wisconsin, Containing an Account . . . of the United States* (Chicago: Western Historical Company, 1881), 845–46.

Camp Arlington Oct 31 1861

Dear Delia & Eva

Returning to Camp this evening after a hard days review i received your verry welcome letters which found me all right. And as I have no news of intrest I will give you a history of our days performance. We left camp at 12 PM in the following order. First the Sixth wis. Second the 7 wis. Third 2 Wis. Fourth 19 Indiana.

That is the order in which we always march. That is the Infantry. There is a Reg. of Cavalry attached to our Brigade which generally takes the advance and to day we found them already on the ground. We marched about three miles to the Potomac River oposite Washington, and formed in two lines. First forming in one line of files two men deep. Then at the order to open ranks the men of the rear rank steped back four paces, the cavalry performing the same manouvre on horseback. We then presented armes. The officers sepping in front four paces and saluting with their swords. The Generals of Division and staf were stationed about one hundred yds in front and oposite the center. As soon as the salute is ended the order is given to shoulder arms, and we all have to remain in that position while the General rides to the extreme right, and down the front and round the rear which makes it a verry tiresome performance on the men. For let me tell you five thousand men and one thousand of them cavalry; makes a good long line if they are in double file. And our generals dont gallop round like our fourth of July soldiers do. They walk their horses and scan the men arms, and accoutrements; very close, and point out every error of dress or any thing else that is unmilitary. After they have been round the Brigade, they take their station again in front. When the order is given to close rank at which the rear rank closes on the front rank to its accostomed place, and the officers take their places. Then the order is given by comp right wheel, which is executed by the right of each company marking time and turning round with the left as it wheels so that when the wheel is executed each company stands in collum, at company distance front each other. Then the word is given forward march. We all march at the word, preserving our exact distance from one company to an other and the men of each company march elbow to elbow preserving a straight front. At the order to march the company on the extreme right wheels to the left. Marches straight forward about fifty yds. Wheels to the left again. When the right guide of the company directs his march so asto pass with the right of his company about ten paces in front of the Gen and staff and marches on past intill the company arrives oposite the place where the extreme left rested when they left the wheel again march forward to where the left stood. Wheel again to the left, and then march right straight back where they started from. Now you must recollect every other com has been following the first at exact company distance wheeling on the same ground they wheeled on and each comp following in the exact trace of the com that preceded it so that we all arrive on the ground we started from at the same time. And when the order is left into line wheel we wheel in a line of two deep on the same ground we started from. I kow you. You will say oh would that i could see it. It is a splendid sight, but it is Devlish hard work and we have it Every week.

You talk of making clothes for the soldiers. Why our soldiers have so many clothes furnished them by unkle sam they dont no what to do with them. The fact is they are over stocked withe clothes. They have each three full suits of chlothes and they talk of sending their grey suit home. The officers buy their own and I can buy good socks for 30 cts per pair, and that is about the cost of the yarn in Wis. We have plenty to eat, and as we officers have to board ourselves. It costs us pretty well. For Butter is 25 cts per lb. Potatoes $1.25 per bush and cussed poor at that. But unkle sam pays us good wages and we will have to stand it. I got vaccinated to day for we have the small pox in camp and i would rather meet the Secesh.

Capt McKee is getting well. The boys of the Seccond & sixth from Grant are right side up with care. I seen Luke Parsons to day. He is better than two dead men yet, i dont no how the story started for he has been in good health all the time. Tell Laura papa read her letter and was glad to here from his little girl. I ordered a photograph of the company roll, to be sent to you from madison. You will get it soon. All you will have to pay will be the Express or postage charges from Madison.[26]

Eva you can have a reading intrest in this miserable thing, and dont complain that I never boared you with a letter. The tattoo is beeting.[27]

My love to all. Good night.

H F Young

NOTES

26. Luke Parsons was in Company C of the Sixth Wisconsin. *Roster*, 1:507.

27. Eva Mills was the daughter of J. T. Mills. She lived with Delia throughout much of the time Henry was absent during the war.

Camp Arlington Nov 15 1861

Dear Friends

Father, I have neglected writing for a longer time than I promised for the reason that I wanted to send you some money. We all concluded to send our money to lancaster by express, to J C Cover, as that was the cheapest and safest. I have sent you one hundred and ten Dollars in treasury notes to Cover, the money is good as goald. This is all I can spare at this time, as I have to buy every thing I use, or eat, at a high price. For instance we pay for Potatoes here one dollar & forty cents per bushel. Butter 28 cts per lb and every thing els in the provision line in proportion. I did not pay Bar the Intrest due last fall, as I told you he would not take curency. When I paid you your goald for the first sales of flour I calculated to have enough to pay all the out standing accounts, but you know how things turned out. The money I send you, use as you think best. I can send you more in January than now, for the reason I had to buy so many things when I came here that I was in debt, when I recievd this payment. I am going to see this war through if I come out not worth the first damed red cent. I would rather spend the last drop of blood I have and let my wife and children have the free government of the united states to live in than to have our government and institutions broken up and be worth millions.[28]

The war news you are as much acquainted with as I am. All I have to say is we are getting the better of the rebble.

The resignation of Scott, and the appointment of McClellen, gives general satisfaction in the army. I hope you are elected to the legislature. I hear that Newick, and Hilton are running independent, if so I feel confident you can Scoup them both.[29]

Gen. George B. McClellan and staff (Library of Congress, Prints & Photographs Division, Civil War Photographs, LC-DIG-ppmsca-34117)

For the time has come that Wisconsin wants her coolest and soundest men in the Legislature. For if the legulature is not sound for the people, the taxes will raise to such a pitch that property will only be a curse to the owner. I think before you get this letter North carolina will be ours.

I may be mistaken. You perhaps think it strange that we are kept here in inactivity. But some troops must hold this point untill the Rebbles leave the Potomac and Kings Brigade are said to be the best Brigade of men in the army of the Potomac. So says McDowl and we consider him good authaurity. His head qrs are at the arlington house. I beleive Woodhouse gave you a description of that house, but the old part which washington used to have full of game and deer, now contains a reg of cavelry. The fences are all burned. And every thing about the place but the house and garden is going to the devil as fast as five thousand men can destroy it. I dont mean to say they have orders to destroy, but there was some four thousand acres of good timber and we are cutting it all down and burning all we want. And timber within 3 to 4 miles of Washington is worth something.

Write soon

Yours & ever

H F Young

NOTES

28. Joseph C. Cover, a prominent citizen in Grant County from Lancaster, served as village president, superintendent of schools, and supervisor of the town for many years. The editor and owner of the *Grant County Herald*, he saw the paper through some rough years before the war, as Cover was an ardent abolitionist, a fact that did not sit well with some residents of the county. Butterfield, *History of Grant County*, 654–59; Holford, *History of Grant County*, 109–10.

29. McClellan replaced Lt. Gen. Winfield Scott as Commander of the Armies of the United States on November 1, 1861. Samuel Newick ousted Jared Warner in the fall elections of 1861 to represent Grant County in the Thirtieth State Assembly District. *OR*, ser. 1, vol. 5, 3; *Blue Book*, 1862, 84.

Camp Arlington Nov 15 1861

Dear Old girl

I have allmost swore for the past two days. Do you want to know why? Its all because I have not got my regular letter from you. We are all well and getting along first if it was not so cursed muddy. We have been paid of for our first two months service in the United States and I sent one hundred & ten Dollars to your Father, and I want you to write me the Magazines you want next year. If you want Harper & Godey together I will send the money for them from here. ~~I go~~ I received a letter from H Bergess this evening and was glad to hear you were all well. I suppose you know we are whipping the Rebbles at all points just at this time. And our General says he thinks that before next pay day comes round we may all go home. I hope it is true for I would like to see you and the babies verry much indeed. I have not seen a child for a month and long for my babies at Evening and wet days, when we can t drill.[30]

I wrote you a history of a review of Kings Brigade, but since that we have had a review of McDowls Division. It was the same manuoeuvres as the one I wrote to you only there were four brigades insead of one making in all some Sixteen Thousand men. It was the grandest military display I ever seen, we were reviewed by McClellan who is now Commander in Chief. We will be sent of from here soon I think, and we may be in the Second Naval expedition.

At all events we must leave here soon for we cant live in tents in this climate in winter. I like to lay down on the soft side of a board, to sleep. And after a hard days drill it is the best kind of a bed. Soldering is hard work and those that go into for the fun of the thing, generally get more than they bargained for, and it is this class of men theat generally make all the fuss about the way soldiers are used.

Woodhouse is officer of the Guard to night and it is Eleven oclock. I must quit writing and cook some Oysters for him. By twelve oclock when I am oficer of the Guard he gets me something to eat at twelve at night and I do the same for him. And oysters ar cheaper here than any thing else. Tell Jared i think I left his sled over head in the smoke house. Tell him to get it and haul wood for his ma. His Grand pa wrote me he got along firstrate. Tell Laura I will bring her a present when i come home. Tell Eva her favourite in the Second is all right.

yours Truly

H F Young

PS write often

NOTE

30. Henry Burgess, Young's neighbor in Cassville Township, was active in local politics and held many positions in the township government in the period from 1860 through the 1880s. Butterfield, *History of Grant County*, 846–47.

Camp Arlington Nov 20 1861

Dear Father

I received your letter last night. Was glad to hear you were well, but sorry to hear you were not elected for the Legislature. I think the people in the district will find out the difference betwen sending their best men, or their do nothing say nothing pets when they find they way their property will be taxed. Newick is just about as good as a wooden man would be in the hands of the legislature that is to assemble this winter. There will be thousands of bills brought against the state for military claims that should never be granted or paid. Our State is keeping agents and as we call them, Dry nurses for they never are known to do anything but board at the large hotells and draw their pay. Randall appointed one with the rank of Col. His name is mansfield. He came here with great pomp, told us he was appointed by Governour Randall, to look after the Wis. vollunteers: had the rank of Col would take up his quarters at Williards hotell. If any thing was wanting he could be found there. I dont think he will ever be called on for if we can go to Willards we can get.[31]

Such appointments are of no earthly use only to spend money, and mind you the United States Government will never pay these useless and unlawful bills. They must know where every dollar goes. We have an extra assistant sergeon appointed from the state. He is of no use only to ride round on reviews; and government wont pay him acent. So you see these men have their commissions from the State and the State will have to foot the bill. I could fill pages with things of mismanagement but it is no use now. If you had been elected i intended giving you a general history.[32]

The money I sent to you, will be at covers. I suppose you will get it before you get this. I would like you to lift bars last year note with it. I owe I G Ury 48 Dollars but as I can send home as much as 50 or 60 dollars a month I will soon get square. Delia wrote about an account to Ballentine. I owed R G Ballentine a balance of twenty nine Dollars. I sent him fifteen, and went to his house to pay the Balance but he was not at home. I met him on the road and paid him fifteen more to which made the principle and one dollar of intrest paid which will him some little intrest but I think it cant be more than one dollar & fifty cents if that. When I paid him the fifteen dollars he promised to bring a grist and come down to the mill Sometime and get it; and I had forgotten all about it. I dont think that I have thought of it for Six months. You perhaps would like to know why I have left these notes go unpaid so long. I will tell you. They were personall notes of my own. When I sold my farm I owed them. I expected to have money plenty to pay them but you know when the mill was built i had not a dollar but was in debt on that. Then i could not pay them without using your money. That I did not like to do and am glad that i did not; for now I can pay them myself. So no debts of mine shall trouble you or any body else.[33]

We had the grandest review yesterday ever had in the world. Europe has had more Soldiers dress in review but they were not volunteers. We were between 70 & 80 thousand. All volunteers. You will get a full history of it in the paper. Give my love to all.[34]

Yours Truly

H F Young

NOTES

31. Louis Powell Harvey, elected governor in November 1861, enjoyed only a very short tenure at the helm of the state. While boosting morale for state soldiers after the Battle of Pittsburg Landing, he fell in the water trying to pass between two riverboats on the night of April 19, 1862. His replacement, Lt. Gov. Edward Salomon, finished his term. The state agent for Wisconsin in Washington, DC, throughout the Civil War was Col. Washington Y. Selleck. By 1862 Selleck also served as the vice president of the Wisconsin Soldier's Aid Society. Young's reference to Mansfield is unclear. Capt. John Mansfield served in Company G, Second Wisconsin, and was later appointed lieutenant colonel in December 1864. *Blue Book*, 1863, 167; Current, *The Civil War Era, 1848–1873*, 2:310; "Wisconsin Soldier's Aid Society," *Weekly Gazette and Free Press* (Janesville, WI), June 13, 1862; *Roster*, 1:345.

32. D. Cooper Ayres, Asst. Surgeon of the Seventh Wisconsin Infantry, was appointed on August 23, 1861. *Roster*, 1:538.

33. Frank Barr, one of six Barr brothers and cousins, moved to Grant County in 1844. Frank lent money to residents in need. I. G. Ury was one of the earliest settlers of the county and built a store in Patch Grove in 1848, which he later sold to Alexander Paul in 1857. Paul married Delia's sister Rebecca on August 22, 1858. George Ballantine, another early settler of the county, was active in local and state politics. He served in the State Assembly before Jared Warner. Holford, *History of Grant County*, 149–50, 163, 565, 567, 614, 617, 618–20, 653; Butterfield, *History of*

Grant County, 855–56, 763; Wisconsin Marriages, 1836–1930, digital image s.v. "Alexander Paul," FamilySearch.org; *Blue Book*, 1860, 34.

34. The Grand Review at Bailey's Crossroads was attended by President Lincoln, cabinet officials, McClellan, and many distinguished visitors, including Julia Ward Howe, with an estimated twenty thousand spectators. Seventy-five regiments passed in review, which reportedly took more than three hours. Nolan, *The Iron Brigade*, 38; Herdegen, *The Men Stood Like Iron*, 43; "The Grand Review near Washington." *Civilian and Telegraph* (Cumberland, MD), November 28, 1861.

Camp Arlington Nov 21 1861

Dear Delia

. . . These were debts of my own contracting before i went to the mill, and i could never pay them without using your . . . no time to attend to it. And I think if I had been there he would have been Elected for we will want such men in The Legislature. Now for the grand review. I send you the repoart of it, but this is only the outsiders that came from washington and the Surrounding cities. Just Picture in your immaganation Seventy thousand troops and 25 or thirty thousand citizens all on a parade ground in plain sight and you will have the grandest sight ever witnessed on this continent. The sight was magnificent beyond description. We pesed the Stand of reveewing officers, in close collum by Division which is two companies marching a brest. All the troops were dressed in their best, and each Reg. did their best to excell. Our boys came of Second to none. Just think of Sixty four Brass Bands all playing it once and when they would stop ninety three Marshall Bands would take their place. The sun shine was bright. The coulors were flying. The guns and bayonets glissened. The Buttons and brass trimings were clean and bright. We had the President member of Cabinett, members of Congress Foreign Minesters; thousands on thousands of fine dressed ladies lined the space around the stand but we marched by with Eyes steady to the front without even a glance at either side. We could hear the exclamations, from some of them to their friends of good, well done, splendid looking fellows & c. It was a specticle such as the world never witnessed, for as we stood there drawn up in lines, we were proud and Haughty freeman. We were all vouluntary placed in that position. We were not forced into the service, but had left our homes to fight for what we consider the best government on earth.

I thought of you and Eva, often during the day, how you would like to have sen it. We were the first brigade on the ground, and last to leave. Just after twelve oclock the cannons began to roar forth the salute, and then the bands began to play. Then came the President McClellan and all the major Gens. and their Staffs something like a hundred of them. They rode past all the reg, down one side and up the other. We wer drawn up in close collum by division so that each Reg occupied but small space. Then between Each row of Regs there was a space of twenty two spaces. It was through these spaces that McClellan and Staff rode. Old Abe looks first rate, and is not a homely man by any means. I think he will live to hang Jeff Davis yet.

Tell Jared i will certainly bring him popgun when I come home and tell Laura i will bring her a present. Kiss the babie dear may. I think i can see her todling round, and once and a while tumbling down on the carpet. Tell Eva she cant scare me any; for there is verry few men worth having left at home, and the girls will all be after them. My love to all with a double share for yourself.

H F Young

Camp Arlington Dec 1 1861

Dear Delia and Eva

I received your ever welcome letters & glad to hear you are all well. Your letter found me all right, but we all get the blues, some times lying here in this cursed mudhole. The State of Virginia is nothing but a mudhole all over; this time of the year any how. You talk about the great expedition. If you only knew how bad we wanted to go with it, we were all on tiptoe for off, for several days; (but McDowel) will never let Kings Brigade go out of his Division if he can keep them. They are undoubtealy the best Brigade of men in the army of the Potomac. As for going into winter quarters here, i we will not do it. If we do it will be only temporary, for we will have Richmond before the first Day of April next; or i miss my guess. You folks at home and many elsewhere think we are doing nothing but you are mistaken. I get the blues sometimes and swear at the whole of our Generals, for not making an advance. And yet i no verry well it will have to be made with large force and great caution; to insure success, for the Rebbles know full well, if we ever pass Manasses, their cause is lost, and this is a hard country to wage war in for the attacting party. It is mountanous and heavy timber, and their fortifications are strong. Many of them in places where it is almost impossible to attackes them, but by sending Expeditions down the coast we will draw off some of their forces from the Potomac. Then we will march rite through them. So we will have to wait for the word march.

Now Eva for your questions. We Officers do have to buy every thing we get rations, books, Candles, chlothes. In fact the government furnish us nothing but our tents. We get all the rest in money. My pay is one hundred and five Dollars per month. Out of that I pay for ever thing i get or use. Every thing comes high. Washing is no small item. In an officers bill we live verry well. We buy beef potatoes Bead, Butter, cheese, coffee, Tea, Sugar Rice & c and hire a cook, to cook them. Sometimes these things cant all be got but we get others, such as Oysters or fresh fish Onions and c.

Now as for cooking. It aint firstrate nor verry clean; but after 3 hours Drill it goes firstrate. I weigh 180 lbs. Two lbs more than i ever weighed before. When we get tired of Camp life; we get a 24 hours pass to the city; take a turn through the Capital and Grounds around it, run round the White House; take a look at the green house, with its Oriental Plants, Flours, & Shrubbery, Fruits & c. Then go to Williards or the National, take a grand dinner; listen to the members of Congress and other big bugs that live on the Public Crib; talk poletics speculate about the war & after supper go to the Theatre if there is any thing worth going to see. I was there the other evening to see the performance of Mons. Hermann the great guglar from India; and all i have to say is, he done more impossible and imposture tricks than Moses or Jesus Christ ever thought of. He is the greatest performer of the age. Then we lumber back to camp, with the consolation of having the world outside of our camp once more. But you must recolect one of these 24 hour passes cant be got only once in twelve days. I have had but two of them since we came to Arlington; but 3 Comissioned Officers & 20 privates can go have a pass to cross the Potomac at one time out of our Regiment. The reason for this is you must recolect there is something over Two Hunndred Regs roung washington and if all the men were permitted to go that wanted; the city would be overrun with soldiers; and many oficers would neglect their comp & Regiments. I have not applied for all the passes i was entitled to. I did not wish to neglect any Drill.[35]

Eat plenty of Hog Furman killed and perhaps you will gain another pound a piece. I would like to kiss you all verry much to night; for it is dark and raining and i am all a lone in my tent. And when i picture to myself how you and Eva are hudling over the stove looking over the last Goody or Harper withe the room all warm and bright, the dear children all tucked away nicely in bed. When I have look at the picture in imagination, and then look round at my tent with nothing of comfort in it but my blanketts and trunk which is all a soldier is allowed transportation or wagon room for. It looks cursed lonesome to say the least. I received a letter from H Bergess. Was glad to hear from him. Will answer it soon. My Love to all of you my dears.

H F Young

NOTE

35. Young attended a show at the Washington Theater that featured Monsieur Herrmann, who, according to the advertisement, was the "greatest living Prestidigitateur." He performed magic tricks that involved sleight of hand. "Washington Theater," *Evening Star* (Washington, DC), November 23, 1861.

Camp Arlington Dec 13 1861

Dear Old Girl

I received your letter of Dec 2 this evening. It found me all right. You talk of my not writing regular, but there is one thing you may set down as signed sealed and delivered. That is, that i write you a letter every week and if you dont get them it is not my fault, i assure you. I am sorry you have the blues, so bad, for i get them myself some times, but keep in good heart, for this war will not last long.

You will see that we are gaining on the Rebbles at all points. You may think that we are doing nothing here but you are mistaken. We are gaining in efficiency every day; and we are keeping the Rebble army from leaving here and going to other places, and as long as McClellan can keep the main part of the Rebble army, watching us on the Potomac, it gives him success everywhere else. We have been out on Pickett for the last three days. We went out near fairfax on the advance lines. We had lots of fun, but had no fight. Our boys behaved firstrate. We were in sight of the Rebbles for the first time. The laying out of nights, without tents was the hardest part of it. We could have advanced and taken fairfax if they had given the word, but the generals would not let us, for we would have to build forts to hold it and that they dont want to do.[36]

Your Father has got the money I sent home before this. At least he ought to have it by this time. I dont no whether i can go home this winter or not. Woodhouse has applied for a Furlough, for twenty days. If he gets it i will have him go down and see you. I would like to go home Oh so verry much but then the parting would be harder than ever for i would have to come back, but if you cant get along without me i will resign and go any how, but I dont want to do that unless you or the children are sick. If you think you can do better dealing at any other store in Cassville than McCartneys why deal there, and let Furman pay them in Flour. And if you cant get what you want that way i will send you money next pay day, which will be first of next month.[37]

Capt McKee arrived here to day and gave us the news from old Grant. He is not verry stout yet. He said J T Mills was going to Farming, Well i just think Unkle Jo will play hell on a farm, and i think Eva had better stay with you. We have got the fancy Encampment on the Potomac. We have cut cedars and set out in rows all through our Encampment, which makes it look firstrate. Our streets are well made and solid. The boys have lots of fiddles and fidlers, and we have a dance in the street every night. When the weather will permit the foks form the city comes out to see us every day that the weather is fine. We have had no snow yet, but the nights are coald. Woodhouse and I bought a Sheet Iron Stove the other day, and it adds greatly to our comfort. It will seame strange to you, to think of a stove inside of a cloth tent but i assure you it is a firstrate institution.

I will send you the Harpers & Godey the first time i can get over in the city and if Woodhouse gets his Furlough i will send you some spending money for Christmas. Oh, how i would like to take my Christmas dinner with you. Wouldent we have a great old time. I think of you every coald morning and feel sad to think how you have to get up and build the fire. I know it must go hard, and i set down as a fact that the weoman that are left at home have equally as hard a time as the men that have left have, but never mind there is a good time coming, if we never see it. Tell Furman that if he dont write to me i will shoot his pet cat when i come home. I want to know if the Old Wheel freezis up this winter, and how the horses gets along, and if old mage, is good as ever, and if the dutch weoman bring their mother pigs to his old boar. There now i have spoiled the whole letter but as this is the third side it will have to go.

I am sorry to hear you lost your Tomatoes, but it is no use crying for spiled milk. You think we live well. If Oysters are so cheap, you dont no how tired we get of them. I would give a bushel of Oyster for one mess of Mexican potatoes baked as we never get baked potatoes here. Tell Eva I always intend that part of my letter is for her and now i want her to stay with you untill i get back, and i want her to write to me often. She wrote she was getting fat. I want to know if her nose is sharp as ever. I think now I had better quit. So good night.

My love to all.

H F Young

NOTES

36. Fairfax, Virginia, is just outside Washington, DC.

37. Orris McCartney, an early settler of the county, eventually settled in Cassville. His son, Alexander, served in Company F of the Seventh Wisconsin. The elder McCartney, active in local town affairs, served on the first town board of Cassville in 1849. McCartney also served on the county board and held many township offices from the 1840s until his death in 1868. Butterfield, *History of Grant County*, 845–47; Holford, *History of Grant County*, 144, 602, 610; *Roster*, 1:560.

Camp Arlington Dec 23 1861

Dear Father

I received your letter yesterday, was glad to hear from you. Your letter found us all well. Capt McKee is here and has taken command of his company. Clark, Cobb, Nasmith Fennicum, Callis, Woodhouse, are well, and we are all absolutely spoiling for a fight. We have been out three days on pickett since i wrote you. We went within two miles of Fairfax, could see the rebble flag flying at their encampment, but not a rebble was to beseen. We wanted to go and stir them up, but the General would not let us. We had to travel nine miles, and there left our reserve, and then threw out our picketts and scouts about two miles in advance of the reserve. The only danger in pickett duty, is from the Rebble Cavalry, which occasionally make a dash on our picketts and drives them in on the reserve and sometimes captures them.[38]

There is some excitement in camp this morning in regard to the news from England. John Bull, talks war and Jonathan has enough to do, if this congress will keep quarling over the damed niger question. You nor i either will live to see this war settled. We are fighting for to crush out rebellion, not for the abolition of slavery. And every man of comon sence knows that as the army advance, the slaves of every Rebble will be set free, and what is the use of their forever harping on the question in Congress. It does us more harm than fifty thousand men in the Rebble army could possibly do. The fact is i wish those agitators of slavery were placed in the ranks to fight. I think that would cure their radical ideas. You must try and do something with N Austin. Cant you get hold of his wheat in some way, or do something for if england pitches into us property wont be worth annything, and hell will be to pay generrally. I cant advise you for you know better what to do than i can tell you, but act, and and promptly, for this war will ruin thousands, and it will ruin many who have been in comparatively good circumstances. I will help you all I can. You can depend on me for some money in a few days. Our money will be due the first of January.[39]

You said you had not received a letter from me for two weeks. There is one lost then for i write regularly every Week.

Give my love to all.

yours truly

H F Young

NOTES

38. McKee was in Company C of the Second Wisconsin; Col. Amasa Cobb was on the Field and Staff in the Fifth Wisconsin; Capt. Samuel Nasmith was in Company C of the Seventh Wisconsin; Capt. John B. Callis and James A. Clark were in Company F of the Seventh Wisconsin; and Capt. Mark Finnicum was in Company H of the Seventh Wisconsin. All of the soldiers were from Grant County. Cobb served in the Wisconsin State Assembly and the US House of Representatives and was later appointed the commander of the newly formed Forty-third Wisconsin Infantry. *Roster*, 1:437, 547, 558–61, 565, 2:723; *Blue Book*, 1860, 8, 1863, 131.

39. The *Trent* incident sparked a rise in tensions between the United States and Great Britain. Two Confederate agents, James Mason and John Slidell, were sent to England to negotiate "all matters and subjects interesting to both nations." The Confederate messengers sailed to Havana and boarded the *Trent*, a British steamer. Capt. Charles D. Wilkes, the commander of USS *San Jacinto*, decided, against the advice of his own executive officer, to seize the two messengers and two other men on November 8, 1861. Tensions quickly escalated; Queen Victoria approved of war preparations, and the British Ambassador to the United States, Lord Lyons, delivered an ultimatum to Secretary of State Seward on December 19. Several delays bought time for a US response. The British government sought an apology from the US government and the release of the four men. A Christmas Day meeting

concluded that the United States would have to release Mason and Slidell. Seward's reply stated that Capt. Wilkes had acted on his own and conceded to a certain extent that he had violated international law. Seward called Lyons to his office on December 27 to deliver the American response. The reply met with the approval of the British government and ended in the release of the men, who finally continued on their voyage to England. Ironically, the settlement left relations between the United States and Great Britain better than before the crisis. Nathaniel Austin was a farmer in the town of Glen Haven. McPherson, *Battle Cry of Freedom*, 389–91; Norman B. Ferris, *The Trent Affair: A Diplomatic Crisis* (Knoxville: University of Tennessee Press, 1977), 3, 18–26, 66, 131–32, 183–88; 1860 United States Census, Glen Haven, Grant County, Wisconsin, digital image s.v. "Nathaniel Austin," Ancestry.com.

Camp Arlington Dec 27 1861

Dear Old girl

I received your letter or rather two letters in one envelope and was glad to hear you were all well. We have been having cold wather which has given me an awful bad cold which is better to day. Except my hourseness and sorethroat, in the curing of which i miss the dear old hand, that used to wrap the wet towl round my neck.

This is the worst feature of soldering for our tents are a poor protection against coald. I often think of you getting up these cold mornings in the cold to build fires, it must go hard, and i feel sorry for you. You will have to provide yourself with plenty of dry wood, to keep you and the children comfortable, if nothing else for heath is worth everything else. I am so glad Eva has got the school, for i know she will be lots of company for you. I have not yet sent money for your books for the reason i have not had a chance to go to the city since i received your answer about them, but i will order them scent the first time i can get to the city. I did intend to send from here, but there is so much complaint, about soldiers money being lost in letters i concluded to wait and get a draft. Did you get the photograph?

I will try and get you a picture gallery, such as you wish when i get to the city. I dont know yet wheather Woodhouse will get his Furlough or not. If he dont i will send you some spending money next pay day anyhow.

We gave the boys of our company an oyster supper on christmas. They enjoyed it firstrate. The bill of Fare was oyster soupe Apples, crackers, coffee, and Pickles with Butter catsup and all other trimings necessary, but i felt lonesome. I would like to have spent it with my wife and babies. I would like to see you all so verry much, you dont no how verry lonesome i get sometimes, as long as there was a prospect of marching it was not so bad, but the thoughts of staying here all this long winter gives me the blues. Well i beleive i had better quit or you will think i am getting homesick. Well the fact is this a verry stormy day; and i will try and do better next time.[40]

My love to you all.

yours ever

H F Young

NOTE

40. One soldier who may have enjoyed the Christmas dinner was William Ray. His journal reflected as much when he stated, "our second Lieutenant is the best drill master in the Regt I think." According to Ray, the men had grown to appreciate Young more the longer they spent in the company. Lance Herdegen and Sherry Murphy, eds., *Four Years with the Iron Brigade: The Civil War Journals of William R. Ray, Co. F, Seventh Wisconsin Infantry* (Cambridge, MA: Da Capo Press, 2002), 37.

CHAPTER TWO

"I came to War to fight for the government"

January 7 to May 8, 1862

Camp Arlington Jan 7 1862

Dear Delia

Here I have been ten Days without a letter or a word from you. When i last wrote i was almost sick with a cold and sore throat, but i am much better, and stand my regular allowance of grubb and Drill.

The weather is cold and Freezing with about two inches of snow on the ground and the Potomac River is Frozen over. But for all that, we get along well. You would not beleive our Small Sheet iron Stoves would make our tents so comfortable, as they do. Day after tomarrow we will get our pay, and you shall have some money this time. I dont know why it is but somehow whenever the weather gets cold and bad, I get the blues, and feel homesick, then is the time i am continually thinking of you and the children, and look Anxiously for a letter. But it is a long time since i got one.

Levi Showalter is going home in a few days. I hope he wont go untill after pay day for i can send you some money with him. He is going on a recruiting service, and he can tell you all about how we get a long. Wesley Largeant has gone home. He got his discharge. I told him to call and see you.[1]

How does Eva get along teaching the young idea how to shoot? Tell her to write me a letter, or i will call her a sharp nosed old maid as long as she lives. I have not any news for you about the war. We were out on pickett last week but did not see a rebble.

There is talk of an advance soon, but that has got to be an old story with us, and we are impatient for the word forward. Knowing at the same time that when it does come, the colission will be awful, and that many of us who go out proud and confident will get our ticketts for the other side of Jordan, but every one is ready for the trial. And when it does come look out for a good account of the Wis 7.

Tell Jared & Laura i would like to see them verry much, and hope they enjon themselves, with their sled. I would like to send them a pressent and will do it the first chance i get. Kiss dear little may for me every day and give my love to Furman & Caroline and to Eva if she writes. If she wont write i wont like her a bit.

yours ever

H F Young

Dear Old girl

I had this letter folded ready for the mail, when i received you long and welcome letter and also one from Furman & Caroline. My questions was to some purpose if they were a little rough. I cant go home for it is impossilbe to get a furlough, and as long as you are Well and the children well I dont want to go. I came to War to fight for the government and i will do it as long as I am able to, providing my Family dnt suffer in my abscence. What you say about Furman was not sharp practice as you call it, for it was perfectly understood by us and him to. I owed Raffauf & Guiger somewhere in twenty dollars. I think twenty 24. I am not certain of the exact amount, and McCartney & Renkie some fifteen Dollars.[2]

Furman was to pay these bills with flour or what ever he chose by the first of February. He was to Pay your bills for the same time. He was to pay John Koll for working on the Dam and the money would be wanted for insurance and Taxes, so that we calculated that it would take about one hundred and fifty Dollars to make all these things right by that time. But your Father will not be exacting enough to make him pay it. I know for it was put in the contract on your account. More than any thing else, for at the time i left home i did not know whether i could ever send any money home and that amount was settled on so that you would have enough to live on and that those other things should be paid.[3]

Your Father will not cause Furman to sacrifice on his Flour to make him pay any thing that is not absolutely necessary at presant, (i will write to him about it). And tell Furman to keep his shirt on, for he will need it if the weather is as cold there as it is here. Write often and try and get your letters to the office sooner.

Yours everr. Good night.

H

NOTES

1. Levi Showalter was in Company C of the Second Wisconsin, and Wesley J. Largent was in Company F of the Seventh Wisconsin. Discharged due to disability, Largent left the service on December 31, 1861. Wisconsin, Adjutant General's Office, *Roster of the Wisconsin Volunteers, War of the Rebellion, 1861–1865*, Blue Books, 2 vols. (Madison: Democrat Printing Press, 1886), 1:353, 560 (hereafter cited as *Roster*).

2. Peter Raffanf and John Geiger operated a general store in Cassville in the 1850s and were joined by Otto Reinke in 1857. Reinke left Raffanf and Geiger in 1860 and joined O. B. McCartney and William McCartney in a store until the end of the Civil War. Consul Willshire Butterfield, *History of Grant County Wisconsin, Containing an Account . . . of the United States* (Chicago: Western Historical Company, 1881), 980–81.

3. John Koll (or Kohl), a farm laborer, lived in the Young household in 1860. It appears that Koll might have accompanied Young as a servant during the war. His service record indicated that from August 1861, while the regiment was still in Madison, through June 1863, John Kohl was listed as servant but not as a soldier. Interestingly, from September 1863 until Young's departure in December 1864, a servant not named served the captain. It is difficult to determine whether John Koll (Kohl) continued in this capacity or someone else served in his stead. 1860 United States Census, Cassville, Grant County, Wisconsin, digital image s.v. "John Koll," Ancestry.com; Compiled Service Record, Henry F. Young, Captain, Company F, Seventh Wisconsin Infantry, Compiled Records Showing Service of Military Units in Volunteer Union Organizations, 1861–1865, Record Group 94, Publication Record M595, Roll 199, Sixth Infantry through Eleventh Infantry, National Archives, Washington, DC.

Camp Arlington Jan 11 1862

Dear Father

I will have to commence as usual. All quiet on the Potomac. Aint you tired of that? if you are not tired of it you may swear we are perfectly sick of it. It has rained for the last twenty four hours, taken off all our snow and left us in mud just twenty inches deep. You cant go out any place in camp without carrying enough of the cursed soil of Old Virginia on your boots to cover a hill of potatoes. We are all well with the exception of colds & coughs, and as for them we might be set down as a regular set of wheezers and barkers. You did well in getting the five hundred from Austin for Bar, for if this war comes to a close soon, property may raise in value. But that is only guss work for we cant tell what six months or a year will bring forth. At all events i would not loose any on that farm now nor as long as you can get Nat to pay the intrest.[4]

You ask if it is so that the Collonels of Reg. each got $1000. I dont know about all of them but i am satisfied ours did and so did the collonel of the Sixt Reg. Cobb would not take it or have any thing to do with it. The way it was found out in our Reg, is our quartermaster is ~~B~~ H Clinton, a Lawyer, and son of the old Clinton, of Rail Road notoriety. And now i dont suppose you will want to anything more than his name and lungae to make up your mind in regard to his honesty.[5]

Well the officers of this Reg was well satisfied in regard to the (honesty of the quartermaster,) but they have made him toe the mark as far as furnishing supplies for the men is concerned. And you must reccollect that So far as we are concerned that is all we line officers have to do with him, for all other conduct he is responsible to the war department. Now note what follows and i will give you a history of a single transaction as near as i have been able to glean the facts. Dan Boss says he is the the Agt of the Fort wayne & Pittsburg R R. Says he paid quarter master Clinton $1000, as a bonus for carrying the 7 Reg. over their R Road, and that it was the understanding that Collonel Vandor; was to have $800 Dollars of the money; and Clinton was to have the other $200. Well it appears that Clinton told Vandor that he did not get the money and he knew Vandor dare not make a fuss about it as long as he was Collonel of the Reg. But vandor left the Reg. and was over in the city; when he found out what Dan Boss swore to; and they called on him about the matter. He then swore the cat tamed quartemaster master cheated him out of his Eight hundred Dollars; and then the Cat Tamed villian signed a petition for him to leaf te Regiment. Vandor sent for Clinton to come over to the city and i suppose they fixed it some how for i have heard nothing since about the matter; and as it is nothing but what they are all engaged in i think they will have no trouble in hushing it up. The fact is swindling the Government is carried on to such an extent, that such small transactions, as the one i have mentioned is hardly noticed. The Collonel of the 6 Reg dont deny getting $1000; and it is strongly suspected that Gov Randall, got a part of the Rail Road fund for all the troops that were carried within the state. I heard this at Madison and have no doubt of it for some times he would send them by one Rail Road, and sometimes by another.[6]

And I have it from good authority that he got $300 of a bonus for every Reg that left Madison or the state; and i have been perfectly satisfied that if it was not for the money that is made by many, and the intrigueing for Military and political power by others this war would be terminated in six weeks. You may think I am gassing but i know it is truth i write. Every person about washington in any kind of business is getting rich. Men that own houses there are renting them at almost fabulous prices. Every man about the city has his hand in the treasuary. Polititians dont want the war put down by the army; for that will turn loose a set of men more popular than they are, and they will Lose their pay from the public cribb and for this verry reason they will quarrel amongst themselves; threw every obsticle they can in the way of any officer that makes a bold push toward putting down the rebellion. It was for this verry reason that Freemont was dismised, and it will be the case with every other man that makes a bold push toward crushing out the rebellion.[7]

Polittions look on this war as a political struggle; and as long as they can make capital out of it they will do every thing they can to keep it on hand. I am writing you a history of only what has come under my own observation, and of which i have formed my own oppinions. I will agree with you. It is a bad state of affairs, but I cannot shut my eyes to the truth. I am convinced of the imbecility of our leaders and have been for some time. They are affraid of each other. The Military officers are affraid of Congress and the Cabinet, & Congress and the Cabinet, are affraid of the Army and is officers. Each is trying to checkmate the other.

You ask are we not fit for self government, (I will answer yes). Provided it is honesty and intelegance we let govern us; and we have enough of honesty and intelegance to govern us you must admit. But for some time we have been governed by Political intrigue, avaris, and every other black and damnable passion, having neither honesty or inteigance about it. And you will find the pople will become convinced of this ere long; and will command a halt; and about face march and will march these intrigueing theiving loafers out of office; and put honest men in their place. When that is done and not before will we have a Government worth a Continental curse. My love to all the friends.

yours Truly

H F Young

I read this to Lieut Woodhouse and he says he believes i have written the facts all round.

NOTES

4. Nathaniel Austin purchased land from Young on September 8, 1858, for $6,000. Grant County Register of Deeds, *Grantor/Grantee Indexes, 1837–1901*, vol. G.2, 558.

5. The colonel of the Sixth Wisconsin was Lysander Cutler, and Amasa Cobb commanded the Fifth Wisconsin. As previously noted, he was a member of Congress and represented southwest Wisconsin. Henry P. Clinton, the first Quartermaster of the Seventh Wisconsin, resigned from the service on November 1, 1862. It was not clear what Young meant by "lungae." *Roster*, 1:494, 437, 538.

6. To secure passage to the nation's capital, several railroad companies exerted pressure in the way of bribes to several colonels of the first regiments from Wisconsin. Congress, led by Rep. Charles Van Wyck of New York, convened a Committee of Government Contracts to check the alleged wrongdoing (Van Wyck Investigating Committee). Young's claim, that Vandor of the Seventh Wisconsin and Cutler of the Sixth Wisconsin were each given $1,000, was to some extent correct. Benjamin Patrick, the ticketing agent for the Pittsburgh, Fort Wayne, and Chicago Railway, testified that he gave $800 to Col. Cutler. Another $200 was given to the Sixth Wisconsin's quartermaster, Isaac N. Mason. Daniel W. Boss, the agent for the railroad, was given $1,000 by Patrick to give to Vandor. Boss testified that he gave $1,000 to the quartermaster of the Seventh Wisconsin, Henry P. Clinton, with the expressed interest that $800 be given to Vandor. The testimony does not specifically state whether Vandor accepted the portion agent Boss wished for him to have as a bonus for using the Pittsburgh, Fort Wayne, and Chicago Railway. Amasa Cobb was not approached by agents because he was known "to be a gentleman, and knowing that no man dare approach him with a bribe." Cutler, however, denied receiving money, at least initially, but later admitted in his testimony that he accepted $400 (in an envelope) from an agent and subsequently used the money to help pay a debt in Milwaukee. G. W. Cass, the president of the Fort Wayne Railroad Company, criticized the practice of paying these bonuses to secure travel contracts from the Wisconsin regiments. Rumors of wrongdoing led Vandor to write the *Wisconsin State Journal* defending himself against the charges. He declared that the "Van Wyck Investigating Committee, . . . found no testimony implicating me with taking money in an improper way." *Congressional Globe*, House of Representatives, Committee, *Government Contracts: Report No. 2*, 37th Congress, 2nd sess., December

18, 1861, 100–103, 106, 332, 71–76; "From Col. Vandor," *Wisconsin State Journal* (Madison, WI), January 17, 1862.

7. Maj. Gen. John C. Frémont declared martial law and proclaimed the slaves of all Confederate supporters free in Missouri. This act, without the approval of or even consultation with the president, forced Lincoln to remove Frémont from his post. Lincoln fretted that such a move would push Kentucky to the Confederacy, something he could ill afford to let happen in his birth state. Many in the North celebrated the measure, hoping that it would hurt the Southern war effort. United States, War Records Office, *War of the Rebellion: A Compilation of the Official Records of the Union and Confederate Armies*, 128 vols. (Washington, DC: Government Printing Office, 1885–1901), ser. 1, vol. 3, 466–67 (hereafter cited as *OR*); James M. McPherson, *Battle Cry of Freedom: The Civil War Era* (New York: Oxford University Press, 1988), 352–54; Mark Grimsley, *The Hard Hand of War: Union Military Policy toward Southern Civilians* (New York: Cambridge University Press, 1995), 124.

Camp Arlington Jan 30 1862

Dear Delia

I received your welcome letter last night. It found me acting officer of the guard, and i wanted something of that kind for i have an awful bad cold and wading round in mud knee deep for twenty four hours has not helped it much. The fact is if it dont stop raining soon we will all be sick. It has rained almost constantly for the last two weeks and it is raining yet, and the mud you can form no idea of it. The whole country is nothing but one vast morter bed.

Woodhouse has gone home and will go and see you. I sent Twenty dollars with him which he agreed to deliver to you in person and i think he will do it. You will certainly get your Godey & Harper soon for i paid the agent for them and you ought to have them by this time. Take good care of the book of photographs i sent you and i will send you some more. You have not answered my question in regard to the photograph of the Company Roll. Let me know if have got it. Dont forget the next time you write. I would liked to have sent you and the children some presants, but i could not get over to the city when Woodhouse left. I met Levi Showalter in the city when he was going home, but there is no knowing when he will get home, for he will have to go where ever his officers send him.

O how i would like to be back home to have one good sleigh ride with you and the babies. Give me the wisconsin winters if they are cold. Why Delia this morning at nine oclock the fog was so thick and dense you could not see ten rods. Damn the country. I would not live in it. Now i have said it. Perhaps i will feel better, but i was out in the mud and wet all night so that i have a good excuse, for my head feels a big as a flour barrel. We are getting good news from Kentuckey. I am glad to hear of our army doing something towards crushing out this Relblion. You talk of going to Susans. Dont forget to comfort her all you can for she feels verry downharted. The fact is it is hard to tell what we are comeing to if they delay this war six months longer. It is no use to send me papers, for i get papers every day in camp.[8]

I will send you a harpers weekly regular once a week after this. I have generally bought one each week but the boys sometimes abused them but since you think so much of them at home i will take care of them and send them to you.

The mail is ready to start.
I must close.
My love to all.
yours Ever

H F Young

NOTE

8. Union gunboat demonstrations from January 17 to January 22 softened the Confederate defenses at Fort Henry in northern Tennessee. Brig. Gen. Ulysses S. Grant, with a force of fifteen thousand, landed several miles below the fort, while Flag Officer Andrew Hull Foote's gunboats attacked from the river. The Confederate commander, sensing the inevitable, directed 2,500 men to nearby Fort Donelson. Grant's force, slowed by heavy rainfall, arrived at the fort after the Confederate surrender on February 6, 1862. As previously mentioned, Rebecca S. Warner (Paul) may have been Delia's sister. *OR*, ser. 1, vol. 7, pt. 1, 1–2; McPherson, *Battle Cry of Freedom*, 396–97; Allen C. Guelzo, *Fateful Lightning: A New History of the Civil War and Reconstruction* (New York: Oxford University Press, 2012), 198; Frederick H. Dyer, *A Compendium of the War of the Rebellion Compiled and Arranged from Official Records . . . and Other Reliable Documents and Sources* (Des Moines, IA: Dyer Publishing Company, 1908), 845 (hereafter cited as *Dyer's Compendium*).

Camp Arlington Feb 6 1862

Dear Father

I must apologize for not writing sooner. My reason for not doing so was the fact of Lieut Woodhouse returning home and he was to call on you and give you the news. And i knew nothing to the contrary, until last evening I received a letter from Art Benett that he had to go to Lacross County. That will go hard with Sam for he was homesick. I sent one hundred & Twenty Dollars with him. One hundred to you and Twenty to Delia.[9]

I suppose he will send it to you, and you can send the Twenty to Delia. We have had two fair days in the last three weeks, but it is raining again this morning. The mud is deep as ever. The road impassible and all of us barking day and night with what the boys calls the damed Potomac glanders.

We get some good news from other places which keeps up our spirits. And there is another thing. The Rebbles in our front are getting awful sick as fast as their time runs out. They refuse to enlist a gain. They knowing that we cant approach them. This weather and roads have removed a number of their men. Now it might happen that we would call on them before they could get those men back. At all events they will be called on as soon as the roads are fit for a move. If it was not for the imposbility of getting provisions to us through this mud we would have moved before this time. I received the Investigators for which i am thankful. As to other papers we have thousands of them from Wis and every other place.[10]

The boys are getting along verry well considering the place we are in. Colonel Vandor has resigned and is Minister to Tahiti. Our regiment has a good feeling existing amongst them both officers and men. The col paid our company a high compliment the other day on dress parade. He marched round and reviewed all the companys and then said the regiment was in very bad condition. In respect to numbers present, arms, clothing and accoutrements, with the exception of company F said he. They always come out with a full company, all in uniform with their arms chlothes and accoutrements always in good condition. And now said the collonel i call your attention to them, and until every company in the line comes up to their standard, i will not sign a pass for either officers or men to go to Washington. And he has been good as his word, for i know of commision officers trying to get a pass since, which he refused, saying when your company is all right you can have a pass but not before. So Co F gets the passes. We had a company of proud boys before but now they hold their heads still higher. We have the best material in the reg and all the boys feel it and do their best. I have no news to write. Give my love to all.[11]

Yours Truly

H F Young

NOTES

9. Alvery A. Bennett was a farmer from Glen Haven in Grant County. The Sam reference was to 1st Lt. Samuel Woodhouse, Company F of the Seventh Wisconsin. 1860 United States Census, Glen Haven, Grant County, Wisconsin, digital image s.v. "Alvery A. Bennett," Ancestry.com.

10. Young's reference to the "Investigators" is unclear. There were a number of newspapers by that name in various places at this time, but none in Wisconsin.

11. Joseph Vandor, scandalized by the railroad bribery fiasco and the mistreatment of his officers, resigned on January 30, 1862. Appointed Consul to Tahiti, Society Islands, Vandor made an annual salary of $1,000. Lt. Col. William W. Robinson assumed command of the regiment on the same date. An incident, related by William Ray but not mentioned to Jared, involved a visit to Washington by Young and two others in which the men returned to camp inebriated. Ray, whose confidence in Young was shaken a bit, decided that all men have faults, including himself, and he decided to drop the "ridiculous affair." *Roster*, 1:538; Lance J. Herdegen, *The Men Stood Like Iron: How the Iron Brigade Won Its Name* (Bloomington: Indiana University Press, 1997), 32; William H. Knight, ed., *Hand-Book Almanac for the Pacific States: An Official Register and Business Directory* (San Francisco: H. H. Bancroft, 1864), 52; Lance Herdegen and Sherry Murphy, eds., *Four Years with the Iron Brigade: The Civil War Journals of William R. Ray, Co. F, Seventh Wisconsin Infantry* (Cambridge, MA: Da Capo Press, 2002), 45–46.

Camp Arlington Feb 9 1862

Dear Delia

I received your letter dated Jan 25 last night. It was just fifteen days from the it was written untill it arrived here. *That is to bad.* I was sorry to hear of the sickness of the children, but verry glad to hear they were better. I know you have a hard time of it and during this muddy weather i some times think of you for hours together. When i last wrote to you i was sick but i am better now and able for duty. The story W Largeant wrote home is simply not true. The night we succeeded in driving old col vandor away from the regiment, we had a high old time, and many of the officers perhaps myself amongst the rest drank more than we had ought to, but none of got so drunk as not to know our duties. For if we had we would have been punished and i have never had a word of reprimand from a superior officer since i enlisted.

I have heard complaints about this Largeant before; and since he has gone we find out he drank vinegar to keep himself poor and pale, and to prevent the doctors medicine from operating so that he could get his discharge. So let him go, but there is one thing you may rest assured of that is Hen Young will never do anything that will disgrace him as a husband or Father, or Officer or Gentleman. So rest easy little one when we meet i will have nothing to be asshamed of. Neither shall you. I have just learned that Lieut Woodhouse was sent to Lacrosse and i dont no where Showwalter was sent, but woodhouse writes me he will go home the first opportunity.[12]

Perhaps he may be there before you get this. At all events you will get your twenty Dollars, for i wrote to your Father to send it to you if Woodhouse sent the money to him. I had thirty five Dollars stolen from me and the Pocket book. It was in with twenty Postage Stamps. I dont no who stole it or where it went. There is plenty that steel every chance they get. I would like to shoot the man that got it.

I dont see why you dont get your Magazines. There must be some mistake some where, if you dont get them soon i will go over to Washington and see the ageant about it. You must write to let me know how much money you will want to get your teeth fixed and i will send it to you next pay day which will be sometime in march. It will be due the first, but we never get it for ten or twelve days after the muster rools are made out.

I am verry glad you have found such good neighbours in the Combs house, but keep in good heart, for this war cant last much longer. We are gaining advantages over the Rebbles at all points. We have good news from Misoure Ky and Tennessee and the Rebbles out in our front are getting verry much discouraged. If we have no Foreign interference th rebbelion will be chrushed by the first of may and when the time comes that peace is declared you may look for me back again and that rite quick to.[13]

The weather is fine overhead but awful muddy underfoot. In fact the whole camp is little better than a swamp. Our company has the character of being the best in the Regiment. The Colonel told the other companys the other day on Dress parade that they were all in bad condition but *Co F*, and untill they came up to the scratch, that he would not give one of them officers or men, a pass to Washington, but that Company F could get all the passes they wanted. Co F was proud and saucy before but that has made them worse. I am glad to hear Eva gets along well with her School. Tell her to be sure and keep her nose well covered up this cold weather or it might freeze, and then it would not answer to fight with.[14]

Tell Jared that when i come home i will bring him a little gun, and drum and a soldier cap, and tell Laura that i will bring her a gipsy hat and a nice doll. And kiss dear little May for me. I have some photographs over in washington. When i get them I will send you one to put in that albium i sent you with Woodhouse. The boys of your acquaintance are all well.

Give my love to all.
yours ever

H F Young

NOTES

12. Wesley Largent, Company F of the Seventh Wisconsin, left the service on December 31, 1861. *Roster*, 1:560.

13. John D. Combs lived in Beetown, Grant County, Wisconsin, and was a gunsmith. The Union victory at Fort Henry was part of the good news referenced by Young. Lebanon, Missouri, was occupied by federal forces on January 22, 1862. 1860 United States Census, Cassville, Grant County, Wisconsin, digital image s.v. "John D. Combs," Ancestry.com; *OR*, ser. 1, vol. 8, 2.

14. The 1868 Grant County Plat showed S. H. (school-house) near the property of Young on the road between Cassville and Beetown. However, this is hard to confirm, as the plat map is dated six years after the letter. Grant County Genealogical Society, *Grant County Plat Map Index, 1868* (Platteville, WI: compiled by Grant County Genealogical Society, 1868), Cassville Township.

Camp Arlington Feb 15 1862

Dear Delia

Your letter dated Feb 2 came to hand this evening and, found us all in usual health. We are having a severe snow storm. In fact it looks more like winter this evening than any time yet. It had just begun to dry up the mud, and this snow will go off tomorrow and make it worse than ever if that were possible. Look at the Harpers weekly i sent you, at the picture, why the Army of the Potomac dont move and you will have a true picture of our situation. We call it the mud blockade. We have got new guns. The famous Austrian Rifles, with minie balls for cartridges and our boys think they can whip any amount of Sesesh. And Lieut Collonel W W Robinson, is promoted Collonel in place of Vandor. All of which makes us feel more conficence in our officers and in one another, for if volunteers have full confidence in their officers and are well drilled they are a match for any regulars in the world. We have been out on pickett since i wrote you last and had a hard time of it, on account of the mud.[15]

Col. William W. Robinson, Seventh Wisconsin Infantry (Wisconsin Historical Society, WHS-1795)

Lieut Woodhouse is home and if he dont call on you as he agreed to, i will whip him the first time i see him. And i will tell him so the first time i write him a letter, and L Showwalter. He did not get away from here as soon as he expected, but i seen Him in the city the day he started and he promised to call and see you. I would have sent you more money and not so much to your Father, if i had known you had to pay money for your wood. I expected Furman would make some trade for the wood, but try and get along with the Twenty Dolls this time and i will send you all you want next pay day. I thought perhaps he would make some trade for bran and shorts, but it will make no difference if you can stand it till i can send you more money. You ask why i did not go into the recruiting business. I will tell you. When i volunteered i did so to fight, and my place is in the camp or on the field, and when i am not wanted any more in camp or field i will go home. When we got this company up i promised to stand by the boys to the last if i had heath and strength to do it and i will keep my word, and i no you will not ask me to brake it. I dont wish to brag on how much the boys depend on me, but i cant refrain from telling you one incident. Our Reg had orders to send a Lieut on detached service, to join the signal corpse. The Adutant told me if i would make the application i could get it. It would take me away from the Reg for several months. I told him if the company was willing i would make the application. I went to the company and not one of them were willing that i should leave. In fact they would not hear to it atall; and you know that many of these boys enlisted with the understanding that i would bee with them, and many of their mothers and friends have confidence in me that i will keep good my word. But lets drop the subject for i know when you wrote that you did not beleive i would come home if i could, or did not want to come home. You did not beleive what you wrote.

But we have such glorious news from the South. Fort Donalson taken with fifteen thousands Prisnors. Roanoak Iland taken with three Thousand Prisnors. Bowling green evacuated and ft Henry taken and general Landers surprise up the River, all within a few days it makes every thing look bright again. The boys are cheering fit to split their sore throats. They have just got the news of the capture of fort Donelson.[16]

I am sorry to hear you have the measles so near you, but if you or the children should get them, you must hire some help immedately. Never mind the cost, and keep in the house. I fear they will go harder with you than with the children, for it takes twelve or fifteen days for a letter to come here from home. And i am afraid you will have them and might die with them before i would know any thing about it, but i will hope for the best, but i will be verry uneasy until i receive your next letter. I wish i was not so far away from home. When i get a letter i look at the date of it and then say o they were all well two weeks ago but some of them may be sick or dying by this time. This is the way i feel every letter i receive since the close of navigation. Tell Jared to bee a good boy and kiss his mama for me and tell Laura i would like to sing old dan tucker to her and be at home once more to rock her to sleep. Kiss dear little may for me, and give my love to all.

Ever yours

H F Young

NOTES

15. A report by Maj. Gen. Irvin McDowell stated that the men of the regiment "lack confidence" in their previous rifle, the Springfield smoothbore musket. William W. Robinson commanded the Seventh Wisconsin from January 30, 1862, to July 9, 1864. *OR*, ser. 1, vol. 5, 708; *Roster*, 1:538.

16. Fort Donelson, Tennessee, fell on February 16, 1862, after a four-day siege. Confederate casualties at Fort Donelson were 15,829 killed and wounded, of which 13,829 became prisoners of war. Brig. Gen. Ambrose Burnside, landing 7,500 men on swampy ground, captured Roanoke Island in early February. The victory cemented, at least for a moment, Burnside's reputation as an aggressive commander. Confederate prisoners from the capture of Roanoke numbered 2,527, while fewer than 300 Union forces were taken. Bowling Green, Kentucky, was abandoned by Confederate forces on February 14–15, 1862. Brig. Gen. Frederick W. Lander led a surprise assault on the Confederate position at Bloomery Gap on February 14, 1862. Lander, who personally led the charge, at great cost to his well-being, forced the Confederates from the area, killing thirteen and capturing sixty-five. In his after-action report, he stated, "My health is too much broken to do any severe work." Maj. Gen. George McClellan noted, "His constitution was impaired by the hardships he had experienced" and led to Lander's death on March 2, 1862. *OR*, ser. 1, vol. 5, 66, 405–6, vol. 7, 2; *Dyer's Compendium*, 845, 972; William F. Fox, *Regimental Losses in the American Civil War* (Albany, NY: Albany Publishing Company, 1889), 549; Guelzo, *Fateful Lightning*, 328; McPherson, *Battle Cry of Freedom*, 372–73.

Camp Arlington Va Feb 22 1862

Dear Delia

I receivd your verry kind letter yesturday. I was glad to hear you were all well and verry glad you seen Liut Woodhouse. Your letter found us all in pety good health and in excellant spirits. You keep what money you need and give the rest to your Father. It is raining here to day as usual, but being Washingtons birth day, there has been a national salute fired from every fort, and every Regiment of the vast Army of the Potomac, and cheers given without number for our recent union victories. The fact is while we are here blockaded with mud, our armies in other parts are crushing out the Rebellion at such a fearful rate that it cant last much longer. In fact our boys are getting affraid that the South will give up the ghost before they get a chance at them, but i think that we will move as soon as possible. And when we do move it will be like the moving of a tornado, sweeping all before it. In firing a salute this forenoon one of our boys got wounded. His name is Wm Atkison. he was shot through the fleshey part of the leg, with a ramrod fired carlessly by one of the boys of the 2 Reg.[17]

Jessee Shipton who lives in Watterloo has got his discharge and starts for home on monday. He has been laid up with rheumatism for a long time. This damp wet weather is begining to tell with fearful effect on our soldiers. In fact i would sooner risk the bullets of the enemy. It will sow the seed of disease in many cases that will carry them off asson as warm weather comes. I wrote a letter yesturday to H Bergess Esq. You ask if i didnt write between the 7 and 30 of last month. I most certanly did and they must be froze up someplace on the road. As for the magazines i paid the money to a man that keeps a bookstore in the city, and asson as the mud dries up so that i can travel i will go and see him. He told me he took all the subscriptions he could get and i supposed it was all right, for he appears to be an honest sort of a man. But i find a great complaint amongst the officers and soldiers of the business men in Washington for never doing what they agree to. I suppose they think they will never see us again. I still feel uneasy about the measles, but i am verry glad you have got plenty of good wood. Get it choped up and piled in convenient places for your use and whenever you want help hire it. Dont use yourself up.[18]

You must lookout in good time for some person to make your garden. Dont have it ploughed untill it is dry. Then have the upper side next the grape vines planted in potatoes this year, and leave the lower side for other things, have the grapevines and cherry trees well taken care of. There is an officer here that has his upper teeth out and a set of put in on gutapercha. He had a set put in on gold plate, but it was to heavy he could not stand it, and he says the gutapercha is lighter and better tasted than the gold plate. The plate of gutapercha is verry thin, but so stout it will bear a persons weight without bending or breaking. You get whichever you think will suit you best. I am sorry to hear of Mrs Furmans misfortune, but tell Furman to cheer up. We will soon end this War and then the price of flour will come up. So will every thing else. The mississipi will be open clear to the Gulf by the time navigation is open in the north. Pork and flour both took a rise on the taking of Fort Donnelson. Tell Jared i will send him a photograph as soon as i go to the city. The fact is i have no money. The Damed curse, that stole my pockett book stole all the money i had but five Dollars.[19]

But pay day will be here again by the time you get this, and then i will get my photographs. I want to send one to Susan and one to Will. We cant drill much now only practice at target shooting. And you had better beleive we are getting awful tired of staying here. When we read the news of what they are doing in other places it make us feel as though we were prisnors. And we are almost as bad, blocked here in this damed infernal mudhole, with no drill, and cant step out of our tents without sinking almost over our boot tops in mud. It is not necessary for me to write you a history of our recent successes, for you will be posted by the papers. But there is one thing certain that those of us who are living will get home some time in may, or i miss my guess entirely. Tell Laura i will bring her a Dolly with toes and fingers on and a dress for it. Give my good wishes to Furmans foks, and tell Eva i dont see as i have gained much by her correspondence, but i am verry glad she gets along well with her School. When i go home i will take her a present of a ginger horse, or a sugar rooster. Kiss may for me and give my love to all the children and except the same for your self.[20]

ever yours

H F Young

NOTES

17. Fort Donelson, at least initially, was not an easy fort to crack, with Foote's gunboats taking a beating from Confederate gun emplacements. Grant called on his old instructor at West Point, Maj. Gen. C. F. Smith, to attack Confederate positions at the fort. Smith's attack, along with the departure of Confederate forces, enabled federal forces to successfully occupy the fort. Brig. Gen. Simon Bolivar Buckner, Grant's classmate at the academy, asked for an armistice, to which Grant, in what would be a trademark of later battles, offered no terms other than "unconditional and immediate surrender." Buckner's reply, "to accept the ungenerous and unchivalrous terms," was no less genuine. William Atkinson was in Company F of the Seventh Wisconsin Infantry. The injury was not serious enough to release him from the service, and he was mustered out of the regiment on July 3, 1865. Ronald C. White Jr., *American Ulysses: A Life of Ulysses S. Grant* (New York: Random House, 2016), 196–98; Ulysses S. Grant, *Personal Memoirs of U. S. Grant*, 2 vols. (New York: Charles L. Webster, 1886), 1:308–315; Geoffrey Perret, *Ulysses S. Grant: Soldier and President* (New York: Modern Library, 1999), 171–73; H. W. Brands, *The Man Who Saved the Union: Ulysses Grant in War and Peace* (New York: Archer Books, 2012), 165–67; *Roster*, 1:558.

18. Jesse Shipton, who was in Company F of the Seventh Wisconsin, was discharged on February 22, 1862, due to disability. Henry Burgess lived near Young in Cassville and, as previously noted, was active in the affairs of the township. *Roster*, 1:561.

19. Gutapercha was a rubbery substance used to make dentures during this period. It was also used to make golf balls until about 1900.

20. The deplorable conditions made drill difficult, and, according to William Ray, Young did his best to help make their lives easier, drilling only when ordered to do so by the colonel. Herdegen and Murphy, eds., *Four Years with the Iron Brigade*, 58.

~

Camp Arlington Va Feb 23 1862

Dear Father and friends

I received you verry kind letter several days ago and was glad to hear you were all in good health. We are in fair health with the exception that nearly every person has got bad colds the natural result of this damp climate and the cursed mudhole we are in.

Fletcher Kidd has been quite sick with fever but is getting better. Jessee Shipton of Watterloo, has got his discharge and starts for home tomarrow. He has been laid up for a long time with rheumtism. In firing a National Salute yesurday in honour of Washingtons birth day, Wm Atkison of our company was wounded by one of the Second Reg boys, carlessly firing without returning his Ramrod. It pased through the calf of Atkisons leg; making a severe flesh wound. All the rest of our Co are able for their allowance. The weather still continues wet and the mud is deep as ever, but we are in gay spirits over our recent glorious successes. We are almost crazy for a chance to try our hands at the Rebbles and i dont think we will have to wait much longer for a chance. This Army of the Potomac is a live and kicking. At least you would think so if you were here some time when the news is being circulated in camp of one of our great union victories as the newsboys cry it of. And while you would be reading it boom boom would go the great guns from our forts, in every direction, making the welcome ring as they belch forth the national salute. And then you would see the companys spring into their streets, and some one would propose three cheers which would be taken up by company, after company, and Reg after Reg untill the whole vast army had echoed and reechoed the same. Then look at the flashing eye compresed lip and cheeks all glowing with excitement. Just listen to what they are saying. Why the Devil didnt they send us to kentucky or missouri says one. Or why in thunder dont they send us down the coast says another, or anywhere that we can have a fight chimes in another. Oh never mind boys says another. We will get to take Centreville and manasses, as soon as we can move. Then they all join in cussing the mud blockade, and adjourn to their tents. Some to reading and discusing the news. Some to cleaning their arms and equipmants. Some others to their favourite pastime of old sledge or euchre, and so the ball rolls on from day to day. All the same which is enough to give the Devil the blues. We have got new Rifles and all the drilling we can do now is to go to the woods and practice target shooting which we do every day when it is not raining. Our guns will carry eight hundred yards so you see we are able to take the Rebbles at any distance short of half a mile either running or standing. I have it from high military authority that it was Gen McClellan plan for all the armies to move at once but we on the potomac were blockaded with *mud* and could not move. The general was over on this side of the river the other day, and said we should have a chance as soon as the teams could follow us with provisions. That is what plays hell with us here. We could advance and take Centreville and mannasses, but you must reccollect that we are marching inland, where we will have to depend on the wagons for all our provissions. You must reccollect that the railroad was entirely destroyed, and we are building one as far as our lines extend and it will be finished that far in a short time. I heard General King say yesturday that he had access to Gen McClellans plans, and they had all come out all right so far according to calculation.[21]

And then an other thing, every commander of a department has the chance to draw all the troops he wants from the army of the Potomac. The army has perfect confidence in McClellan, and we begin to find we have got the right man for Secretary of war. We dont have so cursed many old political friends to hunt offices for as Cameron did. Staunton throws Poaticks out of sight, and appoints no person until satisfide they are deserving and competent. The backbone of the Rebellion is broken. We will march out some of these days take centreville and mannasses. Then the boiler will burst and burn those to deth who started the fire. Then lookout for good times once more. W W Robinson had been promoted to the Collonelcy of this Reg and major Hamilton Lt Col, and Capt George Bill of Co A major. The Governour left it to a vote of the Commisioned officers of the Reg, and made the appointments we reccommended. Give my love to all.[22]

yours Truly

H F Young

Since writing the above i rec your letter of the sixteenth. I was laid up with the sore throat. There was several days i could not speak above a whisper, but i am better now and able for duty. Some Damed infernal scoundrel stole my pockett book with Thirty five dollars in treasury notes. There is plenty in the Reg and every other that ought to be in states prison. I am sure none of Co got it.

H F Y

You may look for us if we are in the land of the living in may. Tell the farmers to sow and plant abundance, for the price will be fair, and we will be there to help harvest it.

NOTES

21. Fletcher S. Kidd was in Company F of the Seventh Wisconsin. *Roster*, 1:560.

22. Simon Cameron was a poor choice as Lincoln's first secretary of war. As a political appointment, he lacked the skills to adequately manage the department. Cameron, to make matters worse, played a part in the corruption and inefficiency of the department that led to an investigation by a House Committee on Government Contracts. His replacement at the post, Edwin M. Stanton, was a prudent pick by Lincoln, especially in the long run. Vandor's resignation on January 30, 1862, changed the command structure of the Seventh Wisconsin. William W. Robinson assumed command of the regiment, while Charles A. Hamilton was promoted to lieutenant colonel, and George Bill, from Company A, was elevated to major. McPherson, *Battle Cry of Freedom*, 260, 324; Guelzo, *Fateful Lightning*, 146, 314; Doris Kearns Goodwin, *Team of Rivals: The Political Genius of Abraham Lincoln* (New York: Simon & Schuster, 2005), 410–15; *Roster*, 1:538.

Camp Arlington Va Mar 5 1862

Dear Delia

I received your welcome letter last night. Was glad to hear from you. Your letter found me all right side up with care, but we have quite a number of sick, many of which i fear will never get well. Fletcher Kidd is verry low with Tyfoid fever, and in the Reg we are having two or more funerals per week. The weather still continues very disagreeable, rain, snow, and blowing alternately all the time. Our Reg is out on pickett. I was left in camp as officer of the guard. William McCartney is here and has gone out on pickett. As to your being expensive, if you only bought what you needed, which i think you would be likely to do, you may rest easy on that score. I will send home money next pay day and send it so that you can get what you need. We are under marching orders, to be ready to march at an hours notice, and we dont know what moment to look for the order to pull up stakes and leave. It has the effect of keeping us in suspense all the time. When we go to bed we dont no but it will be to be called up by the long roll, and when we are up it is the same, every thing is packed up ready. We have got light tents one for every two men, called shelter tents that unbutton and are carried by the men. Each tent weighs sticks and all 8 lbs 3 oz. We dont know where we are to go, but we will find out when we get the order to march. But i think it will be to Richmond, by way of mannasses. You will hear all kinds of rumers and stories affloat for the goverment will let no news of our movements be published at present. So dont let idle rumours give you any uneasiness. Perhaps you will get news of our moveing before you get this but continue to direct your letters to Washington as heretofore.[23]

I never received a letter from Susan Greer but would like to verry much and would certainly answer it, for i answer five or six letters every week. In fact i answer all i get. Tell Jared i am glad to hear he caries wood for mama, for that proves him to be a good boy. Tell Laura she will have a verry nice dolly and to be a good girl. The news from the west is all right. We have just got the news of the evacuation of Collumbus, their strong hold on the Mississippi River, without firing a gun. And Banks has crosed the Potomac, and is advancing on Winchester. Every thing is going all right. I dont think it will last much longer.[24]

You must excuse this short letter for i was officer of the guard last night and slept none. And i have no news anyhow, for i have written so much and so often from here it is hard to find any new to write about. Give my love to all.

ever yours

H F Young

NOTES

23. William F. McCartney lived in Cassville, Wisconsin, and was the son of Orris McCartney, one of the earliest settlers in Grant County. 1860 United States Census, Cassville, Grant County, Wisconsin, digital image s.v. "William McCartney," Ancestry.com.

24. Susann Greer resided in Tafton, Grant County. She was eight or nine in 1862, and her connection to Young at this time is unclear. Columbus, Kentucky, was abandoned by the Confederates on March 2–3, 1862, and occupied by the Union Army. Another political appointee, Maj. Gen. Nathaniel Banks, commanded the Department of the Shenandoah. Winchester, Virginia, was abandoned by the

Confederates on March 11–12, 1862, and occupied by the Union Army. 1860 United States Census, Tafton, Grant County, Wisconsin, digital image s.v. "Susann Greer," Ancestry.com; *OR*, ser. 1, vol. 2, 3, vol. 5, 4, vol. 7, 2; *Dyer's Compendium*, 731, 896.

Camp Arlington Va Mar 17 1862

Dear Delia

Excuse me for not writing sooner for we have been on the march for the last week through mud rain and wet and arrived back here last night all sound, without getting a single shot at the Rebbles. But the paper will keep you posted in regard to our movements. We start to morrow on the Southern expedition. We dont no where we are going, but i will write to you as soon as we ar landed, all about it. I and all the rest of the boys in our company, have stood it firstrate. I sent one hundred and forty Dollars to your Father and wrote to him to let you have what you wanted of it.[25]

I have no time to write more now but this time i will take writing materials with me.

Give my love to all, and you and the children keep in good heart untill i have time to write again.

ever your man

H F Young

NOTE

25. Marching out of Camp Arlington from March 7 through March 11, 1862, Union forces advanced on Centreville, Virginia, and found that the Confederates had abandoned their positions. The men were sorely disappointed at not seeing any action. Herdegen, *The Men Stood Like Iron*, 51; Lance J. Herdegen, *The Iron Brigade in Civil War and Memory: The Black Hats from Bull Run to Appomattox and Thereafter* (El Dorado Hills, CA: Savas Beatie, 2012), 113–14; *OR*, ser. 1, vol. 5, 4.

Camp Arlington Va Mar 17 1862

Dear Father

We are back on our old camping ground, after a weeks absence hunting for the rebbles which we did not find, as they have gone south. We start on the Southern expedition to marrow, where we are going is a sealed book to us. I will write you when we land. I sent one hundred and forty Dollars in treasury notes to you by William N Reed, of Lancaster. I want you to get and let Delia have what she may want and dont forget to pay A Paul back the money he let me have when i started. F Kidd is getting better. The rest of the boys are all well. My love to all. I have no time to write.[26]

yours truly

H F young

NOTE

26. William N. Reed, a surveyor, resided in Lancaster, Grant County. Alexander Paul owned a general store in Patch Grove and, as previously noted, married Delia's sister Rebecca. 1860 United States Census, Lancaster, Grant County, digital image s.v. "William N. Reed," Ancestry.com; Butterfield, *History of Grant County*, 856.

Camp Near Fairfax Semminary Va April 1 1862

Dear Delia

When i wrote to you a week a go just after arriving in this camp i told you we were expecting to embark right off.[27] Well we are here yet still looking for the order to leave. There has over one hundred thousand men embarked and gone; to my certain knowledge since we encamped here. And we will be far on our way south before you get this, or i am much Mistaken. We are all well and as the saying is spoiling for a fight. I hear that the letters of the army have been detained at Washington. I dont know whether it is so or not. I went to Washington before i left camp Arlington, and saw the man i gave the money to for Harpers and Godey. He said he had ordered them sent, and he would see that you got them. Certain now you let me know, for i have got this address and receipt. Lieut Woodhouse has resigned and left the service. He resigned just when he was ordered back to his company. Capt Mckee has been appointed Lieut Colonel of the fifteenth Regiment.[28]

We are having beautiful weather here but the nights are devlish cold to lay out on the damp ground but we stand it firstrate. You must not expect long letters from me, while i have to write on a knapsack for a table. Oh you dont know how much i would like to see you all this beautiful spring morning. Keep in good heart dear. I think there is still happiness in store for us. I have not had a letter for an age.

My love to Jared, Laura, and may, and for your self in particular.

H F Young

NOTES

27. Fairfax Seminary was near Alexandria, Virginia.

28. The Army of the Potomac disembarked from Alexandria on March 17, 1862, to begin the long-anticipated advance on Richmond. McDowell's First Army Corps was left, at least initially, near the nation's capital to guard against a potential Confederate attack. In early April the corps moved to Falmouth, Virginia, and McClellan, who expected all units at his disposal in the peninsula, was not pleased with the development. *OR*, ser. 1, vol. 11, pt. 1, 1; Herdegen, *The Iron Brigade*, 115; Guelzo, *Fateful Lightning*, 163.

Camp Near Fairfax Seminary April 2 1862

Dear Father

I received your letter yesturday. Was glad to hear you were all well. We are all able for our allowance of pork and beans. The sick ones are all better but if you ever saw a lot of birds in a cage, and seen how uneasy they were you can imagine something of our present position. Here we have been for the last two weeks, under marching orders expecting daily to embark, with nothing but these cursed little shelter tents that you can just crawl under to protect us from cold damp or wet. You take a sheet but there is one thing certain. We ought to have caught them at manasses.

yours

H F Young

Direct to Washington till further orders.

Camp Cutler near Bristo Prince William Co Va April 12 1862

Dear Delia

If you will look at the Railroad map some twenty miles south of manasses junction, you will see Warrington. We are encamped between Bisto and Warrington. We have had three days of the worst storm of snow rain and hail i ever seen and we had to lay out in it all. But it has cleared off now.

All verry fine. We did not go down the river, and we dont no where we are going now. We have glorious news from every place where ever the armies move. We are expecting to march on gordenville as soon as the streams fall so that the artillery can cross.[29]

I would like to see your new teeth verry much. You must not expect long letters from me, while we are marching for i am writing seting on a log with a board a cross my nee for a table. Give my love to Jared & Laura and kiss dear may for me. Oh how i would like to see you all. Give my love to all.

Ever yours

H F Young

NOTE

29. Bristoe Station was on the Orange and Alexandria Railroad, between Manassas Junction and Warrenton Junction. Gordonsville, Virginia, is on the same rail line, toward Charlottesville, Virginia.

Camp Falmouth April 23 1862

Dear Delia

I received you welcome letter several days ago and was delighted to hear from you were all well. We are all getting along verry well considering the the roads and weather.[30]

I thought i had seen some pretty tough times in my life but the last two weeks has been the toughest i ever seen. In fact i would not have beleived men could stand what we have stood in that time without getting sick and perfictly used up. It rains nearly every day and the roads are almost impassible and all the streams are bank full. Some days we were all day getting five miles, for we had to wait for the artillery and trains, and they would stick fast and upset in the streams, and it would sometimes take hours to get them acrost. And then we had to lay down at night in our wet chlothes, get up wet and try it again.[31]

Our army is composed of the best stuf in the world, for the only grumbling you could hear was that we could not go faster for they wanted a hand in the big fight that was expected to come of at Fredricksberg. But here we are on Falmouth heights with the Rappahannoc River bank full between us. And all the fight there was, the cavalry and Skermishers had, as they retreated they burned all the bridges across the River. The only man of our Reg that was along was Britton of Plattville, and he was severely wounded by one of the Berdan Sharpshooters. In the skirmish it was before it was light enough to distingwish the uniform and Britton had got on the advance, when Augurs Artillery came up and planted his battery on Falmouth Heights. The Rebbles took a regular stampeede from the city, and the mayor came over and surrendered the city. I am 1 Lieut since the first of Aprile. Our orderly Sergt J W McKenzie is second Lieut and A R McCartney is orderly sergt. Capt Callis has got the Agua and chills and we left A R McCartney at Catlets Station on the other Rail road with the chills and fever. Fletcher Kidd is still at Alexandria doing well. All the rest of your

Capt. John B. Callis, Seventh Wisconsin Infantry (Wisconsin Historical Society, WHS-3904)

acquaintance are well. It is raining as usual and want cant write letters when it rains.[32]

April 27 1862

Sunday and a lovely day. Oh how it makes me think of home. The woods is full of flowers. The fruit trees are in full bloom. Every thing looks like spring. I have had no chance to send off this letter as it was so wet till yesturday that the streams were to high to cross, and the capt is not fit for duty and my time is all taken up with moveing and Mending to the company. Look on your Rail Road map and you will find A Rail Road running from the Aquai creek on the Potomac to Richmond by way of Fredricksberg. You will see a stream called Potomac creek that the road crosses that stream, and will commence in the morning to build it, for it is sixty ft high and one hundred and fifty ft long.[33]

They are having a big fight at yourktown but McClellan will whip them out, and then for Richmond, and i think that will finish the war, and the Rebellion. The other day when we marched throug the town of Falmouth. Nearly every white woman was crying, for they all have friends in the Rebble army, and all the darkies were dancing for Joy. Dont sell the red cow if you can get her milked for it will be hard to find another as good. I am glad the snow went off without a flood. Give my love to all, and let me tell you i would give any thing to see you all to day.[34]

Ever yours

H F Young

NOTES

30. Falmouth, Virginia, is on the Rappahannock River, opposite Fredericksburg.

31. The brigade was part of McDowell's plan to defend eastern and northern Virginia. It advanced from Alexandria on April 4, 1862, but foul weather interrupted the advance, forcing the unit to hunker down for a week. Alan T. Nolan, *The Iron Brigade: A Military History* (New York: Macmillan, 1961), 46; Herdegen, *The Iron Brigade*, 115.

32. William Britton, Company C of the Seventh Wisconsin wounded at Falmouth, Virginia, and discharged on July 22, 1862. Brig. Gen. Christopher Augur's men, advancing ahead of the army, forced their way into Falmouth on April 18, 1862. A committee of citizens met with Augur to arrange the surrender of the city to Union forces. John W. McKenzie and Alexander R. McCartney, both in the Seventh Wisconsin, were promoted to second lieutenant and first sergeant, respectively,

on April 1, 1862. On the same date Young was promoted to first lieutenant. According to William Ray, Young gave a short speech stating he would resign if fourteen men signed a paper requesting it. Instead, he received three cheers from the company. "He was a little tight," slang for drunk, according to Ray. The soldiers were later ordered to headquarters, where their condition made for an interesting evening. *Roster*, 1:548, 558, 560; Nolan, *The Iron Brigade*, 47; Herdegen and Murphy, eds., *Four Years with the Iron Brigade*, 80.

33. Aquia Creek, a tributary of the Potomac River, flowed northeast of Fredericksburg, Virginia. Fredericksburg was connected to the Potomac River by the Richmond and Fredericksburg Railroad. McDowell, who wished to cross into Fredericksburg, was ordered by Secretary of War Stanton to stay put and instead to rebuild the damaged railroad bridges on Potomac Creek. Nolan, *The Iron Brigade*, 47, 49; Herdegen, *The Iron Brigade*, 115–16.

34. The siege of Yorktown, from April 5 to May 4, 1862, was a masterful delaying action by Confederate major general John Magruder. Outnumbered nearly four to one, he convinced McClellan that he had a larger force than was in fact the case by marching the men continuously in their fortifications. Yorktown was evacuated on the night of May 4, 1862. *OR*, ser. 1, vol. 11, pt. 1, 1; McPherson, *Battle Cry of Freedom*, 426–27; *Dyer's Compendium*, 897.

~

Camp near Fredricksberg May 8 1862

Dear Delia

I have not received any letter from you for i dont no how long, and i want one *oh you dont know how bad.*

We are encamped on the Rappahannock River below Fredricksberg, in the most beautiful country in Virginia, and in the land where the oldest settlements were made that we read of in history. The farm Washington was born on lies between us and the city. There is a grave yard near where we are encamped, with monuments in it that mark the burial place of persons that date back two hundred and fifty years. Many of the actors in scenes we read about in history were born on the plantations in this beautiful valley, which one short year a go was all peace and quietness; but now is full of armed forces each bent on the destruction of the other. Almost every day skermishes accur on the oposite side of the River between the advance posts of our army and the enemys picketts in which lives are lost on both sides.

We are having a large army concentrated here. Not less than sixty thousand men are within a few hours march of this place all anxious for the order to march forward to Richmond. But it is doubtful if we find any resistance there, for the Rebbles run from our army wherever we go. If McClellan can drive them to Richmond we may succeed in surrounding them, but a few more retreats like the one at yorktown will ruin them. They may concentrate some where in the cotton states and risk all on one desperate battle, but which ever way they turn they must see nothing but utter ruin and defeat. I cant help but contrast the condition of the dear ones at home with the weoman and children in this country. The men are all away in the Army, and the weoman and old men and children are left unprotected. Our officers have made stringent laws against injuring persons or property, but the forlorn look they usuly weare shew their heart sickness. When we march past their houses in martial array, the old men look pale and uneasy, the weoman will look a short time then burst out crying. Then is the time that i feel perfectly happy the dear ones at home are far from the seat of war.[35]

Capt Callis is getting better. Fletcher Kidd is with us again all right. Clark is all sound so is McCartney, Bergess and all the rest of your acquaintances. The weather is beautiful. The lilack is in full bloom. So is the apple trees dogwood plumb trees and c.[36]

The first of ~~April~~ may brot round another pay day but we have not got it yet. I will send one hundred and fifty Dollars home as soon as we get our pay with orders for you to have what you need. I still think we will be home by the fourth of July. You may think we are going slow but every move we are making now contracts the circle round the enemy, and when their leaders give up and the army find out the exact state of things they will rock under all at once. I think before you get this letter we will be in Richmond.

The fall of New Orleans is a heart sickning blow to the Rebbles in this quarter. The union men we find here are union only while we are here, and it has been so all the way. They are a cowardly sneeking set of Devils, that would submit to annything rather than fight.[37]

Dont forget to plant plenty of Potatoes Tomatoes and every thing else that is good for i have missed a year in the vegetable line and i will want to make it up when i get home.

Write often, give my best wishes to Furman and Carroline ang squire Bergess and lady, and tell the squire that I am waiting anxiously for an answer for that letter I wrote him a long time ago. My best love to your self and the children.

H F Young

PS in reading this letter over i said nothing about the health of Hen young but rest assured he is sound as a Dollar.

NOTES

35. Williamsburg, defended by Maj. Gen. James Longstreet, was evacuated by Confederate forces on May 5, 1862, and occupied by federal forces on May 6, 1862. Early in the war, protection of Southern property was generally the norm, but, as the war progressed, sympathies toward protecting Southern property became less widespread. *OR*, ser. 1, vol. 11, pt. 1, 1; McPherson, *Battle Cry of Freedom*, 427; *Dyer's Compendium*, 898–99; Gerald F. Linderman, *Embattled Courage: The Experience of Combat in the American Civil War* (New York: Free Press, 1987), 182.

36. Andrew Clark was in Company K of the Seventh Wisconsin. *Roster*, 1:572.

37. New Orleans, which before the war was home to a large federal arsenal, later protected by two Confederate forts, was assaulted from the Mississippi River by Flag Officer David Glasgow Farragut. On the night of April 24, 1862, Farragut's flotilla fought its way past the defenses of New Orleans and raised the US flag over the city on April 25. A land force commanded by Maj. Gen. Benjamin Butler entered the city on May 1, 1862. According to Guelzo, "The loss of New Orleans was probably the severest single blow the Confederacy sustained in the war." Guelzo, *Fateful Lightning*, 134, 210–11; McPherson, *Battle Cry of Freedom*, 418–19; *OR*, ser. 1, vol. 6, 437; *Dyer's Compendium*, 743.

May 8 1862

Dear Father

I have not received any letter from you for a long time. We have been moving back and forth considerable since i wrote from Catletts Station. We started the next morning after i wrote my letter, in the rain to march to Fredricksberg, and that was a march never to be forgotten by any of us. It rained for two days. The roads were almost impassible. The streams were overflowing. It took us all one day to get five miles. We encamped two or three days on Falmouth heights, oposite Fredricksberg and then marched out on the Railroad towards Aquia creek, to build bridges on the Rail Road. We cut the timber for the Bridges, and got the road built all but the Bridge across Potomac creek that is four hundred ft long and Eighty five (85) ft high. We were working at that bridge when we received orders to march and we are encamped on the Rappahanock River, about two miles below Fredricksberg. We have got A pontoon bridge across the River but none of our troops have crosed yet.[38]

Pontoon bridge across Rappahannock River (Library of Congress, Prints & Photographs Division, Civil War Photographs, LC-DIG-ppmsca-33280)

I think we will cross the River soon. There is said to be a large force of Rebbles between here and Richmond. All we want is the order to march and we will soon find out for our selves what is between here and Richmond. Capt Callis has been quite sick with chills and Fever. He has done no duty for two weeks but he is getting better. Wm Turnby is better and has been returned for duty. Fletcher Kidd is with us and is all right. We get but little news from yorktown. I think McClellan is keeping every thing two quiet there.[39]

I dont think there can be much of an army there. If there is i dont think there is a large army between here and Richmond. As i have no news of importance and such a cursed unhandy place to write i will quit. Write often. Give my love to all.

H F Young

NOTES

38. Catlett's Station (now Catlett), Virginia, was on the Orange and Alexandria Railroad, between Fairfax and Alexandria, Virginia.

39. William Turnby was in Company F of the Seventh Wisconsin. He was discharged because of a disability on September 2, 1862. *Roster*, 1:561.

CHAPTER THREE

"we are . . . *broken, defeated, and out generald at every move*"

May 15 to October 18, 1862

Camp near Fredricksberg Va May 15 1862

Dear Delia

I received your letter and was glad to hear you were all well. We are encamped on the River oposite Fredricksberg within a Pistol shot of the city and are all in good health.

We are building the bridge across the River, and will have it built in about four days ready for another advance. We were witness of a skirmish the other day on the other side of the River. We were drawn up in line all ready for a start but the Rebbles retreated after loosing fourteen men. We are all mad as thunder for having to go so slow. We have not got teams and cant advance faster than we build the Railroad, and they make us guard all the property of these *damed* Rebbles all round. I tell you it goes against the grain for us to have to guard the fences Pigs and chickens of these men that are fighting against us. The people of this section are the most ignorant of any place i ever have been. They were born and raised here and have never been any where else. I have seen old men in this neighberhood that told me they were never ten miles from home in their lives, and they know nothing of what is being done or what is going on. They have never heard of such a state as Wis. Dident no whether it was a state county or city. I have no news to write. Only we are still successful at all points and i still think we will be home about harvest. I have not received my pay yet. When i do i will send you one hundred and fifty Dollars by express to Cassville. I think Lagrave is the express ageant there, and i want you to send Ury fifty two or three Dollars which is what i owe him and left my note. You can send it by some of the neighbours that is going to Lancaster. That will leave you ninety seven or eight Dollars to pay for your teeth wood & c. Write often. My love to Jared Laura May and your self.[1]

Give my good wishes to Furmans.

H F Young

NOTE

1. Charles L. Lagrave, a merchant in Cassville, opened a commission store in 1847. Isaac G. Ury opened the first store in Patch Grove in 1848 and eventually sold his interests to Alexander Paul. Castello N. Holford, *History of Grant County Wisconsin . . . and a History of the Several Towns* (Lancaster, WI: The Teller Print, 1900), 600; Consul Willshire Butterfield, *History of Grant County Wisconsin, Containing an Account . . . of the United States* (Chicago: Western Historical Company, 1881), 845–46, 856.

Fredricksberg Va May 24 1862

Dear Delia

I received your welcome letter two days ago and was glad to hear you were all well. Your letter found us all right side up with care. We have been in city of Fredricksberg Eight days. Have got the Bridge across the Rappahannoc River finished and the cars running regular from here to Aquia. ~~and~~ This is the greatest old foggy place i ever saw. Every thing has went on from year to year the same. The city must have been finished fity years ago but it is a place of great wealth and beauty. The Residences of the planters are magnifficent and the grounds and walks are all that wealth and taste can make them. That is what makes the place look old and grand. They made their living by furnishing negroes for the Southren market that furnished them with large incomes. So they built themselves beautiful homes and enjoyed them, but i would not like it for myself. I would want a more stering life.

Fredricksberg can bost of two things bautiful, Flowers of every description and pretty Women. There is certainly some of the finest looking women here i ever seen. They sit out on the stoops and varandahs every plesant evening. That is the regular Southern fashion. When we first came here they would not walk on the pavement past our Headquarters because the stars and stripes waved over it from an upper window. But they are getting over that now. They find we are not so bad as what we were represented. In fact many of them will talk with soliders now and cry over their friends in the confedrate army as they allways call it.[2]

Lincoln and Secretary Staunton were here yesturday and they held a council of war at General McDowels Headquarters. But the conclusion they arrived at is not made public, but i am satisfide that we will advance within a verry few days. There is 35000 Rebbles about seven miles from here well fortified and it is expected they will make a stand to prevent us from joining Banks or McClellan. Their picketts and ours have a brush every day. I have just sent you one hundred and forty Dollars by Express. I paid the charges on it and you can get it from the Ageant at Cassville. Now send fifty two or three i dont know which it is to Ury and lift my note. Then pay fore your teeth. Do as you please with the rest. It is the company at the mill that owes Bergess. It was for Wheat that was floured and the account will be paid out of the mill. Give my best wishes to all your good neighbours and except my best love for yourself and the children.[3]

Ever yours

H F Young

NOTES

2. McDowell's men experienced, to some degree expected, disapproval from the local populace as they moved towards Fredericksburg. Alan T. Nolan, *The Iron Brigade: A Military History* (New York: Macmillan, 1961), 49; Lance J. Herdegen, *The Iron Brigade in Civil War and Memory: The Black Hats from Bull Run to Appomattox and Thereafter* (El Dorado Hills, CA: Savas Beatie, 2012), 116.

3. Maj. Gen. Irvin McDowell was ordered by Secretary Stanton to "move upon Richmond" in a telegram on May 17, 1862. Events elsewhere had a profound effect on McDowell's scheduled advance toward the Confederate capital. Maj. Gen. Nathaniel Banks, in command of the Fifth Corps, was attacked by Stonewall Jackson at Front Royal on May 23 and at Winchester on May 25 and was forced to retreat across the Potomac River. This setback had a profound effect on the course of events in the peninsula. President Lincoln suspended McDowell's move from Fredericksburg on May 24, 1862, a move that left McClellan with fewer soldiers than he had hoped to have for his advance on Richmond. United States, War Records Office, *War of the Rebellion: A Compilation of the Official Records of the Union and Confederate Armies*, 128 vols. (Washington, DC: Government Printing Office, 1885–1901), ser. 1, vol. 11, pt. 1, 28, vol. 12, pt. 3, 219 (hereafter cited as *OR*); James M. McPherson, *Battle Cry of Freedom: The Civil War Era* (New York: Oxford University Press, 1988), 455–57; Frederick H. Dyer, *A Compendium of the War of the Rebellion Compiled and*

Arranged from Official Records . . . and Other Reliable Documents and Sources (Des Moines, IA: Dyer Publishing Company, 1908), 899–900 (hereafter cited as *Dyer's Compendium*).

Fredricksberg Va May 29 1862

Dear Father

I received your letter some time since. Was glad to hear from you, we are all well. The 7 Reg is encamped Eight miles from here on the Rail Road to Richmond. I was out there last night. The most of them are doing pickett duty. I am on detatched service with the construction corps. I will have to explain. The corps i am with is the Engineers sapper and miners and construction. It consists of 1 Col, 10 Lieuts and 240 men. Each Lieut com from 20 to 25 men. I have 2 men and a sergeant. We are a divided off for instance. My men are all carpenders and framers. One other party are choppers, an other hewers, an other miners or embankers, an other raisers, an other maks survays, an other lays track, an other ~~lays~~ Runs or Hauls timber stone or any thing that is wanted, and c do as an instance of what we can do. I will tell you of our last exploit Day before yesturday.[4]

We Started from here with a construction train at 1 oclock pm. Run out towards Richmond 6 ms and in just twelve hours work we put in a bridge of ninety 90 ft span 29 ft high and in less than one hour had the track laid and run a train over it. We are laying track about eight miles from here, where the Rebbles tore it up last Saturday. They tore up about ¼ of mile. Piled the ties up then piled the rails on them and burnt the ties and spoiled the iron. I guess the work was to hard for them for they soon quit it. You will want to no how i like my new busi. I objected at first but it was an order from McDowel and I had to go in. You see i had twenty men under my command at the building of these bridges between here and aquia creek. And i suppose old Mc liked my style, and i like it better than lying in camp. I have a tiptop squad of men. I select them out of our own brigade. All Kidd is my Sargeant.[5]

General Gibbons is our Brigade now. We like him firstrate. He is of the regular army. We are in a peck of trouble about Banks. We know he is whiped and has had to retreat but anny how we dont no for they wont let a paper or any news come here since the disaster.[6]

They have sent Shields and Ords Divisions from here to his assistance, which leaves us here with only about twenty thousand effective men. And i think it extremely doubtful whether McDowel will advance with that force at present for from the best information I can get the Rebbles are bound to fight it out in virginia. There is a great change in this city since we came here. The Ladies would take the middle of the street rather than pass under the stars and stripes where they were hung over the pavement. But now they have become quite socible and many of them say they would be sorry to see us leave for they are better protected than when their own soldiers were here. Give my good wishes to all.[7]

H F Young

NOTES

4. From May 25 through September 16, Young was on detached service with the Construction Corps. In the Sixth Wisconsin, two companies were also selected to be part of the Construction Corps. While Young expressed satisfaction with the Construction Corps, others, including William Ray, wished he would return to the company. Wisconsin, Adjutant General's Office, *Regimental Muster and Descriptive Rolls, 1861–1866*, Red Books (Madison: State Militia, Adjutant General's Office, 1865), reel 3, 7th Infantry; Herdegen, *The Iron Brigade*, 115; Lance Herdegen and Sherry Murphy, eds., *Four Years with the Iron Brigade: The Civil War Journals of William R. Ray, Co. F, Seventh Wisconsin Infantry* (Cambridge, MA: Da Capo Press, 2002), 102.

5. Alphonzo Kidd was in Company F of the Seventh Wisconsin, one of the few men from the company to join Young in the Construction Corps. Wisconsin, Adjutant General's Office, *Roster of the Wisconsin Volunteers, War of the Rebellion, 1861–1865*, Blue Books, 2 vols. (Madison: Democrat Printing Press, 1886), 1:538 (hereafter cited as *Roster*).

6. John Gibbon, Battery B, United States Artillery, was promoted to brigadier general and placed in command of the brigade in early May 1862. Gibbon immediately set out to improve the behavior of the men under his command, issuing passes for good turnouts and punishment for wrongdoers. Brig. Gen. King was promoted to the command of a division in the Department of the Rappahannock under McDowell. The defeat of Maj. Gen. Nathaniel Banks at Front Royal and Winchester had the desired effect for Gen. Robert E. Lee as Lincoln suspended McDowell's advance to the peninsula. Nolan, *The Iron Brigade*, 50–1; *OR*, ser. 1, vol. 12, pt. 3, 219–20.

7. Maj. Gen. James Shields commanded the First Division in the Department of the Rappahannock, and Maj. Gen. Edward Otho Cresap (E.O.C.) Ord commanded the Second Division in the Department of the Rappahannock. *OR*, ser. 1, vol. 12, pt. 3, 309–10.

Shenondoah Valley near Front Royal Va June 4 1862

Dear Delia

I have not received any letter from you for some time. You will be surprised perhaps that i am here but our Division moved up from Fredricksberg as soon as Banks Retreat was known. I dont know where the Regiment is at presant as i am on detached service. I am with the engineer and Construction corps. There is 10 Lieuts with 20 men each which forms the corps all under command of a Col. We go in advance as pioneers, build bridges and c. We are at work on the Schannondoah bridge where Col Kenlys Reg was so badly cut up, and where Shields in turn surprised the Rebbles, some of which were yet unburied when we arrived here. We finished the bridge last night but the River is rising so fast that I fear it will take it off. It has rained here for the last three days. Our troops are after Jackson with a strarp stick. They got about one thousand of his men yesturday and day before. In fact there is fighting going on in these mountains all the time, between detached parties of the Rebbles and our men. Ashlys Cavalry are in the Mountains and being ~~behind~~ well aquanted with every pass and cross road they cut off straglers and small parties of our men. There was a capt and private shot between here and the Gap Sunday morning. The capt had seven bullets shot through him, and they were shot with pistols in the hands of men dresed as citizens. But thunder if I had the management of the war i would hang or shoot every Secesionest in this valley. For after our men had protected them and guarded them when Banks retreated they shot our men out of their windows. And i hope they will let us clean them all out this time. I dont think I ever itched to do any thing so much as i did to run off to Freemonts Army the other day when he was driving Jackson. We fell in with Dureys Brigade and was ready for him if he had undertaken to come our way. This is a hard place to drive an army out of. It is such good hiding ground.[8]

I dont know when i will see the Regiment and so i must write to them to send my letters to me. I did not vollunteer for this business. I was placed here by an order from Gen McDowel and i like it much better than lying in camp and then we always ride. I dont stay any lenght of time in one place, so i get to see all that is going on.

I hope you got the money I sent you all safe. Write soon. Direct to Lieut H F Young McDowls Construction Corps Washington. Care of Lieut

Kenady. Give my love to all and except for yourself and the children all the love i have.

Ever yours

H F Young

NOTE

8. Lt. Gen. Thomas "Stonewall" Jackson's campaign in the Shenandoah Valley was successful in that it relieved pressure on Richmond and consequently forced Lincoln to suspend McDowell's move to advance south. Instead, he was to send two divisions, whose intentions were to trap the rear of Jackson's army. Shields and Ord were ordered to aid Banks at Front Royal; however, they arrived too late to have any tangible hope of aiding in rescuing Banks from his predicament. On May 24 Shields suggested a move on Charlottesville, in hopes of catching Jackson's army. The next day McDowell issued an order to Shields to push Jackson from the Valley without uncovering the capital. Shields advanced against Jackson's force east of the Massanutten Mountains while Frémont moved down the west. By early June Jackson had eluded this force on his heels and ended his southward march at Port Republic, Virginia. The Confederate cavalry, commanded by Col. Turner Ashby, burned bridges to delay the federal force; Ashby was killed in one of the rearguard actions. Col. John Reese Kenly resisted fiercely at Winchester before being severely wounded and erroneously reported killed in action. His resistance was a bright spot in the otherwise ignominious defense of Winchester. Brig. Gen. Abram Duryea commanded the Second Brigade, Second Division, under Ord. He arrived May 29, 1862, at Front Royal, three days after the battle at Winchester. McPherson, *Battle Cry of Freedom*, 457–58; Allen C. Guelzo, *Fateful Lightning: A New History of the Civil War and Reconstruction* (New York: Oxford University Press, 2012), 166; *OR*, ser. 1, vol. 12, pt. 3, 222–23, 235–36, 238, 285, 310, 324.

Fredricksberg Va June 18 1862

Dear Delia

I suppose you will be astonished to receive a letter from me here, but here am I, all safe and sound, writing in the same room and on the same table that i used when I wrote you nearly a month ago.

We left the Shenandoah Valley a few days after i wrote you my last letter for this place to build our work over again as the flood had taken off the bridge. We came round by the way of Alexandria and aquia and got here just about the same time our Regiment did. And the best of all our letters. I got two verry welcome ones from yourself one with your fathers and one you wrote after you returned home. Verry glad indeed was i to hear you were all well. We have got the bridge completed and are now engaged in putting in a boom that will insure it from going off again. We have had an awful flood in this country. Some of the sreams rose forty feet, and swept bridges dams and every thing else that came in their course. There is but few troops here. Only part of Gen Kings Division. McCalls Division has been sent to reinforce McClellan. Ords Divission is yet in the mountains. There is a bitter feeling against gen McDowel in this Division. He is considered a perfect curse to the army and every officer under him would leave his Divission if he could. Our Division had a hard march of it all for nothing in bad roads and hot weather. We of the construction corps dont march any. We go by rail Road but we some times have hard work.[9]

I was in the Regiment yesturday and the boys of your acquaintance are all well but are all cursing these long marches for nothing. The account with Savage you speak of i will settle all right but i dont owe him near as much as he claims. He sent me a stateme of indebtedness that i am satisfide was wrong. And the way he arrived at it was by charging 12 pr cent on all the goods i had bought ~~of~~ on credit and all balances from the time they were purchased. I called on him twice for a bill but did not get it. But i will send you some money for him. We are Luxurriating on string beans green Peas Cherries and strawberries all of which are in Fredricksberg in abundance.[10]

The weather is awful hot but i seem to stand it firstrate. I and the rest of the officers of the Corps paid a visit last night to the Gunboat Freeborn lying below the city by invitation of her officers and spent a verry plesant evenning. We had on board a splindid brass band and every thing was conducted supper and all with that life and decorum which well bred officers of our Navy are famous for.[11]

O J Foot has got his discharge and gone home, and i think Frank Brother will have to be sent home. I am not certain whether you are acquainted with either of them or not. Your asking me what i think of Pa selling the mill and letting us take a farm ammounts to this. That i don't think there is anny chance to sell at present, and he aint prepared to give it away. Neither am I. Give my best wishes to all the Neighbours. Tell squire bergess i will answer his kind letter in a day or two. My best love to yourself and the children.[12]

ever yours

H F Young

NOTES

9. Brig. Gen. George A. McCall commanded "McCall's" Division in the Department of the Rappahannock. On April 30, 1862, McCall's Division was ordered to Fredericksburg by McDowell. Ord was relieved on June 8, 1862, and replaced by Brig. Gen. J. B. Ricketts, a brigade commander in McCall's Division. Shields was upset over his treatment during this campaign and sent McDowell's chief of staff a report bluntly stating that, in his opinion, other divisions were featured more prominently in McDowell's report than his own. *OR*, ser. 1, vol. 12, pt. 3, 116, 355, 360.

10. Frederick Savage opened a store in Tafton (later Bloomington) with his brother Harry in 1859. Butterfield, *History of Grant County*, 810; Holford, *History of Grant County*, 633.

11. The *Freeborn* was a naval gunboat, commanded by James Plunkett. "Naval Promotion," *New York Herald*, June 30, 1862.

12. Frank Brother, Company F of the Seventh Wisconsin, returned to the regiment and served for the rest of the war. Orely J. Foot, who was in Company F of the Seventh Wisconsin, was discharged on August 9, 1862, because of a disability. *Roster*, 1:558–59.

Fredricksberg Va June 22 1862

Dear Father

I received a letter from you with one enclosed from Delia several days ago. Glad to hear you were all well. We are all in the enjoyment of talarlby good health, considering the hot weather. Since i wrote you last we have been up on the Shenandoah valley to Strausberg. We were rushed up their day and night through Wet and dry. We built seven bridges from forty to ninety ft long in two days and nights but it was all no go, Jackson escaped. The Shenandoah valley is a beautiful country. We just got there in time to hear the battle between Jackson & Freemont. Our Brigade got no farther than haymarket, some forty miles from the valley. We built a temporary Depot at Front Royal which by the way is the damedest Secesh hole i ever was in. There was about two hundred Secesh prisoners taken by Shields there, and the Ladies of the would join together and get their negroes and carry them the nicest kind of dellicasies. And at the same time would fling all the insult they could at our soldiers.[13]

By the Eternal that trip made me tired of this war the way it is conducted. Men that had their property guarded and claimed to be union as soon as the Rebbles came in sight hoisted the Secesh flag and fired on our soldiers and when we went back their, and the troops were suffering for want of provisions. We had to protect the property of these infernal villians although they themselves had left. The consequence is that whole army officers and men curse McDowel and many beleive him to be a traitor. There is one thing certain and we have settled down to it, that as long as we are under him the only service we will see ~~be~~ will be building Bridges, which i admit is useful, but few can work at that. But the rest will have to keep on building Rebble fences and guarding their propperty. The only troops here are our Brigade, and Augurs, and Doubledays Artillery, and the Harris light cavalry, with the gun boats, in the River. All of which is under the command of Gen King, who by the way is a splendid officer and well liked, but he wants to get his Division out of McDowels Corps awful bad. The fact is McDowel has no friends in the army, and i dont know what in hell the administration keeps him for. I am still in the construction corps, and i feel as if it was the only service i ever done toward putting down the Rebellion, for the army must have provisions and the only way to get them is by rail.[14]

They are just in the midst of harvest here and the crops are good. I went into a field of wheat yesturday where some negroes were running an old McCormick Reaper and i don't think i ever seen finer grain in my life. There will be a great deal of grain that wont be harvested for want of help to do it. The grain was sown last fall when help was plenty but when the confedrate army left many of the masters went with them taking a portion of the Slaves. Most of them that were left have run away since.

This is the finest fruit country i ever saw. Apples Peaches cherries Plumbs Quinces Grapes. In fact almost every kind mature here without any trouble. I have seen old orcherds thrown out in commons entirely surrounded with underbrush, and yet the Apple, the Peach, and Cherrie, and pear trees, were in healthy condition and hanging full of fruit. I have no war news. You will get the news from the about as soon as we do and as for speculating on what we will do next i have quit that some time ago. Give my best wishes to all.

yours Truly

HF Young

NOTES

13. Stonewall Jackson, after his success at Front Royal and Winchester, moved his army south while being pursued by the forces of Frémont and Shields. Jackson's aim was to fight each unit separately. Jackson arrived at Port Republic on June 6 and dispatched Maj. Gen. Richard Ewell to Cross Keys, a few miles northwest of

Port Republic, to meet the force of Maj. Gen. John C. Frémont. A fight between the two broke out at 10 a.m. on June 8, 1862, and by 10:30 a.m. both sides were locked in an artillery duel. On the following day Jackson left Port Republic to meet Shields's force, at that time northeast of Port Republic. In desperate hand-to-hand fighting, Confederate soldiers captured federal gun positions, forcing the Union soldiers from the field. The Battle of Port Republic, a Confederate victory, came at a high price for Jackson. His force of around eight thousand soldiers took four hours to defeat a Union force less than half its size. For his part, Gen. Shields sent a glowing report on the valiant effort of his vastly outnumbered men: "Our men fought like devils. The enemy suffered terribly. The odds were overwhelming." Union casualties were 67 killed, 393 wounded, and 558 captured or missing. Confederate casualties were 78 killed, 533 wounded, and 4 captured or missing. Jackson was ordered to the peninsula on June 17, 1862, but solidified his growing fame through his feat in the valley and thereby deflected any help to McClellan along the way. James I. Robertson, *Stonewall Jackson: The Man, the Soldier, the Legend* (New York: Simon & Schuster, 1997), 428–44; McPherson, *Battle Cry of Freedom*, 458–59; *OR*, ser. 1, vol. 12, pt. 1, 3, 683–85; Douglas Southall Freeman, *Lee's Lieutenants: A Study in Command*, vol. 1, *Manassas to Malvern Hill* (1942; New York: Charles Scribner's Sons, 1970), 454; William F. Fox, *Regimental Losses in the American Civil War* (Albany, NY: Albany Publishing Company, 1889), 543, 549; *Dyer's Compendium*, 901.

14. Brig. Gen. Abner Doubleday was part of a separate command in the Department of the Rappahannock during the campaign, and Augur commanded a brigade in King's division. Harris's cavalry joined King's division in Falmouth on June 24, 1862. *OR*, ser. 1, vol. 12, pt. 3, 309–10, 429.

Fredricksberg July 4 1862

Dear Delia

I received your letter yesturday. Was sorry to hear Laura had the mumps but hope she is all right now. This the dear childs birth day and oh how verry much i would like to see her, and all the rest of you. It is a verry dull fourth to me. We are keeping it as a holliday and the cannon are roaring fourth salutes all the time, but i felt sort of homesick. So i thought i would write you a letter. We are all in good health. The weather is verry warm which i fear will send many to the hospital when we are ordered to march. There is no troops here but Kings Division.

They have had awful fighting at Richmond for several days. I still feel confident that McClellan will succeed. Pope takes command in this department and now we are beginning to look for something to be done, for every boddy is down on McDowell. We have built the R Road bridge across the Rappahannock River the third time. There has not been such a season for floods in this country for manny years. The President has called for more troops, which dont look much like ending the war for some time. The fact is this war will yet destroy this union, at least i verry much fear it. They have two to one against McClellan at Richmond, and fight like Devils. Stone wall Jackson is killed. I considder when they lost him they lost their most dangerous man, that is their best fighter, but the papers will keep you posted.[15]

Glad to hear you got the monney all right. I will send you as much, more in a few days. Do as you think best about painting the house, but i think i would wait till about September as it is better to put on paint when the hottest of the season is over. I want Savage paid forty $40 dollars and no more out of the next money i send home. That will leave you one hundred. If I can send $140, as i expect to be able to, lift the note with Bennett with the ballance if you have it to spare or pay what you can on it. It must be between forty five and fifty dollars. The note was given for something over Eighty Dollars *and I have paid fifty five dollars on it reccollect that.*

It cost us more to live as we go farther south, and more for chlothes. But you shall always have all the money i can spare. I will try and get a Furlough this fall and go home to see you, for i will be entitled to a furlough after a years service. We have new potatoes Blackberries Green corn and c in market. ~~my best wishes~~ Give my best wishes to Furman and Caroline, and to Mr and Mrs Bergess, and except for yourself and the children all my love.

ever yours

HF Young

Just Direct Lieut H F Young McDowells Construction Corps Washington and they will follow me whereever i go.

NOTE

15. Gen. Robert E. Lee, the newly minted leader of the Army of Northern Virginia, attacked Maj. Gen. McClellan's force near Richmond on successive days, in what became known collectively as the Seven Days' Battles. From June 25 to July 1 Lee hit McClellan's army at Mechanicsville, Gaines' Mill, Allen's Farm, Savage Station, Glendale, White Oak Swamp, and Malvern Hill. His only setbacks, the bookends of the assaults at Mechanicsville and Malvern Hill, did not dampen the fact that he had saved Richmond from being captured by McClellan. McClellan, believing himself vastly outnumbered, hesitated throughout the campaign to make any decisive advances on Lee's forces. Union casualties numbered 1,734 killed, 8,063 wounded, and 6,053 captured or missing. Confederate casualties were 3,478 killed, 16,261 wounded, and 875 captured or missing. On June 26, 1862, the Departments

of the Rappahannock, Mountain, and Shenandoah were combined into the Army of Virginia and placed under the command of Maj. Gen. John Pope. For reasons not completely clear, the men of the brigade held McDowell responsible for Jackson's escape from the Shenandoah Valley. The report of Jackson's death was erroneous. McPherson, *Battle Cry of Freedom*, 464–70; Guelzo, *Fateful Lightning*, 166–67; Nolan, *The Iron Brigade*, 59; *OR*, ser. 1, vol. 11, pt. 2, 3; *Dyer's Compendium*, 902; Fox, *Regimental Losses*, 543, 550.

Fredricksberg July 5 1862

Dear Father

I just received your letter of June 28. Glad to get such late news from home and to hear you are all well. Your letter found us all in usual health although there is quite anumber in hospital. The natural result of exposure and hot weather. But the boys of your acquaintance are in good health. Yesturday was a verry dull 4 to me. The most of the officers of the C. C. Corps went to Washington the day before to spend the 4. I thought i could spend the fifteen or twenty dollars it would take to carry there and back, to better advantage by sending it home, so i spent the day if loafing round and in writing a long letter to Delia.

You talk about my not writing oftener. It is not that i dont want to write, but that I have nothing of intrest to write. So like Wilkins Micawber i wait for something of interest to turn up, but the Damed thing never turns up, so i have to commence the same old story. All quiet in McDowells Corps.

Now to answering your questions. Your question why dont McDowell march through to McClellans assistance. You cant be posted in all that is going on or you would not ask that question. Dont you know McClellan jumped McDowell in the way of promotion. Dont you know a regular never forgives another man for jumping him in the way of promotion. Dont you no that when McClellan started for Norfolk he ordered McDowell to follow with his corps in a few days, that his plans were all matured and perfected to that effect.[16]

And further dont you no that as soon as they got McClellan started, McDowell and his friends cheated little Mc out of fifty thousand of his best troops, to give McDowell a separate command to lay round and McCawber like wait for something to turn up. Dont you no it would be the dearest wish of this certain faction to have little Mc defeated so that they could take the credit of steping in and winning glory for themselves after they have frustrated all his plans, and let him be overwhelmed by numbers, as has been the case in the late battles. Dont you no that the reason Jackson escaped was McDowell and Freemont did not go each others assistance for fear the credit would be divided or each was jealous of the other. So they let him escape and pitch into little Mc, but the news is he has played his last card. But this was to much to be stood any longer so now we have got a boss over all of these infernal *Jealous curses* that wont healp one annother. Gen Pope takes command now, and we look for something to be done. Freemont wont stand it, Seigle take his place. Thats all right. We were in hopes McDowell would not stand it, but I hear nothing of him resigning. You may think this a strange way of answering questions but you cant help but understand it. We did have to make rails and build Rebble fences and that on Sunday. And further we arrived after a hard march on the ground at dark and to my certain knowledge there was not a stick of wood within half a mile for the men to cook supper or brakefast with. And they only used sufficient rails to cook with. The next day Sunday we were ordered by Gen Gibbons to send ten men out of each company of the Brigade to make rails and build the fence just as we found it, and we had to obay the order. *That fence is the property of a man that is adjutant Gen in the Rebble army.*[17]

This is a plain statement of the fact, but this is no isolated case, for to protect Rebbles and their property has been the order of McDowell. To that extent that there are many swear him to be a traitor. Now i have answered some of your questions.

I must tell you something else. We have just finished the bridge across the Rappahannock for the third time, and have the boom nearly finished, which will protect the bridge. So your Rev Capt dont turn out verry well. I kow some others that would resign and leave would have done it by this time, but this new call for troops, which will give some of ambitious *patriots* a chance to get appointments in new Reg. as field and staff officers.[18]

And what of myself. I suppose you will think i vollunteered for the war and by the Eternal for the war it is as long as i am able to handle a weapon, i never have asked anny place or office yet and i never will. If attentiveness to duty and good conduct wont win more than pollitical figuring and log rolling, in the way of promotion, it will set better on ones own consience and in the respect and confidence of the me under their command. I will send annother remittance of money to Delia in a few days, as soon as i get it. I will send orders for her to arrainge with you what use to make of it. I owe

Ury, Bennett, and Savage the three together about what one Remittance would ammount to. So you can arrainge it so as to pay it some time. That is all i want. When i look over the list of officers of McCalls Division that i was intimate with two months ago i find almost all of them either killed or wounded. So it is best to prepare for breakers.

Direct to McDowells Construction Corps Washington.

HF Y

NOTES

16. Young's carping about McDowell's not following McClellan to the peninsula was unwarranted. McDowell, who was in Fredericksburg, was ordered to join McClellan on May 17, an order that on May 24 was rescinded when McDowell was ordered to help trap Jackson in the Shenandoah Valley. McClellan, with the backing of Secretary of the Treasury Salmon Chase, was promoted over many others to a position in the regular army beneath only one man, Lt. Gen. Winfield Scott. McDowell, who was replaced by McClellan soon after the defeat at Bull Run, was blamed by many for the loss. The two men immediately clashed with each other, but McClellan named McDowell one of twelve divisional commanders in the Army of the Potomac. The rift between the two men grew as McClellan felt that McDowell and the government had betrayed him in the peninsula. Jeffry D. Wert, *The Sword of Lincoln: The Army of the Potomac* (New York: Simon & Schuster, 2005), 28–30; Wilmer L. Jones, *Generals in Blue and Gray*, vol. 1, *Lincoln's Generals* (Mechanicsburg, PA: Stackpole Books, 2004), 52–53.

17. Maj. Gen. Franz Sigel assumed command of the First Army Corps, Army of Virginia, on June 29, 1862. As previously noted, men in the brigade blamed McDowell for the loss at Bull Run. Another sore spot with the men was the discipline imposed by McDowell and Brig. Gen. John Gibbon with regard to Confederate property, especially when the nearest regiment was tasked with fixing or replacing damaged fences. This, however, eventually had the desired effect as fewer fences were destroyed or stolen after the order was issued. *OR*, ser. 1, vol. 12, pt. 2, 3; Jones, *Lincoln's Generals*, vol. 1, 52; Nolan, *The Iron Brigade*, 51; Herdegen, *The Iron Brigade*, 117.

18. President Lincoln issued a call for three hundred thousand additional men, furnished by the states according to a quota system, on July 1, 1862, in order "to bring this unnecessary and injurious civil war to a speedy and satisfactory conclusion." Roy P. Basler, ed., *The Collected Works of Abraham Lincoln*, 8 vols. (Springfield, IL: Abraham Lincoln Association, 1953), 5:296–97.

Mannasses July 16 1862

Dear Delia

I received you letter yesturday and one from Father several days ago. Glad to hear you were all well. Your letter found us all right. It is most two weeks since i wrote to you. You must pardon the seaming neglect, for a few days after my last from Fredricksberg we were ordered out here. So we came on our old rout by aquia, and Alexandria to mannasses. When we arrived here, we had wagons furnished us to proceed to the Warrington turnpike, to build the bridge across the Bull Run, the Famous stone bridge you have read so much about, as being where the battle was fought nearby one year ago.

We built that bridge and also the bridge across Cub Run, and just got back this morning. And as we had no chance of sending off letters you will kow the reason of the long delay. Pope is concentrating A Powerful Army between here and Warrenton. It is already some 70000 strong yet you see nothing about it in the papers. We now belong to Gen Popes army and probably the first account you will hear of us in the papers is that we are in the neighbourhood of Richmond. But i have quit speculating as to our destination, for we have been deceived so often. It is impossible to tell what the next order will be, but i expect we will be ordered from here some time to day. Our Reg is somewhere in the neighbourhood of Warrenton Junction. I have not seen any of them, but those that are with me since the fourth of July.[19]

I dont no what part we will have to perform in the great drama that is about to come off but I think we will form a portion of the advance. At least i hope so for i would be willing to work Day and night to build bridges to get this Army through to Richmond to help those brave fellows under Gen McClellan.

I have not been paid off yet and dont no when i will, for this movement has disarrainged every thing in the pay department.

When i get it i will send it to you, for you shall have what money you need any how. I will probably send the same amount i did before and probably you can spare your Father one hundred Dollars out of it. If you can that will make four hundred and ten Dollars, i will have paid him since i joined the army. Besides what you have got so that he has no cause to grumble for i have done the best i could. Your Father says you are all as fat as little bears, and seem to get along firstrate. That is just what i like to hear and as i no unkle Sams green backs helps you to live fat you shall have enough of them to keep fat, while i have my health. Write often. Direct as before. Give my good wishes to Mr and Mrs Bergess, and Furman and Carroline and all the Friends and except my love for yourself and the children.

ever yours

HF Young

NOTE

19. According to the Consolidated Morning Report, the Army of Virginia numbered 46,858 men present for duty on July 31, 1862. Cub Run flows into the Bull Run River near Manassas. Warrenton, Virginia, is west of Washington, DC. *OR*, ser. 1, vol. 12, pt. 2, 53.

Warrenton Va July 26 1862

Dear Father and Friends

I received your letter a few minutes ago and hasten to answer it. I am glad to hear you are all well. Your letter found us of the construction corps all well. I have not seen our Reg. for two weeks. They are still at Fredricksberg.

We have been building bridges on the turnpike running from Alexandria to Richmond, and have got this far with our work, and expect to start on to Culpepper tomarrow. We are attached to the engineer corps of Gen Popes Army. Gen Pope is collecting an immense army in this section, but it is yet thoroughly organized. The Army is well pleased with his late orders. That is just what was wanting. There will be no more garding Secesh property, but the Secest is down on Pope. These orders hit them where they live. The fact is we have only been playing with the Rebbles so far, but now the war will be waged on a different principle. We will clean them out as we go, and wont leave them to form gaurilla bands in our rear, to burn bridges and attact our trains. In fact those orders will save us fifty thousand men in Virginia that would have been left to guard Railroads Bridges and C. And the Secesh appear to know Pope verry well for they say he will do what ever he undertakes. And the appointment of a commander in chief is an other glorious good thing for in that way the different Armies can be made to suppoart each other, and operate together. Well take it all round things looks brighter and every body feels in better spirits than they did some time ago.[20]

I have not received my pay yet nor do i know when i will. When i do i will send it to Delia for i can express it through to Cassville, and i will write you and let you no when i send it. You shall have all the money i send, only what is necessary for the suppoart of Delia and the children. I want them to have plenty to live on for they have a hard time of it and so have i. But i think i can send as much as one hundred Dollars for you out of each two months pay, besides what Delia will want. One thing certain i will do the best i can.

As to renting the mill you dont say what price they were willing to pay. I think if Furman will keep it another year, by that time i will be home. And without strong inducements i would not like to rent it for so long a time. It would probably entirely ruin our customer, for ever and probably after the Mississippi River is open, times will be better for millers. But do as you think best.

yours

HF Young

NOTE

20. One such article in the *Rockingham Register and Advertiser* proclaimed, "Evidence of the brutal proceedings of the Yankees in Culpeper County accumulate daily." Later it went on to state, "The high-handed deeds of Butler in New Orleans will hardly bear comparison with the atrocities of Pope and his men in Northern Virginia." "Brutality," *Rockingham Register and Advertiser* (Harrisonburg, VA), August 8, 1862.

Head quarters Engineer Corps Warrenton July 28 1862

Dear Delia

I just received your welcome letter of July 6. Glad to hear you are all well. I was beginning to be real hungry for a letter. We are all in tolarably good health. I came verry near having the fever since i wrote you last, but by taking two or three doses of pills, and not eating any thing but rice for three or four days, i came out all right. I would like verry much to drop in and take supper with you for my teeth are nearly worn out eating hard crackers, and Devilish tough Beef. The fat pork i cant go in hot weather, but i make the beans supper when i am real hungry.

We are in the Engineer Corps under command of maj Houston Topographical Engineer U S Army. After this Direct *Lieut H F Young Engineer Corps third army corps Army of Va, Washington DC.* When directed in that way it will come directly to the Headquarters of our corps. The 6th 7th and 2d Reg. are not with McClellan, but are still at Fredricksberg Va. They are a part of Popes army of Va, and will follow us. You know the Engineer corps are always among the advanced troops. We have been building Bridges here for our heavy artillery to cross. When the Rebbles retreated from here they destroyed every thing in the bridge line even to the foot logs.[21]

Gen Pope has just arrived from Washington, with President Lincoln. We are under marching orders and expect to start tomorrow for Culpepper. We have only been waiting for Gen Pope to arrive when it is known that a forward move takes place. You ask how long i will be apt to remain in the sevice i am in. I dont no. The Engineer Service is the most dangerous and the most laborious & the most active is the service. I got mad the other day and concluded to leave the corps, and go back to the Reg. But when i applied for my papers, the major would not let me go, but said he would remedy the evil i complained of, which he did imediately. So i suppose i am in for it and i like it better than camp life. There is more change more excitement. We are never so long in one place. I am sorry to of Squire Bergess being so sick and hope he will soon get well. Give him and his family my best wishes. I have not got my pay yet. Dont no when i will. Look out for news from the army of Virginia.

Popes orders which you will find in the papers are just the thing. No more guarding or protecting Rebble property line of them as we go thats the talk for us, but it makes the Rebbles have long faces.[22]

Except my love for your self and all the dear ones. Many a long night i lay awake thinking of you and dreaming of our dear home.

ever yours

H F Young

NOTES

21. Maj. David Houston was Young's commanding officer in McDowell's Construction Corps.

22. Gen. Pope issued General Orders 7 and 11 in July 1862. General Orders 7 is of note for its harsh treatment of the local populace and guerrilla fighters: "No privileges and immunities of warfare apply to lawless bands of individuals." Payment

was also expected for any damage done to government rail or property. General Orders 11 called for disloyal citizens to take an oath of loyalty to the Union. Another provision required citizens within a five-mile radius to repair destroyed rail lines. Further, if a house was used for guerrilla actions against federal soldiers, the house was to be destroyed. *OR*, ser. 1, vol. 12, pt. 2, 51–52; "The Army of Virginia, Important Orders Issued by Gen. Pope," *New York Times*, July 24, 1863; Mark Grimsley, *The Hard Hand of War: Union Military Policy toward Southern Civilians* (New York: Cambridge University Press, 1995), 87.

~

Culpepper Va August 10 1862

Dear Delia

I received your letter last night.[23] Glad to hear you were all well. You did well to tell all your griefs at first. Your letter put me in mind of a man i once heard telling his experience in class meeting. He commences with the tribulations and troubles, and ended with the remarks that he was perfectly happy and had all that mortal man could wish for in this eivel world. So with your letter you had the blues when you commenced but i was perfectly delighted to find you had got over them before you finished. For it would grieve me verry much for you to leave the mill. For i know you are better of there than you would be any where else. It is our home and i dont want it to go into other hands, and i would not like to have the mill rented for three years, unless it could be done at a good price and your father did not let me know what price was offered, so that i could not judge of the advantages or disadvantages. But of one thing i was satisfide. That by renting the mill for three years we would probably loose in the long run. It would throw me out of employment during that period, but i wrote to your father to do as he pleased for he knew what the offer was, and i did not. But if you leave the mill you will leave the only home you have, and as for society it is the same every where. But i am only giving advice. You must use your own judgement. As for the team Furman has the use of it only on condition that it should be well taken care of, and that you should have the use of them when ever you wanted them. And if he dont do it i will take the team from him. I will not get my pay till September for we are now in front and our pay master was ordered back several days ago, as it was considered dangerous for men having much money with them on an advance. But i will have more to send when it does come.

We left Warrington a few days after i wrote my last letter, moved out to White Sulpher Springs, built a bridge a cross the north fork of the Rappahannock. Was then ordered out here, and started from here yesturday morning to build a bridge across the Rapidan, twelve miles from here. But when we had got two miles from camp we found the Rebbles had crossed the river in force and were marching on us 60000 strong. Then there was hurrying to and fro i can tell you. Oh it was a grand and exciting seen. We were ordered to fall back with reserve and here we remain yet excepting to start ever moment. I have just been ordered with my men to go to the assistance of the wounded. 4 oclock PM. I have just got back to camp from one of the most horrible jobs i ever was in. Oh it is awful to look on and assist those wounded soldiers. We have (600) six hundred already brought in shot and mangled in every conseiveable manner and they still continue to come.[24]

There is every kind of rumor running in camp and it is impossible to arrive at the truth. But there is one thing certain. Both armies are lying still today taking care of their wounded, and each occupy the ground they did before the battle. (you will get the news before you get this) We lost largely in officers. Augur is wounded. So is Geary. So is price. The fact is Banks Division is pretty much used up, and Banks is said to be wounded. The battle field has its allurements and excitement but not so after it is over. Jared must excuse me for not answering his letter for I have not time. There will be an awful fight to night or tomarow if the Rebbles do not fall back.[25] Give my love to all.

Ever yours

H F Young

NOTES

23. Culpeper, Virginia, is roughly thirty-five miles northwest of Fredericksburg.

24. Lee sent Stonewall Jackson and a twelve-thousand-man force to Gordonsville to counter Pope's thrust by the Army of Virginia. Confederate major general Ambrose P. Hill also arrived, with an additional thirteen thousand men diverted from the peninsula in late July when all was quiet on that front. Two advance divisions of Pope's army, led by Nathaniel Banks, attacked Jackson's force on August 9, 1862, near Cedar Mountain. Initially, the outnumbered Union force drove back Jackson's force until Hill turned the tide with a punishing attack on Banks's men. Banks, whose force fought well, finally gave way and, as evidence of their stubborn resistance, sustained nearly 30 percent casualties. Union casualties were 314 killed, 1,445 wounded, and 622 captured or missing. Confederate casualties numbered 223 killed, 1,060 wounded, and 31 captured or missing. Gibbon's brigade of westerners,

for the first time in the war, witnessed the carnage of war. The brigade spent nearly a week encamped on the battlefield to await the next advance. McPherson, *Battle Cry of Freedom*, 525–26; Wert, *The Sword of Lincoln*, 133–34; Nolan, *The Iron Brigade*, 68–69; Lance J. Herdegen, *The Men Stood Like Iron: How the Iron Brigade Won Its Name* (Bloomington: Indiana University Press, 1997), 77–80; Fox, *Regimental Losses*, 544, 550.

25. Augur was in command of the Second Division, Second Army Corps, under Banks, while Brig. Gen. John W. Geary commanded the First Brigade, Second Division, Second Army Corps. Wounded at Cedar Mountain, Augur was replaced by Brig. Gen. Henry Prince. Augur's and Geary's wounds were severe enough to force them from the field during the battle. Prince, meanwhile, was captured by the Confederates and sent to Richmond as a prisoner. Pope reported that Prince's capture was an accident; he became lost in the dark. *OR*, ser. 1, vol. 12, pt. 2, 134, 137.

Camp Houston Va Aug 15 1862

Dear Delia

Well this is the infernalist unhandy place to write a letter i ever tried. Imagine a man sitting on the ground, crosleged ~~with~~ on the ground with his blanket folded on his knees for a writing desk and you have me as i am at presant. We are encamped at present on the battle ground of Saturday. The dead are all buried and the wounded all removed. It is no use writing about the battle for you will be already informed of it from the papers. Jackson has retreated across the Rapidan. This you will also no, but from the papers you can never know the horrours of the battle field. The excitement of battle wears of after it is over and when it comes to going out and burying the dead by hundreds after they have lain in the sun for three or four days.[26]

It is horrible, but we all feel better over the result for the rebbles suffered terribly. They could not begin to burry their dead in the time allotted to them by the flag of truce, and we buried them after their retreat. We were ordered out this morning to repair the road to the Rapidan. So we started and got out about five miles from camp. Was going along perfectly careless with each detail under its Lieut all scattered along the road feeling perfectly safe, when we received a preemtory order to skedadle back to camp. When we arrived, we learned we had been two miles outside our picketts. Well we had a good laugh over the matter but it was a price of infernal carelessness in the commander who ever he was that ordered us there with only 140 men, for if we had been taken prisoners they would have said it was our own rashness, when we only obaying orders. Our Reg is encamped about a mile from us having arrived day before yesturday. I have seen all the boys and had a good time of it. But when i came to Sec Reg i failed to meet a familliar face that was always amongst the first to welcome me, and when i came to make enquiry i found John Bergess was dead. I was pained to learn the news, for i had lost a dear friend, and the one that always brought home to me the most, for always after the first salutation the question would be whats the news from home. John was a good boy. He had no vices such as young men of his age are apt to fall into in the army, and he was one of those you could place implicit confidence in. The officers of his company and many of his fellow soldiers that were by when his name was mentioned bore testomony to his exemplary conduct as a soldier and a gentleman. Poor fellow when i bid him good by at Fredricksberg i little thought it would be the last time i should see his pleasand face. But such is the fate of many in this vast army every day.[27]

Burnside Arived in Culpepper this evening with his army, and the orders are out for the whole army to move at six oclock to morrow morning. So you will hear of another fight if the Rebbles dont retreat again probaly before you get this. We have had no mail for two day as the cars have all been bringing up Burnside with his troops. When it does come i shall expect a letter. Give my verry best wishes to Squire Bergess and family and except for yourself and the children my unchanging love.[28]

Ever yours

H F Young

NOTES

26. Jackson's retreat was in reality a withdrawal to Gordonsville. Early news reports on the battle at Cedar Mountain were scant in the *Grant County Herald*. The paper initially reported that Jackson had been driven back with heavy losses. The next edition, one week later, gave a better representation of the events of the battle. "Washington, Aug. 10," *Grant County Herald* (Lancaster, WI), August 12, 1862; "Headquarters Army of Virginia, Six Miles beyond Culpeper, Aug. 10," *Grant County Herald*, August 19, 1862.

27. John H. Burgess of Company C, Second Wisconsin, died of disease on July 22, 1862. He was the son of Henry Burgess, a neighbor of Young in Cassville. *Roster*, 1:354.

28. Maj. Gen. Ambrose Burnside was ordered to Washington by General-in-Chief Henry Halleck on August 14, 1862. His Ninth Army Corps, stationed at Falmouth, sent two divisions to support Pope's Army of Virginia. *OR*, ser, 1, vol. 12, pt.

3, 554, 572; John J. Hennessy, *Return to Bull Run: The Campaign and Battle of Second Manassas* (New York: Simon & Schuster, 1993), 39; Nolan, *The Iron Brigade*, 64.

Uptons Hill Va Sept 3 1862

Dear Delia

It is a long time since i wrote you last. At least it seems so to me. And i expect you are verry anxious to hear from me, but you must first know that we have not had any chance of sending off any letters for the last three weeks. Since i wrote you last i have received two letters from you, which did me lots of good I tell you. The last i got yesturday. It was written at fathers. Well here we are in sight of the capital *broken, defeated, and out generald at every move*. Since i wrote you last ~~weh~~ we have built bridges, and destroyed bridges with shels and shot flying thick and fast around us. We have been surrounded and shelled on our retreat, but with the exception of sore feet and torn and dirty chlothes i am all right. I expect two or three of the engineer corps are prisonors but there is none killed or wounded, and our train of pontoon bridges entrenching tools, Engineering tools we got through with all safe.

I have seen many brave fellows bite the dust the last three weeks. Our men with few exceptions fought well, but Pope was out Generald at every turn and Jacksons men fight like devils. They will march to the cannons mouth without flinching. They will march barefoot endure any and every privation. They shout for Jackson. They think and are certain Jackson can and will whip the north and they have been taught their homes and lives and every thing hold near and dear depends on this march of Jackson to the north. And I beleive every man of them if led or told to march on our fortifications would do it. Well here we are just where we ware a year ago perhaps. We hold a few miles further up the river but our lines here are just out side our strong forts. This is the darkest hour our country has seen yet, and every man must nerve himself for the comeing desperate struggle for Jackson must be defeated if it take the whole north to do it. Our brigade fought nobly and held back a whole division of the enemy for some time, but our men were badly cut up.[29]

The Colonel of the Second was killed. The collonel Lieut Collonel and major of our Reg were wounded. Capt Braden of Co B was killed. Capt walker of co E had a ball through his leg. Capt Watthers of co I is severely wounded. In our own co five were kiled. H Ketner Wm Miles L Stephens Ed McDowel and John Lepla and N McPhail is wounde bad. Probaly dead before this time. Serg A R McCartney is wounded in the leg or thigh. Wm Ray in the head. Frank Boyington Perry Gilbert Giles Parker H Miles John Marlow and quite a number of others are wounded but not dangerous. Capt callis had a ball through his hat and one through his pants. Lots of the boys had them through their chlothes, but you will get an account of the affair in the papers, for we have been fighting every day for about three weeks. And between marching lying out at night, starving for our supplies that the Rebbles cut off in our rear and destroyed. That and dust and bad watter has thined our ranks terribly. Orders to pack up immediately. I must go. We are Ordered to work on fortifications.[30]

My love to all.
Ever yours

H F Young

NOTES

29. It was first blood for the westerners, other than the Second Wisconsin, who were present at the First Battle of Bull Run, as they struck at the onset of the Second Battle of Bull Run. Ordered to Centreville on the Warrenton Turnpike, Gibbon's brigade was attacked by Stonewall Jackson near the farm of John Brawner on the afternoon of August 28, 1862. In the pitched battle that followed, the brigade did well to hold its own against the vaunted Stonewall Brigade. Sunset brought the battle to a close for the day. During the fight the next day, Pope sent the attacking federal forces into the fray piecemeal, a colossal mishandling of his command. Even worse, the corps of Maj. Gen. Fitz-John Porter did not enter the attack, even after an order from Pope. These blunders sealed the fate for the federal attack on August 29. Also costly to the final outcome on August 30, thinking that Jackson's force was retreating, Pope ordered another attack, which crashed headlong into Jackson's force, now supported by Lt. Gen. James Longstreet. By the end of the day, Pope pulled the plug on the attack and began a withdrawal to Washington, DC. Gibbon's brigade was tasked with covering the retreat to the capital. Brigade casualties were 148 killed, 536 wounded, and 119 missing or captured. Union casualties at Bull Run totaled 1,747 killed, 8,452 wounded, and 4,263 captured or missing. Hennessy, *Return to Bull Run*, 435–36; Nolan, *The Iron Brigade*, 91–99, 109–10; McPherson, *Battle Cry of Freedom*, 527–31; *Dyer's Compendium*, 907–8; Fox, *Regimental Losses*, 544; *OR*, ser. 1, vol. 12, pt. 2, 262, 380.

30. Col. Edgar O'Conner, commander of the Second Wisconsin, was killed at Gainesville (or Brawner's Farm). Lt. Col. Charles A. Hamilton, Field and Staff of the Seventh Wisconsin, was wounded in the thigh; doctors were not able to remove the bullet and consequently he was forced to resign on March 3, 1863. Maj. George

Bill was wounded and resigned on January 5, 1863. Capt. George Brayton, Company B, Seventh Wisconsin, was killed at Gainesville. Capt. William D. Walker, Company E, Seventh Wisconsin, was wounded and resigned on December 16, 1862. Capt. George H. Walther of Company I, Seventh Wisconsin, was wounded and later promoted to major of the Thirty-fourth Wisconsin on January 30, 1863. Harry Kentner, William N. Miles, Lewis W. Stevens, Edward S. McDowell, John Leppla, and Newton McPhail were all killed at Gainesville. The wounded included Alexander R. McCartney, William R. Ray, Francis A. Boynton, Perry Gilbert, Calvin G. Parker, Isaac L. Miles, William H. Miles, and John Marlow. All of these soldiers were in Company F of the Seventh Wisconsin. *Roster*, 1:345, 538, 544, 554, 568, 558–61; Nolan, *The Iron Brigade*, 197.

Sept 9 1862

Dear Father

We are encamped about ten miles from Washington on the road to Harpers ferry. I suppose you will think this a Devilish long nooning between letters, but i could not help it for we have had no way of sending off letter since we left the Rappidan. I wrote you a letter two weeks ago and carried in my pockett untill it was worn out. Well here we are where we ware a year ago, broken and Defeated. There is no use in disguising the truth. We were completely out Generald at every turn and Gen Pope & McDowell, are completely played out. Pope tries to make out a case against Porter and Franklin for Disobeying his orders at the battle of Friday but if he ordered them in as he did the rest of our division they did perfectly right not to go for it would have been their sure destruction. I was on the battle field that entire day and i know that as fast as our Divisions arrived on the ground they were sent into the battle unsuppoarted and completely routed.[31]

After Pope made the fatal mistake of letting Jackson turn his right flank and get in his rear, he and McDowell acted like men that were perfectly bewildered and went it blind. And yet they knew Jackson was turning our flank. Every officer in the army knew it, but we supposed that Pope was letting Jackson turn our flank for the purpose for getting him in a trap. But when Mannasses was captured with all our supplies and ammunition for the use of the army then these Generals appeared to wake up, for they run us to the right then to the left, marching day and night till they had their army scattered from hell to breakfast. So i will drop the subject for it always mad even to think of it. Well i have built bridges and burned bridges with shot and shell flying thick and fast arround me and our party has been surrounded and shelled when guarding our train but a mis is good as a mile. I am yet untouched. Our Reg is badly used up. You have got a list of killed and wounded before you get this. Our behaved firstrate. Ed McDowell and Harry Kentner are amongst the killed. You knew them both. In fact with few exception our entire army fought well, but Pope threw his men into the fight by brigades unsuppoarted and Jackson kept his all massed together so as to threw a division when necessary against our brigades. Capt Callis is in Command of the Regiment, as all the field officers and the capt of Co E were wounded. Capt Callis is Sen Officer in the Reg. I have made application to return to the Reg, as all the boys say they cant get along without me since the capt is in command of the Reg. As for Callis leaving the company he expected some field office in some of the new Regiments. As to Sam Woodhouse getting back in place again it would be impossible for him to do it. But if Sam would join some newer Reg he would probably do well.[32]

We are going to have hard fighting now. Little Mc is called on second time to stop a victorious enemy and he will do it. He has the entire confidence of the army, and the news of his appointment was received with cheers the first we had given for a long time. But Jacksons men fight like Devils. I have seen them charge right up to the cannons mouth when they were being killed by scores. They think Jackson can do any thing he undertakes. I have four months pay due me now, which i need verry much for i lost some of my chlothes and what i have are worn out. But i will have to wait patiently till it comes.[33]

Jackson is making towards Pennsylvania. If he gets in there i dont think he will ever get back. Give my best wishes to all and write soon.

yours truly

H F Young

NOTES

31. There was plenty of blame to go around after the battle. Pope blamed Porter for not following orders. Porter refused to obey because he thought it would jeopardize his command, and McDowell was indecisive and largely ineffective on August 29. Porter's lack of action led to his court-martial and subsequent dismissal from the service in 1863. Porter, still smarting from his removal years later, asked for another review of his court-martial. The review, with input from Confederate

officers, supported Porter's decision of inaction on August 29, 1862, and his court-martial was overturned. The full transcripts of the court-martial are contained in *OR*, ser. 1, vol. 12, pt. 2, supplement. Maj. Gen. William Franklin, commander of the Sixth Army Corps, stationed in Alexandria, Virginia, was ordered to Centreville and Warrenton on August 26 by Halleck; however, he did not depart until August 29. According to Hennessy, McDowell was one of the most despised commanders in the army. Coupled with McClellan's slow departure from the peninsula, the situation was a recipe for disaster. Ultimately, Pope failed to adequately place his army in a position for success even when the opportunities were available for a favorable outcome of the battle. Hennessy, *Return to Bull Run*, 466–70; McPherson, *Battle Cry of Freedom*, 529–31; *OR*, ser. 1, 12, pt. 3, 676.

32. The fallout from the Second Battle of Bull Run was swift. Pope was sent to Minnesota to deal with a Sioux uprising, and McDowell, feeling that his honor was at stake, demanded a court of inquiry to clear his name. The court convened for sixty-seven days from November 1862 to February 1863 and in the end found no cause for continuing the investigation; McDowell was sent to California. One bright spot during the battle was Gibbon's brigade. Though outnumbered, the men fought well and earned the respect of their adversaries. McPherson, *Battle Cry of Freedom*, 533; Hennessy, *Return to Bull Run*, 463; *OR*, ser. 1, vol. 12, pt. 1, 332.

33. McClellan was again called on to defend Washington after Bull Run. The Army of the Potomac and Department of Virginia joined on September 5, 1862. On the same day, John Pope was relieved of command. McPherson, *Battle Cry of Freedom*, 533; *OR*, ser. 1, vol. 19, pt. 1, 1.

Fredrickscity MD Sept 13 1862

Dear Delia

You will see by the heading where we are. We arrived here this morning. Our advance guard had a brush with the Rebbles and made them scedaddle after an hours fighting. None of our Division were engaged. The rebbles got up a big supper here, said they were just going to take Baltimore and Washington and then got about one thousand men to enlist with them. They were those men that were on the fence ready to join either side which proved the strongest, and now since they have been driven back it makes long faces here i can tell you.

Our army feels more confident and in better spirits. We have had something to eat and good wholesome watter to drink. The men are not marched to death running back and forth. They feel more confidence in their commanders, and will fight better. You ask what you should do if i should be killed. It is a hard question, but i have seen so many men killed and die in the last few weeks that i will give you the best advice i can. *If i should be killed in battle or die while in the service, you as the wife of a 1st Lieut will draw from the government, seventeen Dollars per Month for five years* which is two hundred and four dollars per year. And if you should not live to draw it it would go to the children. Now this is the reason i wanted you so particular to live at the mill, although i never told you of it before for i did not like to speak of it to you. But now you shall know it. While you live there you have a home for yourself and children that noboddy can take from you with having no house rent to pay. The $204 per year will suppoart you and the children well, and by that time the children will be almost out of short chlothes, and by that time should it ever come this question will be settled and probably the mill will pay something. I will have five hundred Dollars due me from government by the last of this month which go a good way towards paying Father.

So now dear if i should run in the way of a bullet and fall which i have no fear but dont no what may happen for i am listning to the sound of battle now. But i have got used to it. Now i can go to sleep with a fight raging within a mile of me. I would advise you to live at the mill and make your home as comfortable on it. If i were a private you would *get but four Dollars per month.*

I was glad to hear you were all well. Oh how i would like to see you all. I often sit down in the evening while the boys are pitching tents and getting supper, and figure out in immagination what you are all doing and how you all look and then i feel so sad to think i cant see you. I get so lonesome. *Oh* you can have no idea of it although you are lonesome. And then comes the march the fight in which we forget home friends in fact everything but our duties as soldiers. Kiss all the children for me and give my best wishes to squire Bergess and family. I am verry sorry to hear he is sick.

Ever yours

H F Young

~~*Camp near Culppep*~~
Sept 18 1862

Dear Delia

I am with the Reg. We have been fighting for three Days. Our company is almost all killed or wounded or sick. Yesturday was the most terrible fight that ever was fought on this continent and our Brigade was in the thickest of it. I went into the fight with only 14 men and lost 6 of them. 2 were killed, and 4 wounded and missing. J Clark and J L Marks, G Cooly, and H A Kaump were killed in Sundays fight.[34]

J W Craig and Lewis Kunty were killed yesturday. The 2d and 6th suffered equally as bad as we did. 2 Lieut McKenzie was wounded in the foot Sunday at south mountain. Capt Callis commands the Reg, which leaves me the only officer in the company. I expect an other big fight to day. What is left of us feel in good spirits for we have got the Rebbles in close quarters.[35]

My love to all.

H F Young

NOTES

34. The dead in Company F for the fight at South Mountain on September 14, 1862, included James A. Clark, John L. Marks, George W. Cooley, and Henry A. Kaump. *Roster*, 1:559–60.

35. 2nd Lt. John W. McKenzie of Company F was wounded at South Mountain. Wesley Craig and Louis Kuntz of Company F were killed at Antietam on September 17, 1862. *Roster*, 1:558–60.

on the battle field near Sharpsberg Sept 20 1862

Dear Father

I joined the Reg on the morning of the morning of the 15 since which time we have been in almost a continental fight. i suppose the great fight of the Rebellion was fought on the 17. At least i hope so for none of us ever wants to see another such, but we whiped them bad. They are lying by thousands on the field of battle but we to suffered terribly. Our men fell thick and fast. I have talked to men that has fought almost every where and all agree that the battle of the 17 was the most terrible they ever were in. Jackson staked his all on the battle, and we did the same. Maryland is clear of Rebbles and we are preparing to cross the river immediately. Our Brigade is allmost used up. I had only 14 men of co F to go into the battle with 2 of them Lewis Kenty, and Wesley Craig, were killed. 2 more were wounded and 1 is missing.

We have lost in killed and wounded on the field of battle out of our Brigade, within the last month over seventeen hundred men and the Rebbles swear they will annihilate Gibbons Brigade and take his Battery if it costs them ten thousand men. Well let them come on. They tried it hard the other day and did not succeed nor do we think they ever will. At least they will have to come on us with five times our number before they do.[36]

You must excuse this miserable excuse for a letter, as i have neither pen ink or paper. I had one or two Devilish close calls in the shape of balls and shell but a miss is good as a mile. Give my best wishes to all.

yours truly

H F Young

NOTE

36. The Iron Brigade sustained the loss of 37 killed, 251 wounded, and 30 captured or missing at South Mountain. Young's figure of 1,700 is relatively accurate; 1,560 casualties were sustained over the three battles. It was at South Mountain that the Iron Brigade was christened. Gibbon's brigade was given orders by Maj. Gen. Hooker to secure Turner's Gap, the summit at South Mountain. Met by withering fire from the Confederate force near the summit, the brigade advanced against excellent enemy emplacements. The last quarter-mile produced desperate fighting for both sides. Capt. John Callis, commanding the Seventh Wisconsin, ordered the men of the regiment to charge Confederate positions with fixed bayonets. The summit was finally secured near dark by the Sixth Wisconsin. Watching the advance were McClellan, Hooker, and Burnside. As they witnessed the superhuman efforts to reach the summit, McClellan remarked, "They must be made of iron." The name stuck and immortalized the brigade forever in the annals of the Civil War as the Iron Brigade. Herdegen, *The Iron Brigade*, 233–36; Herdegen, *The Men Stood Like Iron*, 145–52; Nolan, *The Iron Brigade*, 125–30; *OR*, ser. 1, vol. 19, pt. 1, 184.

Camp near Sharpsberg Md Sept 23 1862

Dear Delia

This is my birth day. Do you think of it? Oh how well i would like to call in and take tea with you. I know you would give me something better than hard crackers, and coffee. Well the fight has been going on at different places since the day i wrote you last, which was the morning after the great battle if I remember right.

We have lost no men since. Our loss in Co F foots up as far as we no at this time in all the fights we have been engaged in at 12 killed, 25 wounded, 2 missing making 39 in all. Of the wounded they will probably most of them get able in time to join us again. Yesturday i got back the 7 men that were with me in the Engineer corps, which gives me quite a company again. All Kidd is back in the company which gives me two Sergt. When all that are sick returns i will have forty men in the company besides the wounded. So you see it dont look so lonesome as it did when we came out of that desperate battle of the 17 when all the men I had was 7. That was an awful lonesome time for us all, but soldiers like we have got used to it. John Harville is waiting to start for home. I send this with him.[37]

Write to co F 7th Reg.

My love to all.

H F Young

NOTE

37. An enumeration of the months fighting showed 12 killed, 26 wounded, and 1 missing. Young's figures were close to correct. Alphonzo A. Kidd of Company F, Seventh Wisconsin, was on detached service with Young in the Construction Corps. John Harville was in Company F of the Seventh Wisconsin. Antietam, one of the deadliest battles in American history, was the victory President Lincoln sought before unveiling a preliminary draft of emancipation. Union casualties were 2,108 killed, 9,549 wounded, and 753 captured or missing, while Confederate casualties totaled 1,886 killed, 9,348 wounded, and 1,367 captured or missing. *Roster,* 1:558–61; Wisconsin, Adjutant General's Office, *Regimental Muster and Descriptive Rolls, 1861–1865,* Red Books, reel 3, 7th Infantry; Fox, *Regimental Losses,* 544, 550.

Camp Near Sharpsberg Md Sept 26 1862

Dear Father & Friends

I received your long and welcome letter this morning. Glad to from you all. We are encamped between the village of Sharpsberg and the Potomac, and are getting recruited up again considerable. What is of us are in good spirits and ready for another fight with the grey backs whenever the order is given. You appear to be some what astonished at the confidence we soldiers have in little Mc and ask what he has done. You charge him with withholding his men from Pope, when we no that McClellan at that verry time had not over (125) men under his command. All the rest having been ordered from him by the war department. And when advised to resign by his friends, he refused to do it saying he would fight for his country in any position he was assigned to. Pope himself alone is responsible for his *Damed*, blunders. His trying to threw the blame on any person else only serves to shew his utter inability to commang or manage a large army. As for the other charges, it is an admitted fact that McClellans plans were interfered with to such an extent as to entirely cripple him. When McDowell was lying at Fredricksberg almost within sound of his cannon at hanover courthouse and when he had been promised his suppoart you no it was not sent.[38]

I will give you a short account of where we have been. The first fire we were under was the second morning after we crossed the Rappahannock River. That night our corps was waked up about ten oclock to go and build a bridge across the river about one mile above the Railroad bridge. It was to be built over a mill pond one hundred and forty ft wide, watter 8 ft deep. We went to work. The night was dark, but we built fires down close to the water under the bank and went to work. We ~~could~~ had sawed stringers and caps but for trussels. We had to cut green timber. By daylight we were just putting in the last trussle or bent but the cursed Rebs had closed up on us during the night and now they opened on us with shell. We had the bridge to plank and guard logs to put on, before the Rebs got the range so as to hit the bridge. Our artillery opened on them from the bank right over our heads so you see were right between the two fires.[39]

The boys displayed more curiosity than allarm for it was hard work to keep them from climbing trees to see what effect our shot had on the Rebbles. At nine oclock the bridge was finished and our battery dashed acoss it when the Rebs withdrew into the woods. And the balance of the day, was used by them in trying to effect a crossing at different points. But they did not succeed, for the two ensuing days the fight was kept up with the river between us mostly with Artillery. Here was where the Rebs, were fooling Gen Pope, for while they were making a feint to cross the River; jackson was marching the main force to turn our right flank. On the morning of the 23 of august, Pope found himself not only out flanked but a quite a large force across the River oposite Rappahannoc Station. We were roused at daylight to go and destroy the Railroad bridge across the Rappahannoc river. The bridge was 80 ft long and from 18 to 25 ft were the length of the bents, owing to the different depths of the River. The night had been one of rain and storm. The river was raising fast. It had already taken off our Bridge built two nights previous. Now on a knoll on the opisite side of the river we had one battery of artillery, and one Brigade of men as their suppoart. The Rebs had opened on these a fierce cononade just at daylight, which they were replying to just as fierce. Pope then ordered some twenty peices of artillery to take positon on the heights on our side of the River, above and below the bridge for the purpose of covering the bridge while our men on the on the other side could get a cross. The Rebs prcevied this at once, and two Brigades were formed in line of battle and commenced, coming forward it at a quick pace to storm the position at their side of the bridge. It was at this mement our Battery on the opisite side of the river ceased firing and came thundering across the bridge followed by the brigade. At the same moment our guns opened on the advancing Rebs, a terrible fire of spherical case and canister their artillery opening on ours at the same time with shell and round shot. I was standing on the bank close by one of our batteries, admiring the courage of the foe for our artillery was making fearful panic in their ranks, but they would close up without any faltering or apparent hesitation. I had not much time to watch the progress of the fight, for it now became apparant to all that the object of the Rebs was to get possesion of the Bridge. As the river was so swollen by this time it was impossible to ford it, and it was equally to our intrest to destroy it, as it would give us several hours start before they could cross. The moment the last man of our brigade was on the bridge I was ordered to burn the bridge commencing at the farther end.[40]

I was detailed by maj Houston to take charge of the destruction of the bridge. And i had ordered a grist mill that stood at the end of the bridge gutted and an arm full of shavens on hand. So when i gave the word all ready; every fellow picked up his load. Some had bolting chest. Some had grain ellevattors. Some had hoppers and one extravagant cuss had the desk out of the office. Others had fire and so forth. Just as the last of the infantry came across at double quick, i heard the voice of Gen McDowell say now for it be quick. I yelled at the men to come on and we started. Just as i got on the bridge a ball knocked of a piece of railing about the center. Before we got across two others hit the bridge, but after that for the space of half an hour i was to busy to pay any attention to the battle. At the end of that time we had the bridge completely on fire at both ends and in the centre. Assoon as the Rebs found they could not save the bridge they fell back. And now i must tell you i have since that been where men were falling thick and fast and a man could not call his life his own a moment, but none of them has ever left their impression as it were so vividly on my mind as the burning of that bridge. None of us on the bridge were killed or wounded, for the reason that the shells did not burst soon enough. But those on the bank suffered severely in both killed and wounded. Assoon as the bridge was thoroughly on fire the retreat of our army commenced, but our corps had to stay at the bridge all day or nearly so untill it was all burned down.[41]

We were the last to leave and the Rebs showed their spite by shelling us as far as they could see us. They wounded two or three of the Penn Boys is all the harm they done us. As it was almost night when we got to camp and we had neither breakfast or dinner. We had to get some supper. By the time we had got supper the rear guard of our cavalry pased us with the not to us verry grattifying news that the Reb Cavalry were crossing the river five miles below, and we have to lookout for ourselves. Now reccollect that we had 16 wagons. Some of them drawn by four mules, and others by four horses. All of slower than the wrath to come and all over loaded. We had all the Engineer apparattus, Bridge apparattice, entrenching tools, instruments & c of Popes whole army. So you see our train would be valueable to the Rebs, and a great loss to us. Maj Houston examined his maps and decided not to take either of the main roads but keep a sort of blind or neigbourhood road. This we kept untill one oclock. By that time our mules refused to go any further. It by this time was raining like the Devil and dark as dungeon. We threw men out in rear and advance. And the rest of us set down by the roots of trees till daylight, when we started on wet, stiff and hungry, for Warrenton, where we arived about noon. And there learned that the Reb Cavalry, had passed in a large boddy just ¾ of a mile from where we were lying in the woods that morning at three oclock. So all that saved us there was Houstans acquaintance with the road. On the 28 of August we were ordered to keep with our train and guard it through if possible. We were between the Penn Reserve Corps, and kings division. The Rebs threw a few shell at the Reserve corps. The Bucktails were thrown out as skirmishers and the Rebs fell back. Then the Reserve turned to the right toward mannasses. We followed, but by some confusion in their amunition train. We got some distance in their rear, and just as we emmerged from the timber, the Rebs opened on us with two guns at a distance of about four hundred yds. We told the drivers to put on the whip and stick to their teams. Then we run across the field and rallied in the woods untill all our teams, got past.[42]

The Rebs could have taken us here, as we were only 125 men. But i think that they mistook our corps, for the advance of kings division. For an hour later when Gibons brigade came up to them they had evidently been waiting for them. For then occurred that severe fight in which our brigade behaved so well, but lost so many men. While the fight was going on we were following after the Reserve corps, expecting every moment to be attacted. But by midnight we found ourselves at what is known as the old Bull run hospital. We now for the first time for several hours knew where we were, and at the same time knew we were surrounded. You may inmagine how we felt. We had become separated from the Reserve corps. We did not know where they were. We knew kings Division to be in the rear, but wheather victors, or defeated we did not know. We dare not build a fire. So we put out picketts each man took his gun in his arms and lay down. And desperate is our situation appears and was. The men were so worn out that many of them were snoring in the next few minutes. At three oclock we were roused. Every man was on his feet and in line in a moment, for the picketts repoarted the advance of a battalion of cavalry. The next moment their advance scouts were halted, when it was found out it was a battallion of Bayards cavalry. We all felt like cheering but dare not say a word for they brought the not verry grattifying intelligence, that a large boddy of Stewards cavalry, were in the immediate vicinity. We formed square determined to give them a warm reception if they made an attack. We stood in possition till daylight, when we started to the stone bridge where we arrived just after Seigle had taken the possition from the Rebs, as this was the place we had been ordered by maj Houston. We cooked breakfast. That is we made coffee to drink with our hard crackers. After breakfast i went immediately on the field of battle.[43]

My object was to find our brigade. As they were at mannasses i did not find them, but i was on the field of battle all day. And although our Gen, claim to have had the best of the fight that day i dont. When i returned at dark, i told the officers and men they need not go to bed, for we would be ordered to build bull run bridge that night. And so we were before an hour just as i was eating some supper the boys had prepared for me. We received the order to build the bridge immediately. Now the impression i had on the field that we were being out generald. Our men fought well, but every division as it arrived on the field was sent forward unsuppoarted and by overwhelming numbers defeated. Jackson kept his troops massed in the woods, where he could move them under cover quickly from one point to an other.

McDowell's railroad bridge, Bull Run (Library of Congress, Prints & Photographs Division, Civil War Photographs, LC-DIG-cwpb-00237)

Pope on the other hand kept his divided and fought them in line of battle. He acted all the time as though he wished to surround the Rebs. That of course weakened his force, and gave the enemy the chance of allways meating the attacking force with superior numbers. We comenced building the bridge immediately. There was no material for to build it on hand. We had to go to the woods for every thing. The bridge was forty Eight ft long and 14 ft high. We had to put in three trussles or perhaps what you would call bents. These we framed with a mudsill for the bottom, and a cap for the top. Then there were three posts. Then the braces the cut represent, one of our trussles framed and braced. Then the stringers on these trussles. Then we had to cut and hew covering for the top. I have been particular in describing this bridge, for this is the way we built most all our bridges. By daylight next morning we had it ready for the covering. I was left with 40 men to cover it while the rest of the corps was sent to build the bridge across Cub run. This morning the battle opened on the left of our line. We could hear it and the shouts of the combattants. But i could not get out on the field for i could not leave my detail, as the men were absolutely worn out, and it took all the energy i had left to keep them at work. By noon the bridge was fineshed. About this time the news came to us that we were driving the Rebs. The boys cheered lustily, but not so with me. I still retained my impression of the previous evening, and i immediately gave the order to march to Cub run, to help finish that bridge. We got that bridge finished before sunset. To speak of the rout and panic, of that evening would take to long. And it is one incident in my life i would lik to forever forget. We were detailed as guard on the bridge in order to prevent the wounded from being crowded off the bridge. I ordered many a stout hearty man knocked off that bridge that night for running over and crowding the wounded. Teams would come rushing down the hill and at the bridge covered with wounded. Their drivers would pay no attention to the orders to halt, and we had to hurl them over them over bank. And in one instance we had to threw a four horse team horses, Waggon, driver and all off the bridge 12 ft high in order to keep him from running over and crushing wounded. I shall never forget the appeals for help made to me that night by men of our own brigade, who could distinguish my voice for it was to dark to reckognize faces by 10 oclock. The wounded were all over. At least those able to walk, and order was being restored. Troops commenced to come back in good order. So we got our men together and marched to centreville where we arrived about twelve oclock. We had no blanketts, so we lay out on the ground, and although cold and wet i slept sound till daylight. The next morning we were marched two miles this side of centreville, and formed in line to prevent straglers from getting to the rear. By evening the panick was over. Each man or squad that had not found their Reg. was hunting it for themselves.[44]

From this time untill the 14th of Sept we were marched in our old place between the Penn Reserve Corps, & Kings Division. On the 14th we were ordered in advance of the Reserve corps, for the Rebs had burned the bridge across a stream about two miles from the foot of south mountain. Reno had thrown over a foot bridge below the turnpike and as the stream was shallow. He had crossed with his whole corps, and was fighting the Rebs at the foot of the mount when we got to the bridge. We went to work at the bridge while the army pased over the foot bridge. Our brigade passed us just after noon. About 5 oclock the fight became general on the side of the mountain about two miles in front of us. At about 7 oclock i was informed that Lieut McKenzie had shot himself in the foot with his revolver. Kowing that left the company without a commissioned officer i immediately left for the battle field. But before i got to the brigade the fighting was over, and our boys suffered severely. The next morning i went to Gen Hooker and got releived of my command in the Engineer corps and orders to join my Reg. Since that time i led Co F and i find them as good and brave a set of boys as ever shouldered a gun. I have also got back All Kidd and all the boys we had on detatched service which makes the co foot up 30 men for duty.[45]

I had intended to give you a history of the fights of the 15 16 and 17 but it will spin this letter out to long. I will have to give it up, but i will say this. That if Gibbons Brigade had of been as strong on the morning of the 17th as we were two months ago, i beleive we could have succeeded in driving the Rebs into the river, for i tell you the troops that releived us did not fight as we did. For we drive them untill our amunition gave out and then held our ground untill we were releived. What do you think of Old Abes prock-lamation? It takes well with the Army here. Now the Rebs, will have to die dog or eat the hatchett. We are all flat broke and would like to see the pay-master. Capt Callis is still in com of the Reg. and get along firstrate. Many of the officers and men that were wounded have gone home on furlough. I will have to stop for want of paper. Dont say this letter aint long enough. I just given you a few of the incidents of our soldier life as it is.[46]

My love to all.

H F Young

Direct as of old to Co F 7th Reg.

NOTES

38. The action or lack thereof by McClellan at Bull Run is debated even today. Ensconced at Alexandria, he finally sent Franklin's corps to aid Pope, but it moved with great caution and did not have an impact on the battle. Some, including President Lincoln, suggested that McClellan deliberately wished to sabotage Pope's command. A reply to the president stated as much when McClellan suggested that the two courses of action were to concentrate forces with Pope or to let him get out of his own mess. McClellan also suggested, with rumors rampant of Confederates between Pope's forces and Washington, that the defense of the capital was tantamount to the fight at Bull Run. It may have been too much to state that McClellan was deliberately working against Pope; however, he certainly did little to aid him. Stephen W. Sears, *George B. McClellan: The Young Napoleon* (New York: Ticknor & Fields, 1988), 254–55; Wert, *The Sword of Lincoln*, 134–36; McPherson, *Battle Cry of Freedom*, 528, 533; Hennessy, *Return to Bull Run*, 239–41, 468.

39. On the night of August 22, 1862, the Construction Corps, under the command of Maj. David Houston, built a trestle bridge eight hundred yards from the railroad bridge at Rappahannock Station. *OR*, ser. 1, vol. 12, pt. 2, 330–31.

40. Brig. Gen. George L. Hartsuff commanded the Third Brigade, Second Division, Third Army Corps, under McDowell, and it was his force that was in danger of becoming trapped on the wrong side of the Rappahannock River at Rappahannock Station. Before McDowell could order the engineers to destroy the bridge, he withdrew Hartsuff's brigade with heavy firing on both sides and a large Confederate force bearing down on them. To make matters worse, heavy rain had destroyed the

trestle bridge built by Young's crew of engineers, and planks crashing into the railroad bridge placed undue stress on the structure. *OR*, ser. 1, vol. 12, pt. 2, 331–32.

41. McDowell, fearing that the Confederate Army would capture the bridge, ordered the destruction of the bridge to allow his army to gain separation from the Confederate Army. Confederate forces, which wanted the bridge intact, "opened a furious fire upon us," according to McDowell. *OR*, ser. 1, vol. 12, pt. 2, 331–32, pt. 3, 631, 647.

42. Brig. Gen. John F. Reynolds commanded a division of Pennsylvania Reserves at Bull Run. They were in advance on the Warrenton Turnpike near Groveton when the fight at Gainesville broke out on August 28, 1862. Part of the Third Division, Third Army Corps, Army of Virginia, they sustained 676 casualties at Bull Run. *OR*, ser. 1, vol. 12, pt. 2, 256; Hennessy, *Return to Bull Run*, 148.

43. Brig. Gen. George D. Bayard commanded the cavalry brigade in the Second Division, Third Army Corps, Army of Virginia, at Bull Run. Bayard was ordered by McDowell on August 30 to march from Manassas to Gainesville to seek out the strength of the enemy and to annoy it if practicable. Maj. Gen. James E. B. Stuart's cavalry provided a screen for Jackson's force before the fight at Gainesville and served as a liaison between the forces of Lee and those of Jackson in the days leading up to August 28. *OR*, ser. 1, vol. 12, pt. 3, 757; McPherson, *Battle Cry of Freedom*, 528–29, 531.

44. Cub Run is a tributary of the Bull Run River west of Centreville, Virginia. The Construction Corps aided troops making their way to the rear and to some extent worked to quell within reason the panic that gripped many. *OR*, ser. 1, vol. 12, pt. 2, 344.

45. Maj. Gen. Jesse Reno commanded the Ninth Army Corps and Hooker, the First Army Corps in the Army of the Potomac at South Mountain. Reno's corps was tasked with securing Fox's Gap, and Hooker's corps was to take Turner's Gap. Ambrose Burnside commanded both corps at South Mountain on September 14. John W. McKenzie of Company F in the Seventh Wisconsin was wounded on September 14, 1862, at South Mountain. Young's detachment in the Construction Corps ended on September 16, 1862, when he was reunited with the men of Company F on the heel of South Mountain. *OR*, ser. 1, vol. 12, pt. 2, 261, vol. 19, pt. 1, 169; Wert, *The Sword of Lincoln*, 151; *Roster*, 1:558; Wisconsin, Adjutant General's Office, *Regimental Muster and Descriptive Rolls, 1861–1865*, Red Books, reel 3, 7th Infantry.

46. On July 13, 1862, President Lincoln, in a private meeting with Secretary of State Seward and Secretary of the Navy Welles, outlined his plan for the Emancipation Proclamation. Meeting with the full cabinet on July 22, Lincoln outlined the preliminary draft of the document. It had not been easy getting to this point, with a whirlwind of issues to face including the course of the war and legal issues related to emancipation. However, by the summer of 1862 Lincoln viewed emancipation as necessary for the North to win the war and so acted using his war powers. Another quandary for the president was the timing of the official announcement of emancipation. Urged on by his cabinet, the president decided to wait for a victory on the battlefield. The Battle of Antietam produced the long-awaited victory, at least strategically. Five days after the battle, Lincoln formally issued the Emancipation

Proclamation, to be effective January 1, 1863, unless the Southern states ended their rebellion against the Union. Emancipation freed only those enslaved Africans in states that were in armed rebellion against the United States. David Herbert Donald, *Lincoln* (New York: Simon & Schuster, 1995), 365–66, 374; McPherson, *Battle Cry of Freedom*, 503–4, 557; Guelzo, *Fateful Lightning*, 174–79.

Camp near Sharpsberg MD Oct 4 1862

Dear Delia

I have waited verry impatiently for the last week for a letter from you, before i would write again. But it dont come. We are encamped on the banks of what is called the upper Potomac, in the roughest country i ever seen. Nothing but hills and hollows. But the location is a healthy one, and if we could get our pay which i think we certainly soon will, we could get some vegetables. We could get a long firstrate. All we officers can buy when we run out of money is what we get from the Brigade commissary, and it is coffee hard crackers sugar & pork, and we get pretty tired of it i can tell you. In fact we dont fare as well as the men, for their provisions are furnished them, while we cant buy from the commissary only when they have a serplus on hand. Now i as i have got my growl over i will write something else.

We were reviewed yesturday by old abe as the boys call him. I tell you it was quite a contrast between yesturday and the last time he reviewed us. It was at Fredricksberg last summer. We were then out with 700 men, while yesturday the Reg had out only 190 men. It looked small i tell you. Our whole Brigade is not as large now as our Reg was then, but we will get recruited up in time. There is 1200 wounded men now at the hospitals out of our Brigade most of which will be back in their Regts during the winter. And we will probably get some recruits from home. We feel in good spirits and are ready for another fight when ever called on. Our Brigade whiped Jacksons famous Stonewall Brigade, at the battle of Anteitam in a fair and square fight. It was them we met in the morning. They fought well, but we hurled them back, broken and in perfect confusion. Many of our own brave comrads fell, but we left the ground literly covered with grey backs, as the boys call them. You may form some idea of the fierceness of the fight. We were meeting each other in the open field, each side commenced firing at the distance of about two hundred yds, when the firing commenced both sides kept it up verry fiercely. At the same time we both kept advancing.

When we got within thirty yds of each other there appeared to be a perfect storm of bullets. It was at this time the 7th changed front, and began pouring in a deadly fire on their flank. At the same time Battery B. was pouring in grape and canister rite over our heads, which was cutting them to peices terribly, when they broke and run. We followed them up and held the position till our amunition gave out and we were releived. We were then marched to the rear, where we got amunition and then were placed in suppoart of a battery where we remained under fire, which did us little damage till dark, when the battle was over for the day. If I was talking to you i could give you a perfect i dea, of all the battles i have been in or seen, but it is impossible to do so in letter for you would not understand the different phases and terms and formations as used on the battle field, or in militair.[47]

This is the finest weather we have had and i dont think we will be long idle. There is some fighting going on across the river every day, and i think there will be a forward movement soon. Give my best wishes to squire Bergess & to Furman and Caroline, and dont forget that this is the fourth letter i have written you since i received one from you. Our wounded boys are all doing well as could be expected.

I dont no what effect the Presidents proclamation will have on the South. But there is one thing certain it is just what was wanted.

And if they dont lay down their arms we will have to annihilate them, niggers cotton and all. It will make hard times for a while but it will forever settle the everlasting slavery question. I would like to see you all this fine morning, and i would not object to taking dinner with you if I could. Well i will have feed on immagination for the present i suppose and put up with my regular hard crackers tough beef and coffee. Take things cool. Dont fret yourself to death, for it will do no good, for we are all creatures of circumstance over which we have no control, and your fretting about my getting killed, wont help the matter. Write often and direct as of old Co F 7 Reg. Give my love to our dear children. Tell Jared i want him to be a good boy and help his mama and tell Laura to kiss may for me.[48]

ever yours

H F Young

NOTES

47. President Lincoln visited Antietam October 1–4. Lincoln reviewed the soldiers and toured hospitals and the battlefield; however, at the top of his list was to urge McClellan to move toward Lee's army and destroy it. McClellan rightfully

sensed this but did little to grant Lincoln's wish. Lincoln, in reply to McClellan's inactivity, sent a curt note on October 13 making reference to McClellan's "overcautiousness" in his pursuit of Lee. This lack of movement led to the eventual sacking of McClellan as commander of the Army of the Potomac. The Iron Brigade played an early role in the battle, again crossing paths with the Stonewall Brigade. As the brigade advanced on both sides of the Hagerstown Turnpike, vicious fighting broke out that lasted through midmorning on September 17 near the West Woods and Dunker Church. The fighting swayed back and forth until both sides were battered and out of action for the rest of the day. Iron Brigade casualties at Antietam were 68 killed, 275 wounded, and 5 missing or captured. Sears, *McClellan*, 330; *OR*, ser. 1, vol. 19, pt. 1, 13–14, 189; Donald, *Lincoln*, 387; Wert, *The Sword of Lincoln*, 175–76; Herdegen, *The Iron Brigade*, 291–92; Nolan, *The Iron Brigade*, 138–43.

48. Reaction to the Emancipation Proclamation was predictable. Northern abolitionists were elated while Democrats saw it as an opportunity to gain seats in the fall elections. Moderate supporters of the Lincoln administration were not happy with emancipation, either. The rank and file had enlisted not to fight slavery but to save the Union. Many soldiers saw it as a practical measure that would help end the war. Emancipation did little to curb the blatant racism among soldiers. Many high-ranking officers, including Gen. McClellan, conservative by nature, were against emancipation. Nolan, *The Iron Brigade*, 145, 195; Wert, *The Sword of Lincoln*, 176; Donald, *Lincoln*, 377–79; McPherson, *Battle Cry of Freedom*, 558–59; Reid Mitchell, *Civil War Soldiers: Their Expectations and Their Experiences* (New York: Viking, 1988), 126–27.

~

Camp near Sharpsberg MD Oct 18 1862

Dear Delia

I received your long delayed letter and was glad to hear from you and to hear you were all well. We have just got in from pickett duty. Last night was quite cool to much so for men to lay out without tents.

We are recruiting up considerable. Some of our wounded are returning to the Reg and the sick and worn out are getting better. Wm Ray, is all right again. I got a letter from him a few days ago. He is able for duty and is detailed in the hospital for guard duty. I got a letter yesturday from Father. He wrote you were all well.

We wont get any pay before next month as the paymaster cant get the money. There is some fighting going on over the river every day mostly skermishers.

Andy Robison, came to see me the other day. He is in 134 Reg Pa Vol. He has got to be a great big stout lubber, and likes soldering very well. They have just got here and dont no any thing about it yet.[49]

I think there will be some move soon. That will give us something to do for we are getting tired of camp. It costs an awful pile of money here to get provisions. Potatoes 2 Dolls per bushel. Butter 40 to 50 cents per pound and every thing els in proportion. There is a new Reg aded to our Brigade the 24 Michigan. It is over 1000 strong and makes quite an addition to our Brigade. If they fight as well as they look, our Brigade will give the Rebs a warm reception when we meet them. I sept none last night and feel to infernal stupid to write or do any thing else. Give my love to the dear ones and write soon.[50]

Ever yours

H F Young

NOTES

49. Andrew Robinson was in Company A of the 134th Pennsylvania Infantry, which was part of the First Brigade, Third Division, Fifth Army Corps. A nine-month volunteer, he was mustered out of the regiment on May 26, 1863. Organized on September 12, 1862, the regiment arrived at Antietam on September 18. Samuel P. Bates, *History of the Pennsylvania Volunteers, 1861–1865*, 5 vols. (Harrisburg, PA: B. Singerly, State Printer, 1869–71), 4:285; *OR*, ser. 1, vol. 19, pt. 1, 175.

50. The Twenty-Fourth Michigan, made up primarily of men from Wayne County, Michigan, joined the Iron Brigade on October 8, 1862. Nolan, *Iron Brigade*, 159–60.

CHAPTER FOUR

"I am not A McClellan man, A Burnside man, A Hooker man. I am for the man that leads us to fight the Rebs"

November 2, 1862, to February 14, 1863

Camp of the 7th Reg in Virginia Nov 2 1862

Dear Delia

This is a pleasant Sunday morning and i cannot help think of home, and the loved ones there. In fact the presence of danger always operates on me in that way, always when going into battle and until i get into the conflict i think of home. But when the conflict begins and we become engaged i foget for the time all else.

Here we are on the east side of the blue ridge, just five miles from Snickers gap, on the road to winchester, and that gap is held by the Grey backs in force. Our Brigade is in advance, and we are expecting the order to move. Every man has got his days rations, in his haverscack and his cartridges in his cartridge box, ready for the conflict, for that gap must be stormed. But it will cost the life of many a brave fellow, that is perfectly careless and indifferent now. Every thing is verry still this morning. Once in a while we hear the boom, of cannon from the gap, for our cavalry are out on a reconnoison and the Rebs, are shelling them.[1]

And once in a while we hear the sharp repoart of a rifle on pickett, for the hostil lines are close together on our left. But you will get the news of a hard fight, or a retreat of the rebs, before you get this. We have been mustered again for pay, and i think we will soon get it when i will be able to send home considerable money. No i would not go in command of negroes, for the reason they are the infernalist set of cowards in the world. We cant trust them as Ambulance drivers, or Amunition drivers, or in fact any where that there is danger, and i would not fight with them for the same reason. It is not on account of their coulour, but on account of their cowardice. There are exceptions but they are rare. The great majority of them would prefer to be slaves rather than fight for their liberty. *Boom boom boom.* The ball is opened. Farewell. Kiss the babies for me and except my love.

Ever yours

H F Young

NOTE

1. The Iron Brigade left Sharpsburg in late October 1862, crossed the Blue Ridge Mountains at Snicker's Gap, and by November 4 settled into Bloomfield on the road to Winchester. At Bloomfield, one era of the Iron Brigade came to an end with the departure of Brig. Gen. John Gibbon. Destined to command a division, he regretted leaving the men of the Iron Brigade. Alan T. Nolan, *The Iron Brigade: A Military History* (New York: Macmillan, 1961), 164–66.

Camp near Warrenton Va Nov 8 1862

Dear Father

I received your last letter long ago, but i had no news to write, so I neglected writing. For the last two weeks we have been moveing every day, and i had no chance to write. We crossed the Potomac River at Berlin and marched round through all the crooks and turns of the blue Ridge. We had skermishes every day with the enemy. They would make a stand with a small boddy of cavalry, and a few pieces of artillery in every available place, so as to annoy us. Our artillery would soon send them back when we would move on again. Our Reg has lost none only those who gave out on the march and they were sent to Washington. We arrived at Warrington night before last. Our advance exchanged a few shots with the rebs when they run away, and left us in possession of the town. We had marched twenty two miles that day but our reg was sent out on pickett. I tell you it was hard. The night was cold and stormy and we dare not build fires. Many of the boys sank down by the roots of trees and in the fence corners, and cold as it was slept from exhaustion. Yesturday morning it was snowing and we had nothing for breakfast. I went to the Brigade comesaries to get some crackers for Capt Callis and my self, but there was none to be had. They had none to isue to the men and consequently they had none to sell to the officers. And as we have no money we will have to wait patiently till it comes. There is one thing we have plenty of fresh Beef. So we are going it on fresh beef and perched corn. We were releived on pickett yesturday at noon, and we came here to camp, which is about one and a half miles from Warrenton on the road to Sulpher Springs. I think the bitterest dose we ever had since we have been in service was yesturday when we came here to camp. We were tired out had nothing to eat and it was snowing and blowing like the Devil, and the ground was covered about an inch deep with snow. And the men have nothing but shelter tents, and the officers nothing but flys, open at boths ends. But we went into the woods and built log heaps and stood round them untill we got thawed out and dry. And now this morning the sun comes out warm and pleasant, which will soon take off the snow, and we are expecting rations up to day. We are all feeling better natured again but i tell you it is making old men of us fast. You can see its effects plainly every day.[2]

They are fighting out in advance of us this morning. The ball opened about daylight. They are fighting with artillery with the Rappahannock River between them. We will be moved on as soon as we get supplies. We had an Election on the 4th. The boys say it is all damed lie about not voting as a man pleases in Virginia for they have tried it. Our company cast twenty five votes. All Strait Republican. The Reg gave (181) one hundred eighty one Republican, to twenty Democrat. There was agents here for to look after the intrest of the democrattic party from Madison, and we have one or two Democratic officers in the Reg. I dont no what has become of young Rice. He was sent to the hospital at Alexandria Va the (23) of Aug with a number of other sick of the Brigade, and we have not herd from him since. He must be living for we would have had notice sent to us, if he had died. Many of our boys in hospital dont write, for want of stamps as they are out of money and cant buy any. I hope they will pay us soon for we are in absolute need, and i think we will get our pay next week. Give my best wishes to all and write often for it is sometimes almost out of the question to send off letters here.[3]

yours truly

H F Young

NOTES

2. The move from their position west of the Blue Ridge Mountains to Warrenton commenced under less than ideal weather. At Warrenton the brigade experienced another problem, a lack of supplies. For two days the regiment was without food

until the situation remedied by illegal foraging among the men, which was overlooked by many officers. Nolan, *The Iron Brigade*, 168–69. Frederick H. Dyer, *A Compendium of the War of the Rebellion Compiled and Arranged from Official Records . . . and Other Reliable Documents and Sources* (Des Moines, IA: Dyer Publishing Company, 1908), 909–10 (hereafter cited as *Dyer's Compendium*); United States, War Records Office, *War of the Rebellion: A Compilation of the Official Records of the Union and Confederate Armies*, 128 vols. (Washington, DC: Government Printing Office, 1885–1901), ser. 1, vol. 19, pt. 1, 3 (hereafter cited as *OR*).

3. The midterm elections of 1862 resulted in a Democratic victory in many states. Lincoln's party saw the gains of 1860 erased in New York, Pennsylvania, Ohio, Indiana, Illinois, and New Jersey. While his party was defeated, the president could take some solace that the Democratic victories were by slim margins in many states. In Wisconsin, three of six congressional seats went to the Democrats. The soldier vote, however, was firmly Republican. In Grant County, the Republican ticket prevailed in nearly all races except that for one assembly seat. Former Democratic governor Nelson Dewey was defeated by Lancaster attorney Joseph T. Mills in the race for district attorney by 588 votes. Skirmishes near Warrenton and Rappahannock Station were reported on November 7 and 8. Benjamin Rice, Company H of the Seventh Wisconsin, was wounded at Brawner's Farm on August 28, 1862, and discharged December 23, 1862, due to disability. David Herbert Donald, *Lincoln* (New York: Simon & Schuster, 1995), 380–83; James M. McPherson, *Battle Cry of Freedom: The Civil War Era* (New York: Oxford University Press, 1988), 560–62; Richard N. Current, *The History of Wisconsin*, vol. 2, *The Civil War Era, 1848–1873* (Madison: State Historical Society of Wisconsin, 1976), 405; "Election Results in Grant County, by Towns," *Grant County Herald* (Lancaster, WI), November 11, 1862; *OR*, ser. 1, vol. 19, pt. 1, 3; *Dyer's Compendium*, 910; Wisconsin, Adjutant General's Office, *Roster of the Wisconsin Volunteers, War of the Rebellion, 1861–1865*, Blue Books, 2 vols. (Madison: Democrat Printing Press, 1886), 1:567 (hereafter cited as *Roster*).

Camp near Rappahannock Station Nov 15 1862

Dear Delia

I just rec you welcome letter and was glad to hear you were all well and enjoying yourselves by a good comfortable fire. As for us poor Devils we are shivering round our camp fires in the cold winds burning one side while the other side is freezing, but we are all sound with the exception of bad colds. And we have all commenced our old trade of barking.

The next morning after writing my last letter we commenced our march, and marched round throug all the crooks and turn of the blue Ridge. The enemy would make a short stand in every available position and commence thundering away at us with his cannon. But when we would get our longed ranged parrots in position, he would always fall back. The weather was cold and we had quite a snow but we all got through safe, but it is making old men of fast i can tell you. There is fighting in front of this morning and we are lying here with three days rations in our haversacks with orders to march at a moments notice. There is considerable dissatisfaction in the army about McClellens removal. I think myself that it was a bad time to remove him when he was pushing forward as fast as he could, but i suppose there is reasons for it that I know nothing about. At all events I have entire confidence in Burnsides, and we will do our best for him. Gibbons has left us. He has been promoted to the command of a Division. Our Brigade is now under command of Col Cutler of the 6th Reg. But it makes little difference to us now who commands us, for we have become so thoughroly perfect in our duties that there is a number of officers in each regiment

Brig. Gen. Lysander Cutler (Library of Congress, Prints & Photographs Division, Civil War Photographs, LC-DIG-cwpb-05196)

competent to command the Brigade. As for the war ending by Chrismas it is all noncense to think of such a thing.[4]

And i have no confidence in the negroes helping us out with it, for i dont beleive they have ambition enough about them to fight for their own rights. But we will have some fighting between here and Richmond and perhaps some at Richmond. But i cant see what is to hinder us from taking Richmond this winter. It is said we have one hundred and forty thousand men on the Pennensula. If that is so and they and us move together Richmond must fall. If that takes place before the 1st of Jan, the cotton states might lay down their arms to save their negroes. Now you see there is a chance for the Rebellion to end. That looks well on paper, but i have no confidence in it, for the best laid plans are often frustrated. But i wish it might be so. There is one thing certain that we cant stand it to winter in these cursed little fly tents this winter in this climate, without suffering worse than death on the field of Battle, so that we must soon move south or go into winter quarters. As to getting a furlough at present the thing is impossible as there an order against granting furloughs excepting wounded men or officers and i dont want one on them terms. There has been quite a number of our wounded discharged and gone home. Geo H Henderson has been discharged and gone home. He will probably call on you. Geo. was a good soldier. Tell him we are nearly opposite the ford on the Rappahannock River where he heard the first scream of a shell. The Rebs built the bridge across the River, where we had so much trouble burning it down, and our cavalry took it the other day, before they had time to destroy it. We have a large force here. Perhaps larger than any force we have had together since last spring when the great army of the Potomac was all together.[5]

You wonder why things are so high here or in Md. I will tell you. The Government has possession of all the Rail Roads and cars, and wont allow any thing to be transported on their roads but army supplies and soldiers. So you see all we get has to hauled through from Washington. This part of Old Virginia is perfectly used up. All the rails are burned. All the pigs and chickens are killed. All the horses and cattle are gone. Most of the houses are deserted and now we are finishing up the contract by using all the corn an wheat thats left, for our horses and cattle.

I am glad to hear that Squire Bergess has got well again. Give him my best wishes for i would rather see him than any man i know the paymaster not excepted. My good wishes to all the neighbours, and my love you yourself and the children.

Ever yours

H F Young

NOTES

4. Maj. Gen. George B. McClellan was removed by the president on November 7, 1862, and replaced by Maj. Gen. Ambrose Burnside. The tipping point for Lincoln was a visit to the army in early October that convinced him that McClellan's removal would not result in a mutiny in the ranks of the army. Two acts helped the president make his decision—Maj. Gen. Jeb Stuart's raid into Pennsylvania and McClellan's failure to follow Lee after Antietam. Angry threats to resign by officers loyal to McClellan amounted to just that—threats but not action. McClellan embarked on a farewell tour of the army on November 10, 1862, and then left the army for good. While at Bloomfield, Virginia, Iron Brigade commander John Gibbon was offered the command of the Second Division, First Army Corps. His immediate replacement, Col. Lysander Cutler of the Sixth Wisconsin, commanded the brigade from November 5 through November 26. *OR*, ser. 1, vol. 19, pt. 1, 3; Lance J. Herdegen, *The Iron Brigade in Civil War and Memory: The Black Hats from Bull Run to Appomattox and Thereafter* (El Dorado Hills, CA: Savas Beatie, 2012), 304–9, 314–15; Allen C. Guelzo, *Fateful Lightning: A New History of the Civil War and Reconstruction* (New York: Oxford University Press, 2012), 327; Jeffry D. Wert, *The Sword of Lincoln: The Army of the Potomac* (New York: Simon & Schuster, 2005), 177–82; Donald, *Lincoln*, 388; Nolan, *The Iron Brigade*, 164–65; *Roster*, 1:494; *Dyer's Compendium*, 285.

5. George H. Henderson, Company F of the Seventh Wisconsin, was wounded at South Mountain and was discharged October 25, 1862, due to disability. *Roster*, 1:559.

Camp near Brooks Station Va Dec 1 1862

Dear Father

I received two letters from you in the last two days.[6] There was two weeks difference in date, and twenty four hours here. Glad to hear you were all well. As for the hard work you do it will probably do you good, if you take it moderate. It will keep your mind from always running on our troubles. But when you wisconsin folk at home talk about hard times privations and the horrors of the War, you have little idea of the real meaning of the language you use. And i hope you may never be called on to witness the destruction of every thing in our own state, for war destroys every thing. You cant immagine the destructiveness of an army. Capt Callis has gone home recruiting. They are going to offer the drafted men all the rights and privledges of vol to come into the old Regiment, for the time the Reg has to serve. I dont no what success they will have. Our Col, Lieut Col, and Maj, are here all ready to be shot again in the next fight. General Gibbons com a Division the 3d Division of this corps, formerly com by Gen Ricketts. Our Brigade is now Commanded by Gen Merrideth. He has always been in the Brigade. He was Col of the 19th Indiana. He always was a favourite, and the Brigade as a general thing likes the change. It has come to light that Gen Gibbons used us harder than than was necessary by threwing his Brigade clear in advance, and then refusing suppoart when offered by other Gen. This is called the best Brigade in Service, but said Gen Reynolds if you have men that never flinch under any circumstances. He did not consider it was good generalship to push them ahead unsuppoarted and have them cut to peices.[7]

Gen Reynolds Commands our corps. We are still the 1st Army Corps. We are in the left grand Division under Franklin. Our division is encamped between Potomac Creek and the Potomac River. The centre Grand Division is between us and the Rappahannock. The right Grand Division is on the north bank of the Rappahannock between Falmouth and Ellis ford. Such is the position of our grand army of the Potomac. Then there is Seigle with a large force between us and Centreville. Then Heinsleman has a large force in and round Washington. We have also a large force at Harpers Ferry under command of General Ricketts, a splendid Artillery officer, and one of the men that will never surrender.[8]

On the oposite side of the Rappahannock River lies the combined armies of Lee, Longstreet, and Hill, numbering from the best information we can get, one hundred and twenty thousand men, and three hundred peices of Artillery. They are threwing Riffe pits and breast works on the high land some two miles from the River, which will give them a great advantage when we attempt to cross.[9]

I am well ~~aq~~ acquainted with the country on the oposite side of the river, and i know the Rebs will have at least fifty per cent the advantage of us, if we attempt to cross any where in our immediate front. For that reason i think there will be a flank movement, by sending a portion of the Army farther south. The position that the Left Grand Division now occupies is such that it could be put on the Board of Transports at Bell Plains and Aquia Creek in a few hours. Then it could be landed any where on Chessapeak Bay, or up the Rappahannoc River within twenty four hours after it was on board. That is the only advantage i can see in our new position, and i consider this a great advantage provided it is made good use of. Such is the possition of affairs at this moment but liable to be all changed within the next few hours. Your question will the Democrats sell us to the traitors. I think not at present. They are not in power yet by any means. In fact their pet scheem of reorganization will not be listened to South. If they were in power and would make the offer to day. But the Administration may feel proud and satisfide of one thing. The Army stands by the old flag and will suppoart the Administration. When our favourite on the field was removed without any appeared cause, for you reccollect that we were on the move when the order was received removeing McClellan, and then all your traitor Dem papers raised the howl that it was done for political purposes. This fuss was all raised for the purpose of demoralizing the Army. But what did it effect? The only thing it did was to shew that the American Soldier is true to his country, true his oath, and resolved to fight the rebellion to the bitter end no difference who commands. And we are still willing to except the order that after this it will only be those who are successfull that will be entitled to command. This army of the Potomac when we come to consider the inteligence of the men composing it is certainly the best deciplined Army in the world. It is positively a fact that this Army would obay any order that was given by a commanding officer, no difference how extravagant the order was. You talk of men resigning. Why that is out of the questions in this Army. The Order reads that only for two causes shall ressignations be excepted. One is disability of boddy. The other disability of mind. Either must be accompanied by a certifficate from the Sergt General. If an officer is not satisfide with this arrangement and makes any complaints he is immediately Dismised the service with loss of all pay; and a dishonourable discharge.[10]

Now you must give the credit of this discipline to McClellan. I know McClellan moved slow in the field, but for drilling and fitting an army he cant be beat, all the editors and newspapers to the contrary.[11]

Father you may think me inconsistent to stand up for Geo B McClellan. I am not A McClellan man, A Burnside man, A Hooker man. I am for the man that leads us to fight the Rebs on any terms he can get. But when i read the Damed infernal lies, in our republican papers of Wis and every other state, it absolutely disgusts me for i see they are becoming a corrput party lying and party loving power. After the Battle of Anteitam McClellan immediately commenced reorganizing the Army, that vast Army were almost destitued of every thing but courage. Now let me give you a true history of my own Co; and is the history of the Reg in fact the history of Hookers entire Corps. On the next Sunday after the battle we had Reg Inspection, to assertain what was wanting. We made out our requisitions for chlothing, and sent teams to harpers ferry after it. The clothing was not there. Now those teams were sent for clothiing every two or three days during our entire stay in Md. At length Gen Gibbons sent the Brigade qr master to Harpers Ferry, with two teams from each Regt in the Brigade, with orders to remain there untill they got our clothing. They had been gone some four or five days and were yet gone when we received orders to march at four oclock. Now let us look at Co F that cold wet morning, when we received orders to march. I had four men that had been excused from duty for some time, for they were entirely barefoot, numbers of the others had theirs writhed on with bark and roaps. Quite a number of my men had no shirts, had no shirts since they had been in Maryland. We had no overcoats. Many of them had lost their oil Blanketts, tents, knapsacks, in fact all they had except what was on their backs. Now these things were not lost carelessly. They were lost on the field of battle. Well the teams came to hand that morning, as there would be no more clothing to be had. They perhaps had one fourth the ammount of clothing sent for, but one lucky thing they got plenty of shoes. So i took co F a share of the chlothes and divided them in such a manner that every one had shoes 1 shirt 1 Drawers, pants and 1 socks. I managed to give those that had neither blanket or tent, an Oil Blanket, and that is the Glorius good condition we were in for marching. And we have been doing our best eversince to get clothing to make the men comfortable in this raw damp climate. There is not more than one fourth of our men have overcoats yet, and i tell you that men want about as much chlothes in this raw damp climate as they do in Wis. The movements of an army of the Magnitude of this is necessarily slow. But when the papers state that our movements were at a snails pace, why dont they also state that the provisions that were to meet us at Warrenton did not get there untill three Days after we did. And then we had to send teams to Mannasses for supplies. When they say the army was well supplied with horses they lie, but dare not publish the truth. But if they dare not publish the truth, they should not publish any thing about it. I know it would have been bad polisy to publish that when we left Warrenton. Burnside had to order one Section of each Battery turned in and shiped round here by rail, for want of horses to draw them. But such is the fact, and our Division has not got their guns yet.[12]

Now when McClellan crosed the Potomac he Ordered that the Rail Road from Aquia creek to Fredricksberg should be taken possession of and repaired. Was it done? No sir. It was not. What is the consequence of this neglect? I will tell you. Burnside then immediately would have crossed the River securing an advantages possition, sure of supplies for his Army he could have waited, Lees attact as retreat as the case might bee. He could have bridged the River and supplied his army anywhere between there and Richmond. The press is already talking about Old Burny being out generald for not taking immediate possessioin of the other side of the river. But Damn their infernal lying pictures. Let them tell the truth. That if we had taken possession of the other side we would have staved or had to retreat. I have many and many times within the last three months bot papers, that spoke of how well we were supplied with chlothes and rations. When i would be reading it some one would hold up a bearfoot, open his coat and shew no shirt. Others would draw round them their thin blouses, and swear the Editor ought never to have an over coat. Sometimes we see something like that when we have not a bite of any thing to eat. Then you ought to hear the boys curse the Editors.[13]

Dec 8

Yesturday and to day I have been sick with cold and Rheumatism. I cant finish this letter as i intended. *We march at Daylight.* Co F has 40 men on hand for rations or fight as the case may bee. I have not seen Clark for a long time. Tell Kassy she deserves some brave soldier and shall have one when the war is over. If you new how infernal bad i hated to anker my stern on a knapsack take a portfolio on my lap and write a letter; you would never think I neglected you.[14]

I dont know where we are going.

My best wishes to all.
yours truly

H F Young

NOTES

6. Brooks Station, Virginia, was midway between Aquia Landing, on the Potomac River, and Falmouth, Virginia.

7. Capt. John Callis left the brigade on November 16 to recruit soldiers in Wisconsin, leaving Young in charge of the company in his absence; Young "by his efficiency of command at the battle of Antietam has proven himself worthy of the trust." The departure of Gibbon elevated Brig. Gen. Solomon Meredith of the Nineteenth Indiana to the position of commander of the Iron Brigade. Gibbon was not

impressed with Meredith's military abilities, an opinion stemming from a dispute in which Meredith expressed displeasure at Gibbon's selection to lead the brigade in May 1862. Meredith, who had the backing of Burnside, was selected as the third commander of the westerners. Gibbon protested the appointment to Burnside, who not surprisingly turned down the request to replace Meredith. Young's claim that Gibbon "used us harder" did not reflect a universal opinion among the soldiers of the brigade, most of whom held the general in high regard. Brig. Gen. James Ricketts commanded the Second Division, First Army Corps, Army of the Potomac, at Antietam. Wisconsin, Adjutant General's Office, *Regimental Muster and Descriptive Rolls, 1861–1865*, Red Books (Madison: State Militia, Adjutant General's Office, 1865), reel 3, 7th Infantry; *Grant County Herald*, November 25, 1862; Nolan, *The Iron Brigade*, 166–67, 171–73; Herdegen, *The Iron Brigade*, 117, 313–14; *OR*, ser. 1, vol. 19, pt. 1, 171.

8. The Iron Brigade became part of the Fourth Brigade (Solomon Meredith), First Division (Brig. Gen. Abner Doubleday), First Army Corps (Maj. Gen. John Reynolds), Left Grand Division (Maj. Gen. William Franklin). Maj. Gen. Franz Sigel, who commanded the Eleventh Army Corps, was headquartered near Fairfax Court House in early December, and Maj. Gen. Samuel P. Heintzelman was in command of the defenses of Washington, DC. *OR*, ser. 1, vol. 19, pt. 1, 3, vol. 21, 57, 146, 847–48, 987, 1121.

9. Lt. Gen. James Longstreet was in command of the First Army Corps, Army of Northern Virginia. The reference to Hill concerned either Maj. Gen. Ambrose Powell Hill or Maj. Gen. David Harvey Hill. Both men commanded divisions in Longstreet's corps. *OR*, ser. 1, vol. 21, 560, 635.

10. Belle Plain, Virginia, was at the confluence of Potomac Creek and the Potomac River. Vitriolic rhetoric appeared in many newspapers after McClellan's removal as commander of the Army of the Potomac. One paper described his removal "as an act of folly, as well as of ingratitude." The paper later asserted that McClellan's removal was "unparalleled in the annals of war and only to be attributed to that insane policy." Others claimed that his removal created great excitement throughout the country and hurt the Lincoln administration. Nolan, *The Iron Brigade*, 189; "Democratic Mass Meeting: Great Uprising of the People," *Bedford Gazette* (Bedford, PA), November 21, 1862; "Intense Excitement in Washington," *New York Herald*, November 10, 1862.

11. Unquestionably, McClellan worked a miracle in refitting the army after the defeat at Second Bull Run. His reorganization invigorated the army when it desperately needed it and showcased his administrative skills. Wert, *The Sword of Lincoln*, 143–44.

12. A local paper stated that McClellan "is a charge against the union party—for inaction is the great crime charged by all parties against the union ticket. And McClellan too is claimed as a democrat—one who would vote to end the war." Another Wisconsin paper wrote, "The true friends of this country will rejoice" at McClellan's removal. Burnside reorganized the Army of the Potomac into three Grand Divisions, a left, center, and right, with the Eleventh Army Corps a reserve Grand Division. Some local publications understood the reasons behind the delay

of the army at Fredericksburg and defended Burnside's slowness. "We make this statement, as it is due to Gen. Burnside's future that the facts involved should be understood by the country from the start." Two corps of his army reached Falmouth on November 17, 1862, but, because there were no pontoons, the troops had to wait until they arrived to cross. However, demands from public and political circles pushing for an advance on Fredericksburg were more the norm. "The Elections in Grant County Considered," *Grant County Herald*, November 11, 1862; "The Removal of McClellan," *Janesville Daily Gazette* (Janesville, WI), November 10, 1862; "Our Military Budget: The Situation," *Evening Star* (Washington, DC), November 20, 1862; Wert, *The Sword of Lincoln*, 185; McPherson, *Battle Cry of Freedom*, 570; Herdegen, *The Iron Brigade*, 315.

13. The army waited until November 25 for the pontoons to reach Falmouth, by which time Lee had fortified the heights west of Fredericksburg. This mix-up was due in part to ambiguous orders from Burnside and General-in-Chief Halleck that resulted from confusion about where the army was going to cross the Rappahannock River. McPherson, *Battle Cry of Freedom*, 570; Wert, *The Sword of Lincoln*, 186; Nolan, *The Iron Brigade*, 175–76.

14. James A. Clark, Company F of the Seventh Wisconsin, was killed at South Mountain on September 14, 1862. Casanna Warner was the fifteen-year-old daughter of Jared Warner. *Roster*, 1:559; 1860 United States Census, Patch Grove, Grant County, Wisconsin, digital image s.v. "Casanna Warner," Ancestry.com.

Camp near Brooks Station Va Dec 3 1862

Dear Delia

I received you letter of Nov 10 last night. It was a long time on the radd but is was verry welcome. I was glad to hear you were all well.

We are now encamped between Aquia Creek and Fredricksberg. We are now on the R Road and get plenty of hard crackers and fat pork. I have been about sick for two or three days with bad cold and Rheumatism. I have just finsished a long letter to Father, and intended writing a long one to you tomorrow, but we are ordered to march at daylight. I would have written sooner but we have been expecting the Paymaster every day for the last week and i wanted to send you some money but he has not showed his presence to our Brigade yet. Capt Callis has gone home recruiting, and when he gets back it will be my turn for a furlough, and i will get one if possible. The Rebs are on the oposite side of the River in force. Where we are going is more than i know. I am sorry to hear of the illness of Sergt McCartney, and hope he will get well. Give him my best wishes and also G H Henderson. Tell them co F has 40 men on hand for rations or fight.[15]

Give my best wishes to Squire Bergess and excuse this short letter for I am pretty well used up, and have considerable to do to be ready to march. I will write you again the first opportunity. Give my love to all the dear ones. It would be no use to tell you how, oh how, verry verry much i would like to be with you once more.

Ever yours

H F Young

NOTE

15. Callis left the regiment on November 17, 1862, to recruit men in Wisconsin. Alexander R. McCartney, Company F of the Seventh Wisconsin, was wounded at Brawner's Farm and discharged from the service on March 8, 1863, due to wounds. Wisconsin, Adjutant General's Office, *Regimental Muster and Descriptive Rolls, 1861–1865*, Red Books, reel 3, 7th Infantry; *Roster*, 1:560.

near Falmouth Va Dec 10 1862

Father

We have just got here. Everything is hurry and confusion. We were ordered to put up our money that we wanted to send home, for we have just been paid off and we have to send the chaplins to Washington with it to night. I sent $460.00 for you to J C Cover, $60 for Delia and $400.00 you.

We are to cross the Rappahannoc River to night. I have a thousand things to attend to.

Addieu.

Your truly

H F Young

Camp near Falmouth Va Dec 17, 1862

Dear Father

Here we are encamped near Falmouth and Devilish glad to get here for we have been in the wrong lox for the last few days. I wont try to describe to you the perfect contempt i feel for the man or men that run us into such a place as we have just got out of. Got out of did I say? Yes, but there is thousands of brave fellows that did not get out, that were sacrificed and butchered. This is perhaps treason but I cant help it if it is for it is truth. We crossed the River on the 12th. The Rebs, lying perfectly still to let us cross. We are the extreem left of the army. Our Brigade is the left Brigade of the army, and the 7th Reg is the left of our Brigade. So that as soon as we crossed the River we filed off down the River. We crosed about two miles below Fredricksberg. Just after we had got a cross the River the Rebs commenced shelling us, but hurt none of our Brigade.[16]

Now I want to tell you something about the lay of the land on the other side of the River. Then let us commence at the falls, above Falmouth. Here the blufs or heights cross the River by the time the River reaches Fredricksberg. The flats or low land is half a mile wide. That is it is about half a mile of flat botom land untill you reach the first raise of ground. As you proceede down the River this flat of bottom land widens untill it gets to be about one mile wide. It is not more than one mile wide at the widest place between the falls at Falmouth and the mouth of the Massaponock creek 7 miles below where the bluffs come to the River. Now on this first range of high land the Rebs had thrown up earth works, but had no seige guns.

This was the line our troops carried, in the centre and on the right. But from ½ to one mile from the hights there is another range of heights higher and more abrupt. It was on this range of heights which is mostly covered with timber that the Rebs had their seige guns and heavy fortifications. But still in rear of this from one to two miles is another range of heights. On the other sided of Massaponock creek the Rebs had this fortified also, and wer working on these hights all the time. We were on the other side of the River when we were not actually engaged in action. This will give you an idea of the lay of the country on the other side of the River. On this side the bluffs or heights are closer to the River. The same as our western or the Ohio river, you no that on the Ohio River where there is wide bottom land on one side of the River. The heights come close to the River on the other side. It is the same here. We lay all night of the 12th just below where we crossed the River. On the morn of the 13th we were formed in line of battle in the following order. The 7th, and 24 Mich, formed the first line. The 2d 6th Wis, and 19th Ind formed the 2d line in our rear. Our line of battle faced down stream.[17]

We had not more than got formed when the order was given to march. We advanced down the river at a steady pace. Battery B, our favourite Battery rite Between us and the 24th Mich. The Rebs would make a short stand when the Battery would pour in a few rounds of shell when they would always fall back. We continued to advance and they to retreat in this way untill we had driven them about three miles, when the order came for us to hold our position but to advance no farther. This was after 12 oclock. Now the reason for this order was this. (but we did not no it at the time) Our men had been repulsed in the centre and on the right, and we were the only ones that could carry the line forward or extend our line. But you will perceive at once that when the centre and right were repulsed it became of vast moment to hold the left. In fact the salvation of the army depended on holding the left. The flat bottom land where our advance was stoped is about one mile wide to where the first range of hills are, which here raises quite abrupt and is thickly covered with timber. And the Rebs, had a line of earth works threwn up just about half way up the first ascent, and an other just at the crest of the first hill. The land between this and the River is flat and has been ditched for drainage. These ditches or drains are on the lowest ground, and in this sandy soil are washed quite deep.[18]

Now as soon as the right and centre was repulsed, the rebs appears to have turned their whole attention to us poor Devils on the left. I say poor Devils for there was only four Brigades of us in a space of more than a mile, and the Iron Brigade had to guard the left alone. Well about this time say 2 oclock they opened up on us one of the most tirriffick cannonades you ever heard of. But if they thought to scare us or make us run, (as they had some eastern troops) they mised it, for we formed our lines of Battle in the ditches where we could ly down, in no verry comfortable condition i admit. But when a man has to choose between laying in a ditch half full of watter or getting his head blown off he will generally lay contented in the mud.[19]

The Rebs kept up this cannonade of shell and grape & cannister untill long after dark and we held our position in the ditch. And they dare not advance on us with their Infantry for then they would have had no advantage of us and we would have given them a little touch of northwestern hell. We held this position untill the night of the 15th when we retreated across the River. I must admit the retreat was well conducted. The Rebs never knew a thing about it until morning, when every man of our army was safe over the River and the Pontoons taken up. The fact is they were so sure of us that they were careless.[20]

The fact is i dont have a verry high oppinion of Lee as a General, for we were there two days and nights on that low flat land with two hundred guns bearing on us, capable of threwing shells, spherical case, and grape and canister, over every foot of land we occupied. He let us lay there two days after our army had been repulsed, when he could have cut our centre in two and that would have cut off the left Grand Division from all chance of crossing the River. I fact that was their intention but they delayed it a few hours to long. They had every thing ready to commence the attact on the morn of the 16th at Daylight. Their program was to force their way to the Bridges where we crossed which they could have done under cover of their guns. Now from the position we occupide you will see that this move would have entirely cut off the left Grand Division.

We of the extreem left were expecting this and had looked out the place where we expected to make our last desperate stand. And desperate it would have been, for it would have been the last stand of the Iron Brigade. After we had got back safe across the River the Rebs to shew us what they could do opened a Battery of Whitworth Guns from their fortifications and threw solid shot 3 miles back of us on our side of the River. This was done just to shew us that they had longer range guns than we had. The 7th had one man killed and four wounded. Co F had one man wounded. Henry Hudson was wounded in the head by a minnie ball. (wound not dangerous) Our Brigade had about 20 killed and about 50 wounded. Now i beleive this is a fair history of the affair as far as we were connected with it, but have a damed poor opinion of those that led us into such a place. I have just got a receipt from Adams express co for our package of money. My love to all.[21]

yours truly

H F Young

NOTES

16. Union casualties at Fredericksburg were 1,284 killed, 9,600 wounded, and 1,769 captured or missing. Confederate casualties totaled 596 killed, 4,068 wounded, and 651 captured or missing. William F. Fox, *Regimental Losses in the American Civil War* (Albany, NY: Albany Publishing Company, 1889), 544, 550; *OR*, ser. 1, vol. 21, 142; *Dyer's Compendium*, 911–12.

17. The Iron Brigade crossed the Rappahannock River on the afternoon of December 12. The brigade formed part of the far left wing of the federal line under William Franklin's Left Grand Division. Its line stretched nearly to the Massaponax Creek and was joined on the right by Maj. Gen. George Gordon Meade's division. Nolan, *The Iron Brigade*, 178–80; Herdegen, *The Iron Brigade*, 315.

18. Burnside, in a meeting with Franklin and Reynolds, ordered the divisions of Meade and Gibbon to advance on the Confederate left on the morning of December

13, 1862. Both divisions advanced and enjoyed early success. Confederate reserves were thrown into the breach, and the federal troops were forced to withdraw. The Twenty-fourth Michigan, advancing from the far left of the federal line, received its first baptism of fire. The regiment carried the lightly defended patch of woods before finding itself confronted by cannon fire from batteries belonging to J. E. B. Stuart. By the late afternoon the brigade was ordered back to a ditch that provided cover from rifle fire but little help from the unrelenting Confederate artillery barrage. Nolan, *The Iron Brigade*, 180–82; McPherson, *Battle Cry of Freedom*, 571, Wert, *The Sword of Lincoln*, 193–95.

19. The main attack, by the federal right and center divisions, flung against the well-entrenched Confederate positions at Marye's Heights, proved disastrous. Casualties in the divisions of Meade and Gibbon approached 40 percent. The Iron Brigade, holding the far left flank, saw little action compared to the desperate fighting in the center and right. Wert, *The Sword of Lincoln*, 196; Nolan, *The Iron Brigade*, 184; *OR*, ser. 1, vol. 21, 450–51.

20. The Iron Brigade, the last of the federal troops to withdraw, finally crossed the Rappahannock on the night of December 15, even as a Confederate force tried to capture it. The Nineteenth Indiana, having advanced beyond its position on December 14, was the last regiment to make it across the river safely. *OR*, ser. 1, vol. 21, 451; Nolan, *The Iron Brigade*, 185–86.

21. Henry Hudson, Company F of the Seventh Wisconsin, wounded at Fredericksburg, returned to duty and was mustered out on September 1, 1864, when his term expired. Iron Brigade casualties at Fredericksburg were nine killed, forty wounded, and sixteen captured or missing. *Roster*, 1:559; *OR*, ser. 1, vol. 21, 138.

Camp near Falmouth Va Dec 17 1862

Dear Delia

I received your letter last night and was verry glad to hear you were all well. Your letter found us just going into camp after our retreat across the river. It found us all well, but almost tired to death.

Our Regiment had one man killed and four wounded, while across the river. Co F had one man wounded. Henry Hudson he was wounded in the head by a minnie ball. (not dangerous)

We crossed the River on the morning of the 12th. Our Division was the extreme left. We crossed the lower Bridge about two miles below Fredricksberg, and immediately filed off down the river, and lay there untill next morning. On the morning of the 13th when the battle commenced we were ordered further down the River. We drove the Rebs about 3 miles down the river. The fight being all together with artillery, for they would not stand on the level flat land next the river. After we had drove them three miles down the river, we were ordered to hold our position to protect the left flank of our army. It is here about one mile of flats from the river to the heights or blufs where the enemy were fortified. About four oclock, after our men had been repulsed on the centre and right the ennemy opened on us one of the most terriffick cannonades you ever heard of. But our brigade was the extreme left. The land had been ditched for draining. We formed our lines of battle in the drains on the low ground where the men could lay in the ditches. And all the shells or grape they could threw they could not move us. And they dare not advance on us with their Infantry, for we would have had an equal chance with them and whiped double our numbers.

We held our positions untill the night of the 15th when we recrossed the river and got to our present encampment last evenning. And now let me tell you that the Iron Brigade sustained its old reputation, of going where ever ordered and staying till ordered away. But i am perfectly disgusted with the man or men that planed the movement for it was the damedest blunder i ever heard of a General making. To think of crossing here and storming those fortified heights, when they could have been easily flanked by the right or left. I cant give you a history of the fight in the centre or rights for i dont no the truth myself. I sent to Washington $460.00. $400 for Father and $60 for you. If that wont do you i will try and spare you some more. I ordered it sent to Cover. We had only abot an hours time to make up the package. So we put all our money in Envelopes, and sent it with the chaplin in one package to be expressed to cover.[22]

I am better than when i last wrote. Strange as it may seam to you, laying out at night with nothing but my rubber blanket between me and the cold damp ground, and nothing over me but one blanket my cold has got better insted of worse. If it is possible for me to get a furlough this winter you may depend on it. I will do it, but unless the army goes into winter quarters the chance will be slim. Give my best wishes to all the friends and neighbours and my love to all the dear ones at home.

Ever yours

H F Young

NOTE

22. Burnside ordered six different assaults on Marye's Heights on December 13, 1862. In desperation, Burnside wished to personally lead another assault with his

own old Ninth Army Corps; however, in the end, he decided against it. Samuel W. Eaton, the chaplain for the Seventh Wisconsin, was a Lancaster native and the Reverend at the Congregational Church. The second man to hold that post, he remained with the regiment until the end of the war. McPherson, *Battle Cry of Freedom*, 572; Guelzo, *Fateful Lightning*, 329–30; Castello N. Holford, *History of Grant County Wisconsin . . . and a History of the Several Towns* (Lancaster, WI: The Teller Print, 1900), 431–32; *Roster*, 1:539.

Camp near Bellplains Va Dec 31 1862

Dear Delia

This is the last night of 1862 and here we are encamped in the infernalest country I ever seen. The fact is there is not level land enough within this whole left Grand Division to set up a tent on. But that is not the worst feature in the arrangement for they wont allow our sutlers to bring us anything to eat. Not even for Christmas or New years. So we have to make the best we can out of what we can buy of the Brigade Commessaries which consists of hard crackers and plenty of bugs in them at that, salt pork tough Beef and coffee and Sugar.[23]

It is over two weeks since i wrote you near Falmouth, but i could not help it. We have moved camp three times. I wrote to you then, and had Pickett duty to do. We came to this camp about a week ago. The weather was fine. So we all went at it to build us cabins, as timber was plenty your humble servant amongst the rest. And I have now got me a shanty ten feet square covered with my fly, which is much more comfortable this cold night than it would be lying out under the open fly. Perhaps you dont know what a fly is, it is a piece of canvas 10 ft wide and 14 ft long. We usually put two forks in the ground and strech it over a hole. Our camp is two miles below Bellplains on the bank of the Potomac River, which is always covered with vessles, and steamers, and men of War, Gun Boats & C. We were put under marching orders to day, that is we were ordered to be ready to move at short notice with three days cooked rations in haversacks. You cant form any idea of how much we dislike to move, or how we suffer when we are moveing in this infernal mud. Then the lying out at night with one blanket, and a Ruber under us, is to bad for the ground is either wet and mud or else frozen. In either case we have to Suffer severely. They wont allow us any teams to haul anything and when you give men a heavy Rifle, 60 Rounds of cartridges, half a shelter tent, Knapsack full of extra clothing for a change, canteen, haversack with three days rations, one Rubber Blanket and one Woollen Blanket. You will see that the men are loaded down with all they can carry, but it is not enough to keep them from suffering in this climate in Winter. The fact is we need about as much clothing in this damp wet climate as we do in the cold dry climate of Wis.

Since writing you last we have one man die Warren W Whitney of Mt hope, and two discharged for being disabled from effects of wounds received in action, F S Kidd, and Collin Chapman.[24]

We have now here forty four men all in tolerable good health with exception of bad colds. Our co is now the largest in the Reg. 2d Lieut J W McKenzie has been discharged from the Service. Eugene Sloat now Sergt Majr has been recommended to fill his place. Sloat will make a good officer. Gen Wadsworth commands our Division. They are eternally *changing changing*. They will displace a good officer that has been tried, for some political favourite that never seen a field of Battle. It is enough to make a man desert and damn the whole institution. ~~they~~ The way they are manageing things at Washington, between demagogues of polotitian Contracters that make money out of the war, and West point Graduates that expect Promotion out of it, they will succeed in ruining the Government Country and everything else. There is one thing certain. The way the war is being managed now will give the South their independence before another New year comes round. The army feel that the men at the head of affairs are going it blind, and are as it were becomeing desperate; and are capable of ordering anything that will have the show or even possibility of winning. The idea of moveing this army now is perfectly ridiculous. We can hardly get provisions here just two miles from the landing in sufficient quantities [illegible phase] our army, through this infernal mud. Well tomarrow the emancipation proclamatin frees all the slaves of disloyal owners. Now we will if the negroes have any ambition to help them selves. I dont beleive they have, and i am sorry for it for if they would raise a little disturbance in the cotton states it would soon disperse Lees Army from Fredricksberg.[25]

It is along time since i received a letter from you but i suppose you are not at home. Did you get the $60.00 i sent you and was it enough for you? We were mustered again to day for pay, but i dont no when we will get it. Let me know when you will want some more. I am homesick as the Devil. I would like to eat my New years dinner with you tomorrow. I fear my chance for a furlough is slim. There has several of our officers applide for furloughs lately, but they have all been denyed at Corps or head Quarters. Give my best wishes to Furman & Caroline and Mr and Mrs Bergess. Give my love to all the dear ones. Tell them i would like to see them verry much indeed. In fact i have had always to cheer the boys up when they got down hearted, but now i have got the blues myself, and i cant see anything cheering ahead. A happy Newyear to you all.

good night

H F Young

NOTES

23. The Army of the Potomac went into winter quarters at Belle Plain, Virginia, located along the Potomac River at the confluence of Potomac Creek. The officers had slightly better quarters than the rest of the troops. The main activity of the winter consisted of picketing along the Rappahannock River. Nolan, *The Iron Brigade*, 189–90.

24. Collins Chapman and Fletcher S. Kidd, both in Company F of the Seventh Wisconsin, were discharged December 7, 1862, and December 5, 1862, respectively, both due to disability caused by wounds received in battle. Warren W. Whitney, Company F of the Seventh Wisconsin, died April 7, 1863, in Frederick, Maryland, of disease. *Roster*, 1:559–61.

25. John W. McKenzie, 2nd Lt. in Company F of the Seventh Wisconsin, was wounded at South Mountain on September 14, 1862, and resigned from service on December 27, 1862. William E. Sloat, Company F of the Seventh Wisconsin, was promoted to second lieutenant on December 27, 1862. Brig. Gen. James Wadsworth received command of the First Division, First Army Corps, Army of the Potomac, on December 22, 1862. *Roster*, 1:558; *OR*, ser. 1, vol. 21, 876, 932; *Dyer's Compendium*, 284.

Camp near Bellplains Va Jan 9 1863

Dear Father

I received your and Delias verry welcome letter last night; and was glad to hear you were all in good health and enjoying yourselves. Your letter found us all right side up with care. We are holed up. Not that we have any orders to build winter quarters, but they encamped us here on these infernal points and hollows on the banks of the Potomac River, where timber was plenty. And we without orders put us up winter quarters. That is we built comfortable log huts and covered them with shelter tents. I have a log shanty ten feet square covered with my fly. I have a fire place, a table made out of a cracker box, a door made out of the same, a bedstead made out of split logs the flat side up. This may appear rough to you, but it is quite different from sleeping out these nights in an open fly. All the boys have built log huts. Four men would join together dig into the bank, (for you must know that there is not level land enough here to build a shanty on) and build their huts ten ft long, and 7 ft wide. They will cover it with their shelter tents. Then they will make a small fire place next the bank, carrying the chimney up the old fashion with sticks and mud. These huts are built in rows, with a street between each co. Here where two weeks a go it was thick timber, is now a city of huts.

We are under marching orders, but we know that we cant march, for if we were five miles from the River or Railroad, all the teams in this corps, could not begin to get our supplies to us. We have to corduroy every foot of roads we use, or every rain that comes it is impassible. So you may set the thing down that we are holed for the winter unless it comes cold freezing weather. Then our Generals probably will be insane enough to turn us out in the snow and frost with one blanket a piece and try crossing the Rappahannock again, if they can do it where we have anything like a fair chance all right. But this thing of storming the heights of Fredricksberg is played out. We have to do pickett duty forty eight hours every ten days, have two or three inspections and Brigade drills a week. The rest of the time we can spend as we please so we dont leave camp. I am verry busy now straitning up the Co books; which were neglected on the march, and making out the final statement papers of those that were killed and those that are discharge. Everything has to be made out in triplicate, which makes a great deal of writing. If it was not that i have so much to do I would have the blues like the verry old nick. For i tell you i aint satisfide with the way they are carrying on this war. The whole thing is one infernal scramble for promotion political power, and money. Those three things will ruin us yet, at least i fear so.

Young Rice is here. He came back a day or two after our retreat from Fredricksberg. He was a prisnor and paroled. He is well. Your question in regard to Capt Callis skulking behind the rocks. I will first explain. I would say there was no foundation for the story, and yet Callis probably take shelter behind the rocks. General Bayard was killed at the Battle of Fredricksberg. While waiting for orders the shels were flying thick and fast, one of his Aids wanted him to take shelter behind some large trees for there was plenty of them where they stood. Bayard scorned the advice, and sat down on the side of the tree next the enemy. In a few minutes he was mortally wounded. He lost his life and the country lost a valuable officer. Now this is the case with Callis. He was waiting for the Sharp Shooters to advance. The Reg had orders to lay down. He steped behind some rocks, for the enemy were sending in their compliments in shape of grape and canister.[26]

For my part I call any man brave that is always ready to obey orders. If it is charge on a battery why go in, if you are sure of being killed the next minute. And if it is ly down i go in for getting as close to the ground as possible. But Callis is not popular with the Regiment. He was not popular at home, and never will be anywhere else. He and I always get along first-rate. I do the work and he puts on style and it suits us both.

The fact is Capt has hurt himself here figuring for promotion, and he ought to be here now for maj Bill has resigned on account of his health be so poor. Callis is the next in rank but the col wont make the appointment. He leaves it to the line officers to elect. I will do what i can for Callis for he is really entitled to the place. General Wadsworth now commands our Division. He could not be elected Governour of Newyork, so he must have a place in the army. Thats the way things are done now. Displace a brave and tried officer thats always fought and managed his Division well, for some broken down polotition that never seen a battle fought. Rosencrantz appears to be given them fits in Tennessee. Good for Rosencrantz, but i am verry sorry to see the name of Lieut Col McKee amongst the killed. I would like the idea you segested of poping in on an old fellow some fine evening verry much, but the Devil is to get the furlough to do it on. After Capt comes back if we aint put in i am going to try it. I can get the col to sign it, and our Brigadeer Gen will sign it and both of them reccommend it. But it has to go through corps Head qrs, then Grand Division Head qrs, then to the Secretary of war, and be approved by all of them before i can get it. I tell you out of the number of applications that is sent in there is Devilish few gets through. Wishing you all a happy New year. I will bid you all good night.[27]

yours truly

H F Young

What is Nat Austin doing? Is he paying up intrest to Bar? Let me how he is making out. I am affraid he will do like bill did get all he can and pay nothing.

NOTES

26. Benjamin Rice, Company H of the Seventh Wisconsin, was wounded at Brawner's Farm on August 28, 1862, and discharged December 23, 1862, due to disability. An article in the *Madison Patriot* insinuated that it was cowardly of Callis, who departed the regiment on a recruiting drive back home, to leave his regiment at such a critical point in the period leading up to the Battle of Fredericksburg. During his absence William Ray remarked, "Lieut Young in command of the company and the only commissioned officer now. As Capt. Callis is in Wisconsin recruiting and hope he will never [return ?] again." On another occasion, Ray commented that "The feeling towards Cap is bitter now, verry. He has sent one man, a good fellow to Fredricsburg jail. . . . He stands very low with the Co." Notwithstanding these comments, in December 1862 the *Grant County Herald* defended Callis by stating, "Capt. Callis is known in this country to possess no part or attribute of a coward . . . and a braver commander never led a host than was this man." In early 1864, twenty-five officers, including Young, sent a letter to Callis that subsequently appeared in the *Wisconsin State Journal*. It stated: "We have been associated in obeying the military call of our country for a period of . . . two years, and now, that you must leave us, causes many regrets." The letter went on to say that, "it is certainly not improper to say, that your urbanity of disposition—your gentlemanly qualities, and your uniformly soldierly bearing, have impressed our minds with a sense of your worth." Brig. Gen. George D. Bayard, struck by a piece of shell at Franklin's headquarters, died the next day. He was five days shy of his scheduled marriage to the daughter of the commander of the military academy at West Point. *Roster*, 1:567; Lance Herdegen and Sherry Murphy, eds., *Four Years with the Iron Brigade: The Civil War Journals of William R. Ray, Co. F, Seventh Wisconsin Infantry* (Cambridge, MA: Da Capo Press, 2002), 162, 120; "The Patriot and Capt. Callis," *Grant County Herald*, December 9, 1862; "Expressions to a Gallant Officer," *Wisconsin State Journal* (Madison, WI), January 13, 1864; Wert, *The Sword of Lincoln*, 204; *OR*, ser. 1, vol. 21, 451.

27. Maj. George Bill, on the Field and Staff of the Seventh Wisconsin, was wounded at Brawner's Farm and resigned from the service on January 5, 1863. His departure opened the door for the promotion of Callis to major on the Field and Staff of the Seventh Wisconsin. The new divisional commander, James Wadsworth, a Union party candidate for governor of New York in the fall of 1862, lost to the Democrat Horatio Seymour by a vote of 306,649 to 296,897. Maj. Gen. William Rosecrans commanded the Fourteenth Army Corps, Army of the Cumberland, during the Battle of Stones River (Murfreesboro), December 31, 1862, to January 2, 1863. Lt. Col. David McKee of the Fifteenth Wisconsin and formerly of the Second Wisconsin was killed in the Battle of Stones River on December 31, 1862. The Fifteenth Wisconsin Infantry was part of the Second Brigade, First Division, and Right Wing in the Army of the Cumberland at Stones River. The commander of the brigade, Col. William P. Carlin, stated that the officers, including McKee, who fell in the battle "were unsurpassed in all the qualities that make up the brave soldier, the true gentlemen, and the pure patriot." *Roster*, 1:538, 804; *Tribune Almanac for the Years 1838–1863*, vol. 2, *1863* (New York: New York Tribune, 1868), 51; McPherson, *Battle Cry of Freedom*, 580, 582; *OR*, ser. 1, vol. 20, pt. 1, 174, 281.

Camp near Bellplains Va Jan 25 1863

Dear Delia

I just received your and Pas verry welcome letter. Verry glad to hear you were all well and enjoying yourselves. You are making quite a long visit, thats right. But when you spoke of our home being forever broken up it made me feel verry sad indeed, for tis the thought of dear loved home that keeps me up. Was it not for the loved ones there and the pictures of them that i continually build in my immagination little would i care what became of me.

And I dont build up hopes of a luxurious home but a humble home with my wife and children with piece and quietness. How i will enjoy it when it is my boon to get it. When out on a lonely pickett post, or on the field of battle, on the march, or in camp, these blessings of home wife and children are ever recurring to my mind. And it is this that keeps my honour unsullied. It nerves my heart to perform my duties, what ever they are. It makes me just and honourable with those that are under my command, for never will wife or child of mine have cause to be other than proud of the husband or Father while an officer in the Federal Government. So bannish that idea from your mind for my sake for if it once gets rooted there we never can have a happy home. As for the children they would at their present age be more under your influence and training than under mine if i was at home. So let us look forward to the time when this infernal war is over, and hope that may be soon. And by being separated so long we will be the better able to appretiate a home when we again get together. At least i will for it appears to me the longer i am away from home the more homesick i become.

Well Delia here we are back in our old quarters after one of the most damnable marches we ever had. It is well represented in some of this mornings commic papers entitled Burnside stuck in the mud. For if ever there was an army stuck in the mud we were. It commenced raining just at dark the day we left camp here we had only got eight miles. It rained all night. A cold rain. We build fires and stood round them all night. Next morning we started in the mud and rain to go six miles above Falmouth. By noon all the roads became impassible for Artillery. The frost had got out of the groung and the mud was half leg deep by the time we got there. The river had raised so that we could not use our Pontoons. The drift wood was thick, so that the whole thing was a failure. Not by the fault of Burnside or any one else, but on account of the rain and mud.[28]

We were out four days and four nights and we never suffered so much in the same length of time since comeing into the service. I would like to of had every northern man that says a campaign can be successfully carried on here in the winter time with us. I would liked to have had them here, had them each take his sixty rounds cartridges, three days rations blanket half tent and Rubber blankett, and in that condition been forced to made that march. It would have been the last of them and the last we would ever hear of winter campaining in this cley fine swampy land. I am sorry it rained for we would have been across the river and took the Rebs completely by surprise if it had not rained. The move was undutedly a good one, but the rebs know better about the country than we do. When General Lee was informed that we were going to flank him, he said the mud would whip us and it did.

Capt Callis is still in Wisconsin and I dont know when he will come back. If he was here i would apply furlough but they wont give a furlough to officers when there is only one left in a co. If Capt gets back before the middle of Feburary there is some show to get one. But i am going to try it as soon as I get an other officer in the Co.[29]

The boys of the Co are pretty well used up with the march but a day or two rest will mak them all right. They behaved well and stuck the thing right through. Wm Ray and Frank Boynton are both back with the Com an are both fat and hearty. I tell you it seems almost like home to get back into my old shanty once more, although we are liable to move again any day. There is a rumour that they are going to send part of this Army down to Gen Foster in north Carolina. I dont know whether it is so or not.[30]

But if it is so i want them to send us. We have been in the part of Va between Washington and Richmond so long we have become heartely sick of it, and going to a new place would suit us better than staying here. The fact is we have burnt all the fences and timber in this part of Va and it is almost impossible to get wood for fires when we are on the march. Then there is nothing left here in the way of forage so that when we move it takes about one half our teams to haul forage for the rest. Give my good wishes to all the neighbours and my love to the children and except the same for yourself.

ever yours

H F Young

NOTES

28. The headline in the *New York Herald* on January 24, 1863, was "Our Army on the Rappahannock—Stuck in the Mud." The paper postulated in a most condescending way that Burnside's army at best might try to flank the Confederate forces at Fredericksburg, but it would take a large movement of the army to have any effect on the enemy. The infamous "Mud March," January 20–24, Burnside's attempt to outflank Lee's position in Fredericksburg, started well, but torrential rains slowed movement to a mile per hour. Burnside had secured the blessings of both Lincoln and Halleck but went against the advice of his own subordinate generals. By the end of the day on January 24, the Iron Brigade returned to camp at Belle Plain. Burnside, incensed over his subordinates' machinations behind his back, issued General Orders 8, calling for the dismissal of Maj. Gen. Joseph Hooker, Brig. Gen. John Newton, Brig. Gen. John Cochrane, and Brig. Gen. W. T. H. Brooks. He put the order before Lincoln, telling him to approve it or accept his resignation; Lincoln relieved Burnside, at his own request, from command of the Army of the Potomac and named Hooker as the new commander. Lincoln, who still needed the services of Burnside, gave him leave and refused to accept his resignation. Young's view of who was to blame was not in line with the thinking of his fellow soldiers, who held Burnside personally responsible for their misery on the "Mud March." *New York Herald*, January, 24, 1863; McPherson, *Battle Cry of Freedom*, 584–85; Wert, *The Sword of Lincoln*, 213–16; *OR*, ser. 1, vol. 21, 752, 998–99, 1004–5; Nolan, *The Iron Brigade*, 191–92.

29. Callis in Wisconsin was on recruitment duty from November 17, 1862, to February 1863; on his return, he joined the Field and Staff of the Seventh Wisconsin. His promotion to major in January 1863 opened the leadership of Company F to Young. Just two months later Callis was promoted once again, to lieutenant colonel of the Seventh Wisconsin. Wisconsin, Adjutant General's Office, *Regimental Muster and Descriptive Rolls, 1861–1865*, Red Books, reel 3, 7th Infantry; Nolan, *The Iron Brigade*, 163, 197; *Roster*, 1:538.

30. Francis Boynton and William Ray, Company F of the Seventh Wisconsin, were both wounded at Brawner's Farm on August 28, 1862. Maj. Gen. John G. Foster, commander of the Eighteenth Army Corps in North Carolina, captured Kinston, White Hall, and Goldsboro December 14–17. *Roster*, 1:558, 560; *OR*, ser. 1, vol. 18, 60.

Camp near BellPlain Va Feb 7 1863

Dear Father

I just receved your last letter. We are here in our old quarters with mud knee deep, with snow one day rain the next freeze the next and so it goes. Our last grand move was a grand failure as you have doutless already learned. It was an infernal hard move on us. We were out four days in one of the infernalist storms I ever was in, and accomplished nothing but the killing of six or seven hundred horses and mules for the Government. It will ever be this as long as our millitary leaders persist in the idea of capturing Richmond from this quarter. The moment our Army is put in motion towards the Confederate Capital, the Rebs having the inside track can bring in an overwhelming force to risist us. It is the same with us if they would march on Washington. We by having the inside track on them, could bring an overwhelming force to defeat their object.

It appears to me in view of the Presidents proclamation that the true polisy would be to strike the Rebelion in some vulnerable part. For instance why not put a force of say fifty thousand men in the forts arround Washington and on line of the upper Potomac which will be amply sufficient to protect Washington from any army the Rebs can spare to send to attact it.

A few Iron clads between Matthias point and fort Washington would be sufficient to keep the lower Potomac from being blockaded. Then let the Rebs have the country between the Rappahannock and the Potomac Rivers and if they wish to occupy it with troops the better for us for the country is entirely cleaned out and will be a damage to them or us either to hold possession of it. Then why not ship the balance of this vast army immediately into the cotton states, and when it gets there let it subsist as far as practicable on the country as we got possession of it. You would soon see the effects of the Presidents proclamation and the traitors would soon feel it. The Rebs would have to keep an army at Richmond to guard against surprise, and if they still kept an army north of Richmond, as i said before all the better for us. For it would give us so many less to content with south. Richmond would not be worth a curse to us if we had it as milliaty point. There is nothing of consequence to be gained by its capture, and its only advantage particularly to the Rebs is that it is their base to opperate against us as long as we are foolish enough to fight them in this mountainous barren region between the Potomac and James River.[31]

And i am of the opinion if this disposition was made of our army it would not be long before the whole state of virginia would be free from the Reb soldiers.

Georgia is said to be the best state of the so called Southern Confederacy. Then why not ship Eighty or a hundred thousand men to Georgia, take possession of the country. Subsist our army on it. Free the slaves. Put them to work for the Government and my word for it we could do more towards crushing out the Rebellion in three months than we could by fighting here in Va three years.[32]

The ninth army corps is in motion but where it is going no person appears to no as yet. I suppose that Hooker is anxious to try his hand at crossing the Rappahannock but the state of the weather and roads wont permit any operations against the Rebs in that quarter for some time. We have had a severe snow storm. The snow was about six inches deep and it froze stormed and blowed equal to any thing we get up in Wis. But it all went off in two or three days. Had we not been in our log huts we would have suffered terribly. As it was however we used plenty of wood had good fires and kept comfortable. Capt Callis is still in Wis prospecting for recruits and it appears to be a slow business, for i have not heard of him getting any yet. He says the war feeling is entirely played out in Wis. I am sorry to hear it is so for i yet think we will get the right man in the right place and then we will whip them out of their boots. You know take hold is a good dog but hold on is better.[33]

But the dissentions and divisions of the north are begining to have a bad effect on the army which is another reason for my thinking that the army should be immediately transfered to the cotton states. The soldiers are well posted on all the questions of the times and such papers as the Newyork herald have a bad influence on them. I have heard men in the New York Regiments swear they would never go into an other fight, that they did not volunteer to fight for negroes & c. This has all come about since the election of Seymore for Gov. If the army was transfered to the cotton states, in moveing we could depend on the country for forage for our teams. Whereas in Va we have to bring all our forage from the north. If the administration would give Gen Butler 75 or 80 thousand men and send him with them into the cotton states, I beleive he would give the Rebellion the hardest blow it ever got. We have had an Election for Majr of our Regt. Capt Fennicum received the reccommend.[34]

The boys of the company are in usual health. I have reccommended Eugene Sloat for Second Lieut of our Co in place of J W McKenzie Resigned. Sloat is the first in rank and has always been a promt and efficient officer. All Kidd is still Acting Orderly and is always on hand and by his promptness and efficiency has always releived me of all the duties he could during the five months that i have been in command of the Company.[35]

NOTES

31. Mathias Point is on the Potomac River east of Falmouth, and Fort Washington is opposite Mount Vernon on the Potomac River.

32. Young's idea of sending an army into Georgia came to fruition the next year when Maj. Gen. Sherman advanced on Atlanta.

33. Maj. Gen. William F. Smith commanded the Ninth Army Corps until Burnside was assigned command on March 17, 1863. The corps, transferred from the Army of the Potomac, moved from Falmouth to Newport News, Virginia, during the second half of February. For a time, the Ninth Corps was part of the Department of the Ohio. The fall elections of 1862, the Emancipation Proclamation, and a string of defeats gave the Copperheads momentum in the first half of 1863. Edward G. Ryan, a Democratic leader, emerged as a leading Copperhead in Wisconsin, especially after a speech in Milwaukee that placed blame for the war on the North. However, few went as far as Marcus "Brick" Pomeroy, editor of the La Crosse *Democrat.* Traveling with Wisconsin soldiers in Missouri and Arkansas, Pomeroy lost "all respect for Lincoln and his generals." Returning to La Crosse, he continued the vitriol and eventually alienated his own followers. *OR*, ser. 1, vol. 18, 149, 539; Current, *The Civil War Era, 1848–1873*, 2:404; Frank L. Klement, *Wisconsin and the Civil War: The Home Front and the Battle Front* (Madison: State Historical Society of Wisconsin, 1997), 41–42.

34. Emancipation fueled much of the hatred felt by the Democrats in early 1863. Newspapers such as the *New York Herald* published editorials discouraging further enlistments and tried to convince soldiers they had no further obligation to serve. One reporter traveling with the army said that the soldiers "will whisper in their dreams the name of their 'Little Mac,' and wish in their hearts his return to command." Such talk advanced the conciliation rhetoric of the Democratic press and policymakers throughout the North. In the midwestern states of Indiana and Illinois, the lower houses, controlled by Democrats, called for a peace conference to end the hostilities between North and South. Maj. Gen. Benjamin Butler authorized several controversial orders in the Department of the Gulf that eventually led to his removal from that post on December 17, 1862. His general orders on confiscating Confederate property and the treatment of women in New Orleans created agitation among the people in the South. Butler was much despised in pro-Confederate New Orleans, and he allegedly committed fraud in his administration of the city before his removal. Mark Finnicum was the captain of Company H in the Seventh Wisconsin and was elected to fill a vacancy on the Field and Staff when George Bill resigned because of his injuries. McPherson, *Battle Cry of Freedom*, 595; "The Army of the Potomac," *New York Herald*, February 7, 1863; Wood Gray, *The Hidden Civil War: The Story of the Copperheads* (Kirkwood, NY: Vail-Ballou Press, 1942), 122; *OR*, ser. 1, vol. 15, 426, 571–73, 611; Donald, *Lincoln*, 425; *Roster*, 1:538; Nolan, *The Iron Brigade*, 198.

35. William E. Sloat, Company F of the Seventh Wisconsin Infantry, was commissioned second lieutenant on December 27, 1862. This letter had no signature. *Roster*, 1:558.

Camp near BellPlain Va Feb 14 1863

Dear Delia

I just received your long and ever welcome letter. Glad to hear you were all at home safe and sound. Your letter found us in our old qurs and all in enjoyment of good health and considering everything in good spirits. We are having beautiful spring weather, but the roads are in an awful condition, and are likely to remain so for some time. Hooker is now in command of the Army of the Potomac, and the probabillity is he will put us in motion as soon as the state of the roads will permit.

I am sorry there is so much despondency and hostillity shown against the war in the north. It has a bad and depressing effect on the soldiers. I sometimes catch the contageon myself. Then when i come to think over other civil wars, and think of the length of time it has always taken to settle them, I again feel hopeful for our cause. When we studdy the magnitude of this rebellion and compare it with others in history, all others dwindle into insignifficence by the comparrison and if the loyal people of the north will hold on and be patient, we will yet get the right man in the right place. And then we will whip them back into the union with or without negroes just as we please. You know the old saying. (take hold is a good dog but hold on is better)

The Ninth Army Corps has embarked here and is gone but it is not known where. I think perhaps to join Fosters force in North Carrolina. The fact is i am of the oppinion that it is no use fighting any more here. This country lying between Washington and Richmond is not worth fighting for now, and as long as we fight them here they have the inside track on us. The moment we start for Richmond they commence prepareing for us. They always choose the ground to fight on which in this mountainous country is equal to one half. And then if we were to take Richmond it would not be worth anything to us as a base for millitary opperations. I think the best thing to be done now, is to put fifty thousand men in the forts round Washington and on the line of the upper potomac, which would be sufficient to protect Washington and Maryland form any army the Rebs can send against it.

Then put a few Iron Clads on the Potomac between Matthis point and fort Washington to keep the lower Potomac from being blockaded. Then let this army be sent south or west. Let it either land in the cotton states or west of the Mississippi River, and my word for it in either case it would be a severe blow to the Rebllion. So dont despair old girl there may be sunshine behind these dark clouds. You know it always the darkest just before dawn of day. You shewed some of the true grit for a soldiers wife when you wrote you did not care how it was ended but you hated to be whipped.

I read that parragraph to a lot of brother officers that was by when i received the letter and they complimented your grit. They thought it had the true ring. So i did not read the rest in the hearing of any one but as you were asshamed of it yourself i wont say any thing about it, for i know that the weoman that are left at home with families have an equally hard time of it with the soldiers.

As for a Furlough. I cant tell when i can get one. Capt Callis is still in Wis. But of one thing you may be assured. I will get one as soon as i can. Sloat has not got his commision yet. Dont know when he will.[36]

To answer your enquires about what would be best to do with the children if we should both die is a hard question to answer. And I think you had the blues awfully or you would not have asked it. What would become of them if we were both at home and should both take sick and die? You perhaps will say you dont know what. Well i can tell you the strong probability is if i should get killed that you would be able with the pension you received from Government to raise your children. And if you should take sick and die which you certainly will some day, if the children are yet under age the pension goes to them, and will go so far towards their suppoart and education.

There is no probability of us both handing in our resignations at once. So the one that is left must do their duty by doing their best to raise the children and have them educated. But always reccollect one thing. (friends are not always relatives, neither are relatives always friends) But let us drop the subject for it has nothing to do with the present, for the reason that i feel confident that at least one of us will be left to a good old age to raise and care for our dear little family. Give my good wishes to squire Bergess and family, and Furmans foks, and all the neighbours. Tell Jared I want another letter from him soon. Kiss Laura and May for me, and write soon and accept for yourself and our dear little ones my love.

Ever yours

H F Young

I have had to write the last two pages of this in a hurry to get it in the mail of today.

NOTE

36. This statement was curious given that Sloat's promotion was dated December 27, 1862. However, it may be that Sloat's notification had not reached him by this date, even though the promotion was already official. *Roster*, 1:558.

CHAPTER FIVE

"We have had three days terrible fighting"

March 1 to July 27, 1863

Camp near BellPlain Va March 1, 1863

Dear Delia

I just got into camp after forty eight hours picktt duty in rain and mud, found your welcome letter waiting for me. Verry glad indeed to find you were all in good health. Delia this the anniversary of our marriage, and I have thought so much about it and let my mind run on home and the dear ones there that i am almost homesick. You dont know how lonesome a person can get out on an out post. There everything is quiet. All an officer has to do is to post his men to guard against surprise, and as there is no chance of sleeping at night on the out post a person has time to think and from thinking to building air castles & c.

We have had a terrible storm since i wrote you last. The snow was just about 1 ft deep and it froze for two days and nights real hard. Then it commenced raining and now the snow is all gone and we have in its place the usual bed of Virginia mud. The roads have become so bad that teams cant go at all. They pack our provision and forage from the landing on mules and horses.

But it will soon be spring. The wind and sun will dry up the mud again. Then will come the marching orders, which to tell you the truth i long to hear, for we have got to fight it out and nothing gives me the blues so much as this being mud bound. And yet i know we cant move untill it dries up. I wish that every northern editor had to march just one day in mud with a knapsack on his back with gun and sixty rounds cartridges, just what our men have to carry. You would never hear them advocating a move in the mud again.

I am sorry about the accident to the mill but i would have it fixed again as soon as possible, and I hope Father will so order. The Grant co Hearld got Sloat appointed Lieut, before he got his com. That all came from my writing to Capt Callis that I had reccommended him. Cover took it for granted that he was com. He is looking for his commission every day. I could not get a furlough if he was commisioned before the middle of march or the first of Aprile. If he had his commission for we have all the officers absent on furlough that existing orders allow us. The orders are that no Regt can have more than two line officers absent on furlough at one time. So the collonel called us down to his tent and classed us off in three classes, putting those that were best entitled in the first class, with the understanding that the first class all got furloughs before the 2d class had a chance to apply. Then each class drew lots for who should go first. I drew No (5) 1st class. But this cutting us down to two absent at a time will bring it the first of April before my time comes round. Then if we are not on the march i will get a furlough. At all events i will get one as soon as I can for i think i want to see you and the babies as bad as you do me.[1]

I am real glad Mr Bergess and family live so near you this winter. Give them my best wishes and tell the Squire to write me a letter. I dont really know but what i owe him one now, but if i do i must of got his last summer when on the march and have forgotton. But tell him a write me a long letter and i will answer. Give my love to the dear ones.

Ever yours

H F Young

NOTE

1. Joseph Cover was the owner and editor of the *Grant County Herald.*

Camp near BellPlain Va March 10 1863

Dear Delia

I received you welcome and interresting letter two days ago. Verry glad to hear you were all well and better pleased to find you were in such good spirits. I have been commisseoned and assumed the title of Capt Young, Co F 7th Regt Wis Vol. Wont you congratulate me? The col said it was well earned and truly deserved which makes it in my case better still. Wm E Sloat will now be 1st Lieut, and I will have All Kidd for Sec Lieut. Comp F will then be well officered if i do say it myself.[2]

Well old gall. It is just one year ago to day since that we broke up camp at Arlington, and as if to commemorat the the 10th of march, we have this morning been put under marching orders. Never did I feel in better spirits about the war than i do now, and that appears to be the general feeling in this army. Every one feels and appears to know that in old Jo Hooker as the boys call him we have got a com of the right stamp. One that will fight it out with the Rebs to the bitter end.

What do I think of the nagur? Now, I say arm and equip them giving them the same pay and all the rights and privliges of white soldiers with the same rewards fo merit, and if there is any fight in them let us have the benefit of it. (will that do)

The late Congress has placed almost unlimited power in the hands of the President and his Cabinet. Now I say sustain them. Let the loyal people of every section, of every coulour, of every polittical party raise in their might, burry their party strife, and come to the suppoart of the administration and we will end this monstrous Rebellion the coming summer. This Army notwithstanding that croakers and peace party men have tried to make it out disorganized, is loyal to the core, and never was an army in better condition, either phisically or in point of military decipline. Gen Hooker has been weeding it out and has sent the disloyal officers and those that always that managed to get sick about the time a battle was to come of home to be taken care of by the Weoman.[3]

The order is to be ready to march without transportation so that we go without wagons. Every man officer and private must carry what he will need, both in the way of provision and tents and blankets. One year ago such an order would have been considered impracticable, now it is greeted with applaus by men and officers. They say go in old Jo weel help you. Damed if i aint willing to starve for a week to whip them out says one. Thems my sentiments says another. Lets pile them through giving them no time to build fortifications says a third. And so it goes. Every boddy except the regular coward appears in good spirits. Lieut Sloat is gone home on a furlough. He got a furlough as Sergt Majr and got off before his commission arived, well knowing that after he got to be a com officer there would be no chance for furlough.

Capt Callis is Majr and as the Lieut Col has been discharged he will now be promoted to Lieut Col, and Capt Fennicum Majr. The roads are in an awful condition. It is certain to rain every night. At least it has rained every night for the last two weeks, and we cant move until we have a few warm days to dry up the mud. But it is coming the time of year to look for dry weather in this climate. I am sorry to hear about the dam being broke but perhaps it is not so bad as it looks. If I ever live to return to take charge of it i will build it more substantial.

I received Furmans letter. Tell him to let his hair grow on top of his head for a few days and i will answer it.

Dear old girl your request for money shall be answered by a remittance of green backs shortly. I have been mustered for four months pay and we are looking for the paymaster every day and as soon as i get it i will send you one hundred dollars, which i suppose will be as much as you want now. I cant see how it is that the 33d Regt suffers so much. They appear to be particularly unfortunate but that is the case with new Regts. We have a new Brigade laying in camp along side of us that burry from one to two men every day while our Regt has not lost a man by deth disease in camp this winter. We pay close attention to airing the clothing and qrs and to cleanliness and have every man change his under clothing once a week. In that way the Regt keeps in good health.[4]

I see that A R McCartney has applied for his discharge. Sorry to lose EK, he was a good soldier and a good officer.[5]

I see GH Henderson is married. Sworn into the service for life. Good for George.[6]

Give my love to the dear ones. You cant immagine how anxious i am to see you all. And if i can get a chance for furlough be assured i will take it unless there is an immediate prospect of an engagement. In which case i would not leave nor would i be likely to get the chance to if i wanted. Give my good wishes to all.

ever yours

H F Young

Come to look over this letter I am asshamed of the writing. I am getting into my old habit of scratching it off as fast as i can think.

NOTES

2. Henry F. Young was promoted to captain on January 5, 1863. Wisconsin, Adjutant General's Office, *Roster of the Wisconsin Volunteers, War of the Rebellion, 1861–1865*, Blue Books, 2 vols. (Madison: Democrat Printing Press, 1886), 1:558 (hereafter cited as *Roster*); Papers of Henry Falls Young, 1861–1902, Wisconsin Historical Society, Madison.

3. After two years of war, two-year as well as nine-month terms of enlistees were expiring, and losses on the battlefield made the draft a military necessity by 1863. On March 3, 1863, President Lincoln signed into law a bill, officially known as the Conscription Act, that authorized the draft. Over time, 292,000 men were drafted, but fewer actually ended up in the ranks. Draftees could hire a substitute or pay a commutation fee of $300 to avoid service. Maj. Gen. Joseph Hooker immediately began the process of reorganizing the Army of the Potomac. Col. Henry A. Morrow, Twenty-fourth Michigan Infantry, meeting with Hooker, urged him to rid the army of all vestiges of Maj. Gen. George B. McClellan's staff. Hooker's reorganization of the army on February 5 accomplished this except for three holdovers, Maj. Gen. John Reynolds, Maj. Gen. George Meade, and Maj. Gen. Darius Couch. Each man, who opposed McClellan's removal, refused to get involved with the power struggle in the aftermath of his sacking by President Lincoln. *Congressional Globe*, 37th Cong. 3rd Sess. (1863), 1,494; James M. McPherson, *Battle Cry of Freedom: The Civil War Era* (New York: Oxford University Press, 1988), 600–601; Allen C. Guelzo, *Fateful Lightning: A New History of the Civil War and Reconstruction* (New York: Oxford University Press, 2012), 459–60; David Herbert Donald, *Lincoln* (New York: Simon & Schuster, 1995), 417–18, 424; United States, War Records Office, *War of the Rebellion: A Compilation of the Official Records of the Union and Confederate Armies*, 128 vols. (Washington, DC: Government Printing Office, 1885–1901), ser. 1, vol. 25, pt. 2, 51 (hereafter cited as *OR*); Jeffry D. Wert, *The Sword of Lincoln: The Army of the Potomac* (New York: Simon & Schuster, 2005), 220–21; Lance J. Herdegen, *The Iron Brigade in Civil War and Memory: The Black Hats from Bull Run to Appomattox and Thereafter* (El Dorado Hills, CA: Savas Beatie, 2012), 330–31.

4. The Thirty-third Wisconsin, commanded by the sheriff of Grant County, Col. J. B. Moore, fought in the west. At one point the regiment mustered only 500 of the original 891 men who left Racine, Wisconsin. In March 1863 more than a quarter of the regiment was sick, and an article stated that "our regiment has lost half her men by sickness." Calvin P. Brainard, "Letter from the 33rd Regiment," *Grant County Herald* (Lancaster, WI), March 10, 1863.

5. Alexander R. McCartney, Company F of the Seventh Wisconsin, was discharged March 8, 1863, due to wounds received at Brawner's Farm. *Roster*, 1:560.

6. George H. Henderson, Company F of the Seventh Wisconsin, was discharged on October 25, 1862, and married Susanna Kidd on February 4, 1863. *Roster*, 1:559; Wisconsin Marriages, 1836–1930, digital image s.v. "George Henderson," Family Search.org.

Camp near Bell Plain Va Mar 21 1863

Dear Delia

I received your welcome letter yesturday and was glad to hear you were all well. I think you must have just about the same kind of weather that we have. We are having another terrible storm. The ground has been covered with snow for the last three days. It is now raining. Then it snows. Then it freezes and so it goes. Lieut Col Callis has got back but he is sick. Lieut Sloat is home on furlough.

We have had one of our boys accidentally killed since I wrote you last. His name was Adelbert Staley. You never seen him. He was killed by falling off a log crossing a ravine with a log of wood on his shoulder. The rest of the boys are in good health. We are all anxious to see the paymaster as there is no money in the Regt. The high prices we have had to pay for what we bought has used it all up. I am verry sorry indeed that i had to disappoint you about my furlough for to tell you the truth I felt almost certain of getting one and the disappointment was a sore one to me. And now I am bound to get one the first one that is offered that is the first time there is a chance for such a thing.[7]

Some of the officers think that there will be furloughs granted rite along 2 for each one hundred men in camp and two officers out of each Regt untill all have had a chance to go home. If that is the case i will get a furlough some time in may. So dont despair alltogether. There is quite a number of women in the Brigade mostly officers wives. There is one from Grant Co; from Platville Lieut Neumans wife of Co C. The Cols wife is also here. If it had not been for our dear ones that you would have had to left at home with no person to take care of I would have sent for you and had you to came down and camped with me this winter.[8]

We have had some fighting on our right for the last few days, mostly cavalry. But it shews us that there is still a large Rebble force on the other side of the River. There is no possibility of moveing yet for the roads are impassible. There is all sorts of rumers in camp about our Brigade leaving this division, but none of them are worthy of confidence. I have no news to write. I might how much i would like to see you all, how I long to kiss and embrace you all. But you know that already. But to tell you the truth i never felt more lonesome and homesick as the boys call it than i do today and yet I never felt in better spirits about the final winding up of the Rebllion than I do now.[9]

I have neglected to answer Furmans letter but will answer it soon. I have no ruled paper at present and i do hate to write letters on this unruled stuff. I am glad to hear you have got such a fine lot of wood, and yo shall have the money to pay for it as soon as the paymaster makes his appearance. My love to all the dear ones.

ever yours

H F Young

If this confounded paper was ruled I would fill it up.

NOTES

7. Adelbert Staley, Company F of the Seventh Wisconsin, was killed in an accident March 12, 1863, at Belle Plain, Virginia. *Roster*, 1:561.

8. Capt. Jefferson Newman, Company C of the Seventh Wisconsin Infantry, was killed in the Battle of the Wilderness on May 5, 1864. *Roster*, 1:547.

9. On March 15 the Eighth Illinois Cavalry was involved in an affair reported at Dumfries, Virginia, with no casualties reported. Frederick H. Dyer, *A Compendium of the War of the Rebellion Compiled and Arranged from Official Records . . . and Other Reliable Documents and Sources* (Des Moines, IA: Dyer Publishing Company, 1908), 913 (hereafter cited as *Dyer's Compendium*).

Camp near BellPlain Va March 26 1863

Dear Father

I rec your last letter last night. Was glad to hear you were all well and was gratifide to learn that the sentiments of the friends at home were so strong and firm for the Union and for a vigorous prossecution of the War. I tell you your Union meetings and Union Leagues are exerting a powerful influence in the army. Thousands of men and officers take their cue from the people at home. You hear of no officers now that want to resign, and the reason is that those that did resign or got dismised the service are looked upon at home as either cowards or traitors. And as long as publick oppinion is on the right side it will have the influence in the army for good and vice versa.[10]

Everthing is being put in readiness for an early move. Where that move is to be or when it is to commence is more than we can tell. Hooker has issued the order to be ready to move at any moment saying to the commissioned officers you must be ready to move at any moment without further orders. And I will hold every commissioned officer in this army responsible to have his command ready to move at any moment without further orders, and that the men must carry with them ten days raitons of bread sugar and coffee in their knapsacks. The beef will be drove with us on foot. Now there is a meaning to all this and speculation runs high that is we all know from the desperate character of the men isuing the order that we are going to make a dash somewhere and that dash is to be made without teams and that we will either win a briliant victory or be devlishly whiped for Hooker is none of your chicken hearted half way men.

Every man is preparing himself for the terrible strugle. We have the utmost confidence in Hooker and we know that thousands of us will perhaps bite the dust and yet there is no murmering. This verry order of marching without transportation which one year ago would have been considered impractible is now hailed with enthusiam both by men and officers, and every one appears to feel that we will whip them out this time. A balloon reconniscence the other day shows a large force on the other side of the river.[11]

Eugene Sloat is 1st Lieut. All Kidd is 2d Lieut Co F. The boys of the co are in good health and spirits. One of co was accidently killed since i wrote you last. His name was Adelbert Staley. He enlisted with us at Lancaster when we first organised. His parents live in Portage. He was a good soldier. Callis is here and is Lieut Col. Fennicum is Majr.

I am glad you have got that Austin place arranged for i was uneasy about it. That is a verry nice Eighty of land you got with plenty of good water and nice young timber on it.

We have got no pay yet and we have nearly five months pay due us and we are begining to feel the want of it. I would have liked a furlough verry much this winter but there was no other officer in the co. Now when I have officers I could not think of excepting a furlough even if I could get one which is not likely. Active service is the order now and i look upon every officer that asks for leave of absence on the eve of an engagement as unworthy to hold a position in the army. I will try and keep you posted in refference to our movements.

Give my best wishes to all.
yours truly

H F Young

NOTES

10. Union Leagues sprang up across the North in response to the perceived threat of secret Democratic societies such as the Democratic Knights of the Golden Circle and the Order of the American Knights. The leagues, created by businessmen and other prominent citizens, ostensibly became an auxiliary of the Republican Party and in some states, including parts of Wisconsin, called themselves the Union Party. Several meetings were called in early March 1863 in various parts of Grant County. The Lancaster League met on Friday, March 6, and another meeting was held in Boscobel on March 20. According to one article, the only requirement for membership was support for the Union and the war. McPherson, *Battle Cry of Freedom*, 599; "Union Leagues," *Grant County Herald*, March 10, 1863.

11. A reconnaissance balloon moved to Falmouth on March 13, according to a correspondent for the *Philadelphia Enquirer*. "From Gen. Hooker's Army," printed in the *Alexandria Gazette* (Alexandria, Virginia), March 16, 1863.

Camp near BellPlain April 17 1863

Dear Delia

I have rec two letters from you since i wrote you last. The reason is that we have been expecting the Paymaster every day this week and i wanted to send you some money before I wrote. But he has thus far failed to shew us his welcome countence. I am glad to hear you were all well, and tell Laura and Jared that papa thinks a great deal of their letters, and says for them to be good children and learn fast and papa will bring them some new books when he comes home. Dear old girl, your wish that I would be more explisit about my going home, shews how little you know military life for I might be promised a furlough tomorrow and some order from the War Department or the Com Genrl, knock it all in the head. The fact is I dont know myself anything about it. Only that if they continue to grant furloughs I will get one some time in May.

We have been having a week of Reviews and Inspections. Old Abe, and lady has been round amongst us, then appeared well satisfide with the discipline and appearance of the Army of the potomac. And well they may for it is certainly in splendid condition.[12]

The weather has been cold and wet untill within the last four days which is warm and windy like spring.

Everything is confounded dul in camp. No news of any kind. I was sorry Sloat did not call on you but he had no chance. He went out with Ury, and

Ury had to go home by way of Waterloo and would not take the time to run round with him. So that he appollogised to me when he returned for not calling as it was part of the program before he left here that he was to call if he could. In selling the cow you did perfectly right if you did not want the milk.

As soon as the paymaster comes I will send your money right to cass-ville by express. The boys in the co are in usual health. Some few have the diarrhoea but none are dangerous.

We are still under marching orders liable to be called out any moment. All the surplus tents, blankets and c have been sent off so that we can start any time on fifteen minutes notice. There is all kind of rumours in camp about our destination but the fact is if Old Jo knows himself he also knows how to keep the secret and that is right. But of one thing all feel the same at least in oppinion, that is that we are to have hard marching and perhaps hard fighting for when Old Jo fights he will win a splendid victory or suffer a terrible defeat. Now that navigation is open it wont take letters so long to go. Write oftener my love to all.

Ever yours

H F Young

TO, MAMA, JARED, LAURA, AND MAY, PAPAS LOVE TO ALL

NOTE

12. Early April brought several reviews of the men in the Iron Brigade. On April 2 the division paraded in front of Hooker and Brig. Gen. James S. Wadsworth. On April 6, 1863, President Lincoln, Mary Lincoln, Tad Lincoln, and Attorney General Bates went to see the Union Army at Falmouth. The president and his party were kept on board the steamer *Carrie Martin* when they arrived, because of a snow-storm. Lincoln spent three days reviewing the revamped Union cavalry, visited soldiers in the hospital, and reviewed sixty thousand men on April 8. The review procession took more than five and one-half hours. The *Daily National Republican* on April 8, 1863, remarked that Tad, the president's youngest son, took to camp life exceedingly well. Ronald C. White Jr., *A. Lincoln* (New York: Random House, 2009), 545; Alan T. Nolan, *The Iron Brigade: A Military History* (New York: Macmillan, 1961), 206; "From the Army of the Potomac, the President and Mrs. Lincoln and Attorney General Bates the Guests of Gen. Hooker," *Daily National Republican* (Washington, DC), April 8, 1863; "The President's Visit to the Army," *Weekly National Intelligencer* (Washington, DC), April 9, 1863.

Camp near BellPlain Va April 17 1863

Dear Father

Your welcome letter has just been rec. Glad to hear you were all well. We are still in camp. We have had our reviews and inspections which always preceed marches and battles. We have all been reviewed by *Old Abe*, and Mrs *Abe*, as the boys call her. From what i seen of the inspections and reviews I must say the Army of the Potomac never looked better, not even when lying in front of Washington under little Mc when we had nothing els to do but put on style.

We have five days light rations (which means crackers sugar & coffee) packed in the knapsack three days rations in the haversack all ready to move at a moments notice. Everything has been turned over to the Q. M. D or sent off, so that we are about in the same condition as if we were already in the field. ~~we~~ All officers and men have one Blanket apiece a change of under chlothing and a piece of shelter tent, carrying with us eight days rations. The teams are ordered to bring five days light rations with them when they come, which makes 13 days rations we will be provided with, or are already provided with to start. This ought to last us to Richmond. If we are successful it will.[13]

But it is no use to speculate. The attact on Charleston is a failure, and ours may be. I have no idea the amt of the enemys forces in our Immediate front. Our cavalry are across the River in the neighbourhood of Culpeper and Gordonsville, but I dont expect much from them as they have never done anything yet. (that is those of them in the army of the Potomac)[14]

The boys are in good spirits and the feeling is general or appears to be that we will whip the Rebs this time. The paymaster is verry much wanted amongst us. The boys would give him a warmer reception than any body else just now.

There is no news in camp. We are all in suspense which is worse even than marching in the mud. The meanest position or the most uncomfortable position which ever you choose to call it, that an officer can be placed in, is just such as we are in now. We have rec our orders and are held responsible for the faithful execution of those orders, and have no Idea when they will come. So that you see there is nothing but suspense. Give my best wishes to all fiends.

yours truly

H F Young

NOTES

13. The Quartermaster's Department was responsible for the logistical support of the army.

14. Several times in 1863 and 1864 the federal army and navy attempted to gain access to the forts in Charleston Harbor. On April 7, 1863, another attempt was foiled by the outlying forts that protected Charleston Harbor, but only after a two-and-a-half-hour engagement. Guelzo, *Fateful Lightning*, 302; *OR*, ser. 1, vol. 14, 241–43; *Dyer's Compendium*, 832.

Camp near BellPlain April 19 1863

Dear Delia

This is a beatitiful day warm and sunshining. I went out in front of my cabin and set down on a stump and for a long time wached the steamers and schooners and brigs on the Potomac when my eye fell on a peach tree in full bloom. This sight carried me back home again. It was on just such bright warm Sunday mornings that we always used to gather flowers together and I always endeavoured to surprise you with the verry first that were in bloom. And I think there are some, in bloom today in the woods in your neighbourhooed and what a pleasure it would be for me to gather them for you. Do you know that I sometimes get to thinking of you in that way and go on and picture it all out in my immagination what you are all doing and how you all look. You verry long well written and ever welcome letter has been received. Verry glad to indeed hear you were all well, but as for your trials and tribulations you talk about I think that they are doing you good. If you had nothing to *combat*, nothing to find fault with or in other words nothing to quarrel with onc in a while you would soon die with the blues.

Not that I think you would seek to quarrel with any body but I have confidence in you that you will take your own part. Now if you dont beleive what I have said about it is true, just pitch into me at the rate of two letters a week for the next six weeks and perhaps at the end of that time you will have proved that i am wrong. Yes as you hold the commission you are certainly Capt. But i will still continue to draw money, that is if our paymaster would ever make his appearance.

If i keep on i will soon have commissions enough to supply a whole family. But my dear old girl, you take care of the com for if any thing should happen me you will find them verry useful.

So your copperheads are beginning to hole up. Thats the best thing for them. Our Regt gave over three hundred votes for Dixon but not one for Cothren. The army is this day the soundest for the union it ever was, and is gaining every day in discipline and patriotism. There has been some movements on our extreme right in the neighbourhood of Ellis ford but as nothing in regard to the movement of this army finds its way into the papers. We dont no what it amt to. We still have our ten days rations packed ready for a move in one hours notice. But when that order will come is more than any of us knows. This suspense is actually worse than marching and now that the weather is good we are all anxious for the word fall in. Then our camp is not convenient any more. All the wood is burned, and as we use brook water as soon as the weather gets warm the water gets bad.[15]

We are having plenty of fresh fish. The boys catch any amount of them in the Potomac and they also catch Eels, which by the way are verry good eating. I pitty C. F. F. Under the circumstances it was Devlish little use of me to advise the letting the hair grow on the top of the head. Poor Devil. How brave he used to be. Who would have thought he would have hauled down his colours to a petticoat at the first broad side. Well i suppose he has the consolation that there is plenty more in the same fix. Rap rap tap tap fall in for Inspection.[16]

My love to all.
Ever yours

H F Young

NOTES

15. Several articles in the April 7, 1863, issue of the *Grant County Herald* railed against the Copperheads. One, "A Copperhead Kicked," referred to Clement Vallandigham going home to Ohio after he lost his reelection bid in the US House of Representatives. Another told of how twenty-five Democrats of New Canaan, Connecticut, had abandoned Governor Seymour of New York and joined a Union League. The spring election for Chief Justice of the Wisconsin Supreme Court pitted incumbent Luther S. Dixon against the Democratic candidate, Montgomery M. Cothren. The Democrats were initially hopeful as Dixon had admonished President Lincoln for suspending the writ of habeas corpus in a case pending before the court. Adding drama to the race was a recent law before the court allowing soldiers to vote in elections, except for judicial races. The legislature, sensing that another change was necessary, amended the law to allow the soldier vote in judicial races as well. This change was fortuitous for Dixon, as Cothren held an advantage on the home

vote of 56,840 to 51,498 for Dixon. The soldier vote, however, was 9,440 for Dixon and 1,747 for Cothren, tipping the balance to Dixon and ensuring his victory. The vote in the Seventh Wisconsin Infantry was 309 for Dixon and none for Cothren. The extreme left of the federal line engaged in operations at Rappahannock Bridge and at Kelly's Ford, Wolford's Ford, and Beverly Ford. "A Copperhead Kicked," *Grant County Herald*, April 7, 1863; Richard N. Current, *The History of Wisconsin*, vol. 2, *The Civil War Era, 1848–1873* (Madison: State Historical Society of Wisconsin, 1976), 405–6; Frank L. Klement, *Wisconsin and the Civil War: The Home Front and the Battle Front* (Madison: State Historical Society of Wisconsin, 1997), 38–39; "How the Soldiers Vote for Chief Justice," *Wisconsin State Journal* (Madison, WI), April, 14, 1863; *OR*, ser. 1, vol. 25, pt. 1, 3; *Dyer's Compendium*, 914.

16. C. F. F. was Cornelius Furman, Young's neighbor in Cassville. Furman, it seems, either elected to get a substitute in order to avoid service or paid the $300 commutation fee.

Camp near BellPlain Va April 25 1863

Dear Father

I this morning rec pay up to the first of march. I have sent off three hundred Dollars. I expressed it to Delia as she is nearest the express office, with orders to pay you $200.00 of it. It will cost you a trip to the mill to get it but that is just what I want for the oftener you call there the better.

I owe I G Ury about fifty Dolls which I wish you to pay the first time you have the money to spare and I will make it all right the next pay day. I have almost two months due now but wont probaly get it before July. We have had rain and flood and mud for the last ten days to our hearts content. I have stood in my cabin door and seen government wagons in mud till the bottom of the wagon box draged in the mud. This and the raise in the Rappahannock River will explain why we are not in motion.

Every thing is ready for a move and is kept so. The health of the Co & Regt is good. There is no news to write.

yours truly

H F Young

Camp near BellPlain Va April 25 1863

Dear Delia

I have just sent to washington $300.00 to your address. I could not pay charges on it as I could get no change. $100 is for you & $200, for father. All well. The Boat is just starting.

ever yours

H F Young

It will go to Lagrave.

~

Camp Below Fredricksberg Va May 4 1863

Dear Delia

We crossed the Rappahannock on the 29th. Our Brigade crossed in open Boats rite in face of the Enemy. Our Regt lost 3 com officers. Co F lost 1 killed and 1 wounded. There is but a small force of us over yet and we have thrown up entrenchments. All well and in good spirits.[17]

My love to all.
ever yours

H F Young

NOTE

17. The Seventh Wisconsin lost two officers during the battle; 2nd Lt. William O. Topping, of Company C, and Capt. Alexander Gordon of Company K, both killed on April 29, 1863, at Fitzhugh's Crossing. Washington Stever, Company K of the Seventh Wisconsin, was wounded but survived his wounds. William O. Ross, Company F of the Seventh Wisconsin, was wounded in battle and died on April 30, 1863, at Fredericksburg. *OR*, ser. 1, vol. 25, pt. 1, 173; *Roster*, 1:547, 572, 560.

~

Monday morning May 4 1863

Dear Father

I write from the field of battle some where below the mouth of the Rapadan River. We crosed the River below Fredricksberg on the morning of the 29 in which I lost one man killed and one man wounded. We held our possition till the morn of the 2d when we were ordered to fall back across the River which we accomplished without loss by 12 oclock PM. We then took up our line of march for this place and arrived here yesturday morn just at daylight and took our position on the extreme right. There was desperate fighting yesturday. The Rebs trying to break our lines, but they were repulsed at all points with terrible loss. They have not yet attactded our part of the line. We took the heights at Fredrickberg yesturday morn. The men are wild with enthusiam. I have no paper or ink till I get some. Adieu my good wishes to all.[18]

H F Young

NOTE

18. Hooker's plan to outflank Gen. Robert E. Lee had three separate pieces. The First, Third, and Sixth Corps would hold Lee's army at Fredericksburg while the remaining four corps would move west along the Rappahannock and cross several fords to roll up Lee's left flank. The Cavalry Corps advanced further upstream in order to disrupt Lee's supply lines. The initial phase of the attack was successful as the First and Sixth Corps crossed the Rappahannock below Fredericksburg. John Reynolds, the First Corps commander, gave the job to cross the river to Wadsworth's division. Wadsworth in turn selected the Iron Brigade to make the crossing, which it accomplished at Fitzhugh's Crossing, under heavy fire from the south side of the river. The Twenty-fourth Michigan and the Sixth Wisconsin were given the task of clearing the opposite shore of rebel infantry. They drove the Confederates from their positions and advanced to the bluff beyond the river, where they and the rest of the brigade dug in late in the day on April 29. The commanders of the Twenty-fourth Michigan and the Sixth Wisconsin were singled out for praise by First Army Corps commander Reynolds for their heroics crossing the river and for their seizure of the bluff beyond. They remained on this front until ordered by Hooker to the federal far right on May 2. They arrived near United States Ford and encamped for the night. That same night, at the far right of the federal line, the Eleventh Corps, under Maj. Gen. Oliver Otis Howard, was attacked by forces under Lt. Gen. Stonewall Jackson and driven back two miles. Wadsworth's division, which replaced the battered Eleventh Corps, arrived in the early morning hours of May 3 and occupied the federal right flank next to the Fifth Army Corps. McPherson, *Battle Cry of Freedom*, 639–42; Stephen W. Sears, *Chancellorsville* (New York: Houghton Mifflin, 1996), 155–59; Nolan, *The Iron Brigade*, 210–17; *OR*, ser. 1, vol. 25, pt. 1, 262.

Camp 1st Army Corps
2 miles below Fredricksberg between the Potomac and Rappahannoc
May 8 1863

Dear Delia

I wrote you a note when oposite here across the Rappahannock River. We fell back across the River the next day after my note to you, without further loss and immediately took up our line of march to the extreme right, where we recrossed the River next morning at 3 oclock and took our position on the extreme right of Hookers line on Sunday morning just at daylight. There was territble fighting all that day. The Rebs the attackting party but they were repulsed with terrible slaughter in every charge. They charged our centre three times with five lines of battle but it was no go. Our men stood firm as rocks.

They did not try our position although we were verry anxious they should. They withdrew from our front sunday night and fell with desperation on Sedwicks forces which had taken the heights at Fredricksberg and retook them monday morning. I think there was some mismanagement there as it was for getting possession of the heights that the forces were sent round to the flank, but where fault rests I cant tell, as everything is kept quiet.[19]

But we all feel that we got the best of them in the fight for we took over Eight thousand prisnors. Besides they lost terribly in killed and wounded in the fight Sunday on the right.[20]

On tuesday we had one of those terrible rain storms which this southern climate can alone produce. And as the country was flat clay land it was but a few hours till the roads were impassible. And as we could not advance through the mud we fell back across the River again without loss except our wounded some of whom had to be left. The Eleventh army Corps Seigles old corps behaved verry bad on Saturday night.[21]

The rest of the army behaved well and appears in good spirits. It was the intention to recross the river to night again but it still continues to rain and it is impossible to move pontoons and Artillery but we must fight here if whiped for we must keep this army from reinforcing Bragg against Rosencrantz.[22]

My love to all.
ever yours

H F Young

(this a scroll but dear i am tired to death so you must excuse it)

NOTES

19. Maj. Gen. John Sedgwick was in command of the Sixth Army Corps at Chancellorsville. His corps crossed the Rappahannock above where the First Corps was situated at Franklin's Crossing. For the first three days of the battle, Sedgwick's Sixth Corps did little until finally ordered by Hooker to advance toward Chancellorsville on May 3. Obstructing his path, Marye's Heights, scene of the December 13 slaughter, towered ominously above his approaching blue coats. On the third attack the heights finally secured, and Sedgwick was able to move beyond the city. Sedgwick, however, extremely cautious, missed an opportunity to roll up Lee's right flank and stopped cold in his tracks at Salem Church, three miles from Chancellorsville. Hooker, who called for a council of war at midnight on May 4, overruled his generals and issued orders to withdraw, and the retreat began in the early morning hours of May 6. Wert, *The Sword of Lincoln*, 246–49; Sears, *Chancellorsville*, 309, 348, 352, 375, 378; Nolan, *The Iron Brigade*, 217–18; *OR*, ser. 1, vol. 25, pt. 1, 156, 802.

20. Union casualties at Chancellorsville were 1,606 killed, 9,762 wounded, and 5,919 captured or missing, and casualties in the Iron Brigade included 11 killed, 46 wounded, and 3 captured or missing. Confederate casualties were 1,665 killed, 9,081 wounded, and 2,018 captured or missing. William F. Fox, *Regimental Losses in the American Civil War* (Albany, NY: Albany Publishing Company, 1889), 544, 550; *OR*, ser. 1, vol. 25, pt. 1, 173.

21. Howard's Eleventh Army Corps was strung out along the right flank of the federal line at Chancellorsville, an inviting target for Lee, who recognized the weakness of Howard's position and sent Stonewall Jackson's corps on May 2 to strike Howard's exposed position. Jackson, with superior numbers, struck with ferocity at 5:45 p.m. and drove the federal troops from their positions. Three regiments of Maj. Gen. Carl Schurz's division, the Eighty-second Ohio, Fifty-eighth New York, and Twenty-sixth Wisconsin Infantry, put up stubborn resistance and withdrew only when outflanked by Jackson's troops. Schurz's force notwithstanding, most federal troops in the Eleventh Corps fired a shot or two before fleeing to the rear and disgracing themselves in the eyes of their fellow soldiers. Schurz, seeking to vindicate his performance, requested a court of inquiry to investigate his command and conduct. McPherson, *Battle Cry of Freedom*, 640–41; Wert, *Sword of Lincoln*, 239–41, 255; Sears, *Chancellorsville*, 268–76; *OR*, ser. 1 vol. 25 pt. 1, 167, 630, 661, 798.

22. Gen. Braxton Bragg commanded the Army of Tennessee, and in early May his army, situated north of Chattanooga, faced Rosecrans's Army of the Cumberland. After the Battle of Stones River, neither Bragg nor Rosecrans seemed interested in mounting or willing to mount any serious attacks on the other until the summer of 1863. Guelzo, *Fateful Lightning*, 351.

Camp near White Oak C. H. Va May 13 1863

Dear Father

I received your welcome letter yesturday.[23] Glad to hear you were all well. When I wrote you last it was on the extreem right up the River near Chancersville. We had a terrible fight up there. The Rebs were hurled back at every charge. They did not charge our Brigade, but I seen them charge on our left with five lines of battle three times in all of which they were repulsed with terrible loss. On monday there was not much fighting till towards night when they charged us again with two lines of battle both of which were sacrificed. Next day we had one of those terrible rain storms which are so frequent in this climate. That night and next morn we recrossed the river without being interfered with. Our division constituting the rear guard. The River was raising fast. The mud was knee deep. We fell back in good order. The men were absolutely astonished at our move for every one felt that we had the best of the Rebs and could hold our possition as the saying is till hell froze over. We left our old camp near Bell Plain on the 28th April at 12 Oclock, marched too within two miles of the Rappahannock River 6 miles below Fredricksberg and there encamped till 2 Oclock AM of the 29th. Then we brok up camp and followed the Pontoons into the River. While they were launching the Pontoons into the River it became light enough see across the River, when the enemys picketts immediately opened on the Engineer Corps that had charge of the Pontoons, driving them back. The 14th Brooklin were ordered to deploy on this side of the River as skirmishers to drive the Rebs out, but they had Rifle pits dug on top of the bank all a long the River and it was impossible to disloge them from this side of the River. Our Brigad was selected to cross the River in the Pontoons and storm the Rifle pits on the oposite bank, and hold the ground till the Pontoons were laid. We striped off our knapsacks haveracks canteens and started for the River, the 6th Wis taking the lead. The 24th Mich next. The 7th Wis next, 2d next then the 19th Ind, all in the same order we had been marching in. Well all i have to say it that we done it in a way that reflects great credit on every man that was engaged in it. It was the most briliant and exciting affair I ever seen. The Rebs did some good shooting for the first round killing and wounded in all about 60 of our men and officers, but most of them seeing their fire was not likely to stop us jumped out of their pits and scampered off. We killed 26 of them Wounding a No of others and took over 100 prisnors. We had two pontoons across in just two hours from the time we got the order to cross. Wm Ross of my Co was killed and Ben Hayden was slightly wounded. I dont think we will move from here for some time. There are some 40 Regts going out of the service which will require a new Organization of a No of Divisions.[24]

The famous Reb Jackson is dead. So much for the fight of Chancellorville. He was worth twenty thousand men to the Rebs in a fight. The whole army feels fine. You cant make any person in this army beleive we were Whiped. And if any of those editors that write such slanderous reports would come down here and intimate as much he would be apt to get his head shaved and be drumed out of camp to the tune of the rogues march.[25]

Give my good wishes to all friends.

yours truly

H F Young

NOTES

23. White Oak, Virginia, was half way between Falmouth and Belle Plain.

24. The Fourteenth Brooklyn Militia was officially the Eighty-fourth New York Regiment, First Brigade, First Division, First Army Corps at Chancellorsville. The first note following the May 4, 1863, letter gives a detailed account of Fitzhugh's Crossing. *OR*, ser. 1, vol. 25, pt. 1, 157.

25. Stonewall Jackson was wounded accidently by his own troops returning from a reconnaissance of federal positions at dusk on May 2. The wound to his left arm, requiring amputation, left Lee without his best field commander. Jackson, who initially rallied from the wound, died eight days later. Young's assessment of the battle generally rang true among the men in the army. The rank and file could not see how they had suffered a "defeat." The Army of the Potomac, while deeply disappointed in the results of Chancellorsville, far from feeling defeated, was even more emboldened to redeem its pride. However, newspaper headlines told a different story. *The Evening Star* on May 8, 1863, reported that the army was greatly "demoralized" by the defeat. Headlines such as "Disastrous News" and "The Retreat is Confirmed" in the *Semi-Weekly Wisconsin* created agony among soldiers who felt they had fought well at Chancellorsville and had been let down by their commanders. James I. Robertson, *Stonewall Jackson: The Man, The Soldier, The Legend* (New York: Simon & Schuster, 1997), 754; Wert, *The Sword of Lincoln*, 254–55; Sears, *Chancellorsville*, 432–34; "Army of the Potomac, Further Details of Hooker's Recrossing," *Evening Star* (Washington, DC), May 8, 1863; "Disastrous News," *Semi-Weekly Wisconsin* (Milwaukee, WI), May 7, 1863; "The Retreat Is Confirmed," *Semi-Weekly Wisconsin*, May 7, 1863.

Camp near W Orchurd May 22 1863

Dear Delia

I rec your welcome letter two or three days ago. Glad to hear you were all well. Your letter found us encamped just where we were when i wrote you last. The rest of our Brigade are out on a reconnoucence and we are held in readiness to march to their suppoart at a moments notice if we are wanted.

The weather is verry warm and manny of us has the diarrhoea myself amongst the rest. It is seldom I have anything of the kind but i have had a pretty severe turn but am all right again. I put in my application for leave but they are granting none at present in our Corps.

I dont think our army will move for some time unless the Rebs do, for there is so many that their time is out. There is some Regt leaving every day.

We have got a beautiful camp. I wish you could see it. You would be astonished to see how neat and tidy our soldiers have become. If I have the good fortune to get home I can then explain to you all about camp life. We are all in good spirits. We soldiers are not like your citizens. We never get excited or elated about anything except when we are charging the enemy, so you see we are not effected with every blast of hot and cold as you are. We pay verry little attention to newspaper repoarts knowing as we do that they are mostly false. My love to the dear ones.

ever yours

H F Young

~

Bivouc near Centreville Va June 16 1863

Dear Delia

This is the first chance I have had of sending off a letter since I returned to the Regt. I reached the old encampment in good season and found our Regt already gone to Rappahannock Station. I repoarted for duty to the Act General and was ordered to pack up the property of the 7th and take command of the men that were left in camp and repoart at Rappahannock Station as soon as possible. After a terrible dusty march we got to Regt on Saturday. Sunday and Sunday night we marched from there to Mannasses Junction. And yesturday we came here. And where next I cant tell. We appear to be watching the motions of Lee, who has troops on the other side of the Bull Run Mts. The boys are all well. Give my good wishes to all. The mail is just starting.[26]

My best love to Jared Laura and May.

Ever yours

H F Young

NOTE

26. Young was granted a fifteen-day leave of absence on May 27, 1863, and returned in time to join the Iron Brigade on its march into Pennsylvania. Wisconsin, Adjutant General's Office, *Regimental Muster and Descriptive Rolls, 1861–1865*, Red Books (Madison: State Militia, Adjutant General's Office, 1865), reel 3, 7th Infantry.

Maj. Gen. John Reynolds (Library of Congress, Prints & Photographs Division, Civil War Photographs, LC-DIG-ppmsca-40576)

Camp near Guilford Station
Louden Co Va June 22 1863

Dear Delia

If you you take the trouble to look on your RR map at the R Road from Alexandria to Leesburg you will find Guilford Station. We are encamped between the station and Goose creek. What we are going to do here is more than I no at pesent.

We are all well but the weather is verry hot. Pleasenton had a set too with the Rebs yesturday in our front and drove them five or six mils. We were in readiness to go to his assistance all day but were not wanted. We are beginning to think that this whole movement of the Rebs was to cover some other move. Perhaps the sending of troops to the south west if that was their object. They have played a bold game and played it well but everything is in the dark with us. We dont know the position of another corps except our own. Give one of my photographs to Furman and 1 to Squire Bergess. My love to Jared, Laura, and may. Write soon. I want to hear from you.[27]

Ever yours

H

NOTE

27. Maj. Gen. Alfred Pleasonton, temporary commander of the Cavalry Corps, was ordered by Hooker to gather intelligence on Confederate advances in the passes of the Blue Ridge Mountains. In three separate engagements, Aldie on June 17, Middleburg on June 19, and Upperville on June 21, his cavalry clashed with that of Maj. Gen. J. E. B. Stuart. Union casualties were 76 killed, 307 wounded, and 208 captured or missing. Wert, *The Sword of Lincoln*, 264; *OR*, ser. 1, vol. 27, pt. 1, 910–12; *Dyer's Compendium*, 919.

Camp near Guilford Station
Laudon Co Va June 22 1863

Dear Father

We are encamped on the RailRoad runing from Alexandria to Leesburg just where the Road crosses Broad Run. What we are here is more than i can tell, for to tell you the truth I have known the least about Army movements since I returned I ever did about any movement that took place. We have had no papers for a week and if there are official orders they do not come to Regt Hd qrs. Genl Pleasenton had a fight with the Butternuts yesturday on the other side of the Bull Run Mts, About 12 ms from here and succeeded in driving the Rebs to Snickers Gap. We were within ten miles of the fight all packed ready to march but up to the present moment it appears we have not been wanted. I know nothing about the movements of other corps.[28]

I arived in camp on Thursday morning after leaving you, found the Regt off on a reconnoucence. I repoarted for duty to A A Genl of the Brigade. I was ordered to take charge of the Guards and camp of the 7th and have everything packed ready to march at a moments notice. We marched Friday morning at two oclock. Got to Rappahannock Station Saturday night and found the Old 7th and my boys of Co F all right. Sunday we marched by way of Sulpher Springs to Warrenten Junction. Sunday night we marched all night and arrived at mannasses just at daylight about the tiredest set of poor Devils you ever seen. That day we marched to centreville and since then we have been shifting round on a circut of ten miles till I am tired of it. Some say the Rebs are in force in the valley of the Schannandoah. Some think it all a front to cover sending off troops to the south west. Of one thing we are certain. Stewards raid scared Pennsylvania and our officials at Washington. At least they act as though they were scared. I sent you some cartridges from Washington by getting the no [number]. You can get what you want at Milwaukie. It is verry hot here. Write soon. Give my best wishes to all.[29]

yours truly

H F Young

NOTES

28. Pleasonton's Cavalry mirrored Stuart's advance from June 17 through June 21 at passes along the Blue Ridge Mountains as the Army of Northern Virginia moved into Pennsylvania. Allen C. Guelzo, *Gettysburg: The Last Invasion* (New York: Vintage Books, 2013), 92–93.

29. On June 22, 1863, Lt. Gen. Richard Ewell's corps reached Greencastle, Pennsylvania, intending to march on the capital at Harrisburg. Guelzo, *Gettysburg*, 95.

Maj. Gen. George G. Meade (Library of Congress, Prints & Photographs Division, Civil War Photographs, LC-DIG-ppmsca-19398)

Gettysburg Pa July 4 1863

Dear Delia

We have had three days terrible fighting. Our victory is complete. Our Brigade suffered terribly. I had two men killed J. Eayers and Darnell and ten wounded. Liut Kidd is wounded, not-dangerous. W. Ray is wounded, Callis I fear is mortally wounded. Our men fought splendid. We are all in good spirits but—tired and hungry.[30]

My love to all.

H F Young

NOTE

30. The Iron Brigade, which bore the brunt of the load early on at Gettysburg, was decimated by day's end and suffered casualties of 171 killed, 720 wounded, and 262 captured or missing. Former Company F commander John Callis was wounded early in the fight and was shot for a third time on the first day, with the bullet lodging in his lung. Miraculously, he survived the wound and resigned on December 9, 1863, because of his injury. However, near the end of the war, he enlisted in the Veteran Volunteer Corps. Alphonzo A. Kidd was wounded and eventually returned to the company. James H. Eayers, Company F of the Seventh Wisconsin, was not killed at Gettysburg and was mustered out on September 1, 1864, when his term expired. Thomas H. B. Darnell, Company F of the Seventh Wisconsin, died of his wounds on July 5, 1863. William W. Ray, wounded for the second time during the war, eventually returned to the company. *OR*, ser. 1, vol. 27, pt. 1, 173; *Roster*, 1:538, 558–60.

In line of battle near Funkstown Md July 11 1863

Dear Father

We had just formed our line of battle with our right resting at the base of the south Mt Range and our left on Anteitam yesturday when I received your interesting letter. Glad to hear you were all well. I have not time to give you a history of events since my last from Guilford va.

You perhaps think I should have written sooner but you have little Idea what I have pased throug since that letter was written. Every spare moment when not in line of battle or on the march I had to devote to the Co for three weeks. Our blanketts and under chlothing were wet. I have not had a chance to change my under chlothing in that time as it is with the trains and they are yet far back towards Washington. We were rushed into the battle the first day of July without suppoart and suffered terribly. Our Brigad was the last to fall back. We cut three lines of battle that were brot up in our front too peices, but we were out flanked. When we left the field the Rebs were in line of battle on both flanks within two hundred yds of us strung along for nearly a mile. We marched off at a right shoulder shift arms men falling at every step. Many of our men that had fought gallantly all day were taken prisnors by not keeping on the road. My first repoarts were wrong for the reason that I took the word of others in many cases. The list stands thus.[31]

Killed	W H Darnell
Wounded severe	Tom Garvy
mortally	Philly Bentts
severe	John Blackburn
"	I C Reamer
"	Wm Ray
"	JA Carrier
Slight	C F Dean
"	B F Hayden
"	D Rector
" and prisnor	J D Runion
had his leg blowed of and wounded in the other	G H Smith
slight wounded	J A Rice
Severe in thigh	Lieut Act Kidd
Prisnors	Sergt Persons
"	" Parker
"	Corp Schloesser
"	private Garner
"	" Huftill
"	" J H Eayres[32]

J H Eayres was first supposed to be dead but he is a prisnor. In fact it was impossible for several days to tell who was killed and who was taken prisnors in falling back the last time, for men were falling thick and fast around us and there was no time to pick them up or look to see who they were. But when we met them on the 2d and third dident we give them hell. Well we did. Our men were perfectly wild with enthusiam. There was one time on the 3d that there was 300 peices of Artillery belching forth at once, and the Iron was coming down almost equal to hail. I think this rather beat your annill salutes for the 4th of July. We as usual were again put in advance and arrived at the famous pass of suth Mt where we fought last fall just in time. Our cavalry was doing their best but there was a collum of fifteen thousand Reb infantry stedily advancing and were within 3 miles of the Gap when our Division commenced to file through and take possition of the oposite side. The Rebs fell back and took up a strong possition on the other side of Anteitam yesturday. We advanced and took our present position. Everything is quiet along the lines this morning. The Idea of baging the Rebs, as expressed by correspondents is all nonscence. We have already inflicted terrible loss on them and the Idea of bucking against the possition they have got and annihilating them would only be to lose all we have gained.[33]

I fear Callis is mortally Wounded. He was shot through the liver the ball remaining in him. Sloat is well and so are the rest of the boys that are with me.

My love to all.
yours truly

H F Young

NOTES

31. The Iron Brigade received orders to move out with rest of the corps on June 12. Their route to Pennsylvania took them through Warrenton, Catlett's Station, Bristoe, Herndon Station, and Guilford Station. On June 30, the brigade crossed the Pennsylvania state line and established a camp at Marsh Creek. The federal cavalry, under Brig. Gen. John Buford, skirmished with the lead elements of Lee's army early in the day of July 1. The brigade, in the vanguard of the federal force, advanced northwest of Gettysburg, where sharp fighting commenced around 10:30 a.m. The brigade, minus the Sixth Wisconsin, routed the enemy force at McPherson's Ridge and captured Confederate brigadier general James J. Archer. For their part, the Sixth Wisconsin advanced on an enemy force in the railroad cut, making prisoners of the survivors. First Corps commander John Reynolds was struck down early in the fight and was replaced by Maj. Gen. Abner Doubleday. His command of the corps did not last long; Maj. Gen. John Newton was assigned to the First Corps later in the day on July 1 and superseded Doubleday's command on July 2. Confederate forces, with the arrival of more troops, were able to flank the Iron Brigade and push them off McPherson's Ridge to Seminary Ridge later in the day. There, behind a barricade, the brigade made a stand before being ordered to Cemetery Hill and to their last stop during this bloody day, Culp's Hill. The casualties in the brigade speak volumes about the heavy fighting experienced during the first day at Gettysburg. Of 1,883 men who went into battle the first day, only 691 remained by day's end. Each regiment's casualties were at or above 50 percent with the Twenty-fourth Michigan at 80 percent, Second Wisconsin at 77 percent, Nineteenth Indiana at 71 percent, Sixth Wisconsin at 48 percent, and Seventh Wisconsin at 42 percent. Nolan, *The Iron Brigade*, 226–28, 230–36, 238–43, 245–49, 252–55; Herdegen, *The Iron Brigade*, 348–55, 365–68, 370, 373, 378–80, 394–400, 402, 403, 405–10, 412, 423–24, 427; Stephen W. Sears, *Gettysburg* (New York: Houghton Mifflin, 2003), 170–71, 180, 210, 217, 220; Guelzo, *Gettysburg*, 147, 150, 152–53, 161, 195, 200, 208; *OR*, ser. 1, vol. 27, pt. 1, 155.

32. Union casualties for the three-day battle were 3,070 killed, 14,497 wounded, and 5,434 captured or missing for a total of 23,001. Confederate casualties numbered

2,592 killed, 12,706 wounded, and 5,150 captured or missing for a total of 20,448. For the period between June 3, 1863, and August 1, 1863, Union forces suffered 32,043 casualties, of which 3,642 were killed or died of wounds. Fox, *Regimental Losses*, 545, 550; *OR*, ser. 1, vol. 27, pt. 1, 193–94; *Dyer's Compendium*, 827–28.

33. In the aftermath of the battle, Meade was seemingly in no hurry to give chase to the Army of Northern Virginia. Lee's army, battling rain and high water, crossed the Potomac River at Williamsport nearly unscathed on July 14, 1863. Meade's Army of the Potomac, a day late to stop the Confederates, was criticized by many who felt he could have dealt the enemy the decisive blow to end the war. Lincoln was intensely disappointed and wondered if McClellan might somehow be part of Meade's delay. Meade's defense, even going against his corps commanders' advice during a council of war, hinged on his soldiers' need for rest and a lack of supplies. Guelzo, *Gettysburg*, 433–40, 446–49; Wert, *The Sword of Lincoln*, 305–9; Doris Kearns Goodwin, *Team of Rivals: The Political Genius of Abraham Lincoln* (New York: Simon & Schuster, 2005), 535–36.

Near Berlin Md July 16 1863

Dear Delia

While setting by the road side to rest I write this. In a few hours we will be in Virginia, following up Lees Army. I did intend to write you a long letter but have not had time. We have been either in line of battle or on the march ever since Gettysberg. I have 20 men left with me in Co F that are all right. We have had no men hurt in Brigade since Gettysberg. The news is glorious from all qrs. My love to all.[34]

H F Young

NOTE

34. Confederate forces at Vicksburg, Mississippi, after a protracted siege, surrendered to Maj. Gen. Ulysses S. Grant on July 4, 1863. Grant's terms to the Confederate force demanded nothing less than "unconditional surrender," to the great dissatisfaction of the Confederate leader, Lt. Gen. John Pemberton. The two generals were not able to reach an agreement on terms of surrender, forcing Grant to change his original terms, and he paroled the nearly thirty thousand Confederate soldiers who surrendered at Vicksburg. Geoffrey Perret, *Ulysses S. Grant: Soldier and President* (New York: Modern Library, 1999), 263–64; H. W. Brands, *The Man Who Saved the Union: Ulysses Grant in War and Peace* (New York: Anchor Books, 2012), 244–45; Ronald C. White Jr., *American Ulysses: A Life of Ulysses S. Grant* (New York: Random House, 2016), 285–86.

Camp near Warrenton Junction Va July 26 1863

Dear Delia

After a day of constant writing and making out reports I must write a few lines to you in answer to your welcome letter I received this evenning. Glad to hear you were all well. I rec one also from Father telling me to write oftenner. I also received eleven others all asking for immediate answers. Some of them from Wounded boys, some of them letters of enquiry from home after wounded or missing ones. All should be answerd but I have not got the time just now to answer anything except to write these few lines to you. Tell mother Ray Wm is not dangerously wounded. He was wounded in the head. I have lost his address. I got a lettr from Gary. Rice. Blackburn. They are all doing well. I heard from Callis this evening. He is comfortable, so writes our sergeon. We arrived here yesturday and have been in camp all day. That is something new for us, but if it is sunday it has been a busy one. We were out of rations when we came here but a train of cars had just got here a head of us, so you ought to heard the boys cheer and shout. Now we will get our hard tack. Now we will get sugar & c. I heard from All Kidd this evening. He had got to his unkles in Salem Ohio. I think he will be home soon. I miss him verry much. Sloat has been acting Adjutant. Parsons is a Prisnor. Parker had his thumb shot off but the Rebs marched him off so that I have been almost bereft of officers. But All Kidd always took more work off my hands than all the rest put together anyhow. I was verry sorry he got wounded. I know it would have done his soul good to see how we cut the Rebble line that was advancing on our front to peices. And when we had done that and were flanked we marched off at a right shoulder shift arms by the right of Cos to the rear and took a new possition by the Seminary and when they brot an other line up in front of us our boys scarcely left a man of them. I never seen a line of battle annihilated as that one was, but it would not save our possition for while we were annihilating the line in front of us all the other troops had left the field and our Brigade cut down to less than a Regt were being rappedly surrounded by twenty thousand men. Then we had to break through their lines not only amidst the fire of the enemy closeing in on us from each side but from the fire of our own guns on cemetry hill. But the closeing scene was the grandest sight I ever seen. It was about 4 oclock on the third that Longstreet and Hill charged our centre with 40 000 men. Three hundred cannon were belching forth and sending a perfect hail storm of shell grape cannister all over our possition and also that of the Rebs. But above all that din we could distinctly hear the savage yell or cheer of the Rebs as they steadly neared our lines. It was an awful spectacle. Oh the Devil. I will quit. I cant convey any idea of it, nor of the feelings it produced. Why Delia at that time I would have threwn myself into the thickest of that fight with a pleasure, (*a sort of fierce calm demoniac pleasure I admit*) but it was the awful stake we were fighting for that made me feel so. For let me tell you that four hours fight desided the fate of our great republic. The papers are down on mead for *letting Lee* recross the Potomac. But damn them. They dont know any thing about it. For my part I am satisfide that there was about ten hours of time that we could nearly ruined them if we had made an attack but the devil of it was to find out when they began to cross the river. I was up in a tree watching their lines when the Signal guns fired for them to commence crossing. They were fired about one mile in front of me and fired at our skermishers. This was about ten oclock. If we had made the attack abot two or three we would have got them but they kept threwing up brest works till night always keeping plenty of men in sight. My light is out in a second. My love to all to Jared to Laura and May.[35]

ever yours

H F Young

NOTE

35. John Blackburn, 2nd Lt. Alphonzo A. Kidd, Thomas Garvey, Calvin G. Parker, Lorin G. Parsons, James A. Rice, and William R. Ray, all in Company F of the Seventh Wisconsin, were wounded at Gettysburg and later returned to duty. Parsons and Parker were reportedly captured at Gettysburg but are not listed on the roster as captured. In the fog of battle the pair, due to either wounds or confusion, may have become separated from the company. Interestingly, the *Grant County Herald* reported on July 14, 1864, that both men were listed as missing. Lee, who hoped to deliver the decisive blow to turn the tide of the battle, ordered the fateful charge by Maj. Gen. George Pickett on the afternoon of the third day at Gettysburg. Lt. Gen. James Longstreet's corps was tasked with storming the federal line. Longstreet, fearing the consequences of the attack, was not in favor but dutifully followed Lee's orders. To bolster the ranks for the July 3 attack, Lt. Gen. A. P. Hill, the commander of the Third Corps, was forced to part with six brigades, a transfer to Pickett that put the attacking force at fifteen thousand troops. The assault, the brunt of which fell on Maj. Gen. Winfield Scott Hancock's Second Corps on Cemetery Ridge, struck the front defended by the divisions of Brig. Gen. John Gibbon, former commander of the Iron Brigade, and Brig. Gen. Alexander Hays. The grand clash of

arms, after an ear-splitting barrage of Confederate artillery, began after 2 p.m. The high-water mark of the Confederate attack, at the Angle in the federal line, was repulsed with heavy loss of life. The headline in the *New York Times* on July 16, 1863, was "The Escape of Lee: How the Movement Was Effected, Our Army Just One Day too Late." Other headlines such as "Gen. Meade's Delay" and "The Escape of Gen. Lee" were common as Lee's army crossed the Potomac River. *Roster*, vol. 1, 558–60; "Losses in the 7th Wisconsin," *Grant County Herald*, July 14, 1864; Sears, *Gettysburg*, 360, 392, 405, 410–11, 450–51; Guelzo, *Gettysburg*, 376–77, 414–15; "The Escape of Lee: How the Movement Was Effected, Our Army Just One Day too Late," *New York Times*, July 16, 1863; "Gen. Meade's Delay," *New York Daily Tribune*, July 16, 1863; "The Escape of Gen. Lee," *Weekly National Intelligencer*, July 16, 1863.

Camp near Warrenton Junction July 27 1863

Dear Father

I rec your interresting and verry welcome letter last night. Glad to hear you were all well. We arrived here Day before yesturday in the evenning. Your letter came to me amongst eleven others. Every one of them said will *write soon*. Well they found me right in the midst of making up my repourts for the year ending July 1st 1863 which i finished at noon to day, so that this after noon must be devoted to answering letters. That is if you call taking a pencil in your hand a book on your lap and setting down on the ground and scribling for hours in absolute misery. I say if you can call that answering letters then consider me in for the balance of this day. I received Letters from J Rice last night. He is at Annapolis Md doing well. Got one from Tom Garry. Tom is doing firstrate. Reamer and Wm Ray are getting along all right. Callis is comfortable. So writes the doctor. All Kidd has started home. Bennetts I fear will die. He is probably the only one of our co but what will recover in some shape of him I have little hope. He was a brave and noble boy when I had to part with him it was like parting with my own child. I dont think that I will lose more than four or five men out of all those wounded at the Gettsburg fight. I think the rest will all be able to joins us in three or four months.[36]

I have 20 men left in the co. All tough and hearty. I got off with a mear scratch on the sole of my right foot, but there was one shell came so close to me that it tooke the heads of the two men in front of me scattering their brains all over my chlothes. We have got Lee in a rather tight place and I think Mead will keep him there. We are cutting his Army off by the piece just as though we had a contract for doing it.

The Paper correspondents that raised the hopes of the country that we were going to capture Lee on the other side of the Potomac are all damed fools. And in place of staying away in the rear should be placed in the front rank in the next fight. I wrote you that it was all nonsence to talk of capturing him before he crossed the river. When I wrote that letter I knew the ground he occupide. I had been over it and I was satisfide that if we made an attack we would be repulsed.

I was in a tree watching the Rebs when they fired the Signal guns to commence crossing the River. Those guns were fired right in front of me just about one mile off. Our line was just about one mile from Funks town and the situation was this. Hills Corps was in our front behind strong earth works. Our Division and corps and the 11th Corps were in their immediate front also behind brest works that we had hastily constructed the night before. Now my oppinion is this. That if we had then attacted the Rebs they would have repulsed us and then retreated in the night. And on the other hand if they had attacted us we would have repulsed them. There was just about ten hours time that if we had attacted them we could have made a good thing out of it. But the Devil of it was to find out when the ten hours was. Of course the newspaper correspondents no when it was, that is after it was over. So did every boddy else know it then but it was too late.

I see that the papers are down on Hooker. That is the way with these damed stay at home cowards. They attact every Genl as soon as he is releived. Hooker is one of the best officers in the world. He is brave and a good disciplinarian. Hooker and Hallick were not friends, but in what condition did Hooker hand over the Army of the Potomac to his successor three days before the fight at Gettsburg? After marching one hundred and fifty miles the Army was in perhaps the best condition it ever was. What was our cavalry before Hooker took command and reorganized it? It was absolutely the laughing stock of the whole army. Now it is an efficient arm of the service. I am no Hooker man. No Mead man nor McClellan man, but I go in to win with who ever is in command and that is the feeling in the army of the Potomac but I dont like to see a Genl run down and abused.[37]

We have had a hard campaign as you must be aware. This continual marching and roughing it is telling on us but all go along cheerfully. The fact is that the news is so good that we all feel that we can see the end of the Rebellion.

So the Irish of Lafayett co have to be whipped. Well this is all right. If the Damed cusses will only stick to it till they get well tharashed. Then they will be perfectly tame.[38]

I think by the time you cipher this out you will have enough for one time. So i will quit and commence on some one else. My love to all the friends. Give my best wishes to the members of our League. Oh yes one thing more. Of all the mean pickaunish low lifed cowardly devils i ever met the dutch farmers around Gettsburg will take the rag off the bush. They are not even fit to be classed with what is known as the dung hill breed. I will give you a history of them when I have more time.

yours truly

H F Young

NOTES

36. Thomas Garvey, James A. Rice, and Isaac C. Raemer, all in Company F of the Seventh Wisconsin, were wounded at Gettysburg, and all returned to duty. Raemer was killed in action at Gravelly Run, March 30, 1865, in one of the last engagements of the war. Phillip Bennett, Company F of the Seventh Wisconsin died of his wounds on July 4, 1863. *Roster*, 1:558, 560.

37. An article, "Gen. Lee's Plans," appeared on July 15, 1863, in the *Chicago Daily Tribune*; it was critical of Hooker's apparent inaction in following Lee, insinuating that Hooker would do little to impede Lee's advance. Hooker, wishing to use the ten-thousand-man force at Harpers Ferry, requested a transfer of the garrison to his command as the Army of the Potomac chased Lee into Pennsylvania. General-in-Chief Halleck refused this demand, and Hooker, still smarting over this denial, requested that he be relieved of command, a gamble he lost when his request was granted. His replacement, George Gordon Meade, commander of the Fifth Corps, received orders to take command of the army on June 28, 1863. Ironically, a similar request for troops was made on June 28 by Meade, and Halleck's reply stated that Meade was in charge of the troops at Harpers Ferry and could place them where he wished. "Gen. Lee's Plans," *Chicago Tribune*, July 16, 1863; Wert, *The Sword of Lincoln*, 220; *OR*, ser. 1, vol. 25, pt. 2, 51, vol. 27, pt. 1, 4, 58–63.

38. Lafayette County, in southwest Wisconsin, is located to the east of Grant County. The county contained many Copperheads who showed their sympathy toward the South by displaying the Confederate flag in prominent locations. They were even brazen enough to launch a raid into the Grant County village of Georgetown, in Smelser Township. The "invasion," according to the *Grant County Herald*, reminded citizens of the danger that was present and raised awareness of the need to be alert for any emergency that could befall the county. It was a source of great agitation for the Union League in the county. "Lafayette County Copperhead Demonstration," *Grant County Herald*, July 7, 1863.

CHAPTER SIX

"but the flag is the most costly and beutiful i ever seen"

August 5 to December 28, 1863

On Pickett at Beverlys ford 3 miles above Rappahannoc Station August 5 1863

Dear Delia

The heading of my letter will indicate our present locality. Our Regt are at present guarding the ford and picketting along the River. We have two Divisions of our corps over the River suppoarting Beaufords Cavalry. The Rebs attacted them yesturday afteernoon but our men drove them back. We have skermishes every day. The Rebs are in plain sight of us about one mile back from the ford. By looking over there now I can see their line of mounted vidетts some 60 or a hundred in plain sight just out of range of our rifles. The weather has been awful hot for the last week. Last night it rained and this morning it, cool and plesant. The boys of the co are in usual health. Phillip Bennetts is dead. He died at Gettysburg before we left there but we did not know it. I was satifide he could not live and had set him down as mortally wounded. He was a brave and noble boy, and was a universal favourite. I dont think I will loose any of the rest of those that were wounded. There will probably be some of them that will never be fit for service again but i dont think any of them will die from effects of their wounds. I hope not at anyrate. We are going to be filled up with conscripts. This is the way to do it. We cant take five or six hundred coms and put them into our old Regt and make them good soldiers in one qr of the time it would take to drill them by themselves.[1]

The Railroad Bridge across the Rappahannock at the Station was compleeted yesturday and the cars crossed just before the Rebs commenced the attack on us. I think they made the attact for the purpose of destroying the bridge. I dont know what meads intentions are but if it means advance on to the Rappadan River we are allmost ready for the move for we have plenty of supplies and the Railroad in good order to keep us in hard tack and coffee & Pork. Col Callis is getting better. His wife is with him. I suppose All Kidd is home by this time under the fostering care of his noble hearted mother and if she dont kill him with kindness he will soon get well.

We are all anxious to see the paymaster but i dont expect him while we are on the move. We are all getting washed up which we verry much needed. I went to the river yesturday in co with majr Fennicum and capt Numan. We took off our under clothing killed the lice on them and then washed them. Perhaps you think we could not wash our under clothes in cold watter but I tell you to take plenty of sope you can wash woolen goods verry well. At anyrate it is all we have to do it with for our kettles are all lost and we will get no more at present for the teams cant carry them. We are all more or less lousy and we cant get rid of the damed Grey Backs as the boys call them, untill we get into camp where we can exchange clothing regularly. I am verry glad indeed that you have got so you can milk, whenever you feel like milking two cows you shall have them. When i get my pay I will send you money enough to buy in your winter supply and you had better buy everything you will want during the winter in the way of apples and vegetables and have them put in the cellar in good condition and then you will have no trouble. I was sorry to hear of the drout in Wis for it will cut the crops short. We had wet weather here. When it was dry with you it rained almost every day for three weeks, which spoiled quantities of grain in Md and Pa.

I have heard nothing from our boys that were taken prisnor. Since capt Hobert succeeded in making his escape he tells me that may of them were slightly wounded. L G Parsons was sightly wounded in the head. Giles Parker had his thumb shot off & c. You ask how many of co F were taken prisnors. I will tell you that there was no more than a fair proportion of Co F taken. The Regt lost 55 in prisnors. Out of that No Co F lost six but it was a large co, and two of them as i have already wrote you were wounded. But the real cause of us loosing any prisnors is this. When we were ordered to fall back through the town our men were in good order although we were almost surrounded. When we got on the road it was narrow and the enemy were firing on us from each side at short range. Just at this time Battery B came Gallaing in right through our ranks and we had to leave them the road, as some of their horses was killed and some of their limbers had to be left rite there. When we gave them the road some of the men went on one side and some on the other so that we got split up and never got together again. I took all that were with me off all right but those that took the other side were taken prisnors. When men loose their officers they are lost. They dont no what to do. As this is all the paper i have here I must finish on it. My love to all.[2]

ever yours

H F Young

NOTES

1. Brig. Gen. John Buford, who commanded the First Cavalry Division, attacked on August 4, 1863, near Brandy Station. In the first assault, Union pickets pushed back 1,500 yards, but in the ensuing counterattack Buford's troopers drove the Confederate force back two miles. Buford reported, "The enemy's reconnaissance was an utter failure." The first draft in American history went into effect on July 1, 1863. Each state, divided by congressional districts, was given a quota, based on population. Governor Salomon disputed the initial quota of 42,462 as set too high given Wisconsin's already generous number of volunteers. Enlistments provided 42,587 soldiers, and only 1,739 were actually drafted. A second call, in the fall of 1863, established a quota of 342 recruits for Grant County; Young's town of Cassville was responsible for 16. Lafayette County, already the scene of antiwar high jinx, provided extra drama, necessitating action by two companies of soldiers that "have been keeping order for a few days in certain towns in Lafayette county, where the copperheads loudly boasted the enrollment should not be made, and organized to resist the draft." United States, War Records Office, *War of the Rebellion: A Compilation of the Official Records of the Union and Confederate Armies*, 128 vols. (Washington, DC: Government Printing Office, 1885–1901), ser. 1, vol. 29, pt. 1, 21–22 (hereafter cited as *OR*); Frederick H. Dyer, *A Compendium of the War of the Rebellion Compiled and Arranged from Official Records . . . and Other Reliable Documents and Sources* (Des Moines, IA: Dyer Publishing Company, 1908), 920 (hereafter cited as *Dyer's Compendium*); Richard N. Current, *The History of Wisconsin*, vol. 2, *The Civil War Era, 1848–1873* (Madison: State Historical Society of Wisconsin, 1976), 324–25; "The Draft—Wisconsin," *Wisconsin State Journal* (Madison, WI), July 15, 1863; "Quota of Volunteer Militia under the Call of October 17, 1863," *Wisconsin State Journal*, November 23, 1863; "The Enrollment," *Weekly Gazette and Free Press* (Janesville, WI), July 31, 1863.

2. Capt. Martin C. Hobart of Company B and Lorin G. Parsons and Calvin G. Parker of Company F were not listed as captured during the Battle of Gettysburg. The latter two, both wounded during the battle, returned to service later. In the confusion that ensued during these first hours, it is entirely possible, given the natural confusion of the battle and movement by both sides, that they were temporarily

within Confederate lines and thus, wounded, did not rejoin the company until after the battle. The Seventh Wisconsin reported fifty-two men captured or missing during the battle of Gettysburg. Wisconsin, Adjutant General's Office, *Roster of the Wisconsin Volunteers, War of the Rebellion, 1861–1865*, Blue Books, 2 vols. (Madison: Democrat Printing Press, 1886), 1:544, 560 (hereafter cited as *Roster*); *OR*, ser. 1, vol. 27, pt. 1, 173.

O Head qrs Pickett line 1st Brigade Aug 13 1863

Dear Delia

I received your welcome letter last evening. Sorry to hear the children have the whooping cough, but as it is a good time of year for them to have it. I am in hopes they will soon be better. I am in command of 170 men from the 7th and 19th Indiana on pickett we are on the south side of the Rappahannoc River just along the Railroad between the River and Brandy Station. The Rebs keep close watch on us. There was a few shells exchanged between them and us this morning, down on our left, but it is all over now. It is just this way whenever either party shew a force of men or horses to close to the lines of the other. They get saluted with a few shell, and as it does not seam to be the program to bring on an engagement at present, those that go close enough to start the dogs to bark generally fall back satisfide that the enemy is still on hand and wide awake.

I sent a check to Father for $150.00 with instructions to pay Frank Bar a note which come due the 1st of Sept which I think amounts to about $24.00 Twenty four Dolls and give the rest or as much as you wanted of the rest to you. There was no express office here and i concluded that was the best way to send it by mail. I did not get as much pay as usual for they took $32.00 off for the time I was home. I received a letter from Lt A. A. Kidd. Glad to hear he is getting better. It is awful warm here and this is a verry poor country for water. I would give almost anything for a drink out of one of those pure cold springs in Old Grant. How does Furman get along? Has he rented the mill for another year? How does old Squire Bergess get along this hot weather? Give him my best wishes for his good health. My love to all.

ever yours

H F Young

Rappahannock st Va Aug 23 1863

Dear Father

I rec your letter yesturday. Glad to you were all well. We are still in camp at the Station and doing pickett on the south side of the River. The weather is verry hot and good water is scarce. The health of the army considering the warm weather is good. The Reb Videtts and ours are but a few hundred yds apart. They and our boys exchange papers and meet and talk when there no officers in the way but there is no shooting. The Rebs are deserting in numbers and appear to be quite indifferent to what they were when we were on this same ground 1 year ago. The other day one of the Reb videtts carelessly let his horse get away from him. The horse run over to our lines. The Reb followed him over and said he either wanted his horse or to be taken prisnor for it would not do for him to stay in the Reb Army after carelessly loosing his horse. The boys talked to him a while and then let him have his horse and he went back to his post. The stories that the north and south could not live peaceably is all noncence. The war has changed the oppinons of the mases of the South. They knew nothing of the character of the people of the north. They were led to beleive the people of the north were every thing that was low cowardly and mean but the war has taught them better. Their leaders will never fool them again. I heard conversation that pased off between a Georgia Reb and one of our boys.

Georgia, so you alls have to go to conscripting yank. yes we have to conscript to make up that 40 000 men Lee took at Gettysberg. Geo come now dont hold us responsible for the lies that are published at the south. We are sick of hearing such stories just such d—d lies got me into this. I tell you we knew nothing of you alls only we were told you were to cowardly to fight and you would steal our niggers. yank, why dont you desert.

Georgia I swore in for three years. My times up next march. I will stay it out if my state stays in the confedracy till then. I will admit I am tired of it and was sold when i enlisted but I have to much honour to back out. And so it goes. The Va soldiers are the most loyal to the bogus Confedracy of any we find. This in many cases is caused by reclessness. Their own state and property are destroyed and they appear to want all their neighbouring states to share the same fate. Charleston has got come this time but perhaps not so soon as many anticipate. Conscripts are arriving every day and when they get under the right kind of officers will make as good soldiers as any.

I am in hopes they will fill us up immediately for now they are making us do the duty of full Regt which keeps just one half our men on duty all the time.

I see you have nominated Lewis for Gov. Solomen would have been the favourite with the Army. I have not yet heard of who the other candidates are, but as the Copperhead tickett is to rank for the soldiers we will suppoart the union candidates whoever they are.[3]

The riots in Newyork and the action of their bogus Gov has opened the eyes of many of those that still clung to the the name of the party. But lately I have heard officers from NY that were Seymore men curs him loud and deep. I think that riot will have a good and lasting effect.[4]

I received a letter form Lieut Col Callis yesturday. He is mending slowly. He will start home soon. I was sorry to hear of the death of Lt Nasmith. He was a good officer. Phillip Bennetts is dead. He died on the morning of the 4th of July whill we were within a mile of him but we did not know it. Garvy, Blackburn, and Reamer are mending verry slow. The rest of the wounded are doing well. Genl Cutler has resigned and gone home, reason he was superrceeded in Comd of the 1st Div by a younger Officer. *A graduate of the great humbug west point.* Cutler did just right i tell you. There are few better Genls in the service than just old Genl Cutler of Wis. Let me know if you got the check for $150.00 and keep me posted on the poletics till Ellection is over, for the d—d copperheads will leave no stone unturned or log unroled. They will use every speices of trickery to obtain some of the soldiers vote. You say it is long between leters. Pleas remember the old adage. Those that live in glass houses should not throw stones. My good wishes to all.[5]

yours truly

H F Young

NOTES

3. At the Republican Convention, several candidates vied for the gubernatorial spot on the fall ticket. In the first informal ballot, Salomon received 134 votes to 122 for James T. Lewis, secretary of state in the Salomon administration. A subsequent motion was made to adjourn to the following morning, but it failed. Thereupon, a formal vote for governor was taken and this time James T. Lewis garnered 135 votes to 134 for Salomon. A second formal vote extended his majority, 143 to 120, and he became the candidate for governor. Jared Warner, Capt. Henry F. Young's father-in-law, was one of the delegates from Grant County at the convention. The convention

nominated Wyman Spooner for lieutenant governor and Col. Lucius Fairchild of the Second Wisconsin, minus his left arm from a wound at Gettysburg, for secretary of state. Henry L. Palmer, a Milwaukee assemblyman, was selected as the Democratic candidate for governor in 1863. "Republican Union State Convention: Official Proceedings," *Wisconsin State Journal*, August 21, 1863; Current, *The Civil War Era, 1848–1873*, 2:327.

4. New York City exploded two days after the first names were drawn for the draft. On the morning of July 13, 1863, draft offices and federal buildings were put to the torch by rioters. For four days the rioters went on a rampage until the War Department dispatched regiments from New York and Pennsylvania to bring order to the city. The fact that New York City was a Democratic Party stronghold with tight commercial ties to the South helped fuel the riots. The death toll, perhaps five hundred or more over the four days, included many African Americans. Reportedly, eighteen African Americans were lynched during the four-day rampage. A smaller riot broke out in Boston but was quickly put down. Barnet Schecter, *The Devil's Own Work: The Civil War Draft Riots and the Fight to Reconstruct America* (New York: Walker, 2005), 3, 251; James M. McPherson, *Battle Cry of Freedom: The Civil War Era* (New York: Oxford University Press, 1988), 609–10; "The Draft Elsewhere: Riot in Boston," *New York Sun*, July 16, 1863.

5. Lt. Col. John B. Callis, still recovering from his wound at Gettysburg, wrote in an article on September 22, 1863, for the *Wisconsin State Journal* that the ball in his right lung "feels like a weight of ten pounds." Lt. Col. Samuel Nasmith of the Twenty-fifth Wisconsin died of disease in Platteville, Wisconsin, on July 22, 1863. Brig. Gen. Lysander Cutler, the commander of First Division, First Army Corps, was relieved on August 5, 1863, by Brig. Gen. Henry S. Briggs, who was himself later replaced by Brig. Gen. James C. Rice on August 28, 1863. Cutler resumed command of the division in October during the Bristoe campaign. *Wisconsin State Journal*, September 22, 1863; *Roster*, 2:282; *OR*, ser. 1, vol. 29, pt. 1, 217, pt. 2, 119.

Rappahannock Station Va Aug 30 1863

Dear Delia

This is a cool pleasant Sunday morning. It makes me think of home everything is so still and quiet. I looked for a letter from you for several days but it has not came yet. Sloat got a letter from his mother last evenning that said you had been to see her. So that explained my not getting a letter for I knew you must have been in Lancaster. That is all right. I hope you had a good visit. Just one year ago today we met with the disastress defeat at Bull Run, and had to fall back before a victorious army to Washington. One year has made quite a change in our favour. Then the Rebs held the Mississippi River and the country on both sides from Iland No 10 to Port

Hudson. Buell was forced to fall back from the line of the Tennessee River. Now look at the change. The Mississippi open to our boats. The country on both banks in our possession. Rosencrantz pushing forward into Georgia, Burnsides into East Tennessee, fort Sumter taken, Charleston the hot bed of Treason bound to be taken or destroyed in a few days. The great country west of the Mississippi almost entirely in our possession and the Rebble armies with perhaps the exception of Lees thoughroly demoralized. Not only this but people of the south are becoming disaffected to an extent that will in a short time destroy every leader of the Rebellion. They are begining to resist the tyrany of the Jeff Davis. Despotism in a way that will soon be felt. As for us we will soon be as strong as ever. The army is fast filling up with conscrits. That riot in Newyork was a good thing for it has taught the disloyal portion of the citizen in the north that we have a Govt that is able and and will enforce her laws. Yesturday there was five deserters shot in the 5th corps. These men all deserted from the army and then sold themselves as substitutes and deserted again. They were shot in presence of the whole corps. It will have a good effect. There will be a No more of conscritps shot in each corps. Then we will hear no more of desertions. Come to look at it all round I feel verry well satisfide with the years work.[6]

We are doing Garrison and Pickett duty on the south side of the River. The Rebs and our boys are on verry good terms. The Picketts are only about two hundred yds apart. A few nights ago one of our men started out to releive his comrad on post. It was dark and raining. He missed his way but kept on the direction that he thought was right when he heard the comd halt, with who the Devil are you? Why I am comeing to releive you if i can ever find you answered the yank. But who are you demanded the sentinel. He told who he was. The other burst into a great laugh and told him to get back Devilish quick for said he we are Rebs here and you are almost across our lines. Our fellow did not wait for a second biding, but got back to our lines as quick as possible. Our army are getting plenty of rations and are in good health and excelent spirits. They isue vegetables and dride apples twice a week. I dont think from present appearance we will move for some time unless Lee makes a move in which case it would be necessary to move. My wounded men are all doing as well as could be expected considering the warm weather we have had since the 1st of July. I have heard nothing lately from those that were taken prisnors. I received a leter from Father a few days ago. He says Jared gets along fine and was almost well of his cough. I received a leter from Lieut Col Callis. He intended to start home the last of this month. He says he is getting better verry slow. I see they have nominated Col L Fairchild of the 2d Regt for Secretary of State, (hurrah for Luce) as the boys call him. I think they got up a verry good ticket in our state all through. I wish I was at home a month to fight it out with that d—d Copperhead Dewey faction in Cassville. But tell Squire Bergess to roll up his sleaves and swear by the great Eternal that they cant have it all their own way for i dont want N Dewey to get a majority in Cassville. And tell Furman to do all he can with the Germans that come to the mill. If they will work they will defeat Dewey in his own town.[7]

Tomorrow we are to be mustered again for two months pay. I have heard nothing from the check i sent to Father yet, but i hope it has went safe and that you will have got what you need of it before you rec this.

Give my good wishes to squire Bergess and family and to Furmans, and my love to the children and write oftener.

ever yours

H F Young

NOTES

6. The riots in New York City and other cities did little to dissuade President Lincoln from continuing the draft. New York governor Horatio Seymour implored him in a series of letters to suspend the draft in New York, wondering whether conscription was constitutional and questioning quotas as unfair in New York. The president, believing conscription a military necessity, was ready to call out the New York militia to enforce the draft. Seymour backed down, and the draft in New York State resumed on August 19, 1863. After the Battle of Stones River, Maj. Gen. William Rosecrans's Army of the Cumberland moved at a glacial pace. All that changed when Rosecrans, whose aim was the railroad line from Atlanta to Chattanooga, advanced federal forces south of Chattanooga, which was at the time occupied by Confederate forces. The resurrected Maj. Gen. Ambrose Burnside, leading the Army of the Ohio, marched his force toward Knoxville in support of Rosecrans's advance and secured it on September 3, 1863. Confederate commander Gen. Braxton Bragg was in a precarious position in Chattanooga and eventually evacuated the city on September 8, 1863. Fort Sumter and Charleston, South Carolina, were under continual bombardment during the late months of 1863. David Herbert Donald, *Lincoln* (New York: Simon & Schuster, 1995), 449–50; Doris Kearns Goodwin, *Team of Rivals: The Political Genius of Abraham Lincoln* (New York: Simon & Schuster, 2005), 537; "Governor Seymour and the Draft," *New York Daily Tribune*, August 12, 1863; McPherson, *Battle Cry of Freedom*, 669–70; *OR*, ser. 1, vol. 28, pt. 1, 1.

7. The Democratic Convention for governor was held in Madison in August 1863. Nelson Dewey, the former governor of Wisconsin, was nominated once again for that post; however, he polled only eighteen votes in the informal first ballot and

four in the subsequent formal ballot. While he was not initially nominated for lieutenant governor, a supporter by the name of Mr. Horn moved that his name be put on the ballot by "acclamation." A flattered Dewey asked that his name be withdrawn as other candidates had already been nominated. As each of the men withdrew their names from consideration, Dewey emerged as the candidate and was nominated by the staunch Democrat Edward G. Ryan and subsequently approved by the delegates. Moved by his nomination for lieutenant governor, Dewey acknowledged this as "the greatest compliment he had ever received from the Democracy of the state." "Democratic Convention," *Wisconsin State Journal*, August 7, 1863.

Rappahannock Station Sept 13 1863

Dear Delia

I received your long and welcome letter several days ago and my reason for not answering it sooner was first I was on outpost duty for 3 days. When i returned I found the Paymaster here and I wanted to get my pay and let you know what I did with it when I wrote. Well I have just put up $220.00 for you by Express to Cassville. I want Ury paid out of it without fail which will take less than $60.00 which will leave you $160.00. You had beter keep what you want at present and let Father have the balance. It will be in hands where you can get it whenever you want it. I have not been well for several days. I have the diarrhoea and it is pulling me down considerable.

There is sterring times times here. Just now they are fighting across the River in our front and we are ordered to be ready to move at a moments notice. Beaufords Cavalry and the 2d Army corps crossed the River this morning, but I think it is only a reconnousance.[8]

If we are allowed to stay here till the 11th we are going to have a grand old time. Some of our friends have got us up a Brigade flag called the Iron Brigade flag and they are to be here to present it to us on the 17th which is the anniversary of Anteitam where we won the name of Iron Brigade.

All Kidd is here but he is not well yet. The boys of the company are in good health. We have been having verry dry weather here. Everything is in such confusion here. I cant write for it is just answer questions and give orders all the time. The news is good from all qrs. I hope the Rebellion will soon end so that I can come home to the loved ones and stay there. My love to all.

ever yours

H F Young

NOTE

8. Skirmishes, on almost a daily basis, occurred between September 10 and September 17, at Stevensburg, Raccoon Ford, Bristoe Station, White Plains, Brandy Station, Muddy Run, Pony Mountain, and Rapidan Station. Action at Culpeper Court House and a federal advance from the Rappahannock River to the Rapidan River kept forces busy during these few days. Casualties at Culpeper Court House on September 13 were 8 killed and 46 wounded. *OR*, ser. 1, vol. 29, pt. 1, 3; *Dyer's Compendium*, 921–22.

Camp near Stevensberg Va Sept 21 1863

Dear Delia

I have not rec any letter from you since my last but I rec one from Father saying you were there. I hope you got the money all right I sent you by express. Delia I have been suffering ever since I wrote you last with the flux. I feel a little better this morning. The sergeon has put in an application to send me for a few days to the Officers Hospital at Georgetown where I can have propper treatment and rest both of which I am in need of. The fact is I need a thorough cleaning out of boil and billious matter and if my leave is granted I will let you know how i get along.

We are encamped between the Rapidan & Culpeper. The Rebs are strongly posted on the oposite side of the River. It has rained blowed and been awful cold and disagreeable ever since we came here till to day. It has cleared up and everything looks brighter. The camp this time of year is a poor place to be sick in. It would soon make anyone homesick. So far I have been extremely fortunate and i think I will come round all right. In this there is one thing certain. I wont take the medicines the sergeons have here and then lay out on the damp ground. I applide for medicine some days ago and they gave me 20 grains blue mass. It was then raining and nothing but the wet ground to sleep on. So I took the medicine put it in my pocket and it is there yet and will stay there and then if does me no good it will do no harm. I am verry careful what I eat and I feel that is curing me faster than any medicine I can take. Write often for when not well is the time I most want to hear from the dear ones at home. My love to you all.[9]

ever yours

Henry

Tell Laura and May that papa often looks at their pictures and sighs to be with them and mama and Jared. Oh if the happy time will ever come when we can all sit down together with our country at peace and nothing to interfere with our happiness. Delia I build many air castles of this kind. Well kiss the children and tell papa loves them verry much and wants them to be verry good children.

NOTE

9. Young did well not to take the blue mass. According to James McPherson, the Civil War was fought at the end of what he referred to as "the medical Middle Ages." Common ailments, such as diarrhea, were treated with barbaric remedies compared to post–Civil War standards. Blue mass, a concoction that contained mercury, was used to treat acute diarrhea. Some in the medical community warned of its effect but left the door open for surgeons in the field to decide about its usefulness. A doctor writing about army medicine stated, "Should, however, the personal experience of the surgeon, or the influence of his previous education induce him to administer small doses of blue pill or of calomel, . . . the effect of the remedy should be carefully watched, and it shall be promptly suspended the moment the gums give the slightest evidence of mercurial impression." Young's illness lasted "for a number of weeks" according to William Ray. McPherson, *Battle Cry of Freedom*, 486; Joseph Janvier Woodward, *Outlines of the Chief Camp Diseases of the United States Armies as Observed during the Present War: A Practical Contribution to Military Medicine* (Philadelphia: J. B. Lippincott, 1863), 222–23; Lance Herdegen and Sherry Murphy, eds., *Four Years with the Iron Brigade: The Civil War Journals of William R. Ray, Co. F, Seventh Wisconsin Infantry* (Cambridge, MA: Da Capo Press, 2002), 220.

Camp near Stevensberg Va Sept 21 1863

Dear Father

I rec yours several days ago while on the march to this camp which is between Culpeper and the Rapidan. I have been suffering with the flux for the last two weeks. I feel a little better this morning. We are under marching orders and if we march at present I will have to be left or go in an ambulance. The Sergeon has made application to send me to the officers Hospital at Georgetown for a few days for treatment and rest both of which I verry much need. Lieut Kidd is here and gets along verry well. He is a little lame yet. The rest of the co are in usual health. We had a flag presentation on the 17th on the anniversary of Antietam which was to have been a grand affair but the march the day before took us away from our beautiful pavilion we had built out of cedar boughs to rec it in.

And then the rain storm here marred the festivities somewhat, but the flag is the most costly and beutiful I ever seen. It was a free gift of our admirers in Wis Ind & Mich. It was presented by Mr Sellick State agent of our state in a neat speach and rec on part of the Brigade by Col Robinson at present Comd the old Iron Brigade.[10]

There are all sorts of rumors affloat as there always is on the eve of any forward movement. But all we know of the facts are that the oposite bank of the Rapadan is held by the Rebs in force and we have not yet succeeded in breaking their lines. The River is pronounced low enough to ford this morning and our cavalry are in motion, so you will probably hear of the army crossing the River before you get this. I sent $220.00 to Delia. I told her Ury must be paid out of it and the balance that she did not want at present to turn over to you and she could always get it when wanted. Write soon. You are not keeping up with your promises in that respect. My good wishes to all.

yours truly

H F Young

NOTE

10. W. Yates Selleck of Milwaukee, the military agent for Wisconsin in Washington, DC, acted as a liaison for the state in the nation's capital. Wisconsin citizens were proud of the brigade and commissioned Tiffany and Company of New York City to produce a new flag. The flag was adorned with the name of each regiment, as well as a list of battles, at the cost of $1,000. Selleck presented the flag to Col. William W. Robinson, the commander of the Seventh Wisconsin, who gave a short speech. Agent Selleck read a letter written by former Army of the Potomac commander George B. McClellan. Lance J. Herdegen, *The Iron Brigade in Civil War and Memory: The Black Hats from Bull Run to Appomattox and Thereafter* (El Dorado Hills, CA: Savas Beatie, 2012), 447, 449; "Flag Presentation to Iron Brigade. From Meade's Army," *Wisconsin State Journal*, September 22, 1863; "Flag Presentation to the 'Iron Brigade.' Eloquent Speech of Col. Robinson," *Wisconsin State Journal*, September 30, 1863.

~

Camp near Raccoon ford Rapadan River Sept 26 1863

Dear Delia

I received your package of dride fruit per Mr Eaton, thank you. That is also the latest news I have from home.[11]

I did not get my leave to go to Georgetown but I am much better than when I wrote last. I think in a few days I will be entirely well. The weather is cool and pleasant. We have moved down on the River and are at our old business of doing pickett on the front. There is just a verry small stream of water here between our lines and the Jonneys.

We have been in the front so long that it dont appear as if we were in place unless we are in sight of the Rebs where we can occasionally exchange papers and the boys blaguard them occasionally. The 12th Corps has gone. It is said to Reinforce Rosencrantz. The 11th is also gone somewhere. I dont know where. Perhaps to tennessee. So that settles any forward movement

Rev. Samuel Eaton, Seventh Wisconsin Infantry (Wisconsin Historical Society, WHS-70748)

from this qr. For those were our largest corps and has taken one third our army. We could advance but our line is to long. It now takes two corps to guard our communication with Washington. The news is not verry flatering from the South west but i think Old Rosa will be able to hold his possition at Chattanooga till reinforced. The boys are in usual heath. The wounded are returning. Wm Ray returned yesturday. He is all right. Lieut Kidd is still some lame. Give my love to all and write soon.[12]

ever yours

H F Young

NOTES

11. Samuel W. Eaton, the chaplain for the Seventh Wisconsin, lived in Lancaster, Wisconsin. *Roster*, 1:539.

12. The Battle of Chickamauga on September 19 and 20 forced the Army of the Cumberland to retreat to Chattanooga. If not for the heroics of Maj. Gen. George Thomas, "The Rock of Chickamauga," the results would have been worse. Rosecrans's headquarters was overrun during the battle, and half of the federal force left the field in the face of the Confederate attack. Secretary of War Stanton convinced President Lincoln to transfer the depleted Eleventh and Twelfth Corps on September 23, 1863, to the Army of the Cumberland. In eleven days Union railroads carried twenty thousand troops to Tennessee, a logistical feat for the day. Maj. Gen. Joseph Hooker was activated to command the two corps. McPherson, *Battle Cry of Freedom*, 672, 674–75; *OR*, ser. 1, vol. 29, pt. 1, 3, vol. 30, pt. 1, 37.

Camp near Raccoon ford Rapadan River Oct 1st 1863

Dear Delia

I rec your welcome letter yesturday. Glad to hear you were in good heath. Your letter found me not well but not sick. My kidneys are effected. The doctor says it originated from billious disorder that the liver rufused to act and that disordered the kidneys. It is verry disagreeable and sometimes verry painful. It is a feeling of continual bearing down as though i wanted to go and use the sink. The feeling is verry uncomfortable and yet i am not sick. My appetite is good and sometimes I feel perfectly well. I think i am improveing and will get all right again in a few days. You had not rec my last two letters when you last wrote. I am anxious to hear from the package of money I sent you to cassville but you will probaly find it there when you go home. I know dear old girl you have a hard and lonesome time. But you know I have only ten months more to serve and if you will live that out in our own home for my sake, i promise you if i live, to come home and stay with you and the dear ones the rest of my days. And it may not be that long for you need not be surprised to see peace before our time is out. It would greive me verry much indeed for you to leave my home and take up your abode somewhere else for I know you would have to suffer great inconvenience. Besides there is no place so independent as ones own home. Cant you get some companionable old maid young girl or widow woman to come and stay with you this winter? I will save twenty five Doll out of my own expenses and send you for the purpose of defraying the expense of such an arrangement. As for the horses it will make no difference this winter for you would have to get furman to take you where you wanted to go. And in the spring if you can find a good quiet nag that you can ride and drive i will send you the money to buy it. Now if you fall in with arrangement the first thing you must do is to look for some person to stay with you. In that case you can take one room for a School room and teach Jared and Laura some every day. In the next place keep money enough to lay in supplies to make you comfortable during the winter. Why if I was only back there for a week I could fix you so comfortable and independent that you could live as smug as a bug in a rug as the saying is.

But if you think you cant stand it another winter at our home you must not go to Susans. You may rent a house somewhere else, but that is to uncomfortable neither wood nor water. Susan worries along with abe and manages to live but it would kill you in three months and I wont allow it at all. Rather than have you go to a place so uncomfortable as that would be I would resign and come home. Now my dear I have given you the best advice i can and I hope you will get along all right. The fact is i have always been proud of my little wife for the way she has managed and got a long ever since I enlisted. When other men have been down hearted about everything going wrong at hom and their wives being in a continual fret, I have often read some of your letters with pride to them to show them what a true hearted patriotic woman could do. And I think you just had the blues just a verry little when you wrote that last letter and you may be sure that I wont shew that to any one. Now my dear I think you must consider this a family letter for I dont think I have room for any other subject and I know of none more interresting. Write soon. Give my love to all.[13]

ever yours

NOTE

13. As previously noted, "Susan" Paul, conceivably Delia's sister Rebecca, lived in Patch Grove and was the wife of Alexander Paul, a local merchant.

Camp near Raccoon ford Va Oct 9 1863

Dear Delia

I just rec your long and interresting letter of Sept 30th. Glad indeed to hear you were all well and enjoying yourselves. Your letter found me if not all right so near it that I have gone to duty again and I am much better. So you were at the fair. All right I am glad of it. I like to hear of your enjoying yourself. You deserve it. We are in the old place doing pickett duty; thats right. Dig your potatoes and get a good supply of vegetables for there is no knowing but what I might spend part of the winter with you. (there might be such a thing as that we would be sent back to *reorganize* and *recruit,*) Lieut Sloat was not sick that is a good reason for not saying anything about him. I am just going out on the lines and the mail starts before i return. If you could just go along I would shew you thousands of Rebs before we got round. My love to all.[14]

ever yours

Henry

NOTE

14. The Eighth Annual Fair and Exhibition was held on September 24–25, 1863, at the fairgrounds in Lancaster. Exhibits included farm animals, sewing, knitting, weaving, and a Miss Addie Durand, who delighted many women with her knowledge of fashion. "Grant County Fair," *Grant County Herald* (Lancaster, WI), September 29, 1863.

Camp near Thoroughfare Gap Oct 23 1863

Dear Delia

I rec your welcome letter last night.[15] Glad to hear you were all well. Your letter found me all right again after marching back and forward or forward & back for a week. Mead fell back. Lee followed him up. Mead took up his possition for fight. Lee fell back mead followed. So it goes. Neither willing to fight without he gets the advantage of the other. Our Regt lost 34 prisnors a few days ago that were on pickett. Our co did not Loose any. They were taken by Stewarts Cavalry. Lieut Col of the 14th NY was in command of the pickett line and he fell back with his reserve without letting those on post know anything about it. And they fought their way back to where their suppoart ought to have been and found they were gone. By this time they were surrounded and had to surrender. The Officer that had charge of the line will be tride by court martial tomorrow and perhaps will get his just deserts. The boys of the co are in good health and spirits. It is no use in me writing about millitary matters for you can learn more from the papers than I can tell you. It is raining and cold at that and I am setting in my shelter tent on a knapsack cramped up in a devilish uncomfortable possition. For that reason you must excuse this miserable scroll.[16]

The talk with the boys now is that we are going home this winter to recruit & fill up. It will all depend on what takes place in the next two weeks. You use your own pleasure about renting your kitchen for a school room but i think you will get tired of it before you get through.

My love to all.

ever yours

H F Young

NOTES

15. Thoroughfare Gap, on the southern end of Bull Run Mountain, was northwest of Gainesville, near the location where the Iron Brigade saw its first action, on August 28, 1862.

16. The Bristoe campaign, Lee's attempt to move around the right flank of the federal line, ended without a major change in positions after eleven days. A Confederate attack at Bristoe Station on October 14 was repulsed by federal forces. Union casualties were 136 killed, 722 wounded, and 1,422 captured or missing. Jeffry D. Wert, *The Sword of Lincoln: The Army of the Potomac* (New York: Simon & Schuster, 2005), 316; *OR*, ser. 1, vol. 29, pt. 1, 4; *Dyer's Compendium*, 923.

Camp near Bristoe Station Va Oct 26 1863

Dear Father

I rec your letter last evening. Glad to hear you were all well. This letter has not been delayed to punish you for not writing to me but for the reason that it is more than three weeks since I have seen my valiese or paper to write with. The fact is for the last three weeks we have been either on the move or in line of battle. Mead & Lee have been playing a game of bluff and for my part I cant see which got the best of it. You will learn the result from the papers.

As for our corps we have had no fighting excepting a slight skermish when our Regt lost one officer and 34 men prisnors.

They were on pickett near Buckland and had just been posted. Killpatrick and Steward were fighting in their front. Fitzhugh Lee turned Fitzpatricks right flank to get in his rear and in that way our boys were surrounded before they kew it. They made a gallant fight but were overpowered, and the d—d Lieut Col of the 14th NY insted of going to the assistance with his reserve as he should have done faced his men and double quicked them off the field. He is under arrest and will be tried by court martial. I hope he may be reduced to the ranks and made to serve 3 years.[17]

I cant tell you the no of men in this army. Lee evidently found us stronger then he expected, our Brigade Nos 1200 men. We have rec a Regt of sharp shooters since the Battle of Gettysburg which gives us Six Regts average 200 men to the Regt. Our Regt Nos 184 men for duty. The boys are in good health and spirits considering that they have marched for the last three weeks throwg cold rains mud and wet. The fact is the men we have with us are so tough that nothing appears to faze them. I have got well again can eat my full ration of hard tack.

We hold the line of the Rappahannock and they are pushing forward the Railroad with all possible speed. The supposition is by those best informed that washington will be garrisoned by the new troops as rapidly as possible and that all the veteran troops will be sent out here to reinforce this army, which will Rendzous on the Rapidann or in the Neighbourhood of Culppeper. And when all is ready move on Lynchburg and occupy that place which would cause the immediate evacuation of Richmond. There is nothing said about this in the papers or in the army. I got it from a friend on the staff so that it may be reliable and it may be speculatioin. This is evidently a bad year for copperheads in the north. I think Wis will still burry them deeper. Seymore has evidently had a revelation since the Election. Keep in good heart for nothwithstanding all the damnable blunders that have been made and will yet be made we will come out all right. Most of our boys has signfide their intention to enlist in the Veteran Corps and probably will be sent home this winter to recruit and reorganize. My love to all.[18]

yours truly

H F Young

NOTES

17. Buckland Mills provided the Confederates with their only bright spot during the Bristoe campaign. As Gen. Lee withdrew to the Rappahannock, federal cavalry units, led by Third Division commander Brig. Gen. Judson Kilpatrick, gave chase. On the south side of the Broad Run, over a stone bridge, lay a Confederate cavalry force under Maj. Gen. J. E. B. Stuart and Maj. Gen. Fitzhugh Lee, who suggested to Stuart that he fall back in order to lure the federal cavalry over a bridge that spanned Broad Run. Kilpatrick took the bait and sent Brig. Gen. George Armstrong Custer's force to secure the bridge and Brig. Gen. Henry E. Davies's force to press forward. Stuart's force pounced on Davies's force, which found itself cut off by Stuart and Lee. The federal units barely escaped the snare and were chased nearly to Gainesville by Stuart and Lee. In this pursuit, elements of the First Army Corps, including soldiers from the Iron Brigade, were captured by their pursuers. Lost also was Custer's baggage, including his table, official reports, and personal letters. Stuart affectionately referred to the action as the "Buckland Races." The *Grant County Herald* reported the loss of thirty-three prisoners in the Seventh Wisconsin Infantry. Wert, *The Sword of Lincoln*, 317; *OR*, ser. 1, vol. 29, pt. 1, 382–83, 387–88, 451–52; Edward Caudill and Paul Ashdown, *Inventing Custer: The Making of an American Legend* (Lanham, MD: Rowman & Littlefield, 2015), 96–97; "The Iron Brigade—More Losses," *Grant County Herald*, November 3, 1863.

18. Horatio Seymour, the Democratic governor of New York, initially used the draft riots in New York City as a pretext to suspend conscription; however, he relented after Lincoln stated he would send soldiers to enforce the measure.

Camp Bristoe Station Va Nov 1st 1863

Dear Delia

I have not received any letter from you since I wrote you last but this is a beautiful Sunday morn and I feel lonesome and will kill time by writing to the dear ones at home.[19] It is ten oclock. We have had Regimental Inspection. Every one that is left of us came out with shoes blacked armes and accoutrements clean and bright and were dismised with the approveing word Capt your co is in good condition. So that from now till time for hard tack and coffee we have nothing on hand. And I imagine that if you have a fine day like this at home that you have your morning work done up, the children washed dressed heads combed, and have just about set down either to answer my last letter or read the Nov No of the Harper. Now this may all be an idle picture but I feel as if it was almost realty.

Yesturday we were mustered for another two months pay which we will get in ten or twelve days. Day after tomorrow is Election. We will all vote the union tickett unless we are in motion. (which is not likely) The Railroad is again compleeted to Warrenton Junction, as also the Branch from there to Warrenton. We are entirely in the dark about the next move. One thing we know that is if we are going to make a forward movement this fall it must be done soon for the wet weather will soon set which will soon make the roads in this clay soil utterly immpaaible. I dont think we will get to go home to recruit. The fact is I never had any confidence in it myself. And the late call for three hundred thousand must be filled up by vollenteers by Jan 1864, or the call will be filled by drafting, so that the Govt is making provision for troops to take our places when we are mustered out. That is as it should be.[20]

So Furman and Father have gone into partnership in the mill for this year. From present prices there ought to be something made this year. Write me in particular how the mill is doing. If I have the luck to get home and nothing happens the mill it will be quite different from what is was when I used to run it. Instead of having to borrow money and being in debt, I will be out of debt and have plenty of money of my own to run it and then I wont be compeled to sell only when the price suits me. And this is what I have long wanted. When I sold my farm I was determined to get out of debt but going into the only served to get me deeper in. Now I have got out and I will stay out. Next summer i will have some person to brake up four or five acres of land on the ridge next Jodys field for an orchard and to raise vegetables. I think it will be a verry good place for an orchard and we can then raise all the vegetables we will want.[21]

The boys are in good health. Those that were taken prisnors at Gettysberg are still at Bell Iland. The last I heard from them they were well. Tell Jared Laura & May papa sends his love to them. Write soon.[22]

ever yours

Henry

NOTES

19. Bristoe Station, Virginia, was on the Orange and Alexandria Railroad between Culpeper Court House and Alexandria.

20. President Lincoln issued Proclamation 107 on October 17, 1863, calling for three hundred thousand volunteers to be furnished by the states by January 5, 1864. Roy P. Basler, ed., *The Collected Works of Abraham Lincoln*, 8 vols. (Springfield, IL: Abraham Lincoln Association, 1953), 6:523–24.

21. Two men, Patrick Joyce and John Shaben, who lived on land next to Young's might be referenced in this letter. However, this is mere speculation based on the

1868 plat book. Grant County Genealogical Society, comp., *Grant County Plat Map Index, 1868* (Platteville, WI: Grant County Genealogical Society, 1868), Cassville Township.

22. Belle Isle Prison, on an island in the James River, contained noncommissioned officers and privates and was connected to Richmond by a footbridge. Soldiers were forced to live in tents as no barracks were constructed. Angela M. Zombeck, *Encyclopedia Virginia*, "Belle Isle Prison," http://www.encyclopediavirginia.org/Belle_Isle_Prison.

Camp near Beverly ford va Nov 13 1863

Dear Delia

I received your welcome letter several days ago.[23] Glad to hear you were all well and in such good spirits, but i fear you will be disappointed about my comeing home. It is true we offered our services to the govt for three years longer or during the *war* beleiveing at the same time that we would not be wanted longer than next fall or winter. And that is my conviction yet that if the old troops were to reenlist and could be sent home to fill up that they could do it and all come out full in the spring, which would do more towards crushing the Rebellion than any thing else that could be done. But it appears our offer has not been accepted. Since writing my last we have been on the march and had some fighting which ended in our facing the Rebs to recross the Rapidan and taking position in their old fortifications. Last Saturday we left Warrenton Junction at daylight and marched to Kellys ford. The 3d corps got the ford and 400 prisnors before we got there. The 6th corps had also stormed the works at Rappahannock Station taking 1600 prisnors and 7 pieces of canon and the Rebble pontoon train.[24]

The Rebs fell back to Brandy Station where they had a high and commanding position early on Sunday morning. We were in motion. Every one expected a desperate fight but I never saw the men feel in better spirits or more confident of success. We could hear the booming of canon and the rattle of small arms between our advance under Killpatrick and the Rebble Picketts under Stewart.

At every discharge the boys would cheer and shout give them hell. Old Kill we will soon be there to help you. But when we got there it was just in time to Killpatrick advance to bring on an engagement. He drove Stewart slowly and cautiously being suppoaarted by infantry but the Reb army had gone. Steward with alarge boddy of cavalry and a few Infantry in light marching order were covering their retreat. In the neighbourhood of Brandy Station the land is cleared and the fences have all been burned. It looks like a prairie. Just before you get to the station the land gradually raises and then continues level from there to Culpeper making it a grand place for mannoeuvreing cavalry. It was here mead intended to fight Lee, and it was not untill several hours after we got in position that we knew to the contrary.[25]

Mead handled his army in splendid style. Sunday was a beautiful day warm and sunshine just such a day as one of Indian Summer in Wis. Now let me tell you what a grand sight it was, in less than half an hour from the time that the first of our troops arrived there. The head collumn of every corps was there comeing in by different routs well closed up, and each taking its appropriate place in line of battle with allacrity but without confusion. Just as if the whole thing was a piece of machinery till in less than two hours the whole army 70 000 strong stood on the plane in lines of battle ready for a desperate struggle as all expected. But Lee declined the chalange and retreated across the Rapidan. Our corps recrossed the River on monday night. The 5th Corps did the same on account of getting supplies. The 6th 2d 3d corps are between Brandy station and the Rapidan. The Railroad will be finished to Culpeper next week. Then if the intention is to cross the Rapidan. This fall will be the time to do it. The boys are all well and in good spirits. Col Callis got worse by the time he got to Washington and had to be sent to Annapolis Md for treatment at the Us Genl Hospital. I fear he will never be able for field service again. I wish I could call in and take supper with you this evening. There has been no sutlers allowed to come out for a month and I am getting Devilish tired of hard Tack fat pork tough beef and coffee. That is of all but the coffee for if it was not for our black strong hot coffee. I dont think unkle sam would have so much nature amongst his boys.

My love to all.

ever yours

H F Young

NOTES

23. Beverly Ford, Virginia, was on the Rappahannock River, just north of where the Orange and Alexandria Railroad Bridge spans the river.

24. A Confederate force, dug in on the north side of the Rappahannock River at Rappahannock Station, was attacked by federal troops on November 7, 1863, and driven across the river by the Union Third and Sixth Corps. More than 1,600

Confederate troops, 2,000 stands of arms, eight battle flags, and four cannons were captured in the attack. Union casualties were 89 killed, 346 wounded, 6 missing. Wert, *The Sword of Lincoln*, 318–19; *OR*, ser. 1, vol. 29, pt. 1, 5, 576, 625; William F. Fox, *Regimental Losses in the American Civil War* (Albany, NY: Albany Publishing Company, 1889), 551; *Dyer's Compendium*, 926.

25. After the loss of Rappahannock Station, Lee decided to concentrate his forces on the south side of the Rapidan River. His previous position, north of the river, did not offer a reasonable chance of success in the next engagement. Wert, *The Sword of Lincoln*, 319; *OR*, ser. 1, vol. 29, pt. 1, 609–11.

Camp near Beverly ford Va Nov 16 1863

Dear Father

Capt Gibson goes home in the morning. I send with him $200.00 in US 6 per cent bonds, to your address to be sent to the express officer at Prairie Duchien. Also a package containing $37.00 and a note from the members of Co F to the wife of James A Simpkins of Millville; which you will please deliver to her at the earliest opportunity. I want you to pay delia what money she may want and keep the bonds all the money that is not needed for her I want to invest in bonds. Then I can use them when I want to. I can get bonds from the paymaster here in place of green backs every pay day.[26]

I want you to keep an account of all the money I send and what you let Delia have, for I have unfortuntely lost my account book and lost the run of the whole concern. A man cant keep anything safe here in the army. One non com officer and one private goes home from each co to recruit. Sergt Eustice of Potosi and private C B Bishop of my co go in the morning. Bishop will go and see you and give you all the news.[27]

The rail Road is again through to Culpepper. There was quite a brisk little fight yesturday bettween a Rebble reconnoucence and Killpatrick. Old Kill drove them back across the Rapidan and made them hunt their heels. The fact is mead is getting the better of Lee at every move and if they did not cripple him at washington I beleive he would winter at Richmond. The Rebs are beginning to find that we not only fall back fast but that we can advance eaqually fast.[28]

One week ago to day the Rebs retreated through culpepper telling the citizens that the yankeys could not hold the town long for the Railroad was entirely destroyed from Warrenton Junction to the Rappahannock and the bridge there was entirely destroyed and that it would take all winter to build it. But this morning just one week the people are astonished to see several trains come puffing and snorting into the town. The Elections were just the thing. Every state did the right thing. Yes I was verry glad to hear Dewey was beat in Cassville. All Kidd cut his foot and is in the feild hospital. All the rest well. Write just as soon as you get the money.[29]

yours truly

H F Young

NOTES

26. Capt. George W. Gibson, Company C of the Second Wisconsin, lived in Boscobel, Wisconsin. James W. Simpkins, Company F of the Seventh Wisconsin, was wounded at South Mountain on September 14, 1862, and died of his wound on October 8, 1862, in Fredericksburg, Maryland. *Roster*, 1:353, 561.

27. George Eustice and Corydon B. Bishop were both in Company F of the Seventh Wisconsin. *Roster*, 1:558–59.

28. A deserter who came into Kilpatarick's camp informed him that Confederate pickets were weak on the other side of the river. This information was corroborated by Davies, the commander of the Second Brigade, Third Cavalry Division. In response, a cavalry detachment reconnoitered the Confederate positions but found little, and no casualties were reported. *OR*, ser. 1, vol. 29, pt. 2, 454.

29. The vote for governor in Grant County went to Lewis by a wide margin. He received 8,404 votes to 1,313 for Palmer. Governor Salomon did not receive a vote in the county. The statewide tally was 72,717 for Lewis, 49,053 for Palmer, and 167 for Salomon. Young, who had earlier written that the men were for Salomon, did not see this play out in the regiment. In the soldier vote, Lewis received 7,766 to 542 for Palmer and only 66 for Salomon. In the Seventh Wisconsin, it was more of the same, with 196 for Lewis and but one vote for Palmer. Nelson Dewey, facing Wyman Spooner for lieutenant governor, did not fare any better. In Cassville, Spooner received 107 votes, while the native Dewey garnered 70 votes. This trend continued at the state level for the former governor of Wisconsin, and Spooner was elected lieutenant governor of Wisconsin. War Democrat and hero Lucius Fairchild of the Second Wisconsin ran for secretary of state and won by an even larger margin than Lewis. Republicans, in a reversal from the previous year, racked up victories in the fall elections in several key states. Wisconsin, *A Manual of Customs, Precedents and Forms, . . . Lists and Tables for Reference*, comp. Clerks of Senate and Assembly (Madison, WI: William J. Park, 1864), 173, 180–81; Current, *The Civil War Era, 1848–1873*, 2:405–8; McPherson, *Battle Cry of Freedom*, 684–88; "Statement: Showing the Number of Votes Polled for Each Candidate," *Grant County Herald*, November 17, 1863.

Camp near Beverly ford Va Nov 21 1863

Dear Delia

Your letter came to hand yesturday. Sorry indeed to hear you were unwell. You must take good care of yourself. I hope to hear of your being better soon. We are all right side up with care. We are almost the rear of the army but are under marching orders and may be sent to the front at any time. We have sent men home to recruit. C B Bishop of Millville and Sergt Geo Eustice of Potosi went from our Co.

I send two hundred dollars in US 6 per cent bonds with Capt Gibson of Co C 2d Wis to Father. I also sent an order for him to pay you whatever money you want and hold the bonds. My object in taking bonds is that I can turn them into cash whenever I want. I intend to invest all my money in bonds after this with the exception of what you want to use. I can get bonds from the paymaster in place of green backs. As you appear to be almost out of money and it may be some time before you see Father I will send you ten Dollars in this letter, which is all that I can possibly spare at present, as I rather stinted myslf in order to send hom the even two hundred in bonds.

Yes. I promise you that when my 3 years is up I will come home and stay till you agree to let me go *again.* Now wont that do you. Col Callis is still at annapolis. He will probably be mustered out of the Service.

my love to all

ever yours

H F Y

Camp near Kelleys ford Va Dec 6 1863

Dear Delia

I have been across the Rapidan for the last ten days and have had no chance to write. I rec your letter. Glad to hear you were all well. We are under marching orders and will probably move to day. The roads are in horrible condition and it is verry cold campaigning but we stand it well, and the men never behaved better.

There were none of our Regt hurt on the other side of the River. We are lying between Kelleys ford on the Rappahannock and Gemania ford on the

Rapidan. When i get in a tent once more I will give you a history of our campaign. I will not let Furman or any other man have money to pay in case he is conscripted. It is men the Govt wants not money and Furman has just as much right to come and fight as any other man, and can come as well and better than thousands of others that will have to come. I hope Congress will knock that three hundred dollar clause to flinders before an other draft takes place. Old Grant raised the Devil with the Rebs at Chattanooga. It is said that Longstreet is back with Lee. If that is true our campaign is not over yet. My love to the children and yourself.[30]

ever yours

Henry

NOTE

30. Commutation was unpopular and consequently was repealed in 1864. Rosecrans, after his defeat at Chickamauga, was replaced by Maj. Gen. George H. Thomas as commander of the Army of the Cumberland. Lincoln, who sought new leadership in the west, created the Division of the Mississippi and placed Maj. Gen. Ulysses S. Grant in command. Unable to capitalize on his victory at Chickamauga, Bragg placed his army along Missionary Ridge and effectively bottled up federals in Chattanooga until Grant's arrival. Grant's plan to secure the mountain involved three forces led by Maj. Gen. William Tecumseh Sherman at the north end, the resuscitated Joe Hooker on the south end, and Thomas at the center. Hooker, looking to redeem himself after his poor performance at Chancellorsville, exceeded Grant's order and captured Lookout Mountain on November 24. Sherman's troops, encountering stiff resistance and having a tough time advancing from the north, forced Grant to order Thomas's men to advance at the center to aid Sherman's troops. Thomas's men, who had been humiliated at Chickamauga, charged the steep center of Missionary Ridge and forced the Confederates to retreat. Union casualties numbered 687 killed, 4,346 wounded, and 349 captured or missing. Confederate casualties were 361 killed, 2,160 wounded, and 4,146 captured or missing. Lt. Gen. James Longstreet's corps was detached to Tennessee on September 9, 1863, and made a failed attack on Knoxville on November 29. Longstreet did not return to the Army of Northern Virginia until April 1863. McPherson, *Battle Cry of Freedom*, 601n21, 675–81; H. W. Brands, *The Man Who Saved the Union: Ulysses Grant in War and Peace* (New York: Anchor Books, 2012), 272–76; Ronald C. White Jr., *American Ulysses: A Life of Ulysses S. Grant* (New York: Random House, 2016), 306–10; *OR*, ser. 1, vol. 29, pt. 1, 398, vol. 31, pt. 2, 25, vol. 33, 4; *Dyer's Compendium*, 866; Fox, *Regimental Losses*, 546, 551.

Camp near Kellys ford Va Dec 16 1863

Dear Father

I rec your letter several days ago but I was so busy getting up a shanty I had no time to answer it and what is worse I had no place to write. Now that I have got a good comfortable shanty you shall hear from me more freequently.

I am sorry to hear of your being so unwell and hope this will find you better. Since writing you last we have been south of the Rapidan as you will learn from the papers. It was bitter cold and we did not accomplish what we went for but it was no fault of ours.

For I never seen the men behave better and all appeared anxious for a fight and I am well sattisfide that the fault of failure rest with the 3d Corps in taking the wrong road the day we crossed the River. Had this corps been on hand to suppoart the 2d corps by 12 oclock as it should have been we would have fought the battle at Robertsons cross Roads where we would have had a fair fight. But this delay gave the enemy time to fall back and concentrate behind their entrenchments on mine Runn. Their position here was a strong one, but still I am satisfide we could have stormed their position. But it would have been at a great sacrifice of life, and Genl mead concluded it would not pay for the taking as he would have to immediately leave it. I had charge of the detail that built three Bridge across the Run. The Run was about the size of the creek at Millville, but on either side it was muckey and swampy for several rods rendering it bad for Artillery to pass. We pushed across oposite our front with two hundred men with arms and I was in command a bout fifty more with axes and shovels to build the bridges. We took the position without much resistance, but as soon as i set my men to work the ennemy opened on us a terrible canonade and our Artillery opened on them with 20 peices of cannon which soon silenced them. But I had to send for three hundred morre men to hold the position untill we got the bridges finished, which we did about 9 oclock pm.[31]

We had 29 men killed and wounded in the fracas. I cant tell how many of the Rebs were killed or wounded but I seen them carry off quite a number on strechers. Besides having a strong position and good fortifications the Rebs had cut down the pine forrest falling the trees with the tops towards us, and they had Sharpened all the limbs that stuck out so that it would have been impossible to have got through in any line of battle. We are now encamped near Kelleys ford on the South side of the Rappahannock the boys have built comfortable huts and are in good health. All Kidd is still in Georgtown hospitall with his cut foot. The rest of are well and ready for anything that turns up. This country as usual for the time of year is one d—d mud hole all over. The get mud any and everywhere to dab their cabins and build chimneys with. *Well what do you think of that pet institution of yours called the union League, d—d Sweet Scented set of cowardly puppies.* Pray dont consider me a member any longer for I have just learned that every one of them that could get off either by fair means or foul did so. I hope Congress will knock that $300 clause to flinders. There are quite a number of our Regt enlisting in the veteran corps. We offered to go in as a Regt and all reinlist four days ago. But mead is opposed to sending organnizations as he cant spare the men as there was applications already in for 25000 men provided he would send them in Organnizations of Regts. There wont in consequence be so many reinlist but still there will be quite a No. Four of my men reinlisted this morning and probably there will be more soon. I think there has about fifty reinlisted in our Regt to day. Have you got the bonds? Write soon.[32]

yours truly

H F young

NOTES

31. After learning that Lee had built entrenchments near the Rapidan, Maj. Gen. George Gordon Meade decided to launch an offensive against his positions. Meade's goal was to either turn Lee's right flank or have the Confederates attack the federal force. Almost immediately his plan hit a few snags. There was a weather delay, and the Third Army Corps, commanded by incompetent drunkard Maj. Gen. William French, fell behind schedule. This stopped the Sixth Corps, which trailed behind. A sharp engagement at Robertson's Tavern between French's Third Corps and two divisions of Lt. Gen. Richard Ewell's Second Corps ended badly for the federal troops, and French consequently accused Maj. Gen. Gouverneur Warren, Second Corps commander, of failing to link up with the federal forces. Lee's official report stated that the advance by French's force had been repulsed. The First Army Corps, including the Iron Brigade, did not arrive at Mine Run until 8 p.m. on November 27. At 3 a.m. on November 28, the brigade was put in line to relieve part of the Second Army Corps. Sharpshooters attached to the brigade pushed across Mine Run and built two bridges across the run. These positions were held until early on November 29, when the brigade was ordered back across Mine Run and ordered to destroy the bridges. Meade, whose force was finally in place on November 28, faced a well-entrenched Confederate force of fifty thousand troops on the other west side of Mine Run, a tributary of the Rapidan River. Warren, of the Second Army Corps,

was tasked with the advance; he personally scouted the enemy entrenchments and was so discouraged by what he saw that he canceled the attack. At first Meade was furious, but he later concurred with Warren's assessment after his own inspection of the Confederate entrenchments, and on December 3 the federal forces withdrew beyond the Rapidan. Wert, *The Sword of Lincoln*, 320–21; *OR*, vol. 29, pt. 1, 689–90, 695, 735–41, 825.

32. The Iron Brigade commander, Lysander Cutler, placed casualties at 3 killed, 33 wounded, and 7 missing. However, the *Official Records* reported casualties of 2 killed and 3 wounded. Union casualties were 173 killed, 1,152 wounded, and 381 captured or missing. Confederate casualties numbered 110 killed, 570 wounded, and 65 captured or missing. The Third Corps, not surprisingly, sustained the majority of the casualties, with 125 killed, 737 wounded, and 71 captured or missing. Some Union League members at home, it seems, took the opportunity to provide a substitute or to pay the commutation fee, to the disdain of Young. The $300 exemption did not sit well with soldiers. Another soldier in the Iron Brigade expressed frustration that "We observe that you talking chaps all pay your $300 or hire a substitute for less and remain at home." Some cities in Wisconsin offered an enlistment bounty of $200 to reach their required quota of volunteers before the January 5, 1864, deadline. *OR*, ser. 1, vol. 29, pt. 1, 678, 682, 689–90; Fox, *Regimental Losses*, 546, 551; *Dyer's Compendium*, 928; George W. Sturges, "What The Soldiers Think . . . The Iron Brigade Wants More Fighters and Less Talkers," in Edwin Bentley Quiner, *Quiner Scrapbooks: Correspondence of the Wisconsin Volunteers, 1861–1865*, 10 vols., electronic reproduction (Madison: Wisconsin Historical Society Digital Collections, 2010), vol. 8, 153; "Out of the Draft," *Wisconsin State Journal*, December 15, 1863.

Camp near Kellys ford va Dec 18 1863

Dear Delia

Griffin Hickok starts home this morning. He will call and see you and give you all the news. We are all well and I am in my own shanty.[33]

He is in a hurry. I have no time to write. Dont cut much of the timber or wood off the land between Jodys field and the race.

my love to all

ever yours

Henry

NOTE

33. Griffin Heacock was in Company F of the Seventh Wisconsin. *Roster*, 1:559.

Culpeper Va Dec 28 1863

Dear Delia

We are occupying this place at present. We had to leave our good comfortable winter qrs and come to front. We are qrts in old houses with no fireplaces and are in the most uncomfortable quarters we ever had in the winter time.

Our forces are picketing to the Rapidan. I cant see the use of making us move. It has been raining for twenty four hours. Mud knee deep and I feel to cross to write so I will quit.

Well I have warmed my feet and feel better natured. I suppose Grif Hickock called on you and gave you the news. If he did not I will ring his neck for him.

So Furman paid his $200 and I see most of the rest did the same. I would have liked to spend my christmas and New years at home with you and the children. I tell you I spent anything but a merry christmas. This place once a hansome town is now one of the most God forsaken places I ever was in. It is full of troops Cavalry Infantry and Artillery. You seldom see a citzen on the street and what few do venture out look [illegible] and no wonder for the place has been taken [illegible] army so often that the poor Devils dont know what minute they will be in the midst of terrible conflict. For they believe that Genl Lee will try to drive us back. The boys are well and tough and hardy nothing appears to faze them now. AA Kidd is still at Georgetown at the hospital. His foot has got well but his wound troubles him yet.[34]

The Veteran enlistment is still talked of. Quite a number of the 7th will reinlist and a number have already reinlisted. The Regt would go in if we could get our furlough now, but we could not get a satisfactory answer when we could go home. I dont think our men we sent home will get many recruits. It appears strange that men wont enlist under the liberal offers now offered and that to when the Rebellion is on its last legs, for I honestly believe that next summer will finish the Rebs. I dont feel like writing. You can see that by my miserable attempt. The fact is i feel homesick. Things are not running to please me. My love to all.[35]

ever yours

Henry

NOTES

34. The previous letter made clear that a number of men at home paid a replacement to serve in the army. Sections on the bottom part of the first page are missing for this letter.

35. Toward the end of 1863, in an effort to increase enlistments, the government offered a thirty-day furlough home and bounty to regiments that reenlisted three-quarters of their men. This induced roughly 28,000 troops in the Army of the Potomac to become part of veteran volunteer regiments. All totaled, federal enlistments topped 136,000 veterans. The Seventh Wisconsin Infantry enlisted 218 of 249 men on their rolls. On January 5, 1864, 201 men of the Seventh Wisconsin departed for a well-deserved thirty-day furlough. The furlough also served as a recruiting mission and added thirty-six new recruits to the ranks of Company F. Wert, *The Sword of Lincoln*, 323; McPherson, *Battle Cry of Freedom*, 720; Herdegen, *The Iron Brigade*, 464–65; *OR*, ser. 1, vol. 33, 358; *Roster*, 1:558–61.

CHAPTER SEVEN

"we will conquer and destroy the Reb Army"

February 16 to May 1, 1864

Camp Utly Feb 16th 1864

Dear Delia

We leave this infernal cold place in the morning for the old place in the front.[1] We have to leave most of our recruits at Madison to be mustered and paid, and i am sorry for it.

I have just expressed a trunk and a sack to Father with my over coat, also Sloats and Alls Kidds, and All has 3 blanketts and some other little articles all marked with his name on them. You will lay them out and keep then till called for.

You will have to get some person to pick the lock of the trunk as the key is lost. You wont get them till you move to Tafton. It is verry cold here. The wind blows right through us. We have all got bad colds and we are all ready to go south. I have felt real lonesome since i came back for it has been so cold. We could not drill or do anything but build big fires and sit by them.

Write soon and direct to Washington DC as you did before. Give my love to Jared Laura & May and except the same my dear little Woman.

ever yours

Henry

NOTE

1. Camp Utley, in Racine, Wisconsin, was one of Wisconsin's training facilities.

Camp Utly Racine Feb 17th 1864

Dear Father

We leave for the old Iron Brigade tomorrow morning at 8 oclock and I am not sorry for this is devilish cold soldiering. I have just sent a trunk and sack full of surplus clothing to Prairie duchien by Express. I had it sent to your address. You send over for it and pay the charges on them and you can send them down to Delia when she gets to Tafton and I will write to her about them. They belong to All Sloat and myself.

yours truly

H F Young

Write and direct as before. We have to leave two hundred of our recruits at Madison. We have about one fifty with us.[2]

NOTE

2. The Seventh Wisconsin returned to camp on February 26, 1864. United States, War Records Office, *War of the Rebellion: A Compilation of the Official Records of the Union and Confederate Armies*, 128 vols. (Washington, DC: Government Printing Office, 1885–1901), ser. 1, vol. 33, 623 (hereafter cited as *OR*).

Camp near Culpeper Va Feb 28 1864

Dear Delia

We are once more in our old position in the front after being run off the track and upset & C. We got here day before yesturday. All well but petty well used up, that is to say tired to death. I would just about as have go through a campaign as to have charge of soldiers from Wis.[3]

I had to leave C Chipman and all the boys from our neighbourhood in Wis. I expect them next week. We are under marching orders but i dont think we will move for some time. At least i hope not for we have lots of work to do in the way of making out Rolls and reports. Tomorrow is muster day and we are busy with the Rolls. The weather is fine as one could ask. We can camp out without inconvenience or freezing. I left $15.15 at Fathers in a letter to M K Young. I advanced the money to Young to pay the intrest and wrote to Father to keep the money. I am anxious to hear form you as i have got no letter yet. You will find 3 over coats in the trunk i sent home from Racine. Sloats Kidds and my own.[4]

You will know Sloats from Kidds by Sloats having the braid riped off the sleave. All but one braid. He had a Cols braid on the sleeve and riped off all but a Lieuts. I suppose you will move about the time you get this. I wish I was there to help you. Excuse this scroll as I am verry busy and I will promise better next time. My love to Jared Laura & may and the same to you my dear old girl.

ever yours

Henry

NOTES

3. The train that returned the men to Washington, DC, ran off the rail, resulting in an injury to the brakeman of the locomotive. Lance J. Herdegen, *The Iron Brigade in Civil War and Memory: The Black Hats from Bull Run to Appomattox and Thereafter* (El Dorado Hills, CA: Savas Beatie, 2012), 469.

4. Charles F. Chipman of Cassville enlisted in Company F on February 6, 1864. Milas K. Young of Grant County was a state senator throughout the war. Wisconsin, Adjutant General's Office, *Roster of the Wisconsin Volunteers, War of the Rebellion, 1861–1865*, Blue Books, 2 vols. (Madison: Democrat Printing Press, 1886), 1:559 (hereafter cited as *Roster*).

Camp near Culpeper Va Feb 29 1864

Dear Father

I just rec your letter. Glad to hear from you. We are in our old position in front, and All Kidd with a squad of men has just gone on pickett. We have just been mustered for the months of Jan & Feb. I think we will all need our pay before we get it. We had quite an acident comeing back. The cars run off the track 20 miles above Ft Wayne about 3 oclock in the morning. We were all a sleep. One of the coaches upset down the bank about 20 ft. It was full of soldiers and what seems strange to me is that they all escaped serious injury. Some had their heads cut eyes blacked, shins backed and c but none seriously hurt. Our Regt is about 350 strong here. We have over 200 men that is Recruits left back in the state. My Co is 48 men present.

The 6th got back last night. They had to leave their recruits. We look for the 19th Ind tomorrow. Then the old Brigade will be all one hand once more. The Papers has had considerable to say about reorganizing this

Army but we find it just as we left it. The same corps and the same commanders. Genl Cutler Comnds our Div and our Col assumed Comnd of our Brigade yesturday. The 6th & 3d Corps are out on reconnoisance to the Rapidan.[5]

And we have orders to be ready to march at a moments notice if anything should turn up that we would be needed. The weather is fine and springlike. The roads are drying up and all we want is a few days drill to break in our Recruits. We will be ready for anything that comes along. There are soldiers leaving on veteran furloughs every day and others returning.

Take two Thousand Dolls insurrance in the Artny for me. Insure on building and machinery. Sell whenever you can get $6000.00 in cash not land.

My best wishes to all.

yours truly

H F Young

NOTE

5. The 226 men home recruiting for the Sixth Wisconsin returned to the brigade February 28. Col. William W. Robinson was only temporarily in command of the brigade, and a complete reorganization of the army took place in March. The Army of the Potomac was reorganized into three corps in the spring of 1864. Disbanded in the reorganization, the First Army Corps transferred three divisions to the Fifth Army Corps, including the Iron Brigade. Maj. Gen. Gouverneur Warren, who had commanded the Second Corps in Maj. Gen. Winfield Scott Hancock's absence, was given command of the Fifth Corps. Brig. Gen. George Armstrong Custer's horse soldiers made a raid into Albemarle County, Virginia, from February 28 to March 1. His cavalry regiments went near Charlottesville before being turned back by a superior force of cavalry and infantry; they were consequently unsuccessful in their attempt to destroy rail bridges over the Rivanna River. However, Custer's force, after withdrawing across the Rapidan, managed to capture various equipages and about one hundred soldiers. On February 29, 1864, the Third and Sixth Corps advanced on Madison Court House to support the cavalry operations of Custer. *OR*, ser. 1, vol. 33, 3, 161–68, 623, 626–27, 717–18, 722–23; Jeffry D. Wert, *The Sword of Lincoln: The Army of the Potomac* (New York: Simon & Schuster, 2005), 329–30; Frederick H. Dyer, *A Compendium of the War of the Rebellion Compiled and Arranged from Official Records . . . and Other Reliable Documents and Sources* (Des Moines, IA: Dyer Publishing Company, 1908), 930 (hereafter cited as *Dyer's Compendium*).

Camp near Culpeper Va March 12th 1864

Dear Delia

I received your verry welcome letter two days ago. Glad to hear from you but the letter was not verry late news as it was near 20 days on the road.

We are still in camp and drilling our Recruits. I have 28 now in my Co. Charles Chipman J Evans H L Sprague Schallenberger Calvert & Garner arrived two days ago all well. Some of the have the mumps & and others the measles but all are doing well. Genl Grant is here stafing with Genl Mead. I suppose reviews will be the order of the day as they always follow the arrival of distingushed visitors.[6]

You must not give currency to Mrs Hortons Scandall for there is no truth in them. The fact is All Kidd did not take any one with him to Potosi. He and an other young man went down in a cutter and returned the same day. Perhaps the other stories are about the same. I dont think i will get my pay in time to send it to you before you move. You had better get your bills and send the money to Furman and let him pay them and send you the receipts. You must get money enough to pay your rent and for your wood. You had better just pay for them at once. I will transmit money to Prairie Duchien as soon as i get it which will be about the 1st of april. Write to me as soon as you can after you have moved, so that i can direct to Tafton. Perhaps you had better send up to Fathers for money, or i will write to him to go down and see you as soon as you get to Tafton and let you have what money you want. You will want to get your garden ploughed and some man to work in it, and i want you to pay down for all you get. You have the money subject to your order and it costs no more to pay as you get things than to buy on credit.[7]

There is no news of importance here. Everything is dull as the weather has been for the last few days, and it was dark murky raining and muddy. Give my love to Jared Laura & May, the same for yourself.

Ever yours

Henry

NOTES

6. Chipman, James H. Evans, Henry L. Sprague, Joseph Schallenberger, Martin Calvert, and John W. Garner enlisted in Company F of the Seventh Wisconsin on February 6, 1864. In March Lt. Gen. Ulysses S. Grant was appointed as General-in-Chief of all Union forces and decided to make his headquarters in the eastern

theater. Maj. Gen. George Gordon Meade retained command of the Army of the Potomac. *Roster*, 1:558–61; Wert, *The Sword of Lincoln*, 326; *OR*, ser. 1, vol. 33, 3.

7. Ann Horton resided in Waterloo, Grant County, with her husband, George. It is hard to say what this "scandal" may have been as it did not make the local newspaper. 1860 United States Census, Waterloo, Grant County, Wisconsin, digital image s.v. "Ann Horton," Ancestry.com.

Camp near Culpeper Va Mar 20 1864

Dear Father

On returning from pickett an hour ago i found your letter. Glad to hear from you. While i was out on pickett the Reb Cavalry made a reconnoicance in our front which had the effect of putting the whole army under marching orders for a few hours till it was ascertained that their force consisted of nothing but cavalry, when all became quiet again. I could not help constrasting the cool indifference of the veteran soldier, with the nervous anxiety of the recruits, when the announcement was made that the Rebs were advancing on us in force. But my recruits on pickett shewed no fear. They appeared to be brave and determined, but still they had that excitement which i beleive is natural to all men when about to meet danger or death for the first time. And when the firing commenced between our videtts and the enemys skirmishers, the old soldiers as usual in such cases began to laugh and joke each other about saying prayers, and about sending some Rebs to Hell, and one telling another now d—d you your times come youl get a throug tickett & c. It was ammusing to see the recruits open their eyes and stare. I was in command of the pickett line of the 1st Brigade and I can assure you if the Rebs had come on our men recruits and all would have given a good account of themselves.

The probability is that the Reb cavalry have started for a raid on our right by going down the Schandoah valley and that the Brigad in our front was for a blind to deceive us. At all events Custers Brigad started for the right last night. Cavalry raids are now the order of the day.[8]

Genl Grant is going to make Culpeper his head qtrs, and I hope he will do something by way of an advance. If Grant goes on his own hook he will probably win. But if he listens to those d—d cowardly curses about washington he will lose all the military fame he ever won in less than three months.

Our Regt numbers 422 enlisted men present for duty. I have 59 enlisted men present fo duty in my Co. 24 veterans & 35 recruits.

Five of my men that were taken prisnors at Gettysberg are among the parolled prisnors at Annapolis MD. L G Parsons & C J Parker are among the no. I have a number of recruits in the State yet.

Col Cobb and McIdoe were here a few days a go. Cobb spoke to me of you as being one of his best friends. I dont like the way they are doing in the way of reccommending men for promotion. Neither do i like the way Governour Lewis is doing the same thing. Every appointment appears to be made through political influence. We have plenty of non commissioned Officers in our Organizations that are fit to fill any position up to Col and they could be promoted to line officers and they deserve it. And whts more they would make soldiers of the recruits in the new Regts in half the time the citizens appointed by the Governour would.[9]

Col. Amasa Cobb, Forty-third Wisconsin Infantry (Wisconsin Historical Society, WHS-52510)

But the Governours pet political friends that dont know any thing about military get the appointment for line officers. Now the appointment of field officers from among the line officers of old Regts is all right, but it is neither the Col Lieut Col or major that drill the Regt and makes it ready for the field. But it is the line or co officers. There are quite a number of Regts home on veteran furloughs but there is more men returning three to one than what are going home. The rumor is that 3 corps from the southwest are to be sent here, but i dont beleive the story. If three corps come from the southwest I think they will be sent to Butler.[10]

All the Blanketts were mine but what All Kidds name was on. You keep a couple. They will make you good horse blankets. Let Delia have what money she wants for i dont want her to have to run in debt. I dont think we will get paid before sometime in april as all moneys at present goes to pay bounties. But that will play out in april.

yours truly

H F Young

NOTES

8. Custer commanded the Third Division of Cavalry Corps. On March 17 and 18 two detached regiments of the First Division, Cavalry Corps, the Sixth and Ninth New York, reconnoitered in Sperryville, Virginia. *OR*, ser. 1, vol. 33, 3; *Dyer's Compendium*, 931.

9. Col. Amasa Cobb began the war on the Field and Staff of the Fifth Wisconsin. On August 10, 1864, Cobb was appointed commander of the newly formed Forty-third Wisconsin and near the end of the war was promoted to brevet brigadier general. In addition, Cobb served in the House of Representatives with Walter D. McIndoe. Cobb represented the Third Congressional District, which encompassed southwestern Wisconsin, while McIndoe's Sixth District ran along a narrow line from La Crosse to Ashland. *Roster*, 2:723; Wisconsin, *A Manual of Customs, Precedents and Forms, . . . Lists and Tables for Reference*, comp. Clerks of Senate and Assembly (Madison: Atwood & Rublee, 1865), 136.

10. Maj. Gen. Benjamin Butler commanded the Army of the James. Part of Grant's plan for spring 1864 consisted of having Butler advance on the Confederate capital from the south while Maj. Gen. Franz Sigel's force in West Virginia was sent to disrupt Gen. Robert E. Lee's line of supply in Staunton; a third force, commanded by Nathaniel Banks, was instructed to capture Mobile, Alabama, thereby prohibiting reinforcements from joining Gen. Joseph Johnston's troops in Georgia. All parts of the plan ended in failure due mostly to poor leadership by each commander. James M. McPherson, *Battle Cry of Freedom: The Civil War Era* (New York: Oxford University Press, 1988), 722–24.

Camp 7th Wis vet vols near Culpeper Va March 21 1864

Dear Delia

I received your welcome letter three days ago and was sent on pickett duty before i had time to answer it. Glad to hear from you, but sorry to hear of Jared being sick. I feel anxious about you and will feel so untill i hear that you are moved and comfortably setled once more. We are having an Equinoxial storm of cold disagreeable weather. The fact is it is uncomfortably cold in our cabins. I rec a letter from Father last evenning. He had rec one from you for money. I wrote to him to give you what money you wanted.

The boys are getting along well. H L Sprague & J Schallenberger have the mumps but are getting well. The recruits are quite tender along side of the old soldiers. L G Parsons & Giles Parker and 3 others of my co that were taken prisnors at Gettysberg are annapolis MD.

We are drilling our recruits. I have 35 in my co and it gives us plenty to do. While i was on pickett the Reb cavalry made a reconnosance in our front which put the army under marching orders for a few hours untill we ascertained their strength then all was quiet again as usual. Delia I want you to get Abee; to make you out a Marriage certifficate and you get it from him dates the same as though he had given it to us when we were married. If i should happen to fall in the Army or die in the service your marriage certifficate is absolutely necessary for you to get your back pay and pension.[11]

I know of officers widows that cant get a settlement at all for want of a certificate. Genl Grant is going to command this Army and we are to be largely reinforced so we expect to have stirring times this spring. I will send this letter to cassville as i dont know when you will move. Give my love to Jared Laura and May and except the same for yourself.

ever yours

Henry

NOTE

11. Preserved Albee, Patch Grove, Grant County, performed the marriage ceremony for Henry and Delia on March 1, 1853. Grant County Genealogical Society, *Marriages for Grant County*, comp. Grant County Genealogical Society, vol. 2, 1987.

Camp near Culpeper Va March 27 1864

Dear Delia

I received your welcome letter last evenning. Glad to hear you were all well. I suppose you have moved before this. At all events i will send this letter to Tafton.

I sent Father $125.00 Dolls yesturday with orders to let you have what money you wanted. By a mistake of the paymaster I did not by $50.00 as much pay as was due me this pay day, but i will get it next pay day. We have had verry disagreeable weather for some days past, the snow fall to the depth of 6 to 8 inches and then it rained for two days. This is the first fair day we have had for some time. Genl Grant is here. They are reorganizing this Army. There are but three corps now. We are now the 1st Brigade 4th Division 5th Corps. The corps is Commanded by Maj Genl Warren. Our Division is com by Brgd Genl Wadsworth our old commander of one year ago.

Our Brigade is comd by Brigd Genl Cutler. So that when you hear news of the 4th Div 5th Corps or of the 1st Brigade 4th Div 5 corps it will mean

Brig. Gen. James Wadsworth and staff (Library of Congress, Prints & Photographs Division, Civil War Photographs, LC-DIG-ppmsca-34138)

us. For as usual we will give a good account of ourselves wherever we are put if it should be at the dinner table. C F Chipman is well L Sprague has been sent to the hospital with the mumps. The rest of the boys of your acquaintance are well. I am just going to let you use your own pleasure about who stays with you in Tafton to go school. You may take as many as you please or none unless you want them. So now if you aint suited dont scold me about it.

If Father does not let you have money enough to get you what is necessary and so that you can pay down for what you get let me know and i will send you money after this myself.

I understand that Parsons is not to teach in the Seminary this summer. But i want Jared and Laura go to school all the time when there is Schooll at either place. I have no news to write. Everyting is dull as a quaker meeting. Give my love to Jared Laura & May and except the same for yourself.[12]

everyours

Henry

I wrote this letter with a darned old quill pen of Sloats.

NOTE

12. Professor David Parsons and his wife, Sophronia, ran the Tafton Collegiate Seminary in Tafton, Wisconsin. A disagreement between Professor Parsons and the trustees led to Parsons's abrupt retirement in the winter term of 1864. Capt. W. W. Likens ran the school for a year, and in fall 1865 W. H. Holford and T. J. Brooks served as associate principals. A final attempt to revive the seminary was made by Professor Charles Newcomb and his wife until the building was abandoned two years later. In 1873 the Congregational Society bought the school and remade it into a church. Castello N. Holford, *History of Grant County Wisconsin . . . and a History of the Several Towns* (Lancaster, WI: The Teller Print, 1900), 645; Consul Willshire Butterfield, *History of Grant County Wisconsin, Containing an Account . . . of the United States* (Chicago: Western Historical Company, 1881), 816.

Camp near Culpeper Va April 7 1864

Dear Delia

I received your welcome letter two days ago. Glad to hear you were all well. We have been having terrible bad weather here for the last week. Rain snow and mud. This morning it has cleared up and looks more like living again. We are busy drilling our recruits. I have 39 recruits now in my co and I draw rations for 64 enlisted men. We have 502 enlisted men for duty in the Regt. It begins to look old fashioned. It looks as if we could do something and i think we will have it to do for on to Richmond will be the order again. But this time we will be suppoarted by two other Colums. Grant is going to attack with overwhelming numbers and I think will succeed.

I suppose you are in Tafton before this, at least I hope you are. I will feel anxious about you untill i hear you are moved and comfortable. We have some fun with our recruits. The old soldiers are always playing tricks on them, but they will get sharp enough after awhile. One anadote will illustrate how green some of them are. I have 8 men from St. Crois Falls or near there some living 10 or 12 miles from the falls, when we were paid off I

Maj. Gen. Gouverneur Warren (Library of Congress, Prints & Photographs Division, Civil War Photographs, LC-DIG-ppmsca-40695)

was putting up their money to express it home for them. One we call Dick lived 12 miles from the Falls and in his envelope he had placed a letter written to his wife. I wanted to know what it was he was sending there. Dick answered innocently that it was a letter informing his wife that he had expressed forty Dollars and where she would find it. He thought he might as well save postage. It was some time before i could get Dick to understand that his wife had better be informed by mail.[13]

This bad weather has given me the Rheumatism in my neck and right shoulder. It troubles me most at night after i go to bed. I think a few days of good weather will set me all right again. Roy Sprague has got well. All the boys of your acquaintance are well. We had an Election tuesday. My co polled 33 votes. All for Jo Mills. The Army are almost unanimous for old Abe as the soldiers call him for President. I tell you we have got a live man for our corps commander Genl Warren, and the boys all like the appearance of Genl Grant.[14]

My love to Jared Laura & May. Tell them papa wants them to be good children.

ever yours

Henry

NOTES

13. Richard H. Turnbull of St. Croix Falls enlisted in Company F of the Seventh Wisconsin on February 18, 1864. *Roster*, 1:561.

14. Henry L. Sprague of Cassville, Wisconsin, enlisted in Company F of the Seventh Wisconsin on February 6, 1864. Joseph T. Mills, Delia's uncle by marriage, was reelected judge of the circuit court by a majority of one thousand votes. Mills served as judge for twelve years in Grant County. He also served as district attorney for Grant County in 1859–60 and 1863–64. *Roster*, 1:561; "J. T. Mills Elected," *Wisconsin State Journal* (Madison, WI), April 15, 1864; Holford, *History of Grant County Wisconsin*, 113–15.

Camp 7th Wis vet vols near Culpeper Va April 17 1864

Dear Delia

I have received two verry welcome letters from you since my last. Glad to hear you are all well and that you have got moved. Sorry to hear you had so much trouble getting your things up, but hope you have got them ere this.

I have ordered the Harpers Weekly sent for one year to Jared. Tell him it is his paper and papa wants him to learn to read it well.

This is a cold disagreeable day for this time of year. We have had thus far nothing that you would call spring. Every thing has been got ready for the Grand advance which may now take place any day. All sutlers citizens surplus bagage & Clothing has been sent to the rear, and we are not waiting for something to turn up like Micawber but we are hard at work to be ready when the order strike tents comes. Delia it is hard to tell what the next 30 days will bring forth. There will be evidently great changes take place. Many that appeared on inspection this morning will in less that 30 days fall in the terriffic conflict which is about to commence. Lee is massing all the troops he can in our front and about Richmond, and Grant is not idle. So that the position of the true soldier and patriot is to look the danger in the face and nerve himself to meet it. Yes meet it with the cool determination to conquer or die. This is no fancy picture. The feeling of conquer ~~of~~ or die never was appearantly so strong before. In fact the general impression is that we will conquer and destroy the Reb Army. The reason of this feeling is this. We will have a column on our left operating in conjunction with us heretofore. We have been alone in our movements and always had to keep between Lee and Washington. Now we will have a chance to flank the Rebs.

My co are in good health. My Recruits drill almost equal to old soldiers. Sloat & Kidd are both well & hearty. I hope you will enjoy yourself now. I feel a great deal better satisfide since you have moved. I always felt uneasy about the children while at the mill. Did Chipman take our house? Charles gets along well. When you get Kassia & Janie you will have plenty of company for both you & the children.[15]

Give my good wishes to John Collier & annt Hannah. Tell old John that I am strong in the faith that we will whip out the Rebs this summer. Papa sends his love to Jared Laura and May not forgetting Mama.[16]

ever yours

Henry

NOTES

15. Casanna M. Warner was the daughter of Jared Warner. There was no Janie in the Warner, Mills, or Paul families in the 1860 census. Jane Morse, the daughter of Abraham and Susan Morse of Tafton, is a possible reference as their daughter was close in age to Young's daughter Laura. 1860 United States Census, Tafton,

Grant County, Wisconsin, digital image s.v. "Cassana Warner" and "Jane Morse," Ancestry.com.

16. John and Hannah Collier lived in Tafton, Wisconsin, and John was employed as a blacksmith. 1860 United States Census, Tafton, Grant County, Wisconsin, digital image s.v. "John Collier," Ancestry.com.

Camp 7th Wis vet vols near Culpeper Va Apl 22 1864

Dear Father

This is the first plesant day we have had for some time. The sprng thus far has been verry wet & cold. The Mts in our front are still covered with snow and the nights are cold and damp and ~~cold~~ disagreeable. I dont think i ever saw a more ~~cold~~ disagreeable spring anywhere than this one here.

We are busy drilling our Recruits and prepearing them for the coming campaign. We have made good use of our time and when the order fall in comes it will find us ready. Our Recruits are good men and they almost equal to old veterans. Our Regt Nos over 500 Enlisted men for duty. My Co has 63 Enlisted men for duty. The health of the men is good and the whole Army is being put in the best possible condition in the way of drill Arms & complete Equipments.

It is useless for me to Speculate on when where or what the next campaign will be. It is questions we ask each other every day but none are able to answer even to their own satisfaction.

One thing we all feel crtain of. That the next campaign will be one of desperate fighting on both sides. Genl Grant is having everything his own way. The War Dept appears to grant him whatever he wants. That being the case I feel quite confident of success. The cavalry are being Reorgannized and heavily reinforced. They appear to be changing commanders by taking Genls from our Cavalry here to the South West and bringing Genls from there to comd our Cavalry here. I feel anxious to hear if you got the money I sent to P Duchien.[17]

I Received a letter from I G Ury a few days ago in relation to that note. He said he had sent the note to A Paul with instructions to take such money on it as he would himself take on the notes due him. He said that Alex Paul sent the note back to him without any explannation and he supposed that you refused to pay it. I am sorry you did not pay it for i am tired being bothered with it and as you and Ury cant come to terms about it. I dont want to pay Intrest on it longer than next pay day. I will have two hundred dollars or more to send home next month so i will send him the money from here unless you succeed in setting it sooner. If you do let me know. Thomas Blunt is here. He will make a good soldier. The Alexander boys are tough & hearty. Genl Wadsworth Comds our Division Cutler our Brigade. We are expecting Governour Lewis to day. Delia has got to Tafton and I am glad of it. She writes that Kassa is going to stay with her and go to school. I am glad of it. They will be company for each other. Give my good wishes to all.[18]

yours truly

H F Young

NOTES

17. Maj. Gen. Philip Sheridan was placed in command of the Cavalry Corps of the Army of the Potomac on April 4, 1864. *OR*, ser. 1, vol. 33, 4.

18. Alexander Paul owned a general merchandise store in Patch Grove that was once owned by I. G. Ury. Cyrus Alexander and Thomas W. Blunt enlisted in Company F of the Seventh Wisconsin on December 31, 1863, and February 25, 1864, respectively. A reception was held in the home of Gen. Starkweather, the first commissioned colonel of the Wisconsin Infantry, on April 22, 1864. Attending the gala were Wisconsin senators Doolittle and Howe, eight generals, former governor Randall, and many others. "The party separated about one o'clock, all well pleased with the entertainment." Butterfield, *History of Grant County*, 856; *Roster*, 1:558; "A Distinguished Party and a Pleasant Time," *Evening Star* (Washington, DC), April 22, 1864; "Our Washington Letter," *Wisconsin State Journal*, April 27, 1864.

Camp near Culpeper Va May 1st 1864

Dear Delia

I received your welcome letter three days ago. Glad to hear you were all well and that you had got comfortable settled in your new home. We are still in our old camp with six days rations on hand as per Genl Order. Ready to move at a moments notice.

We dont where or when we are going. Burnsides with his Army are said to be at Warrenton Junction and Bristoe Station. That move has knocked our theory and speculation on the comeing campaign into a cooked Hat.[19]

We have been fortifing to some extent here in plain sight of the Rebs. I am inclined to think it is only for a blind for the works would be of little use to us unless it is the intention to leave a force here to hold this point when the army moves. Our Rebs in Culpeper feel verry certain that Genl Lee will shortly pay us a visit, and i am satisfide nothing would suit us better.

Yesturday was muster day for the months of March and april. Our Regt is larger now than it has been since Aug 1862.

One year ago today we were fighting the Battle of Chancellorsville. The Rebs and us occupy the same lines we did then here in Va. In other sections we have gained great advantage but then and now the mainstay of the Southren Confederacy is in our immediate front for Lees Army is all that keeps the Rebellion from going to pieces. They hold all the gaps and heights in our front and have them well fortified. It would take three times their No to take them by assault and a flank movement is what we must have.

This is a beautiful day. I wish I was at home to gather flowers for you as I used to do on a pleasant Sunday. I often think of those dear old pleasures that we both so much enjoyed. Every early spring flower i see brings them fresh to my memory and I sigh to think they were so short. I often wonder if we will ever be permitted to renew them again. And I always feel hopefull and yet I cannot shut my eyes to the danger of the coming struggle. Many will fall, and if it should be my misfortune to fall, it will be in the line of my duty as becoms a true soldier. And I will have the proud satisfaction that I have been true to my wife and family as well as to my country.

If this should befall us you will have to struggle hard to raise our Family. It will look dark and dreary to you at first but I feel that you are equal to the task. Endeavour to give each a good substantial education & teach them to be true Patriots. As for myself all I ask is that you should remember my good quallities if I have any and forget my faults.

I wrote to Susan long a go and also to Will. Tell Sue I shall expect to see something xtra in the young Grant. Did you get the Harpers Weekly? Tell Jared when he learns to read it well I will send him something else. Dont let him get into the habit of running round. If you do it will give you a great trouble. His Grand pa wrote me that he left there without saying anything about it and I felt quite uneasy about him untill I received your letter. Tell him pa says he is a naughty boy and he must do so no more. This everlasting drill and putting on style as the boys call it has become a perfect bore. We are all tired of it. The army is in splendid condition. The roads are dry and hard. The weather warm and pleasant. The newspapers are harping for the army to move, but they may scold and fret to their hearts content. Grant will give the order to move when he gets ready. What he is waiting for is more than I can tell but I feel confident he must have good and sufficient reason therefor.

The boys are in good health and appear anxious for the order to march. John W Garner was sent to hospital some time ago. He is getting better. All the boys of your accquaintance are in good health. I will send you the Photograph of one of my particular friends. You take care of these photographs and I will send you a larger album the first opportunity. Give my love to Jared Laura and May and except the same.[20]

ever yours

Henry

NOTES

19. Maj. Gen. Ambrose Burnside's Ninth Army Corps arrived from Tennessee on April 29, 1864. Burnside, who outranked Meade, was given an independent command and at least initially reported directly to Grant. Wert, *The Sword of Lincoln*, 330–31.

20. John W. Garner was in Company F of the Seventh Wisconsin. *Roster*, 1:559.

CHAPTER EIGHT

"My dear little woman if I am so unfortunate as to fall my last thoughts will be of you and the dear ones"

May 13 to August 6, 1864

On the field of Battle near Spotsylvania Court H May 13th 1864

Dear Delia

I am alive yet and as the saying is worth two or three dead men. I was slightly wounded the first days fight on the B[r]east and on the right arm, but i did not leave the field. We have been in front for 9 days continually fighting almost night and day. The Rebs are quiet this morning and are said to be falling back. I have lost over half my Co in Killed & wounded. There are four missing that I dont know whether are killed or wounded for they fell into the hands of the Rebs on the first days fight. James Evens was severely wounded and was I fear taken prisnor.[1]

C F Chipman	severe wound and got to hospital
H L Sprague	the same
Wm R Ray	wounded
C B Bishop	wounded
A M Hutchinson	wounded
J L Taylor	Do
Web Cook	Do

Well I cant enumerate them. There is just 30 wounded that got to our hospital. There was none of your accquaintances killed. The fighting is almost entirely in the thick timber where we have to fight them at great disadvantage. We had a terrible fight yesturday drove the ennemy & captured a number of guns and several thousand prisnors but we are completely worn out. Our loss must be near fifty thousand in killed wounded & missing. My love to all.[2]

ever yours

Henry

NOTES

1. The Battle of the Wilderness, May 5–7, was the opening salvo of the Overland Campaign. The federals slipped across the Rapidan River at Ely's and Germanna Fords. The opposing armies ran into each other in the early morning of May 5. Maj. Gen. George Gordon Meade ordered Maj. Gen. Gouverneur K. Warren to attack, an order delayed for more than two hours. The federal attack started well enough around 1 p.m., but soon after the balance shifted to the Confederates, who had a more intimate understanding of the tangled undergrowth than the federals. The brigade came to a clearing, Saunders' Field, on the south side of Orange Turnpike and met withering fire. Panic ensued in the ranks of the men, and for the first time in the war they fled from the fighting. In the advance, the Iron Brigade's line extended beyond the two brigades on either side of it. This gave Confederate soldiers a perfect opportunity to roll up the flanks of the brigade and sent them reeling to the rear. Because of the large number of new recruits in their first action, this outcome was perhaps inevitable. A second attack that day, by Warren's Fifth Corps and Maj. Gen. John Sedgwick's Sixth Corps, ended with similar results. On day two of the Wilderness, Lt. Gen. Ulysses S. Grant, using Maj. Gen. Winfield Scott Hancock's Second Corps, shifted the main attack to the Confederate right, while Brig. Gen. James Wadsworth's division advanced on the left flank of Lt. Gen. Ambrose P. Hill's corps. Initially, the attackers caught the Confederates off guard and advanced until the arrival on the field of Lt. Gen. James Longstreet's corps. His timely arrival and an attack from a concealed railroad bed sent the federals to the rear once again. James Wadsworth, attempting to rally his division, was fatally shot in the head and died. The day was equally costly for the Confederates; Longstreet took a bullet in the abdomen, an injury that sidelined him for five months. James H. Evens of Company F was wounded at the Wilderness and died of disease on January 28, 1865, in Salisbury, North Carolina. James M. McPherson, *Battle Cry of Freedom: The Civil War Era* (New York: Oxford University Press, 1988), 724–26; Jeffry D. Wert, *The Sword of Lincoln: The Army of the Potomac* (New York: Simon & Schuster, 2005), 335–37, 340–41; Lance J. Herdegen, *The Iron Brigade in Civil War and Memory: The Black Hats from Bull Run to Appomattox and Thereafter* (El Dorado Hills, CA: Savas Beatie, 2012), 479–80, 482–83, 488, 490, 492; Gordon C. Rhea, *The Battle of the Wilderness, May 5–6, 1864* (Baton Rouge: Louisiana State University Press, 1994), 160–63; United States, War Records Office, *War of the Rebellion: A Compilation of the Official Records of the Union and Confederate Armies*, 128 vols. (Washington, DC: Government Printing Office, 1885–1901), ser. 1, vol. 36, pt. 1, 190–91 (hereafter cited as *OR*); Frederick H. Dyer, *A Compendium of the War of the Rebellion Compiled and Arranged*

from Official Records . . . and Other Reliable Documents and Sources (Des Moines, IA: Dyer Publishing Company, 1908), 933–34 (hereafter cited as *Dyer's Compendium*); Wisconsin, Adjutant General's Office, *Roster of the Wisconsin Volunteers, War of the Rebellion, 1861–1865*, Blue Books, 2 vols. (Madison: Democrat Printing Press, 1886), 1:559 (hereafter cited as *Roster*).

2. Skirmishing between the two armies continued on May 7 when Grant, acting differently from his predecessors, turned the army south toward Spotsylvania Court House. About a mile to the northwest of Spotsylvania, the Iron Brigade and the rest of the Fifth Corps, supported on the left by the Sixth Corps, were ordered to take Laurel Hill, the left flank of the Confederate lines. The Confederates on Laurel Hill, in their well-fortified position, successfully beat back two attempts by Warren's Fifth Corps on May 10 and 12; many felt this was a futile move by the brigade. Fierce fighting at a salient in the Confederate lines, the "Mule Shoe," took place for most of the day on the federal left, involving the Second and Sixth Army Corps. The apex of the "Mule Shoe," where the fighting raged morning, afternoon, and night, acquired a new name that day, the "Bloody Angle." Union casualties at the Wilderness were 2,246 killed, 12,038 wounded, and 3,383 captured or missing. Casualties at Spotsylvania numbered 2,725 killed, 13,416 wounded, and 2,258 captured or missing. In seven days the Union Army had casualties of 36,065. Wert, *The Sword of Lincoln*, 345–354; Herdegen, *The Iron Brigade*, 501–2, 504–5; William F. Fox, *Regimental Losses in the American Civil War* (Albany, NY: Albany Publishing Company, 1889), 546; *Dyer's Compendium*, 933–34.

In Line of Battle near Spotsylvania CH Va May 17 1864

Dear Delia

I am all right yet and the fight goes on. We are east of Spotsylvania CH just one mile. The Rebs are in stong possition just between us & the CH. We are gradually forcing them back having to fight for every foot of ground we get. It has rained six days & the roads are in horrible condition. Our Brigade has been the front line of Battle ever since the fighting commenced and we lose some every day. Since my last I have had two men wounded. They were brothers by the name of Forra. Lee tells his men they must fight it out with us here for if he has to fall back to Richmond he would have to surrender.[3]

Excuse these short letters for I have not slept for 12 days. Only what I could catch lying down with my clothes on & arms by my side ready for use at a moments notice. My love to all.

Henry

I have had no mail for 3 weeks as it comes no farther than Washington.

NOTE

3. George and Richard Faurre, Company F of the Seventh Wisconsin, were wounded at Laurel Hill, Virginia, on May 8, 1864. *Roster*, 1:559.

In line of Battle C near Hanover Junction May 24 1864

Dear Delia

I am still on duty and as ever with the Regt in the front Line next the ennemy. We crossed the north anne River yesturday about noon at this place.[4]

Last night the Rebs attacked us with terrible yells and a heavy Column and tried to drive us into the river. They knowing that only the 5th Corps had crossed and they attacked us before we had got in possition. We defeated them with terrible slaughter. Our Regt lost 3 killed 13 wounded 4 missing. I had one man M McHugh severely wounded and one man Wm J Garner missing. This campaign is trying our endurance as well as our courage. I never knew how much I could stand before. I have not had a change of clothing for more than three weeks and most of that time we have up and moveing or fighting night and day. We are so worn out that we go to sleep in line of Battle under heavy Artillery fire.[5]

The people of the north can have no idea of the hardship to be endured in such a campaign as this where every foot of ground is hotly contested. I would write to Father and rest of the friends but I have neither time or paper envellops or anything else and cant get them till our teams comes up. When that will be is hard to tell. So let them get their news from you.

The papers will inform you that we are getting the better of the Rebs. If it was not for that to cheer us on we would fall by the wayside. I am to tired and sleepy to write more.[6]

My dear little woman if I am so unfortunate as to fall my last thoughts will be of you and the dear ones. My love to all.

ever your

Henry

NOTES

4. After Spotsylvania, Grant attempted to put himself between Lee and Richmond and skirted around the Confederate right flank. Lee positioned his army just

ahead of the federal advance and crossed the North Anna River and prepared his defenses. Warren's Fifth Corps, leading the army, crossed the North Anna at Jericho Mills. Brig. Gen. Lysander Cutler, the new divisional commander after the death of James Wadsworth, arrayed his forces on the south side of the river and put the Iron Brigade in front. Col. William W. Robinson was the new commander of the brigade. Around 5 p.m., A. P. Hill sent a division against the Iron Brigade. The attack sent more than half the brigade running for the river; only the Sixth Wisconsin conducted an orderly withdrawal. Federal artillery and Warren's other divisions put a stop to the Confederate advance. Gen. Robert E. Lee's defensive formation, an inverted "V," was perfect for the terrain, and after several limited attempts Grant decided to move around Lee's right flank once again. For the period from May 22 to June 1, the Seventh Wisconsin lost 20 killed, 95 wounded, and 17 missing or captured. Union casualties at North Anna were 186 killed, 942 wounded, and 196 missing or captured. Herdegen, *The Iron Brigade*, 508–12; Wert, *The Sword of Lincoln*, 358–60; Joseph Wheelan, *Bloody Spring: Forty Days That Sealed the Confederacy's Fate* (Boston: Da Capo Press, 2014), 257–58, 260–63; *OR*, ser. 1, vol. 36, pt. 1, 158.

5. William J. Garner, Seventh Wisconsin Infantry, was not listed as missing or captured during the campaign. He was mustered out of the regiment at the end of the war. Michael McHugh, Company F of the Seventh Wisconsin, was wounded at the Wilderness, returned to duty, and was mustered out of the regiment at the end of the war. *Roster*, 1:559–60.

6. While inaccurate, one morning headline reinforced Young's view that the battle had ended more favorably than in reality. The *Wisconsin State Journal* (Madison, WI), on May 24, 1864, stated, "A Rebel Midnight Attack, Are Fearfully Repulsed, Our Guns Mow Them Down." Another headline, in the *Janesville Daily Gazette* (Janesville, WI), on the same date announced, "The Rebels Get Punished!" Both headlines did little justice to the real events of the Overland Campaign.

May 31 1864

Dear Delia

We are in line of Battle this morning on the Road from Newcastle to McClanicksville between the Pumunkey & the Chickehomeny and about 5 miles from the latter place. Our Corps is the extreeme left of our Army and Ewells Corps attacted us yesturday with the intention of turning our left. But they found us prepared for them. They were repulsed with heavy loss. Genl Ramsey Comdg the old Stonewall Division was killed and was left on the field. Since my last i have had four men wounded. Corpl T C Alexander Corpl J C Raemer Geo W St Claire & Joseph Schallenberger. None of them dangerous.[7]

I received your welcome letter last night after the fight. Glad indeed to hear from you. I also received one from Father and it is all the blank paper I can raise to write this on. Tell them all that I dont forget them but I cant at present write as I have not got paper Envelopes or anything else and we are working marching and fighting day & night. Our Regt has lost 330 men 33 are missing 297 killed & wounded. We are getting men almost every day prisnors & men that were in hospital.[8]

Give my love to Jared Laura May & Janie. It almost makes me homesick every time i think of our dear old home.

ever yours

Henry

NOTES

7. Grant disengaged federal troops from the North Anna River on the evening of May 26 and marched around Lee's right flank once again. Lee, who at first thought Grant was heading to the southwest, adjusted and aligned his force along Totopotomoy Creek in a well-entrenched defensive position while Grant's troops crossed the Pamunky River, only eight miles from Mechanicsville, by May 28. Maj. Gen. Jubal Early, whose Confederate troops were at the far right of Lee's line, saw an opportunity to strike at Warren's Fifth Corps, in the hope of cutting it off from the federal move around Lee's right flank. Maj. Gen. Stephen Ramseur, one day shy of his twenty-seventh birthday, led the former division of Jubal Early in the May 30 attack. It did not go well. As they drew near, federal artillery ripped into the assaulting Confederate force, halting its advance; with no orders to withdraw, the unit continued to advance, despite heavy casualties, until it finally withdrew. Thomas C. Alexander, Isaac C. Raemer, George W. St. Claire, and Joseph Schalenberger, all in Company F of the Seventh Wisconsin, were all wounded at North Anna. Wert, *The Sword of Lincoln*, 360–62; Wheelan, *Bloody Spring*, 280–81; *Dyer's Compendium*, 939–40; *Roster*, 1:558, 560–61.

8. Capt. Henry F. Young's estimate of casualties was a little low—in fighting between May 5 and June 1, casualties in the regiment numbered 425 men killed, wounded, captured, or missing. *OR*, ser. 1, vol. 36, pt. 1, 125, 143, 158.

~

June 5 1864

Dear Delia

I have not recived any letters from home since I wrote you last. Am looking for one anxiously. We are in line of Battle about four miles from little medow Bridge on the Chickahomeny. Our Corps is the extreeme right our left resting on the Chickahomeny. There has been some desperate fighting since my last.[9]

Our Regt has been skirmishing and building brest works all the time. Our works and the Rebs are so close together here that we shoot from one line of Battle to the other. The consequence is we have both to keep under cover as much as possible. Lieut Sloat was severely wounded yesturday. The ball passing through the thigh between the bone & the main artery making a severe and painful though not dangerous woung. On the 3d Copl W*m* H Miles was shot through the leg below the knee breaking the bone.[10]

Those are all the Casualties in my co since my last. Lieut AA Kidd is Division ordenance officer. He gets a horse to ride and will get along first rate. It is five weeks to day since I had a clean shirt. What think you of that? Well I feel in good spirits. I may fall but it is with the firm conviction that we will win and that my children will be the gainers, and I am satisfide that you will get along bravely though lonely. If i should fall you must not get down hearted but meet it bravely as we meet the Rebs with a determination to conquor or die.

Give my love to all the friends and to the dear ones Jared Laura May & Janie. Tell them papa longs to see them and often dreams of them but wakes to find his arms in his hands instead of the little carresse of his dear ones at home. Accept for yourself as ever my love.

ever yours

Henry

NOTES

9. As the two armies raced toward Cold Harbor, the Fifth and Ninth Corps occupied the federal right near Bethesda Church. On the afternoon of June 2, Lee's left flank struck the Fifth and Ninth Corps, resulting in 1,366 Union casualties. That same day, Grant wanted to attack Lee's right at Cold Harbor, but the Second Army Corps was not ready, having just arrived late the previous evening. The delay gave Lee another day to dig in and prepare for the assault. When it came, at 4:30 a.m. on June 3, Lee's men were well entrenched. Several federal advances failed to dislodge the Confederates, leading to horrific casualties for the attackers. Union casualties were 1,844 killed, 9,077 wounded, and 1,816 captured or missing, similar to losses at the Wilderness and Spotsylvania, except that at Cold Harbor most of the casualties came in the first hours of the battle. Wheelan, *Bloody Spring*, 291–96, 300–306; Wert, *The Sword of Lincoln*, 361–65; *Dyer's Compendium*, 941; Fox, *Regimental Losses*, 547.

10. 1st Lt. William E. Sloat and William H. Miles, Company F of the Seventh Wisconsin, were wounded at Bethesda Church and Cold Harbor, respectively. Sloat's injury was severe—he resigned on September 14, 1864. William H. Miles

recovered from his wound and was mustered out of the service at the end of the war. *Roster*, 1:558, 560.

On Pickett on the bank of the Chickahomeny near the West Point Railroad Bridge

June 8 1864

Dear Father

I have rec two letters from you since this campaign commenced but I had no materials for writing and I will further acknowledg i had no time nor inclination to write. I am sleepy this morning, but I will try and write you a short letter. The chickahomeny here is about 30 ft wide but deep. The Rebs are on the south. We on the north. By mutual agreement we are not firing any on our part of the line but the boys are doing a brisk business in the way of trade. I have been reading the Richmond papers of yesturday. They feel sore over the capture of Staunton by Hunter but say that everything must be kept here to defeat Grant for if he is defeated they can soon get back all the other places they have lost. But if they lose Richmond they loose all together. I think the one hundred day men will be sent to the front to work on intrenchments. There are several Regts here already. Grant will fight all the force he can get. That is the way to do it[11]

I got to my carpet sack yesturday and got the first change of shirts & drawers I have had for 35 days. All the officers in the Brigade were in the same fix.

Talk about being lousy & dirty, *Oh ye Gods.* Our Div has marched & counter marched till the distance amts to over 300 miles. This is not allone a campaign of courage. It is more trying on the endurance than on the mere courage or pluck on the field.

I told you long ago that the last battle of the Rebellion would be fought in Va. We are kind of resting at present. That is yesturday and to day and I can assure you we need it. We only repoart one man as killed dead on the field but it my own oppinion that E Moses R Blakeley & Peter Francis were all killed. But I am not certain only in case of Francis. The others I repoart as missing. Frank Brother was taken prisnor. There are four or five men that were slightly wounded the first day that have returned to the co. The following comprises the list of wounded that are absent in hospital several of which are reporated dead.[12]

T C Alexander	Severe
Wm H Miles	"
Wm R Ray	"
T C Ramer	"
N Bradberry	"
C Alexander	Slight
Geo Atkinson	Severe
John Bradley	Slight
A Bishop	severe
C B Bishop	slight
Bruce Biran	"
H Bonham	"
W Cook	"
A Conner	verry severe perhaps mortal
G Corrick	mortally since dead
C Chipman	severe
J Endicot	slight
J Evens	wounded severe left on field probably dead
J Folk	severe
G Fourra	slight
A Fourra	"
A Hutchinson	"
T F Kinney	"
A Morse	"
T W Riley	severe
H Rupkee	slight
H L Sprague	perhaps mortally
J Schallenberger	slight
Geo W St Clair	slight

We have 30 absent wounded or that have died of wounds 3 missing 1 killed. There is scarecely a man in the co but what has been hit. Lieut Sloat is severely wounded in the thigh. Lieut Kidd is Div ordnance officer and is all right. He sends his good wishes. I was struck on the right Brest & knocked down making quite a Bruise. I was also slightly wounded on the right wrist and two days ago i was struck on the shoulder with a piece of lounding case shot. They are all slight. If I get no worse I will come out all right. This is as near correct as I can come at it now. We have had 4 officers killed & 14 wounded.

The cannons are beginning roar down the River. I think it is Sherredions Cavalry trying to cross at Bottoms Bridge. I have over $400 due me from Govt but dont know when I will get it.[13]

Delia writes me she has some debts unpaid at Cassville. Now those debts must be paid. In my anxiety to pay you & get out of debt I sent her to little money for her to get along with, and she says you scold her so she wont ask you for money to pay them. Now that is no use for those debts must be paid the sooner and as you have money belonging to me, let her have sufficient to pay her debts and enough to live on.

And if I fall in Battle try & trade of my half of the mill for land in some sutable locatity where with it and the pension of $20 per month she can live comfortable. I have been so fortunate thus far that is has become a common saying amongst my Brother officers that I will get killed dead the next punch i get. I hope not. At all events I will fall if fall. I must as becomes the true soldier.

My love to all.
yours truly

H F Young

NOTES

11. In the aftermath of Cold Harbor, Grant did not attempt to gather the wounded and the dead until June 5. Grant hoped that unarmed soldiers could retrieve the dead and wounded, but Lee rejected this idea. Lee proposed that Grant collect troops anytime under a flag of truce, but Grant vehemently opposed this because it suggested defeat. Grant, by June 7, finally caved in and called for a truce at 8 p.m., four and a half days after the battle. Maj. Gen. David Hunter, commander of the Department of West Virginia, was part of a plan to disrupt Lee's line of supplies. It called for Hunter to enter the Shenandoah Valley, destroy a supply depot in Lynchburg, and then link up with Grant near Richmond. Hunter met with early success, capturing one thousand Confederate soldiers in Piedmont, Virginia; he then moved to Staunton and Lexington before getting to the all-important depot at Lynchburg. Lee correctly saw this as a serious threat and consequently sent Jubal Early's Second Corps to defend Lynchburg. The federal troops tested the defenses at Lynchburg and withdrew into West Virginia, essentially sealing the fate of Hunter, who subsequently lost his command. The *Richmond Enquirer* stated, "there comes bad news from Staunton. Gen. Hunter, . . . has been reinforced and marched up the Valley." It went on to say, "It is very distressing that the beautiful Valley of Virginia should be subject to the devastation of the enemy." *Richmond Enquirer*, June 7, 1864; Wheelan,

Bloody Spring, 314–15, 320–22; McPherson, *Battle Cry of Freedom*, 737–39; Wert, *The Sword of Lincoln*, 371, 377, 386; *OR*, ser. 1, vol. 37, pt. 1, 1.

12. Robert Blakeley, Peter Francis, and Frank Brother were all soldiers in Company F of the Seventh Wisconsin. Blakeley was captured during the Wilderness and died at Andersonville, Georgia, November 14, 1864. Francis was killed at the Wilderness, May 5, 1864, and Brother was not listed as missing or captured during the entirety of the Overland Campaign. *Roster*, 1:558–59.

13. Bottom's Bridge was a crossing on the Chickahominy River. The Army of the Potomac cavalry commander, Maj. Gen. Philip Sheridan, working in tandem with Hunter in the Shenandoah Valley, set out to destroy the Virginia Central Railroad and eventually link up in Charlottesville, Virginia. However, Hunter bypassed Charlottesville, while Sheridan dueled with Confederates at Trevilian Station. To make matters worse, Hunter's withdrawal into West Virginia left the entire Shenandoah Valley open for the subsequent advance of Jubal Early's Second Corps into Maryland and Washington, DC. Wheelan, *Bloody Spring*, 320–23; McPherson, *Battle Cry of Freedom*, 737–39; *Dyer's Compendium*, 942.

Behind Breast works in line of Battle south of Petersburg Va June 20 1864

Dear Delia

You will see by the heading of this where we are. It is about 1½ miles to Petersberg, the spires of which are in sight. Two hundred yds in front of us are the Rebs in fortification bristling with canon.

On the 18th we drove them out of two lines that are now in our rear and charged on those in front but were repulsed. Our Regt suffered severe loss.[14]

My co loss was as follows. Sergt C Giles Parker was carring the colours and fell. We supposed he was killed and went out at night to get him and he had been removed and some of the Regt said he had been carried off the field and was only wounded. I hope it is so and will find out as soon as possible and let his folks know.[15]

We through out a line of battle after night within 50 yds of the Reb works so as to get off our wounded & killed. We were in the line and the orders were to carry all back without regard to co or Regt and bury the dead and take the wounded to hospital.[16]

So that we cant tell where our men are yet as we are still under heavy fire and a man cant lift his above the works in daylight. Corpl J D Runion was killed. Wm P Pauly killed.[17]

wounded	Sergt	F A Boynton
Do	"	Geo Eustice
"	Private	Jas Stonehouse
"	"	Thos Blunt
"	"	M Calvert
"	"	A Morse slight
"	"	J C Miles "
"	"	O Weymouth "
"	"	H P Green severe

Edward Whitney missing. Tell Mrs J L Taylor her husband is in a rebble hospital. Left foot amputated doing well. About one more charge on Rebble fortifications and our Regt will be out of service entirely. Give my love to Jared Laura & May & Janie and accept the same.[18]

ever yours

Henry

NOTES

14. On the evening of June 12, 1864, Grant, wishing to secure the vital railroad lines at Petersburg, removed troops from positions in Cold Harbor and sent them yet again southward. On June 15, the Eighteenth Corps, led by Maj. Gen. William Smith, advanced and occupied the outer set of trenches near Petersburg. However, the overcautious Smith, fearful after the bloodletting at Cold Harbor, did not follow up on his success, giving Gen. Pierre G. T. Beauregard a chance to reposition his troops to another line of defenses. Hancock's Second Corps met with little success on the next day, and on June 17 another attack by Maj. Gen. Ambrose Burnside's Ninth Corps was driven back after some initial success by a Confederate counterattack. By June 17, Lee, who was at first confused about Grant's intentions, rushed men to the defense of Petersburg. The main assault on June 18 was unsuccessful in carrying Confederate entrenchments, eventually leading many to question the tactic of storming such fortified positions. The day also brought recriminations from Meade to his corps commanders for their failure in the assault. Warren took personal exception to this, and the animosity between the two men, who were never close, only grew as a result. Casualties in the Seventh Wisconsin for the June 18 assault at Petersburg were 12 killed and 52 wounded. Union casualties numbered 1,188 killed, 8,513 wounded, and 1,185 captured or missing. McPherson, *Battle Cry of Freedom*, 739–41; Wert, *The Sword of Lincoln*, 367, 370–73; Wheelan, *Bloody Spring*, 330–37, 340–41; *OR*, ser. 1, vol. 40, pt. 1, 225; Fox, *Regimental Losses*, 547; *Dyer's Compendium*, 943–44.

15. Calvin Giles Parker, Company F of the Seventh Wisconsin, who carried the regimental banner into action, was killed at Petersburg on June 18, 1864. Herdegen, *The Iron Brigade*, 514; *Roster*, 1:560.

16. The Seventh Wisconsin, situated on the left flank of the Iron Brigade, was caught between the lines after the assault on Confederate entrenchments on June 18. For ninety minutes, using only a ravine for shelter, the men dug entrenchments with tin pans and even their bayonets. Before they could finish, an enemy skirmish line, moving on their exposed left flank, forced them to flee back to their original lines from earlier in the day. Herdegen, *The Iron Brigade*, 514–15.

17. William B. Pauley and John Runion, both in Company F of the Seventh Wisconsin, were killed on June 18, 1864, at Petersburg. *Roster*, 1:560–61.

18. Edwin E. Whitney, Company F of the Seventh Wisconsin, was wounded on June 18 at Petersburg and was mustered out with the company at the end of the war. Lorenzo Taylor was captured on June 21, 1864, at Petersburg and, presumably paroled, was mustered out at the end of his term on September 1, 1864. *Roster*, 1:561.

Laying about loose about one & half miles from Petersburg Va June 27 1864

Dear Father

I set myself down on a cool bank of sand with the thermometer at about 150 in the shade to write you a long letter. At least that was my intention when i took this seat. If I should fail in interresting you just consider the circumstances by which i am surrounded. I am within point blank rang of Rebble musketry & shell but that I have got so used to that if my next neighbour was hit I would not think of moveing for the reason that one place is just as safe as an other. Then we have had no rain for about a month and the dust is about an inch thick on everything and the Rebble shot and shell pecking our brest works keeps up a continual cloud of dust. But notwithstanding all these difficulties I feel fine this morning for be it known that I got a clean shirt and drawers on yesturday the 2d change I have had since the 3d of May. And I not only shed my duty clothing but i sent off a good crop of lice with them, but as far as that is concerned by tomorrow I will have new and more hungry set for the whol country is covered with them.

We are behind breast works west of the Norfolk & Petersberg RR about 1½ miles from the city. The Rebs are in our front behind strong fortifications. The distance from their line to ours is about 300 yds on the right of our Division & 500 on our left. It is within easy range from one line to the other with our Rifles, and whenever a head is raised above the works on either side crack go a dozen of Rifles at the unfortunate owner. For several days our causalities have been small as we keep pretty well under cover. This seiging is going to be slow work as the Reb possition is a strong one and they have a larg army. We compell them to evacuate by cutting their RR but if they lose Petersburg Richmond is gone up. We have got a good base to operate from. We can put cars on the Norfolk RR and having the James River we can ration our army here with less expense than we could at Culpeper then. This is a better country than any in which this army has been in Va. If Grant seiges them out of this place you must not get impatient for it will be a long job if they can get supplies. But it is the only way to do it for I am perfectly disgusted with bucking their fortifications. I consider that we lost 2000 men of our corps half of them of our division on the 18th just uselessly. That is we were bucked against fortifications that we could not take and we could not have hold then if we had succeeded in carrying them. Our Genls some of them want to go to fast. We had with artillery and musketry drove the Rebs from their first & 2d lines and into their main line of works, and I think the Genls should have halted and made a reconnosance before rushing us on. Had we accomplished anything I would have been satisfide but where we lost over 2000 men I dont beleive the Rebs lost (200). Our Regt 2 officers Lieut Thomas Co H Killed S Phillips Ajt mortally wounded since dead. Capt Pond wounded and 52 enlisted killed & wounded. My co lost[19]

Corpl J D Runion	killed
Wm Pauley	"

Sergt C Giles Parker supposed to be killed. In fact I am satisfide of it. Martin Calverd shot down and left on the field supposed to be dead. We were thrown forward after dark to hold the ground while we got the wounded & dead. In that way in the dark men burried men without knowing who they were. One thing is certain. The Rebs got none of our men for we lay down and formed a line after we found we could not carry their works so close to them that we kept their heads down till we got our wounded away. The wounded were[20]

Sergt	F A Boynton	Severe
"	Geo Eustice	bruised by shell returned to duty
	Thomas Blunt	slight
	Isaac L Miles	"
	Josseph Stonehouse	leg amputated
	H P Green	arm "
	A C Morse	slight head

E Whitney	severe leg
O Weymouth	Slight "

No Causalities since in my co. I have 15 men for duty. I dont know what they are going to do with these old Regts. We have only 130 muskets in our Regt. The probability is that at the expiration of the first 3 ys all those that did not reinlist will be mustered out of the service, and all surplus officers will also be mustered out. So unless you get a chance to do well with the mill dont do anythin till the 1st of Sept.

What do you Freemont men think of your favourite now that you see him in his true coulours? I am sorry they dont send the Wis 100 day men down here. They would have had a good chance to see the elephant. Our men that is is the men of the old army of the Potomac will charge rite over Beauregards or Brackinridges men. They will take brest works or anything else from them, and it is just the same with the Rebs. They cant get them to charge one of our old corps in works if there is only a single line, but they will charge rite over Butlers or Smiths or Gilmores men with a yell.[21]

I was on out post one evening when they came up in three lines of Battle charge. As soon as they got upon the ridge our artillery opened on them and they all lay down. Their officers beged coaxed & swore at them to get them to charge but is was no go. They told them we had all gone but a skermish line, and I heard one of them yell out he knew better for by G—d the yanks dident have artillery on their skermish line. There are thirty men under comd of Leiut Brooks 6th Wis. All of our Brigade gone on a raid to burn the Bridge across the Staunton River at Roanoak Station. I am getting uneasy about them as they were to join Sherredin but he failed to get to Danville. Lorenzo Taylor of my co is one of the No. They were volunteers and good men and are well mounted and have each a grey uniform to put on in case of nececesity. They all understand that if taken they would pull hemp. J L Taylor John Folk James Evens & Robt Blakeley of my co are in Locust Grove Hospital wounded and doing well. The Rebs permit our own sergeon to attend them and they get plenty supplies through the sanetary com.[22]

I have just learned that we are building a railroad from citty Point here and that one half our line is to be releived every 48 hours. That is we have two lines of battle, one will lay in the trenches 48 hours and the other will rest in rear within suppoarting distance. This looks as if grant was going to seige them out. Well I uppose we will have to seige them somewhere and this is the most convenient place for us. We are out of paper ink and everything else. This this is paper Perry Gilbert stole out of Prince Georges Court House. Just where our line of Battle crosses the R Road is a large Ice house full of Ice. It was put up for market. There is quite a stream and by daming it up at different points they had succeeded is packing quite a quantity of ice. This house is 30 × 40 with from 5 to 6 ft of ice. It is in layres about 4 in thick. Our boys go for Ice every day and when there is many of get in the Rebs will open on them with artillery. They are at it now and the boys climb up the steps with a big chunk on ice and shake it at them. And when they see the flash run down where they of course are perfectly safe. By thunder Ill quit. I am sweating like a horse and my feet are both assleep and more the sun has flanked me.[23]

My good wishes to all.

H F Young

NOTES

19. The Iron Brigade assault started at 3 p.m. on June 18 and advanced to within seventy-five yards of the enemy entrenchments before being severely hit by both infantry and artillery fire. By 5 p.m., the advance halted and the brigade withdrew to its original entrenchments, except the Seventh Wisconsin, as previously stated, which sought shelter in a ravine, before being flanked by Confederate skirmishers and forced to run to its original lines. 2nd Lt. Tanner Thomas, Company H of the Seventh Wisconsin, was killed on June 18, 1864. Samuel J. Phillips, Adjutant on the Field and Staff of the Seventh Wisconsin, was wounded at Petersburg and died at City Point on June 21, 1864. Capt. Levi E. Pond, Company E of the Seventh Wisconsin, was wounded at Petersburg and discharged on December 30, 1864, due to disability. Herdegen, *The Iron Brigade*, 514–15; *OR*, ser. 1, vol. 40, pt. 1, 474–75, pt. 2, 176; *Roster*, 1:565, 538, 544.

20. Martin Calvert, Company F of the Seventh Wisconsin, was killed on June 18, 1864, at Petersburg. *Roster*, 1:558.

21. The Radical Republicans in Cleveland nominated former general John C. Frémont for president as a third-party candidate on May 31, 1864. Calling themselves the Radical Democratic Party, they wanted reconstruction in the hands of Congress, not President Lincoln. Even Grant was floated as a candidate, but he refused consideration. Beauregard manned the lines at Petersburg before the arrival of Lee's main force and skillfully kept the federal force at bay. Maj. Gen. John C. Breckinridge, former vice president of the United States, departed Lee's lines in May and defeated a federal force at New Market, Virginia. Maj. Gen. Benjamin Butler commanded the Army of the James, and Smith, who commanded the Eighteenth Army Corps, was relieved on July 11 for his poor performance at Petersburg. Maj. Gen. Quincy A. Gillmore commanded the Tenth Army Corps in the Army of the James, whose failed assault on Petersburg on June 10 led to his dismissal on June 14 by Butler for

failing to carry the works at Petersburg, even though he had volunteered for the duty. Grant later modified the order, and Gillmore was relieved at his own request and eventually was sent to Washington to await new orders. McPherson, *Battle Cry of Freedom*, 715–16, 724; David Herbert Donald, *Lincoln* (New York: Simon & Schuster, 1995), 494, 534–35; Allen C. Guelzo, *Fateful Lightning: A New History of the Civil War and Reconstruction* (New York: Oxford University Press, 2012), 462; Doris Kearns Goodwin, *Team of Rivals: The Political Genius of Abraham Lincoln* (New York: Simon & Schuster, 2005), 659; Wert, *The Sword of Lincoln*, 375; Wheelan, *Bloody Spring*, 331; *OR*, ser. 1, vol. 40, pt. 1, 2, 23.

22. Edward P. Brooks, Adjutant in the Sixth Wisconsin, led a hand-selected group of thirty-two soldiers from the brigade on a raid to destroy bridges on the Danville Railroad. On June 22, 1864, they captured a Confederate officer, whom they later paroled. The detail had stopped at a farm for lunch when the paroled Confederate officer returned and demanded their surrender. Brooks, who failed to put out guards during lunch, complied, thinking the officer had more men with him than he did in reality—the officer had farmers, armed with shotguns. Robert Blakely, James H. Evans, John Falk, and James L. Taylor were all in Company F of the Seventh Wisconsin. Taylor, who was wounded at the Wilderness, was mustered out at the end of the war, and Falk, who was wounded at the Wilderness, was absent when he was mustered out of the regiment. Evans was captured on June 21, 1864, and died of disease in Salisbury, North Carolina, on January 28, 1865. Blakeley was captured during the Wilderness and died of disease in Andersonville Prison on November 15, 1864. Herdegen, *The Iron Brigade*, 521; *Roster*, 1:494, 558–59, 561.

23. Perry Gilbert was in Company F of the Seventh Wisconsin. *Roster*, 1:559.

near Petersberg Va July 2d 1864

Dear Delia

I have neglected you for some days but i have been so busy that i could not find the time to write. Our teams came up and we had to make out muster and pay Rolls and monthly returns and repoarts of every description.

My health is good but I am worn out. I weigh less than for ten years, and it is so hot and dusty here it is almost impossible to breathe. We lay in the trenches 72 hours and then we are releived for the same length of time. So you see we have some time to our selves. Out brest works and those of the Enemy are not more than 300 to 500 yds apart so that it is heads down when we are in the brest works. They are issuing plenty of good rations now and we can get our clothes washed so that we are feeling better. Our men ammuse themselves nightly by either threwing moter shells inside of the Reb breastworks or by shelling the city. I dont think it is much ammusement for the Rebs, but it keeps them from going to sleep. This seiging is slow work but they will eventually have to succumb for they cant drive us away from here.

We have had no causualities since my last. Sargt Eustice was not seriously wounded. He was briused and stuned by a shell that exploded within 2 ft of him. I feel almost certain the C J Parker was killed and Martin Calvert. We buried Corpl Runion & Wm B Pauly but the other two must have been caried off and buried by some other Regt while we were in line close under the Enemys breast works. Wm Ray & Webster Cook returned to the co yesturday. They look fine. I suppose Sloat is home as he wrote to me from washington. There is considerable excitement here amongst the officers of the veteran Regts. They are all used up till they dont amt to more than one or two good companys and the rumuor is that one half or more of the organizations will be broken up and the surplus officers mustered out. Well the the thing causes quite a flutter particularly with officers that want to get out. Many others that want to remain are fretting over it. For my part i am easy about the matter. If the Govt want my services and will give me a command that suits me I will stay. If not i will go home, but this is speculating for there is no knowing what will turn up between now and the 1st of Sept. Lieut Kidd is quite lame with his old wound he says it is so painful at night he cant sleep. The marching at the start used him up. I hope you will have had rain before you get this for a short crop will make hard times in Wis with everything at such high prices. It is verry dry here. It has not rained for over thirty days and in this warm dry sandy soil it is terrible. The dust is setled on the leaves of the trees, so as to completely discoulour them, and good water is getting scarce.[24]

We are expecting the 19th army corps here within a few days. It will yet turn out as i told you long ago that the last fighting will be done in Va. Both sides will concentrate all their available force here for a desperate struggle. Our Cavalry is playing the mischief with their RR and communications. I cant see how they are to stand it long here without they have made provision for standing a seige before hand which I dont think they have. But they are putting forth mighty efforts and will continue to do so till after the Presidential Election.[25]

I suppose you have seen some of the boys of my Co before this as there are a number of them home on furlough. Give my love to Susan. Tell her I will write to her the first opportunity but the fact is i am stealing the time to write this when i ought to be in bed. There has so much writing and business accumulated for the last two months that I dont know when i will get through with it.

Give my good wishes to John Collier & Aunt Hannah. ~~tell~~ Ask old John what he thinks of that pet of his John C Freemont. Give my love to Jared Luara May & Janie and acept the same for yourself and by wishing you all a pleasant fourth of July I will bid you a verry good night.

Ever yours

Henry

NOTES

24. George Eustice was not listed as wounded; each of the other men, Calvert, Parker, Pauley, and Runion, all of Company F, died in the assault on Petersburg on June 18. William W. Ray, wounded for the third time, survived the war and was mustered out with the regiment in 1865. *Roster*, 1:559, 558, 560–61.

25. The Nineteenth Army Corps spent most of July shifting operations from Louisiana to Virginia. The first troops began to arrive on the steamer *Crescent* at City Point on the afternoon of July 11, under the command of Quincy Gillmore. Once there, Grant changed his mind and sent them to Washington to defend the capital against Jubal Early's raid. This was the same Gillmore relieved by Butler after his failed assault at Petersburg. Grant, trying to cut Lee's supply lines to the south, ordered Brig. Gen. James Wilson and Brig. Gen. August Kautz on a raid to destroy portions of the Southside Railroad on June 22, 1864. The raiders successfully destroyed sections of the railroad before nearly being surrounded near Reams's Station, leading to the capture of one thousand troops. They rejoined the army near Petersburg on July 1. Marc Leepson, *Desperate Engagement: How a Little Known Battle Saved Washington, D.C. and Changed the Course of American History* (New York: St. Martin's Griffin, 2007), 161; Wert, *The Sword of Lincoln*, 375–77; *OR*, ser. 1, vol. 37, pt. 1, 170, 283–85.

In the Trenches in front of Petersberg Va July 15 1864

Dear Delia

I would have written sooner had I not known my letter could not leave Washington. We still spend half our time in the trenches. In our front there has been no firing of infantry, for the last ten days, both sides became tired of it and quit it. But we have plenty of artillery and morter shelling. We have had no causualities in my co since my last. The boys that are here are in good health. Glad to hear you had a pleasant 4th. Ours was dull as a Quaker meeting. We are putting up immence fortification & the Rebs are doing the same. Each have large details working every night. Ours for attack. Theirs look only to defense. We have no rain yet. Every thing is drying up. The Reb raiders are giving them a regular scare in Baltimore & Washington. Our men ought to capture the whole party.[26]

There will be a terrible battle here soon. It will probably be the greatest Artillern fight the world has ever yet seen. Many will unavoidably fall for in many places the guns of the two armies are not more than four & five hundred yds apart. We have artillery enough to fill the air with hissing grape & Bursting shells and the Rebs have apperantly the same.

This is a bad place to write. I quit. Give my love to Jared Laura May & Janie. I would like verry much to see them paymaster.

ever yours

Henry

NOTE

26. Jubal Early's corps was dispatched to the Shenandoah Valley to meet the threat of Hunter's force, which was then near Staunton, Virginia, and advancing on the valuable supply hub of Lynchburg. Forcing Hunter into West Virginia opened the valley for Early and his raiders to threaten Washington, DC. On July 6, the raiders defeated a federal force at Monocacy, and by July 11 they were on the doorstep of the capital, just outside Fort Stevens. President Lincoln visited the fort on July 12 and watched a sharp engagement that afternoon in which a doctor near him was shot in the leg. A future Justice of the Supreme Court of the United States, Oliver Wendell Holmes Jr., reportedly told Lincoln, "Get down, you damn fool, before you get shot!" While it is true that Lincoln peered at Confederate forces over the parapet, it is not entirely clear that Holmes uttered the famous remark to Lincoln that day. The raid succeeded in some fashion as Grant sent the Sixth Corps, then at Petersburg, to defend the capital. The raiders, after departing Washington, DC, defeated a federal force in the Second Battle of Kernstown, destroyed homes and businesses in Chambersburg, Pennsylvania, and returned to Virginia by the end of July, without facing any serious effort to stop them by federal forces, which failed to coordinate their efforts. Depending on their allegiance, the newspapers had a field day with the raid. The *Weekly National Intelligencer* on July 21 referred to the raid as "The Late National Humiliation." Another stated that "It is too early yet for us to make up our minds whether we ought to laugh over the denouement . . . , or whether we should feel a devout thankfulness for a great deliverance." William Ray's account of the Fourth of July differs from what Young reported to Delia. The day was fine "except some of the officers getting drunk. I am sorry to see some of the officers is so bad repute. Especially Cap Young." Ray, as he clearly stated, did not like this side of Young and believed other men felt the same way. Leepson, *Desperate Engagement*, 1, 199–203; Wert, *The Sword of Lincoln*, 386; McPherson, *Battle Cry of Freedom*, 756–57; *OR*, ser. 1, vol. 37, pt. 2, 155–56; "The Late National Humiliation," *Weekly*

National Intelligencer (Washington, DC), July 21, 1864; "Review of the Rebel Raid," *Evening Telegraph* (Philadelphia, PA), July 15, 1864; Lance Herdegen and Sherry Murphy, eds., *Four Years with The Iron Brigade: The Civil War Journals of William R. Ray, Co. F, Seventh Wisconsin Infantry* (Cambridge, MA: Da Capo Press, 2002), 287.

near Petersberg Va July 26 1864

Dear Father

I received your letter several days ago. Glad to hear you were all well, and hear you had rain. I have delayed writing untill the question was settled in refference to our muster. The orders are to retain the officers of all Veteran Regts. ~~Officers~~ So you had better rent the mill for one year if you can do so to suit yourself.

We are *diging diging diging*. It is nothing but dig. You cant realize the ammount of work we are doing building fortifications sunken roads saps & c—.

We are well pleased with the call for 500000. I think we will get them this time. We want the full quota without any shuffling or fizzle. The health of our men is good. We have been having rain lately. The weather is cool and pleasant. We have had no casualities since my last. There is Regts being mustered out every day whose term of service has expired.[27]

We have every confidence in being able to rout the rebs out of this in time. But seiging is had work and awful slow. We take a 1000 men work all night threwing works that command some portion of the enemys works. The next night they will threw up counter works, and so it goes the unnitiated would suppose we were each trying to out do the other with pick & shovel but there will in all probability be a grand opening some of these mornings. We will have 400 peices of artillery ready to open at once, some of threwing 100 lbs of shell. And the Rebs have no scarcity to answer back but when we open the city of Petersberg is doomed.

We have good news from Sherman. Hope he will wipe out Hoods army. The Rebs are becoming uneasy about our mining their works and well they may be for if nothing happens they will soon realize the truth of their fears. My good wishes to all.[28]

yours truly

H F Young

NOTES

27. President Lincoln issued Proclamation 116 to add five hundred thousand soldiers for one-year, two-year, or three-year enlistments. The states had until September 5, 1864, to meet their quotas. Roy P. Basler, ed., *The Collected Works of Abraham Lincoln*, 8 vols. (Springfield, IL: Abraham Lincoln Association, 1953), 7:448–49; McPherson, *Battle Cry of Freedom*, 758.

28. Maj. Gen. William Tecumseh Sherman's federal force approached the outskirts of Atlanta by the end of July. Sherman managed to outmaneuver Gen. Joseph E. Johnston nearly every step of the way. Gen. John Bell Hood replaced Johnston on July 17, 1864, and went on the offensive, with little success except in the Southern press, which saw his defeat by Sherman as a victory. Sherman's army by July 28 was only two miles from downtown Atlanta. McPherson, *Battle Cry of Freedom*, 754–55; *OR*, ser. 1, vol. 38, pt. 1, 957; *Dyer's Compendium*, 714–15.

near Petersberg Va July 26 1864

Dear Delia

I rec your welcome letter last night. Glad to hear from you & to hear you were all well. We are still in front of Petersberg *diging diging diging*.

The health of the Regt is good and the casualities are few. There has been none in my co since my last. The 2d Corps crossed the James River this morning and they appear to be doing considerable fighting over there today. I dont no what the result is yet. We have to be verry vigilent in front in consequence of the 2d Corps withdrawing.[29]

We are having our usual amt of Picket Morter & artillery firing, but there has been no ration demons to shew that they have missed any of our troops. You would be astonished to see our fortifications. We are diging the whole country over.

I told Furman we would buy his house provided we wanted it for a miller and perhaps i will do so when i return for then I will probably want it. But i dont want it now neither do i want any property in Tafton. If was to buy it i want it where it is. This war will close immediately after the Presidential Election if not before, and if I live to get home i will want all the money i can raise at the mill and i would rather have property there then than in Tafton.

Look out for a comfortable house and do the best you can. If you have to winter in it you had better one thats comfortable if it should cost double what a poor one would. Give my love to Jared Laura & may and accept the same.

ever yours

Henry

NOTE

29. This movement was a demonstration by the Second Corps on the north side of the James River from July 27 to July 29. Fighting occurred at Darbytown, Strawberry Plains, and New Market Road. Casualties amounted to 62 killed, 285 wounded, and 85 captured or missing. The once highly vaunted Second Army Corps, racked with casualties, performed poorly during the campaign. McPherson, *Battle Cry of Freedom*, 756; *OR*, ser. 1, vol. 40, pt. 1, 2; *Dyer's Compendium*, 948–49.

Camp near Petersberg Va Aug 4th 1864

Dear Delia

I received your long and interresting two days since. Sorry to hear of your indisposition but hope this will find you better. My health is good. That of the boys the same. We moved day before yesturday from the centre of the line in front of Petersburg to the extreeme left of our line where we are at presant doing garrison & pickett duty.[30]

I tell you it is quite a releif to get out of reach of the enemys bullets once more after laying exposed to them continually for six weeks. We have a pleasant camp with plenty of good water and although we have heavy pickett details and have to be verry vigilent to guard against a surprise by a flank movement. It seems almost like freedom again when we can walk round set up and eat our meals lie down to sleep without crawling into holes without fear of being shot.

The men are begining to show their old life and animation. Last evening they had a game of ball. I must say that never till this campaign did i know what men under such circumstances could stand. When i have read in history of men going through what we have this summer or something like it i did not beleive it.[31]

On the 30th we made a grand assault on the enemys works. It commenced by us succssfully blewing up a large fort in the enemys works. The blewing up of the fort was a perfect success and was the thrilling sight perhaps ever witnessed. Our line was just 800 yds from the fort that was blown up that is the line occupied by our Brigade. We were in front line of works and our orders were to open musketry fire on the line in our immediate front as soon as the fort went up. The time had passed and a knot of officers of us were standing on one of the parrapets of our forts discussing the probable reason of the failure when we felt the ground tremble then saw the fort guns men and all raise in one mighty mass of ruins some two or three hundred ft in air. It looked for a moment like a vast column of muddy water. Then all was shut out by dust & smoke. At the same moment two hundred canon opened from our side and thousands of musket. Amidst this tirriffick din and confusion a Division charged and carried both lines of the enemys works where the breach was made. Up to this time everything was a perfect success and we were all jubilent over the taking of Petersberg which we looked on as ours certain. But the next divission threwn forward to suppoart the division already established were negroes. They went forward in good order till they came to the first breast work when they met a stuberon resistance. Instead of overcomeing which they broke and fled like a flock of sheep or huddled together behind the enemys breast works to be cut to peices by the enemys grape & canister. The enemy seeing their demorralized condition charged them in front and although they had to fall back themselves from under our terrible artillery fire they succeeded in scaring a way the coloured Divison. The white Division held their ground for several hours during which time the enemy made 3 unsuccessful assaults on them and not till they were almost surrounded did they fall back. Thus was lost the fruits of near a months labour. Had Burnside kept his negroes away we would have carried Petersberg. My oppinion is that negro troops with white officers will not do for the following reasons. Now this couloured division advanced to the first line of the enemys works in good order. But as soon as they came in close quarters the enemy shot nearly all their white officers knowing that the negroes would be worth nothing without their officers and so it proved as soon as their officers were not there to lead them the negroes were no better thay a lot of scared sheep. We cant blame the negroes for they will go whereever their officers lead them, but an officer of a couloured Regt is a conspicuous mark to what the same officer would be in a white Regt. And the Rebs have learned that all is necessary to defeat the couloured troops is to shoot down their officers and they will act upon it.[32]

Our regt had 1 officer wounded 4 men killed 3 wounded on the 30th. None of which belonged to my co. We are expecting the paymaster soon and we need him verry much for every officer is heels over head in debt. It costs something to live in the army. Unkle sam has raised his prices almost equal to sutlers prices. I will feel anxious about you till i get another letter. Keep in good heart. When we get that other 500000 men we will make short work of the Rebellion.[33]

The 38 & 37th Wis were in the storming Divison on the 30th & lost heavily particularly in officers. New Regts will suffer terribly in officers as long as officers will persist in going into a fight in full dress. After they have been in a year or so they will addopt the fatigue suit to fight in. Give my love to Jared Laura May & Janie and accept the same.[34]

ever yours

Henry

NOTES

30. The Iron Brigade, along with the rest of Warren's Fifth Army Corps, was situated between the Norfolk and Petersburg Railroad and Jerusalem Plank Road throughout July. In early August it changed positions and moved into an area formerly occupied by the Second Army Corps. Herdegen, *The Iron Brigade*, 522.

31. By the 1860s baseball had become popular throughout the country. In August 1864, contests took place throughout the United States. In Philadelphia, the best eighteen players took part in a game at Fairmont Park. In New York a contest played between Mutual of New York and Eureka of Newark resulted in a win for Mutual, by a score of 15–10. However, not everyone was thrilled with the new game. Great mortification occurred in Irasburgh, Vermont, when a game was played on the Sabbath. "A Match Game," *Evening Telegraph*, August 5, 1864; "Base Ball," *New York Herald*, August 7, 1864; "Desecration on the Sabbath," *Orleans Independent Standard* (Irasburgh, Vermont), June 17, 1864.

32. Lt. Col. Henry Pleasants, Forty-eighth Pennsylvania, Ninth Army Corps, presented a plan to Burnside to dig a mine under the Confederate fort in their front. His unit consisted of coal miners from Pennsylvania, and he was given the green light by Burnside, Meade, and Grant to continue. The dig, completed on July 23, measured 525 feet in length with two lateral lines of nearly 40 feet each. Burnside had selected Brig. Gen. Edward Ferrero's United States Colored Troops to lead the assault after the detonation. However, Meade and Grant, not convinced of the fighting ability of black troops, in addition to the potential fallout politically, requested that white troops advance first. Burnside protested, but in the end three divisions of white troops were given the task to advance after the explosion. Also, Pleasants had requested six tons of explosives, which melted away to four in the end. At 4:44 a.m. on the morning of July 30, 1864, a tremendous explosion created a crater 170 feet wide, 60 feet across, and 30 feet deep. The first troops, flabbergasted by the destruction caused by the explosion, disregarded their original orders and went into the

crater rather than around it. Confederate artillery and infantry, after the initial shock, responded savagely, especially when Burnside ordered his remaining division, the United States Colored Troops, to advance. The crater filled with disorganized men under intense fire from Confederate gunners. Total casualties in Ferrero's Fourth Division were 1,327, of whom 209 were killed in action. He later pointed out that the black soldiers had had scarcely two weeks of training before the battle and "that my troops are raw." There exists conflicting evidence about the level of training the black troops had received before the Battle of the Crater. Richard Slotkin stated that "The most significant factor in the 4th Division's performance was not that its men were Black but that its units were 'green.'" Gen. Grant summed up the debacle when he succinctly stated, "It was the saddest affair I have witnessed in the war." A court of inquiry was convened almost immediately in the aftermath of the Crater. It was held in the headquarters of the Second Army Corps and lasted seventeen days. The court found that failure resulted from a variety of factors, including poor use of troops, troops' stopping in the crater before advancing, poor leadership at the top, and lack of a leader at the scene of the assault. Most of the blame for the disaster rested on Burnside's shoulders. The historian Earl J. Hess concluded that Meade's meddling with Burnside's plan in addition to Burnside's method of selecting the advance division contributed greatly to the failure at the Crater. Others held accountable were Edward Ferrero, Col. Z. R. Bliss, and Brig. Gen. Orlando B. Wilcox. The Crater effectively ended the military career of Ambrose Burnside. Wert, *The Sword of Lincoln*, 380, 382–85; Richard Slotkin, *No Quarter: The Battle of the Crater, 1864* (New York: Random House, 2009), 96, 331; Earl J. Hess, *Into the Crater; The Mine Attack at Petersburg* (Columbia: University of South Carolina Press, 2010), 54–55; 216, 223, 244; McPherson, *Battle Cry of Freedom*, 758–60; *OR*, ser. 1, vol. 40, pt. 1, 2, 17, 46, 93, 125–29, 248.

33. The Seventh Wisconsin had 6 wounded for the period July 1–31. Union casualties at the Battle of the Crater numbered 504 killed, 1,881 wounded, and 1,413 captured or missing. *OR*, ser. 1, vol. 40, pt. 1, 256, 249; Fox, *Regimental Losses*, 547; *Dyer's Compendium*, 949.

34. The Thirty-seventh and Thirty-eighth Wisconsin, part of the First Brigade, Third Division, Ninth Army Corps, suffered 174 casualties at the Battle of the Crater. *OR*, ser. 1, vol. 40, pt. 1, 247.

Camp 7th Wis Vet vol near Petersberg Va Aug 6th 1864

Dear Father

I received your letter. Glad to hear you were all well. We are once again in camp we are encamped on the Norfolk & Petersberg RR about two miles in rear of where our former position was. We were releived in front by a portion of Burnsides Corps on the 1st of aug. We are the extreem left of our line and to keep out a strong Picket force. In fact it takes just half our

Brigade on pickett all the time. But as the saying is we are thankful for small favours for now we can run round without fear of getting in the way of a Reb shell or bullet. Only those that have lain under continual range of an enemys guns for 6 weeks can know the feeling of releif on experiances when they can travel round write eat & sleep and know there is no danger of being shot. You will have heard of the blowing up of the fort on the 30th of July and the grand assault made on the enemys lines. The blowing up of the fort & the first assault were all that was ever claimed for them. They ammounted to the destruction of a large fort with its garrison & guns and the carrying of the Reb lines for some distance on each side of the breach. The whole attack was the most Terriffick sight & sound perhaps ever witnessed. But we lost the possition after we had carried it. Ah thats the rub. We should have held it. We should have taken the whole line then Petersberg, but instead we lost what we got. True we punished the enemy verry severe when he charged time & again on our line to retake it. I myself saw two of his lines of battle almost annihilated and thouroughly repulsed by the Division of white troops in the breach. Had there been no couloured troops in the assault I am confident we would have carried the entire line on the left, fortifications, and Petersberg, into the bargain.[35]

And yet I have nothing to say against the courage of the negro Division. But in such a place as that where everything depends on quick manouvres no troops should be pushed forward as storming party without thoroughly understanding what is expected of them. And then they should be troops that can be handled and maourved on the run. Farreroes Division of negroes made the first advance and carried the 1st line of the enemys works in good style but there was an inner line but a few yds from the 1st line. From behind this line the Rebs shot nearly all the white officers in the Division. The negroes without their officers huddled together like a lot of sheep and instead of charging over and carrying the next line became perfectly demoralized and run back right in the way of the suppoarting column. That had they had sense enough to lay down behind the works five minutes would have saved them and the works too. But in their hasty retreat they forced back the suppoarting column which was compelled to break to let the couloured Division through. By this time the Rebs had got up suppoarts and our advantage was lost, and the order was given to Warren not to attempt to carry the line in his front.[36]

Warren was ready to advance as soon as Burnside suppoarted by the 10th Corps carried his part of the line, and his disposition of his troops were such as to insure success. We had been keeping the heads of the Rebs down in our front all morning not letting them fire on Burnsides storming party and we did it completely. And if old Burnys men had carried their part of both lines they could have fire along the works and kept down the Johneys while we would have charged, and I can assure you if we had got their works in our front we would have held them.

I wrote you about the mill. Do the best you can. To tell you the truth I am heartily tired & sick of the service but this is no time to whine or back down. I see and hear to much of that and I almost get the blues sometimes and yet I know that the true soldier should never get downhearted.[37]

Old Abe has given his ultimatum to the peace croakers. Its style suits me exactly and I will stand by it and fight for it and if the country dont suppoart him in it those of us who remain true and loyal will go down with our coulours flying. It has been known to us for some time that the Rebs was mining one of our forts. We counter mined the fort, and after they put the powder in our men took it out leaving just enough to make an explosion without injuring the fort. Then our artillery and men were mased in the fort. Well the great looked for event came off last evenning. I did not see it but heard the firing. Those who saw it say that after the explosion which was so arrainged as to give the appearance of having blown up the fort. A Brigade of Rebs massed for the purpose charged forward with a yell to occupy the supposed ruins. Our men let them come till they got within a few rods when they opened on them and just everlastingly slayed them.[38]

Our boys that were slightly wounded are returning. There has quite a No returned to my co. I have 23 men for duty all in good health. We are getting anxious to see the Paymaster. My good wishes to all.

yours truly

H F Young

NOTES

35. It was truly a scene of confusion after the first assault. At 9:45 a.m. Meade requested the withdrawal of the Ninth Corps to its previous position. Ironically, another dispatch, at 10 a.m., stated that Burnside, at his discretion, could withdraw at any time. The fighting raged for two hours in the crater before Burnside gave the order for the black soldiers to advance. Wert, *The Sword of Lincoln*, 384–85; *OR*, ser. 1, vol. 40, pt. 1, 144.

36. Considering how little training the black soldiers received before the battle, they generally performed well under the circumstances. However, an inspection of

the Ninth Corps two weeks before the Crater stated that the men were apathetic to drill, discipline, and performance of duties. Burnside stated that "from what I can learn no officers or men behaved with greater gallantry than they did." Brig. Gen. Hartranft said they went "to the front as well as any troops; but they were certainly not in very good condition to resist an attack." A telling report was given by Col. Henry G. Thomas, commander of the Second Brigade, Fourth Division, on the withdrawal of the USCT soldiers from the crater. "The black and white troops came pouring back together. A few, more gallant than the rest, without organization, but guided by a soldier's instinct, remained on . . . our line and held the enemy at bay some ten or fifteen minutes until they were nearly all shot away." When the United States Colored Troops entered the crater, the Confederate counterattack was in full swing, cutting down black troops in droves. Magnifying their difficulties, Southern soldiers, incensed over the sight of black troops, shot some who had surrendered. *OR*, ser. 1, vol. 40, pt. 1, 64, 102, 599; Wert, *The Sword of Lincoln*, 384–86; McPherson, *Battle Cry of Freedom*, 760.

37. Neither the Fifth nor the Eighteenth Army Corps entered the crater. Part of this was due to vague orders from Meade to both corps commanders. According to Warren, there was not enough room to operate, and a move by these troops to enter the crater would have compounded an already bad situation. He also stated that even if he had acted independently, there were too many men in the crater to make an effective advance. Back-and-forth orders between Meade and Warren resulted in little movement by the Fifth Corps in the crater, and eventually Meade suspended any effort by the Fifth Corps to enter the fray. Warren's own personal assessment of the disaster rested on the time spent getting troops into the crater and securing the flanks once the crater crested. Slotkin, *No Quarter*, 150; Hess, *Into the Crater*, 138–39; *OR*, ser. 1, vol. 40, pt. 1, 78, 81.

38. In the summer of 1864, there were illusions of a peace overture from the South. Two former members of Congress, Jacob Thompson of Mississippi and Clement C. Clay of Alabama, and Professor James P. Holcombe of the University of Virginia were in Niagara Falls, Canada, apparently discussing possible peace talks. President Lincoln did not trust that they had the authority to act on behalf of the Confederate government but nonetheless thought it necessary to check on the sincerity of their claims. He sent Horace Greeley and John Hay, who presented Lincoln's "Whom it may concern" letter of July 18, 1864. Lincoln stated that he would be for "Any proposition which embraces the restoration of peace, . . . and the abandonment of slavery." The Confederate ambassadors had little power to negotiate, and nothing came of the peace effort. On August 5, 1864, a mine detonated forty yards in front of the Eighteenth Army Corps at Petersburg. Deserters from the Confederate army had warned Union leadership of this attack as early as August 2, and Warren ordered the preparation of a counter mine in response on August 3. There was little damage, and the assault was repulsed by Union troops. McPherson, *Battle Cry of Freedom*, 762, 766; Donald, *Lincoln*, 521–22; Goodwin, *Team of Rivals*, 646–47; Basler, ed., *Collected Works of Abraham Lincoln*, 7:451; *OR*, ser. 1, vol. 42, pt. 2, 24, 26, 52.

CHAPTER NINE

"This morning I received the sad news of the loss of our darling child"

August 23 to November 23, 1864

In Line of Battle west of the Weldon RR 5 ms south of Petersberg Va Aug 23 1864

Dear Delia

We have had severe marching and fighting since my last. We had a hard fight here day before yesturday. We fought behind breast works and whiped the Rebs badly with verry little los to us.[1]

I have lost no men by bullets since we started. Webster Cook was sun struck and is gone to the hospital. A no. of others gave out the day we came out here but there are none of them dangerously ill. I rec yours from Annamosa. You did right to go. Hope you enjoyed yourself. I sent Pa a draft for $400.00 Hope it will arrive safe. Sloat has just got back.[2]

It has rained here every day for two weeks. The roads are in horrible conditon. My love to the children. Tell Laura I will answer her letter soon.

ever yours

Henry

NOTES

1. On August 18, 1864, Maj. Gen. Warren's Fifth Corps was given the task of advancing on the Weldon Railroad link at Globe Tavern, also known as Yellow Tavern, and cutting off the Confederate supply route from North Carolina. A division in Warren's Corps was assaulted by Confederate major general Henry Heth's soldiers, after which they broke and ran, leaving the rest of the Fifth Corps to stop the advance. Additional attempts made by the Confederates on August 19 and 21 proved unsuccessful. Union casualties at Weldon Railroad were 251 killed, 1,148 wounded,

and 4,278 captured or missing. In the Seventh Wisconsin, 3 men were wounded while casualties for the entire Iron Brigade numbered 217. The Fifth Army Corps recorded 3,609 casualties at Weldon Railroad. Jeffry D. Wert, *The Sword of Lincoln: The Army of the Potomac* (New York: Simon & Schuster, 2005), 387–89; Lance J. Herdegen, *The Iron Brigade in Civil War and Memory: The Black Hats from Bull Run to Appomattox and Thereafter* (El Dorado Hills, CA: Savas Beatie, 2012), 527–28; War Records Office, *War of the Rebellion: A Compilation of the Official Records of the Union and Confederate Armies*, 2 vols. (Washington, DC: Government Printing Office, 1885–1901), ser. 1, vol. 42, pt. 1, 125–26 (hereafter cited as *OR*); William F. Fox, *Regimental Losses in the American Civil War* (Albany, NY: Albany Publishing Company, 1889), 547.

2. Webster Cook, Company F of the Seventh Wisconsin, was mustered out of the company on July 3, 1865. Anamosa, Iowa, is ninety miles from Cassville and sixty-three miles southwest of Dubuque, Iowa. Wisconsin, Adjutant General's Office, *Roster of the Wisconsin Volunteers, War of the Rebellion, 1861–1865*, Blue Books, 2 vols. (Madison: Democrat Printing Press, 1886), 1:559 (hereafter cited as *Roster*).

Camp 7th Wis Vet Vols near yellow tavern on the Weldon R Road Sept 2d 1864

Dear Delia

I have received no letter from you since your letter from Annamosa. Hope you are all well. We have had some severe fighting here for this road the Rebs seem determined to have it. Grant is equally determined to hold it. We are strongly fortified and expect more fighting. So far I have not lost a man in these fights.[3]

The men of our Regt who did not reinlist were discharged yesturday and started home under command of Lt Col Fennicum. You will probably see some of them. If Lincoln sends in his 500 000 or all he can get of them soon we will soon finish up this Rebellion, but if he does not enforce the draft he is polittically dead with the soldiers in the field.[4]

I would like to quit and go home. Three years is long enough to serve but I feel as though I would not be doing right to leave now when my services are most needed, and when so many are trying to shuffle out "*ass* backwards and every other way. This has been a trying Campaign. Some times almost disheartning to the best soldiers, but things are looking brighter now. There is a rumour in camp that McClellan has received the nomination at Chicago. If so and old Abe dont enforce the draft Mc will get a large soldier vote. The fact is the polisy of the President in calling out 100 Days men and militia for short seasons men who do us no good has become verry obnoxious to the soldiers at the front. I will suppoart the administration myself and always have done so but it is not so with others. I put in an application to go home with the soldiers, but Col Fennicum got the Privlige. His wife was sick and in that case i did not press my claim but I will come home after the campaign is ended if I live to see it ended. Give my love to Jared Laura & May.[5]

ever yours

Henry

NOTES

3. The Second Corps was sent to destroy the tracks at Reams's Station on the Weldon Railroad on August 25, leading to a near rout of federal forces. The third attempt by the Confederate force sent the federals running away, and Maj. Gen. Winfield Scott Hancock, attempting to rally his men, sent in two brigades from Maj. Gen. John Gibbon's division, which also performed badly. Other units prevented a total rout, and Hancock withdrew his Second Corps east during the night. Union casualties were 140 killed, 529 wounded, and 2,073 captured and missing. Confederate casualties numbered 720 in cavalry, artillery, and infantry. Wert, *The Sword of Lincoln*, 388–89; Frederick H. Dyer, *A Compendium of the War of the Rebellion Compiled and Arranged from Official Records . . . and Other Reliable Documents and Sources* (Des Moines, IA: Dyer Publishing Company, 1908), 951 (hereafter cited as *Dyer's Compendium*); Fox, *Regimental Losses*, 547; *OR*, ser. 1, vol. 42, pt. 1, 130, 940.

4. Col. William W. Robinson resigned as commander of the Seventh Wisconsin on July 9, 1864, and was replaced by Lt. Col. Mark Finnicum, of Fennimore, Wisconsin. Robinson's resignation was triggered by battle fatigue in addition to lingering questions concerning his performance at North Anna. *Roster*, 1:538. Herdegen, *The Iron Brigade*, 529.

5. George B. McClellan, the former commander of the Army of the Potomac, was nominated for president at the Democratic Convention in Chicago on August 30, 1864. The rift in the Democratic Party between war and peace factions led to a disjointed convention. McClellan, a War Democrat, became the nominee, while the peace faction of the party crafted a platform that hoped to bring an end to the war. His chief rival for the nomination, New York governor Horatio Seymour, garnered little support in the end. Democrats hoped that McClellan's standing with the soldiers would elect him, but President Lincoln felt he had developed a bond with the soldiers that would override the once popular general. McClellan issued a letter in which he stated he would not end the war at any cost. It had the effect of pitting the two factions of the Democratic Party against each other and all but ensured his defeat. McClellan received 202½ votes; there were 23½ for Seymour. George H. Pendleton of Ohio, who was against the war from the start, was selected as McClellan's running mate. Lincoln's chief rival for the Republican nomination, Salmon Chase, served as his secretary of the treasury. Chase built the machinery to

challenge Lincoln in 1864, but popular support in state legislatures, newspapers, and Union Leagues throughout the North effectively undermined any chance Chase had of being nominated. The convention, held in Baltimore, dumped Hannibal Hamlin and nominated the Tennessean Andrew Johnson for vice president. David Herbert Donald, *Lincoln* (New York: Simon & Schuster, 1995), 494, 506, 530; James M. McPherson, *Battle Cry of Freedom: The Civil War Era* (New York: Oxford University Press, 1988), 713–17, 765, 772; Doris Kearns Goodwin, *Team of Rivals: The Political Genius of Abraham Lincoln* (New York: Simon & Schuster, 2005), 663; Ronald C. White Jr., *A. Lincoln* (New York: Random House, 2009), 640; "The Chicago Convention," *Weekly National Intelligencer* (Washington, DC), September 1, 1864.

Camp 7th Wis Vet Vols on the Weldon RR Sept 5th 1864

Dear Father

My last was written when in line of Battle preparatory to our advance here, but we did not know where we were going and our surmises proved to be all wrong.

The papers have posted you in regard to our advance here and severe fighting we had for the first few days to mentain our position. Now we are ready for them. We have strong fortifications. So strong that Rebs cant drive us out without being heavily reinforced.[6]

We have just got the news of the capture of atlanta by Sherman. Everything is looking bright again. If Old Abe will enforce the Draft and bring us 300 000 men we will finish this little work verry soon. But if he dont enforce the draft and get the men Father Abaham is pollittically dead with the soldiers. The nomination of Pendleton is going to hurt the McClellan tickett with the soldiers, but McLellan has many warm friends in the army.[7]

I have had but one man wounded since my last. Our old Division whipped 3 Brigades of Rebs with verry small loss to us. On the 21st of Aug we were behind entrenchments. Those of the Regt who did not reinlist have gone home. Col Fennucum went with them. I would not trade with Furman & Scott without you get the worth of your half of the mill. Rent it till Sept 1st 1865 and if I live i will be home by that time to take charge of it.

Did you get the draft for $400 I sent you? I am anxious to hear from it. The news is that they are volunteering fast in some portions of Wis. How is it in Old Grant?

I am looking for an other swing round to the left which will cover the South Side R R which will undoubtly cause the evacuation of Petersberg. The copperhead papers may speculate as much as they please about grant falling back from this line but you may rest assured that Grant will never give up till the Rebs are driven across the Appomatix. Some think the entire Rebble army will be here within the next two weeks and that they will put forth their entire strength to dislodge grant. If so it will be their ruin for no army can long stand bucking against fortifications such as we have here.

I have wrote this in a hurry as the mail is just going out. My good wishes to all.

yours truly

H F Young

NOTES

6. The headline in the *Wisconsin State Journal* (Madison, WI) on August 26, 1864, was, "Weldon Road Utterly Destroyed."

7. On August 26 Maj. Gen. William Tecumseh Sherman orchestrated an end run around Atlanta, leaving one corps to give Gen. John Bell Hood the impression that most of the federal soldiers had gone. His march put him twenty miles south of the city. When Hood realized the true disposition of Sherman's force, he attacked on August 30 and met strong resistance and was repelled. Sherman attacked the next day, and Hood fled the city on September 1 before becoming trapped. Federal troops entered the city the next day. It had been nearly four months to the day since Sherman began the campaign for Atlanta. At 6 a.m. on September 3 Sherman telegraphed Maj. Gen. Halleck: "So Atlanta is ours, and fairly won." It was not received in Washington until 5:30 p.m. on September 4. McPherson, *Battle Cry of Freedom*, 774; *OR*, ser. 1, vol. 38, pt. 5, 777.

Camp 7th Wis Vet Vols Sept 15th 1864

Dear Delia

I received your verry welcome letter several days ago. Glad to indeed hear you were all well. I have been verry bussy for the last week. I have had 400 men under my command building Curturoy Roads. We have built miles of the best Roads here you ever seen. We have also got the R Road through from City Point.[8]

The Rebs wont know this country when they see it. There are a number of our officers going home, by being mustered out. It makes me verry home sick i cant tell you.

Capt F L Warner got his discharge this morning. I was laying on my bunk of poles thinking of you and the dear ones at home when he came in with it. And I tell you it was quite a struggle in my own mind which i should do ask my discharge on my three years service or write you a letter.[9]

I concluded at length to stand by the old flag during the present campaign for i still beleive if we get plenty of men this war will end with the reelection of Old Abe. I think McClellans chances are slim. The drag of having Pendleton on the tickett would kill the most popular man in the Union. If Father cant rent the mill to suit him let Furman run it till I get home. Which in that case will be early in the winter, for I am to near used up to stand annother winters campaign. We are fighting some every day but have got so used to it we dont mind it much. I send Laura a picture. Pleasant dreams. It is a lovely picture tell her that was for remembering papa with her letter.

I suppose some of our discharged men have got home by this time. All Kidd is discharged and has gone home. I tell you it is beginning to be real lonesome here. I expect Sloat will go out next.[10]

Have you moved yet and how do you like your shanty? You talk of high prices. They are high. We sometimes indulge in Potatoes at $9.00 per bushel Butter $1.00 pr lb and other things in proportion. Give my love to Laura Jared & May. Tell them I would like to kiss them all and then stay with them.

ever yours

Henry

NOTES

8. Warren reported that "400 men [were] assisting the engineers in building a new wagon road" on September 10, 1864. *OR*, ser. 1, vol. 42, pt. 2, 778.

9. Capt. Frederick L. Warner, Company G of the Seventh Wisconsin, was mustered out on September 17, 1864. *Roster*, 1:561.

10. 2nd Lt. Alphonzo A. Kidd and 1st Lt. William E. Sloat, both in Company F of the Seventh Wisconsin, resigned on September 10 and 14, respectively, due to earlier wounds. *Roster*, 1:558.

Camp 7th Wis Vet Vols On Weldon R Road Sept 19th 1864

Dear Father

I rec you kind letter several days ago. Glad to hear you were all in good health. We are still on the weldon Road strongly fortified. In fact we are so strong we want the Rebs to come on and drive us off as soon as they please. The sooner they try it the better it will suit us. So the draft commences in earnest this day. That suits us. It makes Lincoln stock rairse 100 per cent with the soldiers. In fact Lincoln will get most of the Solider vote. The Newyork Hearld by its strong union articles and bitter denunciation of the peace faction has helped Lincoln with the soldiers. It may suppoart McClellan but its bitter denunciation of the men that nominated him will overbalance all it can say in little Mcs favor.[11]

A A Kidd & Lieut Sloat have been mustered out of the service. In fact most of the officers who have been in three years have been mustered out or have ~~been~~ made application to be mustered out. I can muster out any time as my term of service is out and I wont remuster three years in the same grade I have served. But I dont feel like leaving the service now. Some how my hope is large, and I still hope to see the Rebellion crushed before winter. The draft and Recruits will fill up the army by Nov, then I look for the Election of Lincoln which in its self will be a crushing blow at the Rebellion. Let him be elected and at the same time let Grant, Sherman, & Sherridan be heavily reinforced and ready to strike the decisive blow and down will the Rebellion. At all events this is not the time to falter while the Govt is calling for men. Is not the time for me to leave the service. Although i am free to confess i am tired of it and some times verry home sick.

If you cant rent the mill to your satisfaction let it stand till winter. By that time the new Recruits will be well in the field and I can feel better sattisfide in quitting. But if you can rent it for a year or till next spring I would like to have it done. I can see nothing ahead but high prices and hard times. Those that will be best off are the ones that have small farms that they can cultivate themselves and are out of debt. I think we will have to take to raising sheep & Flax and go in on the old homespin and raise our own Sugar Tabacco & c. It costs an officer $1.00 per day to live here at the presant prices of provissions, and we live poor at that.

I am sorry to hear that they are still raising new organnizations in Wis. I should think the fate of the 36 37 & 38th would have given them enough of sending new troops into the field with undrilled officers. My good wishes to all.[12]

yours truly

H F Young

NOTES

11. In the article "A Call upon McClellan for More Light," the *New York Herald*, on September 17, 1864, presented a clear picture of what it hoped would happen regardless of who won the election. "Whoever may be elected the next President of the United States will have either to acknowledge the independence of the South or destroy their power. The power of Jeff. Davis must be destroyed at all hazards, or the nation is lost forever."

12. The Thirty-sixth, Thirty-seventh, and Thirty-eighth Wisconsin were organized in Madison on March 23, April 9, and April 15, 1864, respectively. They all took part in the bloody fighting of the Overland Campaign and the assault at Petersburg, and the Thirty-seventh Wisconsin suffered heavy casualties at the Battle of the Crater. More than half of the officers in the Field and Staff, eight of fourteen, had combat experience before joining the regiment. However, the same was not true of the company officers in each regiment, only 30 percent of whom had served in other regiments before joining their new companies. *Roster*, 2:578–653; Edwin Bentley Quiner, *The Military History of Wisconsin: A Record of the Civil and Military Patriotism of the States, in the War for the Union* (Chicago: Clark and Co., 1866), 824–25, 835–36, 845–46; Fox, *Regimental Losses*, 14, 400–401; Charles E. Estabrook, ed., *Wisconsin Losses in the Civil War: A List of the Names of Wisconsin Soldiers Killed in Action, Mortally Wounded, or Dying From Other Causes in the Civil War* (Madison: Democrat Printing Company, 1915), 173–85; *Dyer's Compendium*, 949.

Camp 7th Wis Vet Vols near Weldon R R Va Sept 27th 1864

Dear Father

I received yours of Sept 12th. Glad to find you are sound & strong for the administration, for now is the time for every man to stand firm. A few more such rattification meetings such as Sherriden has given them in the valley will entirely destroy McClellans prospects with the soldiers. Our army is in motion and fighting has been going on for 48 hours. But we have no news as the fighting is on the right and we are on the extreeme left. We have been sending troops to the right for two days. We are in the front line now, and we are strung out till we aint more than a good skirmish line, but we have good strong works with abbetus in front. Rumours of success come from the right but I can get nothing reliable but you will get the news good or bad by telgram before you get this. Enclosed I send $200.00 draft. We have just our pay up to Aug 31st. I hope you have succeeded in selling the mill either all of it or your half of it.[13]

My Idea for your selling your half to Scott & Furman is this. First if you can sell to them for $4000 I look upon it as just saving that much from the wreck. Furman says Scott wont turn out his old homestead. If he wont do that he would not be able to buy more than half the mill. In the 2d place you will not spend any more money on it and I would not feel like spending 12 or 1500 Dolls myself to put the mill and race in condition.[14]

But I will do it as partners if for no other purpose. I will do it for the purpose of getting rid of it to the best advantage and I think I can manage Furman so that we can get the custom back that he has lost.

The mill is a bad bargain for us and if we can turn half the bad bargain over to some others we will be gainers and it is not necessary to let the question of ownership stand in the way of what is for the best. If you can trade off my half instead of yours do so and I will be obliged. Not that I want to get away from you as my partner, but that the one half of that mill is enough for one Family. Col Fennicum has returned to his post. Capt Monteith of Co H has gone out the Service. It is getting lonesome here. There are so many of the old officers going out. The chaplin goes home on a leave this day.[15]

yours truly

H F Young

NOTES

13. Lt. Gen. Ulysses S. Grant's attacks on the north and south sides of the James River forced Gen. Robert E. Lee to withdraw a division from Lt. Gen. Jubal Early, consequently putting Early's troops at a disadvantage in the Shenandoah Valley as they faced Maj. Gen. Philip Sheridan's cavalry. Sheridan's horse soldiers seized the initiative, struck Winchester, Virginia, on September 19, and drove Early's force twenty miles south. Three days later, at Fort Fisher, south of Strasburg, Sheridan routed the Confederate force again and sent them reeling further south. Grant's fifth offensive ended without the capture of Petersburg; however, the capture of a Confederate fort put the federal force within six miles of Richmond, creating panic in the capital. McPherson, *Battle Cry of Freedom*, 777–78; Wert, *The Sword of Lincoln*, 387, 389–90; *Dyer's Compendium*, 949.

14. Samuel Scott, a farmer in Tafton, may have been Furman's partner in a deal for the mill that never reached fruition. Caroline Furman, the wife of Cornelius Furman, was the daughter of Samuel Scott. Consul Willshire Butterfield, *History of Grant County Wisconsin, Containing an Account . . . of the United States* (Chicago: Western Historical Company, 1881), 952; 1850 United States Census, digital image s.v. "Samuel Scott," FamilySearch.org.

15. Capt. Robert Monteith, Company H of the Seventh Wisconsin, was mustered out on September 26, 1864. Chaplain Samuel W. Eaton was mustered out at the end of the war, on July 3, 1865. *Roster*, 1:565, 539.

Camp 7th Wis Vet Vols near Weldon R Road Va Oct 6th 1864

Dear Delia

Here am I in the same place I was when I wrote my last letter but we have not been here all the time. We have been over west of the R Road for the last week. We were not engaged with the enemy so that luckily i have no casualities to repoart in our Regt.

But our advance on the west side was quite successful but not so much so as it would have been had it not rained continually for two days and nights making it almost impossible to move artillery in level clayey country. We still hold the position we gained at Poplar Grove church which commands the South Side R Road.

I am glad to hear Eva has been making you a visit and that you have had a good time. You talk of your poor pen that you are in. That gives me more unneasiness than anything else for it wont do for you to winter in such a place as that. You and the children would catch your death of colds.

But I still think we will finish this Rebellion as soon as the Presidential Election is over. At all events I dont think you will object to my staying till that time to see what will turn up.

I sent Pa $200 the other day but I dont want you to spend much on the house you are in for you must not stay there this winter. I am verry sorry to hear Jared is such a naughty boy to run away from home. In the way you speak of tell him there are thousands of little boys like him in this southren country that have no homes nor nothing to eat and if he dont be a good boy his papa wont care about seeing him. I see that the majorship still sticks in the mind of the little woman. I tell you I wont except a promotion that will fasten me for another three years without your consent. Wont that satisfy you for the present. There is some talk of consolidation again. If they do consolidate I will make tracks for Wisconsin in a hurry for there then will be a surplus of officers. Every one speaks of dull hards time in Wis. I am sorry to hear it and yet i expected it. I look for a crash soon that will carry most of the speculators with it. I have come to the conclusion that after I leave the service i will always raise about two or three acres of potatoes for my own use for it appears we cant get enough of them here. We had a mess for dinner at the round rate of $9 pr bushell 15 cts pr lb. Give my love to Jared Laura & May and accept the same for your own dear self.[16]

ever yours

Henry

NOTE

16. Several manufactured products did well in Wisconsin during the war—farm machinery, leather, beer, and pork. However, other industries were not so fortunate. "Many of the areas of manufacturing hardly held their own. The flour-milling industry made slow progress, and Wisconsin continued to market wheat rather than flour." Another source of concern at the end of September was a banking crisis in Chicago in which two banks went under. A mob went so far as to attack one of the failed banks and demanded their money. Frank L. Klement, *Wisconsin and the Civil War: The Home Front and the Battle Front* (Madison: State Historical Society of Wisconsin, 1997), 117–19; "Chicago Market," *Wisconsin State Journal*, October 1, 1864; "Panic in Chicago," *Daily Intelligencer* (Wheeling, WV), October 6, 1864; "A Chicago Banking House Attacked by Mob," *New York Herald*, October 2, 1864.

Camp 7th Wis Vet Vols near Ft Howard Va Oct 13 1864

Dear Delia

I received your welcome letter. Glad to hear you were all well. This is a cold windy day. Real fall weather. It begins to feel like overcoats and mittens would be comfortable. I feel verry lonesome to day. This morning the 19th Indiana Regt went to the 2d Corps; they being consolidated with the 20th Indiana Regt. They have been along side of us every day for over three years. Their history and our own have been identical. We have ever formed a part of the famous Old Iron Brigade. Between us there were warm friendships. The friendships that are formed in camp and on the field of danger are stronger than they are in civil life. I seen officers and men of the gallant Old 19th shed tears this morning in parting with us, and I have seen those same men stand firm and swing their hats and cheer when charging on the enemy amidst a perfect storm of bullets.[17]

Thus they go. There will soon be nothing of our once splendid Brigade left together. The three or four old officers left of the 7th look at each other and feel almost as if we could not stand it much longer. I wrote to Furman in refference to his house. While I am in the service I cant buy it. There has been no fighting in our front since my last except the usual Pickett firing in which the casualities have been light. There has been none in our Regt. Birney has been fighting on the Right near Richmond with some success. Our line is now 44 miles long all the way well fortified. The Rebs have a corresponding line in our front. In fact a greate deal of both lines are doubled. Grant will take Richmond this fall. Of that i have no doubts at all.

Then we will elect Old Abe President and then you may look upon the Rebellion as played out. What a Gloriously happy day that will be for the soldiers and their families.[18]

Give my love to Susan and all the little pets and the same for yourself.

Ever yours

Henry

NOTES

17. By the fall of 1864, the Iron Brigade was a shell of its former self. Depletion in the ranks by deaths, wounds, and the expiration of terms forced a reorganization of the brigade. Only three of the original regiments were left, the Twenty-fourth Michigan, Sixth Wisconsin, and Seventh Wisconsin. They became part of Brig. Gen. Samuel W. Crawford's Third Division and supplemented their ranks with the 143rd, 149th, and 150th Pennsylvania Infantry and a battalion of New York sharpshooters. Herdegan, *The Iron Brigade*, 539; *OR*, ser. 1, vol. 42, pt. 3, 461.

18. The Darbytown Road engagement on October 13, 1864, involved elements of the Tenth Army Corps, commanded by Maj. Gen. David Birney. Shortly thereafter, Birney died of an intestinal hemorrhage in Philadelphia. *Dyer's Compendium*, 955; *OR*, ser. 1, vol. 42, pt. 1, 690–91; Wert, *The Sword of Lincoln*, 392.

Camp 7th Wis Vet Vols near Weldon R Road Va Oct 21 1864

Dear Father

It appears you have changed your *Religion* or Tactics. I cant say which it should be called for instead of doing as you would be done by, you get me to write all the letters you can, and on your part write as few as you can. I am willing to admit your letters are interresting but Ill be *cused* if they keep good Three weeks in this climate. In your last you noted in pencil that you had received one from me and after that I sent you another containing a draft for $200 which I am anxious to hear from. And for the neglect of answering which I would like a pull at that old Patiarchal beard.

Ah by the way Bill Trembly was here the other day to see me. He is Capt in a N Y Regt. He requested me to remember him to you & tell you he was sound for Lincoln & Johnson. And further to say to you that he had a turn of the measles that stuck to him much longer than that dose of religion did that he caught in the Pocket. Bill made me quite a visit. He is greatly improved and after we had drank to Lincoln & Johnson and the cause in general about twice *round*, he was verry sociable. The fact is I have come to the conclusion that the great equalizer in the army is forty rod Lightning comesary Whiskey. I have seen it bring Genls down as low and flat as Privates could *get*, and I have seen it elevate the lowest till they felt as big as the President.[19]

Well Sherradin has had another Peace meeting in the Valley in which as usual he used *solid sharp* and over whelmingly convincing arguments. Bully for Sherradin. I reccollect last spring at Culpeper of hearing that some person had asked Grant who Sherridan was. Grant answered Sherradin is a Thunderbolt. His fighting shews Grant understood his man.[20]

I suppose we are getting the strongest works here on both sides that the world ever seen. We have works so strong and Intricate that we can leave them take care of themselves. *This saves rations* well. At all events we have nothing in some of them but artillery & pickett line and yet Lee might buck his entire army against them, and he would fail every time.

Our morter firing at night is the grandest sight ever witnessed. I have seen as much as 100 morter shells in the air at one time. It is a grand & interesting sight. Our Picketts and the Rebs are working on each other all the time. They dig down about four ft deep 8 ft wide. That threws up quite an embankmenet next the enemy. When either of the parties get to close, the other side will take fifteen or twenty of these little four inch morters place them in their Pickett pits. Then will commence one of the most interresting fights ever seen. They threw them up and after the range is secured. They drop them in the pits every time. Then there is nothing left for the poor Devils thats attacted but to run back to their own pits which are all Bomb proof. The boys are all well.

Hurrah for old Abe.
yours truly

H F Young

NOTES

19. Capt. William L. Trembly of the 104th New York Infantry enlisted in 1861 and was wounded at Antietam. Commissioned captain in October 1863, he was mustered out in Washington, DC, on July 17, 1865. New York State, Adjutant General Office, *Annual Report of the Adjutant-General of the State of New York for the Year 1902: Registers of the One Hundredth, One Hundred and First, One Hundred and Second, One Hundred and Third, One Hundred and Fourth, One Hundred and Fifth and one Hundred and Sixth Regiments of Infantry* (Albany: Argus Company, Printers, 1903), 1,048.

20. Sheridan's horse soldiers were by the middle of October busy laying waste to barns and farm machinery and driving cattle and sheep for federal soldiers' consumption. The fighting became personal, with marauding bands of Confederate guerrillas nipping at the edges of Sheridan's force, killing an aide and a medical inspector. Meeting with Grant near Harpers Ferry, Sheridan had drawn up further plans that impressed Grant so much that he did not bother to pull his own plan from his pocket. Sheridan also impressed Grant during the Battle of Cedar Creek on October 19; federal troops were in headlong retreat when Sheridan arrived on the battlefield. He immediately went to the front and turned a near defeat into a victory. By the end of November, the Shenandoah Valley was secured thanks to the actions of Sheridan's cavalry force. McPherson, *Battle Cry of Freedom*, 778–79; Ulysses S. Grant, *Personal Memoirs of U.S. Grant*, 2 vols. (New York: Charles L. Webster, 1886), 2:327–28; *Dyer's Compendium*, 956; H. W. Brands, *The Man Who Saved the Union: Ulysses Grant in War and Peace* (New York: Anchor Books, 2012), 328–29.

Camp 7th Wis Vet Vols near Weldon R Road Va Oct 22 1864

Dear Delia

Here am *I*. The worst disappointed man you ever saw just because I received no letter this morning. Neither have I received any since my last and I set myself down to bore you with a letter with as little news in it as possible just to pay you for neglecting me. Now old girl how do you like that for a commencement. Next in order. It is a cold raw morning and my fire which is in front of my tent smokes without any considerations for my comfort. Next in order. Capt Hoyt my bedfellow is on picket and I had to divide our scant bedding with him so that I Devilish near froze last night. And every time I waked up cold my mind would wander off to Wisconsin to where I had a good bed and a bedfellow that dont go on picet. Sherradin has had another *Peace Convention* with the Rebs in the valley in which he has ~~as useul~~ as usual used verry convincing arguments. He has nearly ruined the Deomcratic Party. Little Mc. Poor fellow. Puts me in mind of the Ladys little dog. She used to take him in her lap and pat him "*Oh* your a nice little dog a pretty little dog but you can never be a big dog. I still think that the Election of Lincoln unless our Genls make some blunder will crush the spirit of the south. The other evening on our picket line our boys Hurrahed for Lincoln. The Rebs took it up an cheered for McClellan, and from cheering they got to abusing each other quite lively and from that to picket firing and from that to Artillery and moter firing.[21]

I heard a soldier that was out on the line swear that he yet beleived Mc to be a true and Loyal man, and he had intended to vote for him. But said he Ill be d—d if I vote for any man the rebs will fight for. Genls Grant and Mead were here skylarking round yesturday. The boys think they can see a fight a head within the next few days, but I dont look for much fighting untill Sherradins forces return from the valley. The boys of the co are in good health and in good spirits.

Chaplin Eaton has just returned from a visit home. Eaton takes a lively interest in Polatics & War, and by the way is the most popular Chaplin I know of in the army.

Lieut Col Fennicum was severely bruised by being thrown from his horse. He is in Hospital and is improving. I wrote your Father three weeks ago & sent him a Draft for $200. I would like to pull his whiskers untill he answers it. My love to all.

ever yours

Henry

NOTE

21. Capt. George S. Hoyt, Company K of the Seventh Wisconsin, was wounded in two separate battles, South Mountain and the Wilderness, and promoted to major on December 29, 1864. *Roster*, 1:538, 572.

Camp 7th Wis Vet Vols near Weldon R Road Va Oct 30th 1864

Dear Delia

I am verry busy making out my muster & pay Rolls as tommorrow is muster day, but I must take time to write you a few lines. I received your welcome letter three or four days ago, glad to hear you were all well. We have just returned from a movement on the left which from some cause at present unexplained proved a failure. That is if it was intended as anything more than a reconnoisance. Our Corps was not engaged only in skemmishing. We came back to camp all right with 200 prisnors. Dont make to much calculation for wintering in Tafton till you hear from me again. For as soon as F Boynton gets his commission as Lieut I will muster out if they will let me. And under existing orders, they cant help it. The fact is I cant stand another winter campaign. It will kill me with Rheumatism. I have it now whenever I lay out on the damp ground. I actually beleive I am getting *old*. My love to all.[22]

ever yours

Henry

NOTE

22. An engagement at Hatcher's Run on October 27–28 did little to change the calculus around Petersburg. The Seventh Wisconsin lost one man captured in the engagement. Union casualties were 166 killed, 1,028 wounded, and 564 captured or missing. Francis A. Boynton, Company F of the Seventh Wisconsin, was promoted to captain on December 13, 1864. *Dyer's Compendium*, 956; *OR*, ser. 1, vol. 42, pt. 1, 157, 160; *Roster*, 1:558.

Camp 7th Wis Vet Vols Weldon R R Va Nov 5th 1864

Dear Delia

As I am on duty to night I will drop you a few lines just to while away the hours till one oclock in the morning when I will be releived. You will perhaps wonder why I can write while on duty. Well I am on duty and yet I am in my cabin. The men are in their cabins setting by their fires talking poletics but are not allowed to go to bed. Their guns are stacked in the co street so that at the first allarm on the picket line our breast work will be bristling with Bayonets. The Johnys have been massing troops in our front to day as though they would like to punch a hole through our lines. Let them come. We are ready for them. The next 48 hours will settle the great Presidential question of 1864 and will go far toward setling the Rebellion. For I am sure Old Abe will be reelected for another 4 years and that will dishearten the Rebs more than the winning from them a great victory would. The men have built comfortable quarters covered with their shelter tents and are cheerful good natured & happy and all wishing the Jonnys would buck up against our works. The weather for the time of year is warm & pleasant. We have had a remarkable fine fall so far. Verry little rain or mud. Our Regt will vote almost unanimous for Old Abe. Little Mc is at a great discount in the army. Pendleton and the Chicago platform is tomuch of a load for any man to carry. It would break down the best man in the world.[23]

Oh, but I am sleepy. I hope to see you and the rest of the dear ones soon. My love to all.

Good night *dear*.
Ever yours

Henry

NOTE

23. George McClellan, the Democratic candidate for president, was in a no-win situation by October 1864. Union victories in Atlanta and Sheridan's campaign in the Shenandoah Valley greatly aided the incumbent Lincoln. To add insult to his chance of victory, he was often at odds with the peace faction of the party. Copperhead intrigues, real or perceived, in Canada also made victory elusive for McClellan by the end of October. McPherson, *Battle Cry of Freedom*, 771, 775, 783; Goodwin, *Team of Rivals*, 656; White, *A. Lincoln*, 640.

Camp 7th Wis Vet Vols Weldon R R Va Nov 7th 1864

Dear Father

I received yours of Oct 29th this morning. Glad to hear from you. Your letter left me verry uneasy. You speak of all being well but Laura and state Delia had wrote me about her. I have had no letter from Delia for more than a week and your intimation of all being well but her leaves me verry uneasy. It has always been a source of uneasiness with me the dread of accident or sickness in my family.

Tomorrow is the eventful day of the Election. I think it will not only wind up little Mc but will be a telling blow to the Rebellion. I see from a Richmond paper that there is likely to be a regular split amongst the Rebs about the arming of the negroes. Davis and his gang have grown Desperate for anything and now go in for freeing and arming two hundred & fifty thousand negroes. The Planters & Slave owners cant see it as they contend that it will ruin the institution of slavery forever. The other side contend that in case of the reelection of Lincoln they will have neither Confederacy Slaves or anything else soon if they dont do it.[24]

Our late movement to the left was a failure. It is no use disguising it to you by any other name although it goes as a reconnoisance. Well that is all we got out of it. For we found the Rebs had two lines of works fifteen miles long in front on the south side R Road & had their cars to run their troops to any given point on the line to man their works at short notice.[25]

We made no attack and consequently lost but few men. Deserters say they intend to attact us tomorrow to prevent our voting. If so they will us ready. If they will just buck against our lines enough to prevent our voting we will agree to finish the Rebellion on this line within the next 48 hours.

I wrote you about Fennicum being hurt by a fall from his horse. He is still unable for duty. We have just received a batch of new commissions. 1st Sergt F A Boynton is commissioned 1st Lieut of my Co and will be mustered as such in a few days. We are not entitled to a 2d Lieut. I am looking for the consolidation of our Regts, as soon as the Election is over. They have Consolidated the Regts form Indiana, but between you & I, they would not have been consolidated till after the Election if they had been allowed to vote. Consolidation is not satisfactory to officers or men. When their Regt looses its designation and the smaller Regt being absorbed by the larger and addopting its men often puts old and honrourable organizations into new organizations that have no renown attached to their No. But it is the only policy to adopt to save the Govt vast expense as long as the Governours of States are permited to adopt the suicidle policy of making new organizations, so that they can pay off their political friends with the offices. I am verry sorry you did not say what was the trouble with Laura. If she is sick dangerously leave nothing undone for her that can be done. Your letter has left me verry uneasy blue & home sick.

yours truly

H F Young

NOTES

24. As the manpower dwindled in the South, considerable debate ensued in Richmond over conscription of slaves into the Confederate army. Although it was unthinkable at the beginning of the war, by 1863 several backers, including Maj. Gen. Patrick Cleburne, recommended arming the slaves. However, many soldiers were not convinced that this was a good policy. Sentiments ran high on both sides of the issue, and by November 1864 some Southern politicians and generals reluctantly stated that it might become necessary to use the slaves as soldiers. Judah P. Benjamin, secretary of state for the Confederacy, stated that the use of slaves as soldiers is "always best settled by degrees," and if they did fight Southerners "should emancipate them as a reward for their services." A Richmond newspaper defended the use of slaves in paternalistic terms by stating "That the negro will fight more faithfully for his master than for the Yankee, no one can doubt who has seen the

attachment of the slaves towards their masters in camp." In the early days of 1865 necessity seems to have won over even Gen. Lee, who endorsed the use of slaves as soldiers. On March 13, 1865, a bill to use slaves as soldiers reached the desk of Confederate president Jefferson Davis, leading him to state that "Much benefit is anticipated from this measure, though far less than would have resulted from its adoption at an earlier date." Reid Mitchell, *Civil War Soldiers: Their Expectations and Experiences* (New York: Viking, 1988), 190–91; McPherson, *Battle Cry of Freedom*, 832, 834–36; *OR*, ser. 4, vol. 3, 959, 1012; "Negro Conscription," *Richmond Enquirer*, November 4, 1864; Confederate States of America, *Journal of the Congress of the Confederate States of America, 1861–1865*, 7 vols. (Washington, DC: Government Printing Office, 1904–5), 4:704.

25. The unsuccessful movement on October 27–28 was the engagement at Hatcher's Run.

Camp 7th Wis Vet Vols near Weldon R R Va Nov 10 1864

Dear Delia

I just received your letter. Sorry to hear of Lauras sickness but verry glad to hear she was getting better. I am glad to hear you have got into a comfortable house.

The Election is over. Our Brigade cast 1291 votes of which Lincoln received 946 & Mc 345 giving Lincoln 645 majority. The rest of the army voted about the same. Tomorrow we will begin to get the news of how the states went. I am looking for Lincoln to have a larger majority than at his 1st Election. Frank Boynton has got his Commissin as 1st Lieut but he has not mustered yet. It is still my intentin to muster out as soon as he musters and I can get things fixed for it. It will take me some time to settle my accounts with the Govt, everything has to be done under the infernal *red tap system*.[26]

Frank has been a week trying to muster in and it will perhaps take a week longer before he accomplishes it. All because the mustering officer is Judge Advocate of a court martial. We have nothing new in the way of consolidation but are looking for an order to that effect.

I received a letter from your Father two days since. He wrote of you all being well but Laura. It made me verry uneasy untill I received your letter. I am anxious to get home so as to make some arrangements about the mill, so as to be ready to go to work next spring.

Furman wants to buy half of the mill. I will sell him my half if we can agree about the terms.

I have the Rheumatism every time I get wet and i tell you its verry uncomfortable for the cursed thing dont stop when I lay down but pains more than ever.

I look for a move in the army soon. Perhaps within the next week, but what will be the point of attack. I cant pretent to say. My love to all Jared Laura & May.

ever yours

Henry

NOTE

26. In twelve states, including Wisconsin, the soldier vote was tabulated separately. Soldiers in the Seventh Wisconsin recorded 147 votes for Lincoln and 30 for McClellan. The soldier vote in Wisconsin was 11,372 for Lincoln and 2,428 for McClellan; nationwide the soldier vote was 119,754 for Lincoln and 34,291 for McClellan. In Wisconsin, 68,887 voted for Lincoln and 62,586 for McClellan. McPherson, *Battle Cry of Freedom*, 804–5; *OR*, ser. 1, vol. 42, pt. 3, 577; Wisconsin, *A Manual of Customs, Precedents and Forms, . . . Lists and Tables for Reference*, comp. Clerks of Senate and Assembly (Madison: Atwood & Rublee, 1865), 171–72.

Camp 7th Wis Vet Vols Weldon R R Va Nov 13th 1864

Dear Delia

This morning I received the sad news of the loss of our da[r]ling child. It was entirely unexpected as I had received no dispatch and your last letter left me the impression that the dear child was out of danger and after that I had gave myself no uneasiness. I had just got her a hat made out of corn husks. I got it yesturday evening and was anticipating how well she would look and what pleasure she would have in shewing her Rebble gipsey hat. I went to sleep thinking about it, and when I awoke I found yours and Fathers letter on my table, with the mournful inteligence that I should never see my darling more. Had I received your telegram I should have gone home on a leave of absence but now I will remain till I can get mustered out. Frank Boynton was mustered ~~in~~ 1st Lieut day before yesturday. I will have to remain here untill the paymaster comes and pays us off, as there are some of the men have unsettled accounts, and could not well get them settled without I was present. And our co have clothing stored at Alexandria Va which we have sent for and I have qr masters stores there for which I am responsible that I have sent for so as to turn them over. All of which I will do as quick as possible so as to get mustered out & return home to stay with the *loved ones.*[27]

I feel verry thankful to our friends & neighbours for their kindness to you through the trying ordeal you have passed. I feel so greived to think I was not with you to assist you and see our darling child once more. I cant write more at present. My love to Jared & May and tell them papa will soon be home.

ever yours

Henry

NOTE

27. Laura Eva Young died on November 5, 1864, in Tafton, Wisconsin, of diphtheria. "Deaths," *Grant County Herald* (Lancaster, WI), November 22, 1864.

Camp 7th Wis Vet Vols Weldon R Road Va Nov 20th 1864

Dear Father

Your last letter with its sad news has been received. It was unexpected and sorrowful news to me as I received no dispatch and Delias last letter led me to beleive that all danger was past. It has ever been a source of anxiety to me to know what to do in case of the sickness of my family. And perhaps it is better under the circumstances that I did not receive the dispatch, for I could not have got home in to see my dear child and I certainly should have went. While I mourn the loss of my child I am pleased to no that all was done for that kind hearts and loving hands could do. I think I will go out of the service next month. I owe it to my family and I will go. I have faithfully served my over three years and my wife has nobly performed her part, but now she says come home and a man must not neglect his family.

We were just on the eve of a move this morning but the rain has stoped it. Where we were going is all speculation. Some say two or three corps are going to Wilmington & c. My own theory is that it is merely a demonstration to keep Lee from sending troops to operate against Sherman.

I never saw this army in as good spirits as now. The overwhelming defeat of the copperheads, the advance of Sherman, the depression of the Rebs on pickett in our front, all contribute to raise the spirits of our men.

You hear no whining or grumbling at the administration or anything else. All feel satisfied that we can whip the Rebs in our front, since our friends at home have so crushingly defeated the enemy in our rear. Your segestion to stay till spring and then muster out—does not meet my approbation. My military carrear I feel proud of, and what you recommend is what I have often cursed officers for. In fact it was carried to such an extent last spring that Grant published an order dismissing all officers dishonourably from the service asking for discharges—of course you did not understand this or you would not have reccommended it.

Allow me to thank you and mother for your kindness to my family in their affliction. My best wishes to all.

yours truly

H F Young

~

Camp 7th Wis Vet Vols Weldon R R Va Nov 23 1864

Dear Delia

It is a week since I received yours & Fathers letter with the sad news of Lauras death and you dont no how anxious I am to hear from home.

It has rained for the last five days & last night it cleared up cold freezing hard during the night.

We were under marching orders but the rain stoped the contemplated move. And it is well we did not get started for we would have suffered terribly during the storm, but in our cabins we have got along verry well. I have a severe cold otherwise I am all right. We hear of a terrible storm in the north. I am anxious about you and the children during the cold weather with no person to get your wood and build your fires. I will try and start to Washington about the 1st of Dec so you need not answer this letter unless you hear from me again for unless something unlooked for happens your letter would not arrive in time to find me here.

There is great anxiety in the army to hear from Sherman. The Rebs dont publish a word about him for if they did we would get it. They are bad off in our front and desertions these dark nights are quite frequent. All tell the same story of want and destitution. If Sherman succeeds in getting through to Savanna or Charleston the Georgia & South Carrolina troops wont stay in the Reb army so that I think the end is at hand. I would like verry much to take my thanksgiving dinner with you tomorrow. I have lost yours & Lauras pictures. I am verry sorry for it especially Lauras.[28]

I had them in a Book and some person carried off the book with them in. I am in hopes it was Sloat as the book belonged to him and I missed it just after he left. If so I will get them.

I dont know what arrangements I can make about the mill and will make none till I get home. But the way times are I cant afford to be long idle and I will do what is best toward getting along comfortably.

I will write you as soon as I get to Washington as it will take me perhaps a week to settle up with the Govt as I have been a long time in command and everything has to be done through the red tape system. My love to Jared & May and for yourself the same.[29]

ever yours

Henry

NOTES

28. Sherman proposed a march to the sea to counter Hood's army to his rear. A reluctant Lincoln, Halleck, and Grant acquiesced only when Sherman sent the Army of Tennessee to guard his rear against Hood's movements. Sherman left Atlanta on November 15, 1864; his march to the sea ended with the capture of Savannah on December 21, 1864. Sherman provided Lincoln with an early holiday present when he cabled, "I beg to present you, as a Christmas gift, the city of Savannah." McPherson, *Battle Cry of Freedom*, 808–10; *OR*, ser. 1, vol. 44, 783.

29. The departure of Young was not welcomed by William Ray. However, he understood the reason, and he could not "blame Capt Young any for his business at home was in such a bad condition that he must go & him going gives me a chance to rise some in the scale of Military Promotion." Ray did not relate in his journal whether he knew the other compelling reason behind Capt. Young's departure from the service. Lance Herdegen and Sherry Murphy, eds., *Four Years with the Iron Brigade: The Civil War Journals of William R. Ray, Co. F, Seventh Wisconsin Infantry* (Cambridge, MA: Da Capo Press, 2002), 340.

Epilogue

For Captain Henry Falls Young, the war was over. Young, with a heavy heart, made his way through the camp of the Seventh Wisconsin one last time for final goodbyes before trudging north, to Washington, DC, and departure from the service. He served his company, regiment, state, and country dutifully, but now it was time to reunite and heal a family he had left three long years earlier.

Young was discharged on December 3, 1864. That he was a survivor of the war when so many others had perished marred what should have been a joyous occasion, touched also by the loss of his dear child. Equally heart-wrenching was the cruel injustice he felt knowing he could do nothing to help his daughter in her greatest hour of need. Lt. Col. Hollon Richardson of Chippewa Falls, Wisconsin, was in command of the regiment at the time of Young's departure. Certainly, his commanding officer knew Young well enough to know the real reason behind his somewhat abrupt departure from the company, especially considering his recent enlistment in the Seventh Wisconsin as a veteran volunteer. The Seventh Wisconsin commander offered praise for the Company F commander, writing on the back of Young's discharge paper that "he is a brave and has ever been a very useful Officer."[1]

Young returned to the mill in Grant County, the subject of many letters home during the war. By all accounts, the postwar years were filled with a certain degree of happiness along with the usual twists and turns of life. Henry and Delia operated the mill for the next twelve years; a fourth and final child, Harry Warner Young, was born on February 28, 1869. Tragedy, never far away in the nineteenth century, struck again with the death of their oldest child, Jared, on January 14, 1870, at the age of thirteen. In 1878, perhaps tiring of the mill, the family moved to the farm of his father-in-law, Jared Warner, near the village of Patch Grove. The move, likely welcomed by both men, put Delia closer to family and relieved the everyday burdens for Warner, then in his sixty-sixth year. The farmstead, consisting of about 280 acres in 1877, remained in family proprietorship until the death of Harry Young in 1944.[2]

While vocal in his politics, Young made few forays into government in the years after the war. In 1875–76 he served as Grant County coroner, and in 1881 he served, along with three other men, as justice of the peace in Patch Grove Township. Around this same time, Young also served on the executive committee of the Blake's Prairie Agricultural Society. The society's mission was to hold and promote an annual fair and to display the bounty produced within Grant County each year. His interest in the politics of the day did not go beyond Grant County, and he reportedly turned down many offers to serve in government. Henry did attend a county Republican convention in Boscobel during the fall of 1868 that supported the candidacy of Amasa Cobb, former colonel of the Fifth and Forty-third Wisconsin Infantry, to represent the third congressional district of Wisconsin. The convention also resolved to back the Republican candidate for president, Gen. Ulysses S. Grant, largely because of his "honesty, abilities, and patriotism." He was a member of another organization, the Free Thought Society of Patch Grove, where Young and others debated the issues of the day. In religious belief, he was an avowed agnostic; he believed and hoped there was something after death but was uncertain what the afterlife held for him.[3]

With the passing of the years, several former comrades reached out to Young. His replacement as commander of Company F, Francis A. Boynton, wrote to see how he liked the transition to civilian life and to update his former comrade on company affairs. One letter in April and another written in June 1865 illustrate Boynton's frustration at not being mustered out of the service soon enough. Boynton, breathing a bit of fire, wrote, on the subject of the short-term enlisted men, "to think that these d—d *Draften* and Subs all one year *Cowards* are to be sent home and the men that have been Here for nearly 4 years and been through everything but—Hell, must stay *God Knows How Much Longer.*" Young, who was not shy when it came to matters of duty, likely shared these sentiments. What Boynton really wanted, as the date of the soldiers' departure neared, was "a Glass of

Beer." As he awaited discharge, it is easy to believe that he was not alone in this desire.[4]

Their wait finally ended on July 3, 1865, when forty-eight men in Company F of the Seventh Wisconsin were officially mustered out. Before their official leave, the men took part in the Grand Review on May 23–24, 1865. The review, lasting a full six hours, took place on a beautiful day where "The sun shone brilliantly." Thousands of citizens, many of whom had traveled from others cities, witnessed the grand spectacle of "a continuous moving line as far as the eye could reach." The reviewing stand was filled with dignitaries, including President Johnson and members of his cabinet, along with Generals Grant, Sherman, and Meade and other high-ranking military officers. Salutes and enthusiastic cheers greeted the men, and children gave bouquets of flowers to the soldiers near the White House. Of the original 104 officers and enlisted men who joined Company F in 1861, only six were mustered out in July 1865. One man was mustered out on August 29, twenty-two on September 1, and Young on December 3, all at the end of their three-year terms of enlistment. The remaining seventy-six men either were killed or wounded or left the service before their term of service ended.[5]

In 1881, another former soldier, Lorin G. Parsons, wrote to Young reminiscing about the days spent in the military and trying to catch up on a piece of his past. Fond of his former commanding officer, Parsons confided that he would be more contented in his life if he could see him again. He remarked that Young was "kind of a second father" and wondered aloud how the original boys were getting along. He recounted an interesting incident that occurred at the onset of Gettysburg; a woman had baked a loaf of bread for the unit, and in the haste and confusion of battle he jokingly wondered what had happened to it. The men's sacrifices, Parsons noted, were not lost "when they gave up their lives how long the battle would have to be fought before Southerners acknowledge that our nation was spelled with a capital 'A.'"[6]

In 1887, Young received three letters from another company commander, who late in the war was promoted to the headquarters of the Seventh Wisconsin. Lt. Col. Mark Finnicum, originally from Fennimore, Grant County, wrote to Captain Young about an injury he had suffered at Laurel Hill in 1863. Finnicum, who had migrated to Pulaski County, Kentucky, after the war, was seeking Young's help. Needing proof for his disability claim, he hoped Young would write a deposition, with details of the injury, to the government. To help jog his memory, Finnicum went so far as to remind Young about what he had said to him after seeing his wound. Young reportedly had stated, "Old fellow you have got it this time, I have been expecting it for some time." Writing back, he helped furnish Finnicum with the necessary documentation he needed to fill out the affidavit. In his last letter to Young, Finnicum expressed gratitude for Young's help and ended by asking Young whether he planned to attend the dedication of a monument commemorating the twenty-fifth anniversary of the Iron Brigade at Gettysburg. No evidence is available about whether Young made the pilgrimage to Gettysburg.[7]

George W. St. Claire, a private in Company F, also made a request. St. Claire, a late recruit, enlisted in Tafton in January 1864. He had lost his discharge papers when the regiment was mustered out in Washington, DC, in July 1865 and hoped Young could furnish him with a duplicate set so that he could apply for a pension. St. Claire had been wounded at North Anna in 1864, and in his letter, written on June 11, 1895, he complained that his "Health is no good." It is not clear whether Young provided any assistance, but St. Claire is listed as an invalid on pension forms, and after his death his wife continued to collect a pension until her death in 1923. St. Claire, who also went by the name William B. Sickels, moved to South Dakota after the war.[8]

First Lt. Amos D. Rood, Company K of the Seventh Wisconsin, wrote to Young in 1899, inquiring about the men in the regiment and wondering how many were still alive. Focused on the legacy of the Seventh Wisconsin, he wanted their deeds remembered, stating, "and we *must hustle* and get out our '*History of the Iron Brigade*' and not let the 2nd and 6th boys *monopolize all of its* space!" These sentiments, expressed by Rood, were certainly approved by Captain Young.[9]

A stroke in October 1894 left Young an invalid for the remaining eight years of his life. In 1900, likely in an effort to make him more comfortable, he and Delia moved to Bloomington, formerly Tafton, in Grant County. He met this last challenge with the same determined demeanor he had displayed as a soldier. The final bugle call for Captain Henry Falls Young arrived on February 5, 1902, when he was seventy-seven years of age. Soldiers of the Grand Army of the Potomac performed a service for Young, and many family and friends attended the service. A close friend and soldier, Reuben B. Showalter, delivered a fitting eulogy for Young. The Rev. F. W. Schoenfeld, presiding over the ceremony on February 8 at the

Congregational Church, remarked, "All the ends which Mr. Young aimed at were the welfare of his country and family." He went on to say, "He worked hard to sustain a government which should secure to every citizen the rights . . . of this commonwealth, . . . and which should guard these rights with equal vigilance, both against the oppression of the many and the tyranny of the few."[10]

Following his death, Delia remained in Bloomington until her death in 1924 at the age of eighty-seven. May, born the year before Young's enlistment, became a nurse, eventually moving to Manitowoc, Wisconsin, where she cared for her second cousin, Eva, the oft-mentioned young woman in Young's letters. She returned home to care for Delia in her last years. May, who never married, died in Bloomington in 1941 at the age of eighty. Harry Warner Young, the youngest child of Henry and Delia, ran the family farm in Patch Grove until his death in 1944 at the age of seventy-seven. His marriage, to Emma Lambert in 1889, produced a son, who died in infancy. Harry Young's death, which was preceded by that of Emma, ended the direct line of his descendants. Perhaps the best tribute to Young can be found in a

Henry F. Young headstone (photo by Micheal J. Larson)

letter from his former charge, Lorin G. Parsons, which closes, "with much love for my honored Captain, I Remain As Ever Yours To Command."[11]

NOTES

1. Henry F. Young Discharge Papers, December 3, 1865, Papers of Henry Falls Young, 1861–1902, Wisconsin Historical Society, Madison.

2. It is interesting to note that no deed was drawn up for the land when Henry, Delia, and their children moved to the farm near Patch Grove. Two years later, Jared Warner passed away, and his wife, Mary, on November 11, 1880, sold part of Warner's estate to his three daughters, Delia, Rebecca, and Casanna, along with their husbands, for $627.60. On the same date, eighty acres adjoining the first parcel of land were sold to James Hicklin of Patch Grove for $400. Apparently, some arrangement was made that gave possession of the farm to Henry and Delia; the 1895 plat of Patch Grove Township showed only Young as proprietor of two hundred acres. 1870 United States Census, Cassville, Grant County, Wisconsin, digital image s.v. "Harry Young," Ancestry.com; "Deaths," *Grant County Herald* (Lancaster, WI), January 25, 1870; "Henry Falls Young," *The Weekly Teller* (Lancaster, WI), February 20, 1902; *Atlas of Grant County Wisconsin* (Red Wing, MN: Warner & Foote, 1877), 61; C. M. Foote and J. W. Henion, *Plat Book of Grant County Wisconsin* (Minneapolis, MN: C. M. Foote and Co., 1895), 9; Grant County Register of Deeds, *Grantor/Grantee Indexes, 1837–1901*, vol. 89, 157, 170; "Harry W. Young," *Bloomington Record* (Bloomington, WI), January 26, 1944.

3. The Blake's Prairie Agricultural Society held an annual fair from 1868 until 1968, when the fair was reorganized with a renewed focus on youth participation and was rebranded the Blake's Prairie Junior Fair. In 2017 it celebrated its 150th Anniversary. Consul Willshire Butterfield, *History of Grant County Wisconsin, Containing an Account . . . of the United States* (Chicago: Western Historical Company, 1881), 500, 820, 859; Castello N. Holford, *History of Grant County Wisconsin . . . and a History of the Several Towns* (Lancaster, WI: The Teller Print, 1900), 143, 650; Rachel Mergen, "A Look Back: 150th Blake's Prairie Fair Is Here," *Courier Press* (Prairie du Chien, WI), July 10, 2017; "Republican Congressional Convention—Third District," *Wisconsin State Journal* (Madison, WI), September 3, 1868; "Henry Falls Young," *The Weekly Teller*, February 20, 1902.

4. Francis A. Boynton to Young, April 27, 1865; Boynton to Young, June 8, 1865.

5. "The Grand Review," *Wisconsin State Journal*, May 24, 1865; "The Grand Review in Washington," *Daily Intelligencer* (Wheeling, WV), May 24, 1865, http://chroniclingamerica.loc.gov/lccn/sn84026845/1865-05-24/ed-1/seq-3/; "The Grand Review," *Janesville Daily Gazette* (Janesville, WI), May 25, 1865.

6. Lorin G. Parsons to Young, February 12, 1881.

7. Mark Finnicum to Young, June 25, 1887; Finnicum to Young, July 25, 1887; Finnicum to Young, December 12, 1887.

8. George W. St. Claire to Young, June 11, 1895, National Archives, *Organization to Pension Files of Veterans Who Served 1861–1900*, Electronic Database, s.v. "George S. St. Claire," Fold3.

9. Amos D. Rood to Young, November 19, 1899; Wisconsin, Adjutant General's Office, *Roster of the Wisconsin Volunteers, War of the Rebellion, 1861–1865*, Blue Books, 2 vols. (Madison: Democrat Printing Press, 1886), 1:572.

10. *The Weekly Teller*, February 20, 1902.

11. "Mrs. Delia Young," *Bloomington Record*, March 5, 1924; "May B. Young," *Bloomington Record*, October 29, 1941; "Harry W. Young," *Bloomington Record*, January 26, 1944; Wisconsin, County Marriages, 1836–1911, digital image s.v. "Harry W. Young," FamilySearch.org; Parsons to Young, February 12, 1881.

Bibliography

"1850 United States Census." Database. http://ancestry.com: 2009.

"1850 United States Census." Database. http://familysearch.org: 2016.

"1860 United States Census." Database. http://ancestry.com: 2009.

"1860 United States Census." Schedule 5, Products of Industry, Cassville Township, Grant County, Wisconsin.

"1870 United States Census." Database. http://ancestry.com: 2009.

Adams, Michael C. C. *Our Masters the Rebels: A Speculation on Union Military Failure in the East, 1861–1865*. Cambridge, MA: Harvard University Press, 1978.

Aley, Ginette, and J. L. Anderson, eds. *Union Heartland: The Midwestern Home Front during the Civil War*. Carbondale: Southern Illinois University Press, 2013.

Atlas of Grant County Wisconsin. Red Wing, MN: Warner & Foote, 1877.

Axelrod, Alan. *The Horrid Pit: The Battle of the Crater, the Civil War's Cruelest Mission*. New York: Carroll & Graf, 2007.

Ayers, Edward L. *The Thin Light of Freedom: The Civil War and Emancipation in the Heart of America*. New York: Norton, 2017.

Baker, Thomas R. *The Sacred Cause of Union: Iowa in the Civil War*. Iowa City: University of Iowa Press, 2016.

Barton, Michael, and Larry M. Logue, eds. *The Civil War Soldier: A Historical Reader*. New York: New York University Press, 2002.

Basler, Roy P., ed. *Collected Works of Abraham Lincoln*. 8 vols. New Brunswick, NJ: Rutgers University Press, 1953.

Bates, Samuel Penniman. *History of Pennsylvania Volunteers, 1861–1865; Prepared in Compliance with Acts of the Legislature*. 5 vols. Harrisburg, PA: B. Singerly, State Printer, 1869–71.

Bledsoe, Andrew S. *Citizen-Officers: The Union and Confederate Volunteer Junior Officer Corps in the American Civil War*. Baton Rouge: Louisiana State University Press, 2015.

Boatner, Mark M. III. *The Civil War Dictionary*. Rev. ed. New York: Vintage Books, 1991.

Bowery, Charles R. Jr., and Ethan S. Rafuse. *Guide to the Richmond–Petersburg Campaign.* US Army War College Guides to Civil War Battles. Lawrence: University Press of Kansas, 2014.

Brands, H. W. *The Man Who Saved the Union: Ulysses Grant in War and Peace.* New York: Anchor Books, 2012.

Brendel, Johnny. *Swamp Hogs: The Civil War Journals of Johnny Brendel.* Edited by William Thomas Venner. Goshen, OH: Larrea Books, 1995.

Butterfield, Consul Willshire. *History of Grant County Wisconsin, Containing an Account . . . of the United States.* Chicago: Western Historical Company, 1881.

Carmichael, Peter S., ed. *Audacity Personified: The Generalship of Robert E. Lee.* Baton Rouge: Louisiana State University Press, 2004.

Caudill, Edward, and Paul Ashdown. *Inventing Custer: The Making of an American Legend.* Lanham, MD: Rowman & Littlefield, 2015.

Chick, Sean Michael. *The Battle of Petersburg, June 15–18, 1864.* Lincoln, NE: Potomac Books, 2015.

Cimbala, Paul A., and Randall M. Miller. *The Northern Home Front during the Civil War.* Santa Barbara, CA: Praeger, 2017.

———, eds. *Union Soldiers and the Northern Home Front: Wartime Experiences, Postwar Adjustments.* New York: Fordham University Press, 2002.

Confederate States of America. Congress. *Journal of the Congress of the Confederate States of America, 1861–1865.* 7 vols. Washington, DC: Government Printing Office, 1904–5.

Congressional Globe. 37th Congress, 2nd Session, "House of Rep., Report No. 2, Government Contracts," 1861–62.

Congressional Globe. 37th Congress, 3rd Session, 1863.

Current, Richard N. *The History of Wisconsin.* Vol. 2, *The Civil War Era, 1848–1873.* Madison: State Historical Society of Wisconsin, 1976.

Dawes, Rufus R. *Service with the Sixth Wisconsin Volunteers.* Marietta, OH: E. R. Alderman & Sons, 1890.

Dillard, Philip D. *Jefferson Davis's Final Campaign: Confederate Nationalism and the Fight to Arm Slaves.* Macon, GA: Mercer University Press, 2017.

Donald, David Herbert. *Lincoln.* New York: Simon & Schuster, 1995.

Dorsey, Chris. "Of Iron and Stone: A Comparison of the Iron and Stonewall Brigades." *Journal of America's Military Past* 27 (Winter 2001): 48–67.

Durden, Robert F. *The Gray and the Black: The Confederate Debate on Emancipation.* Baton Rouge: Louisiana State University Press, 1972.

Durrill, Wayne K. *War of Another Kind: A Southern Community in the Great Rebellion.* New York: Oxford University Press, 1990.

Dyer, Frederick. *A Compendium of the War of the Rebellion . . . and Other Reliable Documents and Sources.* Des Moines, IA: Dyer Publishing Company, 1908.

Eicher, John H., and David J. Eicher. *Civil War High Commands.* Stanford, CA: Stanford University Press, 2001.

Estabrook, Charles E., ed. *Losses in the Civil War: A List of the Names of Wisconsin Soldiers Killed in Action, Mortally Wounded, or Dying from Other Causes in the Civil War.* Madison: Democrat Printing Company, 1915.

Etcheson, Nicole. *A Generation at War: The Civil War in a Northern Community*. Lawrence: University Press of Kansas, 2011.

Faust, Patricia L., ed. *Historical Times Illustrated Encyclopedia of the Civil War*. New York: Harper & Row, 1986.

Ferris, Norman B. *The Trent Affair: A Diplomatic Crisis*. Knoxville: University of Tennessee Press, 1977.

Foote, C. F., and J. W. Henion. *Plat Book of Grant County Wisconsin*. Minneapolis, MN: C. M. Foote & Co., 1895.

Foote, Lorien. *The Gentlemen and the Roughs: Violence, Honor, and Manhood in the Union Army*. New York: New York University Press, 2010.

Forsberg, Grant. "Women's Education at Knox." https://www.knox.edu/about-knox/our-history/perspectives-on-knox-history/womens-education.

Fox, William F. *Regimental Losses in the American Civil War*. Albany, NY: Albany Publishing Company, 1889.

Frassanito, William A. *Grant and Lee: The Virginia Campaigns 1864–1865*. New York: Scribner, 1983.

Freeman, Douglas Southall. *Lee's Lieutenants: A Study in Command*. Vol. 1, *Manassas to Malvern Hill*. 1942; New York: Charles Scribner's Sons, 1970.

Furgurson, Ernest B. *Chancellorsville 1863: The Souls of the Brave*. New York: Knopf, 1992.

———. *Not War but Murder: Cold Harbor 1864*. New York: Knopf, 2000.

Gaff, Alan D. *On Many a Bloody Field: Four Years in the Iron Brigade*. Bloomington: Indiana University Press, 1996.

Gallagher, Gary W. *The Battle of Chancellorsville*. National Park Service Civil War series. Conshohocken, PA: US National Park Service and Eastern National, 1995.

———, ed. *The Fredericksburg Campaign: Decision on the Rappahannock*. Chapel Hill: University of North Carolina Press, 1995.

———. *Lee and His Army in Confederate History*. Chapel Hill: University of North Carolina Press, 2001.

———. *The Union War*. Cambridge, MA: Harvard University Press, 2011.

Gallagher, Gary W., and Caroline E. Janney, eds. *Cold Harbor to the Crater: The End of the Overland Campaign*. Chapel Hill: University of North Carolina Press, 2015.

Gallman, J. Matthew. *The North Fights the Civil War: The Home Front*. Chicago: Ivan R. Dee, 1994.

———. *Northerners at War: Reflections on the Civil War Home Front*. Kent, OH: Kent State University Press, 2010.

Gates, Paul W. *Agriculture and the Civil War*. New York: Knopf, 1965.

Glatthaar, Joseph T. *Forged in Battle: The Civil War Alliance of Black Soldiers and White Officers*. New York: Free Press, 1990.

———. *General Lee's Army: From Victory to Collapse*. New York: Free Press, 2008.

Goodwin, Doris Kearns. *Team of Rivals: The Political Genius of Abraham Lincoln*. New York: Simon & Schuster, 2005.

Grant, Ulysses S. *Personal Memoirs of U.S. Grant*. 2 vols. New York: Charles L. Webster, 1886.

———. "An Undeserved Stigma." *North American Review* 135 (December 1882): 536–46.

Grant County Genealogical Society. *Grant County Plat Map Index, 1868*. Platteville, WI: Grant County Genealogical Society, 1868.

———. *Marriages for Grant County*. Compiled by the Grant County Genealogical Society. Vol. 2, 1987.

Grant County Register of Deeds. *Grantor/Grantee Indexes, 1837–1901.*

Gray, Wood. *The Hidden Civil War: The Story of the Copperhead*. Kirkwood, NY: Vail-Ballou Press, 1942.

Greene, A. Wilson. *The Final Battles of the Petersburg Campaign: Breaking the Backbone of the Rebellion*. Knoxville: University of Tennessee Press, 2008.

Grimsley, Mark. *And Keep Moving On: The Virginia Campaign, May–June 1864*. Lincoln: University of Nebraska Press, 2002.

———. *The Hard Hand of War: Union Military Policy towards Southern Civilians 1861–1865*. New York: Cambridge University Press, 1995.

Guelzo, Allen C. *Fateful Lighting: A New History of the Civil War and Reconstruction*. New York: Oxford University Press, 2012.

———. *Gettysburg: The Last Invasion*. New York: Vintage Books, 2013.

Hadden, Robert Lee. "The Deadly Embrace: The Meeting of the Twenty-fourth Regiment, Michigan Infantry and the Twenty-sixth Regiment of North Carolina Troops at McPherson's Woods, Gettysburg, Pennsylvania, July 1, 1863." *Gettysburg Magazine*, no. 5 (July 1, 1991): 19–33.

Hardee, William Joseph. *Rifle and Light Infantry Tactics; For the Exercise and Manoeuvres of Troops When Acting as Light Infantry or Riflemen*. Philadelphia: Lippincott, Grambo & Co., 1855.

Harris, Loyd. "With the Iron Brigade at Gettysburg." Edited by Lance J. Herdegen and William J. K. Beaudot. *Gettysburg Magazine* 1 (July 1989): 29–34.

Harsh, Joseph L. *Sounding the Shallows: A Confederate Companion for the Maryland Campaign of 1862*. Kent, OH: Kent State University Press, 2000.

———. *Taken at the Flood: Robert E. Lee and Confederate Strategy in the Maryland Campaign of 1862*. Kent, OH: Kent State University Press, 1999.

Hattaway, Herman, and Archer Jones. *How the North Won: A Military History of the Civil War*. Urbana: University of Illinois Press, 1983.

Hebert, Walter H. *Fighting Joe Hooker*. Lincoln: University of Nebraska Press, 1999.

Heidler, David S., and Jeanne T. Heidler, eds. *Encyclopedia of the American Civil War: A Political, Social, and Military History*. New York: Norton, 2000.

Hennessy, John J. *Return to Bull Run: The Campaign and Battle of Second Manassas*. New York: Simon & Schuster, 1993.

Herdegen, Lance J. *The Iron Brigade in Civil War and Memory: The Black Hats from Bull Run to Appomattox and Thereafter*. El Dorado Hills, CA: Savas Beatie, 2012.

———. *The Men Stood Like Iron: How the Iron Brigade Won Its Name*. Bloomington: Indiana University Press, 1997.

Herdegen, Lance J., and William J. K. Beaudot. *In the Bloody Railroad Cut at Gettysburg: The 6th Wisconsin of the Iron Brigade and Its Famous Charge*. El Dorado Hills, CA: Savas Beatie, 2015.

Herdegen, Lance J., and Sherry Murphy, eds. *Four Years with the Iron Brigade: The Civil War Journals of William R. Ray, Co. F, Seventh Wisconsin Infantry*. Cambridge, MA: Da Capo Press, 2002.

Hess, Earl J. *Civil War Infantry Tactics: Training, Combat, and Small-Unit Effectiveness*. Baton Rouge: Louisiana State University Press, 2015.

———. *Into the Crater: The Mine Attack at Petersburg*. Columbia: University of South Carolina Press, 2010.

Holford, Castello N. *History of Grant County Wisconsin . . . and a History of the Several Towns*. Lancaster, WI: The Teller Print, 1900.

Huets, Jean. "The Iron Brigade." *New York Times*, July 23, 2013.

Hurn, Ethel Alice. *Wisconsin Women in the War between the States*. Madison: Wisconsin History Commission, 1911.

Jamieson, Perry D. *Death in September: The Antietam Campaign*. Abilene, TX: McWhiney Foundation Press, 1999.

Jones, Joshua. "'Absent so long from those I love': The Civil War Letters of Joshua Jones." Edited by Eugene H. Berwanger. *Indiana Magazine of History* 88 (September 1992): 205–39.

Jones, Wilmer L. *Generals in Blue and Gray*. Vol. 1, *Lincoln's Generals*. Mechanicsburg, PA: Stackpole Books, 2004.

Kahn, Matthew E., and Dora L. Costa. "Cowards and Heroes: Group Loyalty in the American Civil War." *Quarterly Journal of Economics* 118 (May 2003): 519–48.

Keegan, John. *The American Civil War: A Military History*. New York: Knopf, 2009.

Klement, Frank L. *Wisconsin in the Civil War: The Home Front and the Battle Front, 1861–1865*. Madison: State Historical Society of Wisconsin, 1997.

Knight, William Henry. *Hand-Book Almanac for the Pacific States: An Official Register and Business Directory*. San Francisco: H. H. Bancroft and Co., 1864.

Krick, Robert K. *Chancellorsville—Lee's Greatest Victory*. New York: American Heritage Publishing Co., 1990.

Leepson, Marc. *Desperate Engagement: How a Little Known Civil War Battle Saved Washington, D.C., and Changed the Course of American History*. New York: St. Martin's Griffin, 2007.

Legate, George H. "Never Defeated Yet." Edited by Paul Kallina. *Lincoln Herald* 89 (Fall 1987): 117–22.

Levine, Bruce. *Confederate Emancipation: Southern Plans to Free and Arm Slaves during the Civil War*. New York: Oxford University Press, 2006.

Linderman, Gerald F. *Embattled Courage: The Experience of Combat in the American Civil War*. New York: Free Press, 1987.

Longacre, Edward G. *The Cavalry at Gettysburg*. Lincoln: University of Nebraska Press, 1986.

Manning, Chandra. "Wartime Nationalism and Race: Comparing the Visions of Confederate, Black Union, and White Union Soldiers." In *In the Cause of Liberty: How the Civil War Redefined American Ideals*, edited by William J. Cooper Jr. and John M. McCardell Jr., 87–104. Baton Rouge: Louisiana State University Press, 2009.

———. *What This Cruel War Was Over: Soldiers, Slavery, and the Civil War*. New York: Knopf, 2007.

Marvel, William. *Burnside*. Chapel Hill: University of North Carolina Press, 1991.

Matrau, Henry. *Letters Home: Henry Matrau of the Iron Brigade*. Edited by Marcia Reid-Green. Lincoln: University of Nebraska Press, 1993.

McK., J. M. "'The United States Has' and 'Remarks.'" *Washington Post*, April 24, 1887.

McPherson, James M. *Battle Cry of Freedom: The Civil War Era*. New York: Oxford University Press, 1988.

———. *For Cause & Comrades: Why Men Fought in the Civil War*. New York: Oxford University Press, 1997.

———. *Crossroads of Freedom: Antietam, the Battle That Changed the Course of the Civil War*. New York: Oxford University Press, 2002.

Merk, Frederick. *Economic History of Wisconsin during the Civil War Decade*. Madison: State Historical Society of Wisconsin, 1916.

Military, Compiled Service Records. Civil War. Carded Records, Volunteer Organizations. Records of the Adjutant General's Office. Record Group 94. Publication M594, Roll 199, Sixth through Eleventh Wisconsin Infantry. National Archives, Washington, DC.

Mitchell, Reid. *Civil War Soldiers: Their Expectations and Their Experiences*. New York: Viking Penguin, 1988.

———. *The Vacant Chair: The Northern Soldier Leaves Home*. New York: Oxford University Press, 1993.

Murray, Williamson, and Wayne Wei-siang Hsieh. *A Savage War: A Military History of the Civil War*. Princeton: Princeton University Press, 2016.

National Archives. *Organization Index to Pension Files of Veterans Who Served between 1861–1900*. Electronic Database. Fold3.

Neely, Mark E. Jr. *The Fate of Liberty: Abraham Lincoln and Civil Liberties*. New York: Oxford University Press, 1991.

———. *The Union Divided: Party Conflict in the Civil War North*. Cambridge, MA: Harvard University Press, 2002.

New York State. Adjutant General Office. *Annual Report of the Adjutant-General of the State of New York for the Year 1902: Registers of the One Hundredth, One Hundred and First, One Hundred and Second, One Hundred and Third, One Hundred and Fourth, One Hundred and Fifth and One Hundred and Sixth Regiments of Infantry*. Albany: Argus Company, Printers, 1903.

Nolan, Alan T. *The Iron Brigade: A Military History*. New York: Macmillan, 1961.

Nolan, Alan T., and Sharon Eggleston Vipond, eds. *Giants in Their Tall Black Hats: Essays on the Iron Brigade*. Bloomington: Indiana University Press, 1998.

Paludan, Phillip Shaw. *"A People's Contest": The Union and Civil War, 1861–1865*. New York: Harper & Row, 1988.

Partridge, George W. Jr. *Letters from the Iron Brigade: George Washington Partridge Jr., 1839–1863, Civil War Letters to His Sisters*. Edited by Hugh L. Whitehouse. Indianapolis: Guild Press of Indiana, 1994.

Perret, Geoffrey. *Ulysses S. Grant: Soldier and President.* New York: Modern Library, 1999.

Pfanz, Harry W. *Gettysburg: Culp's Hill and Cemetery Hill.* Chapel Hill: University of North Carolina Press, 1993.

———. *Gettysburg—The Second Day.* Chapel Hill: University of North Carolina Press, 1987.

Quiner, Edwin Bentley. *The Military History of Wisconsin: A Record of the Civil and Military Patriotism of the States, in the War for the Union.* Chicago: Clarke & Co., 1866.

———. *Quiner Scrapbooks: Correspondence of the Wisconsin Volunteers, 1861–1865.* 10 vols. Electronic reproduction. Madison: Wisconsin Historical Society Digital Collections, 2010.

Rable, George C. *Fredericksburg! Fredericksburg!* Chapel Hill: University of North Carolina Press, 2002.

Reardon, Carol. *With a Sword in One Hand and Jomini in the Other: The Problem of Military Thought in the Civil War North.* Chapel Hill: University of North Carolina Press, 2012.

Rhea, Gordon C. *The Battle of Cold Harbor.* Fort Washington, PA: US National Park Service and Eastern National, 2001.

———. *The Battle of the Wilderness, May 5–6, 1864.* Baton Rouge: Louisiana State University Press, 1994.

———. *The Battles for Spotsylvania Court House and the Road to Yellow Tavern, May 7–12, 1864.* Baton Rouge: Louisiana State University Press, 1997.

———. *Cold Harbor: Grant and Lee, May 26–June 3, 1864.* Baton Rouge: Louisiana State University Press, 2002.

———. *In the Footsteps of Grant and Lee: The Wilderness through Cold Harbor.* Baton Rouge: Louisiana State University Press, 2007.

———. *On to Petersburg: Grant and Lee, June 4–15, 1864.* Baton Rouge: Louisiana State University Press, 2017.

———. *To the North Anna River: Grant and Lee, May 13–25, 1864.* Baton Rouge: Louisiana State University Press, 2000.

Robertson, James I. Jr. *Stonewall Jackson: The Man, the Soldier, the Legend.* New York: Simon & Schuster, 1997.

Rose, C. B. Jr. "Civil War Forts in Arlington." *Arlington Historical Magazine* 1, no. 4 (1960): 14–27.

Schecter, Barnet. *The Devil's Own Work: The Civil War Draft Riots and the Fight to Reconstruct America.* New York: Walker, 2005.

Sears, Stephen W. *Chancellorsville.* New York: Houghton Mifflin, 1996.

———. *George B. McClellan: The Young Napoleon.* New York: Ticknor & Fields, 1988.

———. *Gettysburg.* New York: Houghton Mifflin, 2003.

———. *Landscape Turned Red: The Battle of Antietam.* Boston: Houghton Mifflin, 1983.

———. *To the Gates of Richmond: The Peninsula Campaign.* New York: Ticknor & Fields, 1992.

Shortell, Michael. *The Civil War Letters of Corporal Michael Shortell, Company G. 7th Wisconsin Volunteer Infantry*. Compiled by Mary Wanty Frazier. Bowie, MD, 1992.

Slotkin, Richard. *The Long Road to Antietam: How the Civil War Became a Revolution*. New York: Liveright, 2012.

———. *No Quarter: The Battle of the Crater, 1864*. New York: Random House, 2009.

Smith, John David. *Lincoln and the U.S. Colored Troops*. Carbondale: Southern Illinois University Press, 2013.

———, ed. *Black Soldiers in Blue: African American Troops in the Civil War Era*. Chapel Hill: University of North Carolina Press, 2003.

Sommers, Richard J. *Richmond Redeemed: The Siege at Petersburg*. Garden City, NY: Doubleday, 1981.

Stanley, Matthew E. *The Loyal West: Civil War & Reunion in Middle America*. Urbana: University of Illinois Press, 2017.

Starr, Stephen Z. *The Union Cavalry in the Civil War*. Vol. 2, *The War in the East from Gettysburg to Appomattox, 1863–1865*. Baton Rouge: Louisiana State University Press, 1981.

Stout, Harry S. *American Aristocrats: A Family, a Fortune, and the Making of American Capitalism*. New York: Basic Books, 2017.

Sullivan, James P. *An Irishman in the Iron Brigade: The Civil War Memoirs of James P. Sullivan, Serg., Company K, 6th Wisconsin Volunteers*. Edited by William J. K. Beaudot and Lance J. Herdegen. New York: Fordham University Press, 1993.

Taaffe, Stephen R. *Commanding the Army of the Potomac*. Lawrence: University Press of Kansas, 2006.

Tribune Almanac for the Years 1838–1868, Inclusive; . . . Making a Connected Political History for Thirty Years. Vol. 2. New York: New York Tribune, 1868. http://archive.org/details/tribunealmanac01unkgoog.

Trudeau, Noah Andre. *Bloody Roads South: The Wilderness to Cold Harbor, May–June 1864*. Boston: Little, Brown, 1989.

———. *Gettysburg: A Testing of Courage*. New York: HarperCollins, 2002.

———. *The Last Citadel: Petersburg, Virginia, June 1864–April 1865*. Baton Rouge: Louisiana State University Press, 1991.

United States. War Records Office. *The War of the Rebellion: A Compilation of the Official Records of the Union and Confederate Armies*. 128 vols. Washington, DC, 1880–1901.

Warner, Jared. Papers, 1836–1880. Madison: Wisconsin Historical Society.

Welcher, Frank J. *The Union Army, 1861–1865 Organization and Operations*. Vol. 1, *The Eastern Theater*. Bloomington: Indiana University Press, 1989.

Wert, Jeffry D. *A Brotherhood of Valor: The Common Soldiers of the Stonewall Brigade, C.S.A., and the Iron Brigade, U.S.A.* New York: Simon & Schuster, 1999.

———. *The Sword of Lincoln: The Army of the Potomac*. New York: Simon & Schuster, 2005.

Wheelan, Joseph. *Bloody Spring: Forty Days That Sealed the Confederacy's Fate*. Boston: Da Capo Press, 2014.

White, Jonathan. *Diary of a Soldier, Jonathan White, 2nd Wisconsin Volunteers, Civil War, 1862*. Compiled by Frances Dugger Rowan. Bishop, CA: F. D. Rowan, 1996.

White, Ronald C. Jr. *A. Lincoln*. New York: Random House, 2009.
———. *American Ulysses: A Life of Ulysses S. Grant*. New York: Random House, 2016.
Wisconsin. Adjutant General's Office. *Regimental Muster and Descriptive Rolls, 1861–1865* (Red Books). 57 vols. Madison: State Militia, 1865.
Wisconsin. Adjutant General's Office. *Roster of Wisconsin Volunteers, War of the Rebellion, 1861–1865* (Blue Books). 2 vols. Madison: Democrat Printing, 1886.
Wisconsin. *A Manual of Customs, Precedents and Forms, . . . with Indices*. Compiled by L.D.H. Crane. Madison: James Ross, State Printer, 1860.
Wisconsin. *A Manual of Customs, Precedents and Forms, . . . with Indices*. Compiled by L.D.H. Crane. Madison: E. A. Calkins & Co., 1861.
Wisconsin. *A Manual of Customs, Precedents and Forms, . . . Lists and Tables for Reference*. Compiled by John H. Warren and John S. Dean. Madison: Smith & Cullaton, 1862.
Wisconsin. *A Manual of Customs, Precedents and Forms, . . . Lists and Tables for Reference*. Compiled by Clerks of Senate and Assembly. Madison: Atwood & Rublee, 1863.
Wisconsin. *A Manual of Customs, Precedents and Forms, . . . Lists and Tables for Reference*. Compiled by Clerks of Senate and Assembly. Madison: William J. Park, 1864.
Wisconsin. *A Manual of Customs, Precedents and Forms, . . . Lists and Tables for Reference*. Compiled by Clerks of Senate and Assembly. Madison: Atwood & Rublee, 1865.
Wisconsin. *A Manual of Customs, Precedents and Forms, . . . Lists and Tables for Reference*. Compiled by Clerks of Senate and Assembly. Madison: Atwood & Rublee, 1866.
Wisconsin. *A Manual of Customs, Precedents and Forms, . . . Lists and Tables for Reference*. Compiled by Secretary of State. Madison: Atwood & Rublee, 1867.
Wisconsin. "County Marriages, 1836–1911." Database. FamilySearch.org, 2016.
Wisconsin. "Wisconsin Marriages, 1836–1930." Database. FamilySearch.org, 2014.
Woodward, Joseph Janvier. *Outlines of the Chief Camp Diseases of the United States Armies as Observed during the Present War; A Practical Contribution to Military Medicine*. Philadelphia: J. B. Lippincott, 1863.
Young, Alfred C. III. *Lee's Army during the Overland Campaign: A Numerical Study*. Baton Rouge: Louisiana State University Press, 2013.
Young, Henry Falls. Papers, 1861–1902. Madison: Wisconsin Historical Society.
Zombek, Angela M. "Belle Isle Prison." In *Encyclopedia Virginia*. Article published June 27, 2010, and modified June 8, 2011. http://encyclopediavirginia.org/.

Newspapers

Alexandria Gazette, Alexandria, Virginia
Bedford Gazette, Bedford, Pennsylvania
Bloomington Record, Bloomington, Wisconsin
Chicago Tribune
Civilian and Telegraph, Cumberland, Maryland

Courier Press, Prairie du Chien, Wisconsin
Daily Intelligencer, Wheeling, West Virginia
Daily Milwaukee Press and News
Daily National Republican, Washington, DC
Evening Star, Washington, DC
Evening Telegraph, Philadelphia
Grant County Herald, Lancaster, Wisconsin
Janesville Daily Gazette, Janesville, Wisconsin
Manitowoc Daily Tribune, Manitowoc, Wisconsin
New York Herald
New York Sun
New York Times
New York Tribune
Orleans Independent Standard, Irasburgh, Vermont
Philadelphia Enquirer
Plymouth Weekly Democrat, Plymouth, Indiana
Richmond Enquirer, Richmond, Virginia
Rockingham Register and Advertiser, Harrisonburg, Virginia
Semi-Weekly Wisconsin, Milwaukee
Weekly Gazette and Free Press, Janesville, Wisconsin
Weekly National Intelligencer, Washington, DC
The Weekly Teller, Lancaster, Wisconsin
Wilmington Clinton Republican, Wilmington, Ohio
Wisconsin State Journal, Madison, Wisconsin
Wisconsin State Patriot, Madison, Wisconsin

Index

Printed in the United States
By Bookmasters